The Conditions for
Economic Recovery

JOHN CORNWALL

The Conditions for Economic Recovery

A Post-Keynesian Analysis

M. E. SHARPE, INC.
Armonk, New York

First published in the United States in 1983 by
M. E. Sharpe, Inc.,
80 Business Park Drive,
Armonk, New York 10504 USA

Library of Congress Cataloging in Publication Data

Cornwall, John.
  The conditions for economic recovery.

  Bibliography: p.
  Includes index.
  1. Economic history – 1971 – . 2. Unemployment –
Effect of inflation on.   3. Wage-price policy. I.   Title.
HC59.C726   1983   339.5   83-12802
ISBN 0-87332-263-0
ISBN 0-87332-264-9 (pbk)

Printed in Great Britain

For Wendy

Contents

Preface

This study focuses on the various forces that have led to the current crisis of capitalist economies. Following a period of unprecedented prosperity, developed capitalist economies have for over a decade been plagued by the problems of inflation and economic stagnation. What limited success there has been in resolving these difficulties has been bought at great cost – prolonged periods of high unemployment. This book explains the breakdown in the developed capitalist economies and offers a solution.

It marks the third phase of an effort to explain the main macroeconomic developments in mature capitalist economies over approximately the past century. An earlier book, *Growth and Stability in a Mature Economy*, discussed why capitalist economies were not frequently subject to depressions of the 1930s variety.[1] Centrally planned economies, no matter how inefficiently run, are understandably able to solve the problem of adequate aggregate demand. But it struck me at the time as most amazing that economies characterized by decentralized decision making had been subject to only one severe and prolonged depression over a period of approximately 100 years.

Modern Capitalism: Its Growth and Transformation dealt with the 'golden age' of capitalism – roughly the 1950s and 1960s.[2] Never before had so many economies grown so rapidly and for so long as during this period. Moreover, this was not just a time of rapid and sustained growth on a wide scale. It was also a period of transformation in which new industries, new sectors and new 'life styles' devel-

---

[1] J. Cornwall, *Growth and Stability in a Mature Economy,* Martin Robertson, London, 1972.

[2] J. Cornwall, *Modern Capitalism: Its Growth and Transformation,* Martin Robertson, London, 1977.

oped, resulting in an economic landscape vastly different from that of pre-World War II.

During the time I was recording these events (1974–76), I became increasingly aware that something had gone quite wrong and expressed this unease in a chapter entitled 'Closing Time in the Gardens of the West', a title repeated in the present book. This unease was apparent in my attitude towards the restrictive aggregate demand policies then (as now) in effect, aimed at 'whipping the inflationary psychology once and for all'. It seemed to me at the time that the only likely result of these policies was that governments would recreate conditions similar to those in Britain during the inter-war period. To quote but one sentence from that study:

A concern with an inflation that cannot be handled by managing aggregate demand (together with some form of temporary incomes policy) will, at best, lead to a similar situation of prolonged high unemployment and stagnation.[3]

Events since 1976 have only strengthened that conviction.

This book explains the major macroeconomic developments from the late 1960s until the present. While the previous two books concentrated on the economics of output, attention here is centred on the macroeconomics of price or inflation. However, since I believe that the stagnation of today is primarily the result of misguided policies to bring inflation under control, the slow-down in the rate of growth of output and measures to end stagnation are discussed at some length.

I have long believed that the primary task of macroeconomic theory is to explain historical processes. However, this involves more than the application of conventional dynamic macroeconomic theory: it requires that economic theory be supplemented by an institutional approach. Institutions are important in determining economic outcomes since they act as constraints on the manner in which problems can be solved. Moreover, one thing that should be apparent is the accelerated rate at which the institutional framework evolves today and old problems are replaced by new difficulties. These developments are but a natural part of the evolution of an economy. An adequate understanding of the important macroeconomic events cannot, therefore, be handled within a framework that assumes a given set of institutions. To put the point in language

[3] ibid., p. 211.

more familiar to economists, the rate at which tastes, technologies, endowments and institutional constraints change is so rapid in modern times relative to the rate at which an economy adjusts to any set of underlying institutional and structural factors, that any inherent convergence tendencies are of very secondary importance and interest. Furthermore, when institutions alter so must policies, if a rational approach to problem resolution is to be adopted.

Having said this, it should be clear that in setting out to explain the important macroeconomic developments during a period of rapid change, the standard neoclassical framework is most inappropriate. An outstanding (and unfortunate) feature of this mode of analysis is its assumption of exogenous tastes, technologies and endowments that change, if at all, in an artificial and predictable way. The relevance of this framework for analysing macroeconomic developments is questionable for an additional important reason – the reliance of neoclassical analysis on the competitive model. These particular issues are discussed in detail in the Introduction to Part I.

This emphasis on institutions and their evolution in understanding on-going economic events quite naturally leads to a multidisciplinary approach to the problem of stagflation. For example, in Part II of this book much is made of the policy implications of economic developments. The growing power of unions and oligopolies generates inflationary pressures that can only be controlled by political means. On the other hand, it is pointed out that political developments and institutions today greatly constrain the set of economic policies that are politically feasible and in so doing, greatly determine the likely course of economic events.

But there is more to it than this. Having compared the economic development of a number of mature capitalist economies, I concluded that very basic changes are needed to redress the current difficulties. These changes must affect the very institutions themselves, especially in English-speaking countries, to reflect the tight inter-relationships between political, economic and social matters. As seen in Part II, institutions of consensus and cooperation are required to provide the framework in which the needed economic policies can work. In many countries this means additional policies to develop and strengthen such institutions.

The fact that findings from several disciplines must be brought together has made it necessary to carry out the discussion in as non-technical a manner as possible. Certainly, with 35 million unemployed predicted for 1984 in the OECD countries, it is absolutely essential that the debate be carried out in such a way that everyone knows what the issues are.

The book divides into two parts, 'Analysis' and 'Policy'. I have added an introduction to each part to give the reader an immediate grasp of the central issues. It will be noted that a certain amount of mathematics has had to be used in the early chapters. However, it is of a fairly elementary kind and is used to enhance the reader's understanding of the issues. Nevertheless, numerous references are scattered throughout the book allowing those who prefer a more technical approach to satisfy their need.

In general, the book strives to follow the dictum that 'if a thing can be said, it can be said clearly'. What will soon be obvious is that the exposition often takes a forceful tone. This has been deliberate. The most widely adopted anti-inflationary policies today are restrictive aggregate demand policies that find their justification largely in monetarism. Monetarism, in turn, is the application of neoclassical principles to the macroeconomic problems of inflation and unemployment. Because I find these policies and their theoretical basis so inappropriate and damaging, I have felt it necessary at times to adopt an aggressive style. I can only hope that I provide adequate support for my views and that the exposition does not strike the reader as being in any way shrill and harsh. But, given my belief that economists today are actually doing a great deal of harm, I have felt that I could not proceed otherwise.

I wish to extend my thanks to the Research Development Fund at Dalhousie University for financial assistance. I would also like to take this opportunity to thank S. Amirkhalkhali, Ronald Britto, Melvin Cross, J. S. Metcalfe, Lars Osberg, A. P. Thirlwall, Alasdair Sinclair, R. M. Sundrum and Brendan Walsh for their helpful comments. I am particularly grateful to Wendy Maclean who read the entire manuscript and made numerous helpful criticisms.

PART I

Analysis

Introduction

By general agreement, the economic orthodoxy of today is neoclassical, a mode of analysis or paradigm that now pervades all sub-branches of economics in English-speaking countries and one that has made important inroads elsewhere. Consider the following: the neoclassical approach continues to dominate growth theory, replacing the empiricism of Marx, Schumpeter and the Keynesians; the Heckscher-Ohlin doctrine of comparative advantage has been the virtually unchallenged basis of trade theory until the recent development of the 'neotechnology' theory of trade; and general equilibrium theory has been without challenge as an explanation of how markets are coordinated, resources allocated and the economy is organized. Today, the dominant view of inflation and unemployment is monetarist, an application of neoclassical precepts to these macro problems.

This is an unfortunate trend for it is the central tenet of this study that economics will never come of scientific age until the neoclassical framework has been largely discarded. This is not to deny that the neoclassical mode of theorizing has made a major contribution to economics. It has sharpened our techniques and tightened our definitions in a number of areas. For example, the introduction of marginal analysis and the related distinction between total, average and marginal concepts was a major achievement in the pre-Keynesian era of economics and would not have been possible without the application of neoclassical principles. Moreover, in an effort to introduce rigor and simplicity to economic theory, neoclassical analysis has shown how economic events can be modelled with an economy of assumptions and with clearly articulated conclusions.

However, neoclassical theorizing has become a victim of its own early success. Having accomplished much it turned inward, developing more elaborate and sophisticated techniques rather than attempting to expand the analysis to include the more important developments in the evolution of capitalism. The result has been that the technical success of neoclassical analysis have been purchased at a great cost, that of simplifying to such a degree that the approach has very limited explanatory power. This has an important corollary; economists will never understand the forces generating stagflation today nor formulate a policy for relieving economies of its burdens, unless they are first freed from the intellectual predispositions of neoclassical thinking. The qualifying adjective 'Post-Keynesian' is used in the title of this study to suggest an alternative to the neoclassical explanation of stagflation.

HARD-CORE NEOCLASSICAL ECONOMICS

What can be described as the neoclassical paradigm or hard core of neoclassical economics is best summarized in terms of its basic assumptions, those that define the 'competitive model': atomistic competition (or, more generally, all traders are price takers); exogenously determined tastes and technologies that are fixed within the period of analysis or change between periods in some unexplained way; consumer and worker sovereignty; and independent preferences.[1]

Going further, the neoclassical view sees the economy as one of interconnected markets in which economic activities are coordinated by the 'price mechanism'. Changes in relative prices reflect the interplay of shifting demand and supply curves and provide the signals needed to organize the economy efficiently. Furthermore, economic actions are influenced by prices so as to lead individuals to react quickly and effectively to this price information. To put the matter differently, with given tastes, technologies and endowments, amounts demanded and supplied in factor and goods markets are functions only of some relevant price, and reactions lead to market clearing prices.

---

[1] The discussion of scientific paradigms and their replacement has received a good deal of attention in recent years from social scientists. See T. Kuhn (1970) *The Structure of Scientific Revolutions*, 2nd Edn, University of Chicago Press, Chicago, and M. Blaug (1975) Kuhn versus Lakatos, or paradigms versus research programmes in the history of economics, *History of Political Economy* No. 4. A discussion of 'worker sovereignty' is found in D. Gordon (1972) *Theories of Poverty and Underemployment*, D.C., Heath, Lexington, Mass.

To this hard core, neoclassical analysis appends a collection of more restrictive assumptions, most but not all of which are then retained in the different studies. The assumptions of perfect foresight on the part of all traders and perfect mobility of all factors and the introduction of very simple and well-defined functions describing the goals of consumers, workers and producers and equally simple and well-defined constraints on the means of obtaining these objectives are most prominent among them. Having introduced some such collection of assumptions, the procedure is to relax one (but seldom more than one) of them to determine its importance in the analysis.

The result is a highly abstract framework tailor-made for rigorous model building and of the kind that formulates economic problems within the optimizing framework, i.e. given some assumed goal and constraints on behaviour, the rational or efficient way of achieving that goal is then derived. This point has loomed large within the economics profession recently as neoclassical writers are given to assert that their models, and only theirs, model rational behaviour. As will become clear, they are quite mistaken in this regard.

SOME APPLICATIONS

General Equilibrium Theory (GET) exemplifies neoclassical analysis in its purest and mathematically most elegant form. Devoid of almost any institutional consideration (other than perhaps the assumption of private ownership), describing household, worker and business motivations and goals in the simplest of terms, limiting the constraints on the attainment of these goals to the barest minimum, it is able to show with great precision how a set of endogenous prices and quantities can emerge that reflect an efficient allocation of resources and an ordering of production exactly satisfying consumer demands.

The basic framework of analysis of GET has been extended in different ways to areas of economics outside of pure theory. As a result, it is possible to think in terms of a neoclassical approach to growth theory, trade theory, labour markets, inflation and unemployment, etc. Here, the various assumptions of the competitive model are often only implicit but none the less critical, e.g. the assumption in neoclassical growth and Hecksher-Ohlin trade theory of full employment is based on the continuous and instantaneous market-clearing assumptions of GET. The exogenous tastes and technology assumption is also an integral part of the neoclassical theorizing in these two areas. For example, the macrodynamic version of GET, i.e. neoclassical growth theory, is really nothing more than the addition of an aggregate production function, a fixed savings relationship and given, exogenous rates of growth of labour and technical progress to the static, competitive structure of GET. The result is a form of theorizing about growth with limited explanatory power. Differences in growth rates turn out to be functions of differences in exogenously determined rates of growth of labour and technical progress, a conclusion of scant use to policy makers.

In spite of continuous structural and institutional changes throughout the history of capitalist economies, neoclassical theorists have been reluctant to abandon the competitive model arguing that in some sense it is still relevant. This question begging procedure has had an important and unfortunate result. Adherence to a form of theorizing that assumes the competitive conditions has lead to a lack of concern with evolving institutional characteristics of economies. As a result of this neglect of institutional changes, neoclassical economics puts insufficient emphasis on new constraints on behaviour resulting from changing conditions or new means or goals of conduct.

THE RELEVANCE OF THE COMPETITIVE MODEL

Why model builders chose to treat prices (including wages) as endogenous, freely varying phenomena but tastes and technologies as exogenous is not clear. In the pre-capitalist era, there is evidence that wages did not move in response to market forces of demand and supply.[2] The competitive model thus captured an important change in labour markets, one that began during the early stages of capitalism. Furthermore, in the very early days of capitalism, before the development of powerful business monopolies and labour groups, of sophisticated, highly fabricated consumer and capital goods or of a factory system that required a highly skilled, well-coordinated labour force, prices may well have behaved somewhat along the lines suggested by the competitive, neoclassical model. In these early days, non-price aspects of competition would be less important in goods and labour markets, with one unit exchanged much like any other. It might even have been useful to model capitalist economies as if tastes and technologies were exogenous and not likely to change abruptly, at least in the period before industrialization and rising per capita incomes.

[2] See E. Phelps Brown (1968) *A Century of Pay*, Macmillan, London, chapter IB.

Industrialization and the rise of the factory system changed all this, if for no other reason than the growing ability of employers to act as price makers in both the labour and product markets. But in addition, the increased importance of non-price aspects of competition in both goods and factor markets would certainly reduce the usefulness of the competitive model. In the chapters to follow, it will be argued that the rise of large-scale, powerful organizations, the increased importance of non-price forms of competition in product markets and the development of production processes requiring a highly skilled, yet highly integrated work force – to name but a few of the important institutional changes – have not just made the competitive model largely irrelevant. These and other changes it will be argued, have made its replacement an absolutely essential precondition for a clear insight into the nature of current problems. For it is literally impossible to correctly appraise and administer to the problems of inflation and unemployment as long as it is held, for example, that amounts of labour demanded and supplied depend only upon real wages, that changes in money wage rates reflect the interplay of shifting demand and supply curves, and that firms are constantly adjusting prices to satisfy the short-run marginal conditions.

The assumption of exogenous (fixed) tastes and technologies is even more difficult to justify by a study of history. Neoclassical economics developed during a period of tremendous and abrupt changes in production techniques and tastes. An important characteristic of capitalist development then (as now) was the quickened pace of invention and innovation compared to earlier periods. And this pace was closely related to economic conditions. Moreover, once a stage had been reached in which per capita incomes were rising, tastes began to change as households reallocated their budgets towards newly available goods with high-income elasticities and away from 'necessities'. As later chapters will point out, such cavalier treatment of two of the most outstanding features of development does much to explain the inappropriate and incorrect treatment of the impact of aggregate demand on the growth of productivity and supply by many economists. It does much to explain our inability to come to grips with the problem of stagnation as well.

'AS IF' THEORIZING

It is at this point that neoclassical economists often have recourse to what has become known as the 'as if' doctrine. The argument here is that in spite of noticeable institutional changes, it is not necessary to alter the competitive, neoclassical framework. Rather it is sound scientific procedure to allow, for example, that labour demanded and supplied is still simply a function of the real wage, that atomistic competition describes markets, etc. This, however, is not to be justified because of the belief that these assumptions about markets are true or even realistic, but because somehow the economy and markets behave 'as if' the model of atomistic competition still holds.[3] This view requires further discussion.

If true, the 'as if' doctrine has important practical implications. In terms of day-to-day activities of the ordinary economist, it means that the time, effort and frustrations involved in understanding institutions, how they work, their impact and evolution can be circumvented. For example, if the rise in labour unions is really of no importance in wage setting, if unions act 'more like a thermostat than a furnace', then most labour economists had best redirect their interests.

At a more theoretical level, what is involved here is the matter of 'negligibility assumptions'.[4] Negligible assumptions are assumptions whose inclusion in the analysis is of little consequence in the sense that their inclusion is not likely to be the source of a discrepancy (should there be any) between the predictions of the model and happenings in the real world. What advocates of the competitive, neoclassical model must be positing in their support of the 'as if' doctrine is that seemingly important discrepancies between the real world and the competitive assumptions are really of such little consequence that the predictions of the models will not be refuted by real-world events in any important way.

If, in fact, a correspondence between the predictions of this model and the real world is lacking then the proper scientific procedure is to conclude that the empirical relevance of the competitive model is, at best, restricted to economies of earlier times.[5] In this case the erroneous predictions indicate that the assumptions (i.e. the competitive assumptions) have not been negligible. Galileo's law of falling bodies is often cited as a parallel example illustrating what is

---

[3] The spurious correlation is a special case of the 'as if' doctrine. For example, a high correlation between wine production in France and foxes killed in hunting in Ireland indicates that the world behaves 'as if' fox hunting influences wine production (or vice versa).

[4] See A. Musgrave (1981) 'Unreal Assumptions' in economic theory: The F-twist untwisted, *Kyklos*, No. 3.

[5] ibid.

involved. This law is formulated in terms of the behaviour of bodies falling in a vacuum. To say, in this case, that the real world operates such that falling bodies behave as if falling in a vacuum is but to say that in most circumstances air resistance is of no consequence. And this can be readily tested in physics.

Unfortunately the important issue about assumptions, i.e. whether they are negligible or not, has become confused with the issue of their realism or truth. Thus, one writer espousing the 'as if' doctrine in support of the competitive model has argued that the realism of the assumptions of a model, in this case the competitive assumptions, are of no consequence.

Truly important and significant hypotheses will be found to have 'assumptions' that are wildly inaccurate descriptive representations of reality, and, in general, the more significant the theory, the more unrealistic the assumptions (in this sense).[6]

Clearly, this fails to distinguish between the realism of assumptions and their negligibility. The correct inference is not the more unrealistic the assumptions the more significant the theory. Unrealistic assumptions must lead to unrealistic conclusions and insignificance ('garbage in – garbage out'). Instead the inference to draw is that the more insignificant or negligible the assumptions, the more significant the theory.[7]

---

[6] See M. Friedman (1953) The methodology of positive economics in *Essays in Positive Economics,* University of Chicago Press, Chicago, p. 14.

[7] Unfortunately, social life is not so simple and attempts to test economic theories by means of the correspondence between their predictions and the real world are difficult. For example, in what follows it will be argued that unions have an important impact on wage settlements and the inflationary process. Among other things, they cause wages to be much less sensitive to aggregate demand, especially to declines in aggregate demand, a view that would not be accepted by many neoclassical economists. In this case, a test of this (and the competitive) hypothesis is the real-world behaviour of wage inflation in the face of the current restrictive policies being pursued throughout the OECD. By this test, the 'as if' assumption that unions have a negligible impact on wage settlements on the economy would seem to fail badly. Modern-day stagflation is but the coexistence of wage inflation with rising unemployment rates.

However, as chapter 3 reveals, modern-day neoclassical economists specializing in inflation and unemployment problems; i.e. the monetarists, are quite unconvinced by all this. By allowing for what has come to be known as 'price' or 'supply' surprises, the coexistence of rising wages and prices and unemployment can be explained within a modified neoclassical framework that assumes 'flex-price' markets. In the final analysis, the choice between the monetarist explanation of stagflation and that offered here must be determined by both the realism of the assumptions and the predictions of the theories.

AN ALTERNATIVE APPROACH

The analysis to follow incorporates two important and radical divergences from the neoclassical framework. First, the view that something worthwhile can emerge from a framework that assumes tastes and technologies are exogenous while prices are endogenous and vary freely to clear markets, organize production and allocate resources is discarded. As already pointed out, models of exogenous tastes and technologies are appropriate only for pre-industrial societies. In this study tastes and technologies are endogenously determined and are constantly changing. Furthermore, because of pervasive institutional changes, most markets no longer operate in the manner assumed in neoclassical analysis. In general, price movements while explicable in economic terms, seldom reflect the interplay of shifting demand and supply curves, thereby allowing the 'price mechanism' to organize economic activities. This quite obviously has important implications for an analysis of inflation.

This leads to the second main divergence of this study from neoclassical analysis. Historical developments leading to institutional changes in the nature of production, work, leisure and economic power relations cannot be ignored in studying any economic problem of significance. Proponents of the competitive model have an unyielding faith in the forces of competition to bring about a definitive, predictable form of economic organization, provided the invisible hand is allowed free play. 'Markets are markets' whatever else has taken place historically, they argue. Hence, efforts to study institutional changes are wasted efforts. Quite a contrary view is adopted here. What is to be argued is that the real world cannot be finessed. The problems of inflation, stagnation and unemployment cannot be explained and alleviated by looking, say, at the money supply. Rather these difficulties can only be understood and combated when seen within the institutional context in which they arose. These are points to be developed in some detail. They are relevant at this stage, however, in clearing up two methodological issues that have become obscured in neoclassical writings. These issues are the distinction between rational means and rational ends, on the one hand, and *ad hoc* theorizing and *ad hoc* theory, on the other.

RATIONAL MEANS VERSUS RATIONAL ENDS

The process of optimizing has played a critical role in model building in economics for over a century. Related to it is the concept of rational behaviour. Workers, firms or consumers are said to be behaving irrationally if their behaviour is non-optimizing, etc. From this non-controversial matter of definitions, neoclassical economists leap to an unwarranted conclusion; only the kinds of behaviour modelled within their framework can be considered optimal or rational.

Two points must be made, one with regards to means compared to ends, the other concerning constraints. First, optimization is merely a consistency criterion, a framework used to relate means to ends. Given certain constraints on behaviour, optimization techniques merely determine whether, given the stated ends, the means chosen are those most efficient for achieving them. If they are, then the economic agent can be said to be optimizing or behaving rationally (by definition). The point to notice is that rationality refers to means not ends. To refer to goals or ends as rational or irrational is to engage in moral philosophy, not science.[8] Thus, if a firm in an industry with many competitors sets a goal of short-run profit maximization and is completely unconstrained in its behaviour except by the technology adopted, then it would be expected that the price it charges will vary freely (and continuously, if necessary) to equate marginal cost and marginal revenue.

On the other hand, suppose that the firm in question has a good deal of market power and its managers organize their activities with multiple goals or ends in mind. For example, the ends of their activities are profits and a concern that their activities be consistent with some national goal, e.g. a war effort or export success for the nation as a whole. If it is further assumed that these goals can be made explicit in the form of some kind of objective function and that the only constraint on behaviour is technology, then optimizing, rational behaviour need not and is not likely to imply continuous price

---

[8] Consider the following quotation from a recently published monetarist text (my italics):

Households maximize their utility and firms, their profits. *This means* that the lower the real wage, the more labour will be demanded, and the higher the real wage, the more labour will be supplied.

The first sentence in the quote means no such thing. For example, backward-bending supply curves are a possibility even in neoclassical analysis. In reality workers as heads of households have much more complicated utility functions than suggested by the second sentence. As a result, the means by which they go about maximizing is a good deal more involved than that described in a neoclassical world. The same is true of firms.

See M. Parkin (1982) *Modern Macroeconomics,* Prentice Hall Canada, Scarborough, Ontario.

adjustments that bring marginal costs and revenues into line. What kind of behaviour is rational or irrational will be derived from close inspection of the nature of the objective function and the constraints. But under no circumstance can the economist say that the goals or ends are rational or not. Neoclassical models tend to make rather restrictive assumptions about the goals of economic activity. As the above example makes clear, it is not necessary to use neoclassical models to represent rational or optimizing behaviour.[9]

The example just given can be expressed in terms of a profit maximizing goal subject to an additional constraint; namely, that certain national goals be advanced. This leads to a second point and that has to do with the nature of the constraints on behaviour assumed in neoclassical economics. One of the important points to emerge from the later chapters is the endogenous nature of labour productivity, in which emphasis is given to the importance of morale on output. Now, morale is partly a function of workers feeling that they were paid a 'fair' wage which is, in turn, related to the wages paid to other workers. Going further, when firm-specific, on the job training is involved, management has a strong interest in reducing turnover. This is to a large extent a morale problem, one of convincing workers that they are being well-treated. Therefore, because of these kinds of influences in the real world, management is constrained in its wage behaviour. If it tries to reduce money wages whenever excess supply develops, this is considered unfair. Labour's long-run productivity response will be such as to adversely affect costs and, therefore, profits. Other arguments are given in chapter 5 to indicate why wages are often not adjusted to eliminate excess-demand conditions.

All of this is but to say that when some of the relevant institutional complexities of modern-day economies are recognized, it is necessary to introduce both economic and non-economic constraints on wage (and other) behaviour. The constraints, in this case, are implicit (long-run) contracts between buyers and sellers guaranteeing fair treatment all around, largely in the interests of long-run profit maximization. The reluctance of neoclassical analysis to take account of

---

[9] There is a large and important literature that questions the appropriateness of modelling human behaviour in terms of the rational means–ends, optimizing framework. In a world of uncertainty (in contrast to measurable risk), people may not optimize but satisfice. See H. Simon (1978) 'Rationality as process and as product of thought, *American Economic Review, Papers and Proceedings,* May, and H. Leibenstein (1976) *Beyond Economic Man,* Harvard University, Cambridge, Mass. These important views are not considered in the text.

the institutional framework leads it to ignore important constraining influences on behaviour. The neoclassical view of the labour market corresponds to a view of cheap, untrained, undifferentiated labour being bought and sold in markets characterized by atomistic competition. In the real world of today, an unwillingness to adjust money wages to market clearing levels is not the result of irrational behaviour or a willingness to 'forego perceived benefits from trade'. Such conclusions are based on overly simplistic and poor modelling of labour markets. In truth the reluctance to adjust money wages is better interpreted as an attempt to behave rationally, i.e. to maximize profits, in a complex, uncertain world.[10]

AD HOC THEORY AND *AD HOC* THEORIZING

The rational means–rational ends distinction helps to clarify another misunderstanding. Consider what has become known as the *ad hoc* theorizing. This is said to consist of constructing macro behavioural relations between variables that cannot be rigorously and consistently derived from micro optimizing behaviour of individual consumers and businessmen. Now neoclassical analysis is often given high marks when the issue of *ad hoc* theorizing is brought up.[11] As any number of texts make clear, the world of atomistic competition lends itself very well to rigorous micro modelling. Anyone must be impressed with the rigour and precision of, say, indifference curve analysis and the theory of the firm under pure competition. But the point implicit in the previous section is that this rigour is obtained at

[10] Two additional methodological points came to mind. First, it is fairly common practice among economists to argue that if in response, say, to a shift in the demand curve for a good or for labour, price is not quickly adjusted to equate marginal revenue and costs or the real wage is not altered to clear the labour market, this is due to 'transactions costs'. Similarly, if it is found that consumer purchases do not reveal some kind of marginalist calculation indicating equalization of marginal utilities, this is due to the 'disutility of calculating utilities'. Unfortunately, in both cases, such a procedure leads to non-refutable hypotheses or tautologies. If there is, for example, a cost in changing a price it must be specified in advance if testable hypothesis are to ever be formulated.

Second, modern-day contract theory illustrates all too well that economists are constantly involved in reinventing the wheel. A reluctance to mistreat workers has long been an important consideration in the minds of most business men and has been common knowledge among economists willing to work with primary data for half a century.

[11] See M. Pesaran (1982) A critique of the proposed tests of the natural rate–rational expectations hypothesis, *The Economic Journal*, September, pp. 531–2.

a great cost. The micro basis of economic behaviour has been formulated usually as if there are not multiple goals to activities or complicated, various constraints on behaviour. As just argued, neoclassical economists are reluctant to extend their modelling into those domains that allow institutional considerations to impinge upon behaviour through the incorporation of additional goals and constraints. But once such extensions are undertaken, the subject matter no longer lends itself to such precise, explicit modelling. Furthermore while its micro modelling has become highly developed, aggregation procedures within neoclassical economics involve the same grossly unrealistic assumptions or restrictions as within, say, Keynesian economics. The alleged superiority of neoclassical economics in this matter is nothing more than illusion.[12]

None of this should be understood to imply that micro foundations of a theory may not be valuable parts of any study. However, the critical issue is whether the micro-analysis chosen has explanatory power. This suggests a distinction between *ad hoc* theorizing as defined above, and an *ad hoc* theory. The latter is meant to signify a theory constructed with little prior attempt to ascertain its empirical relevance to the problem at hand. To use some earlier terminology, *ad hoc* theory is little concerned with whether its assumptions are negligible or not. Because of this lack of concern with the importance of its assumptions, neoclassical analysis has developed models that assume means, ends and constraints of slight relevance for contemporary economies.[13]

THE MONETARIST, NEOCLASSICAL VIEW

The preceeding discussion is needed to understand why there is so much confusion among economists over the causes of the current stagflation and so many contradictory policies offered as solutions.

---

[12] For example, consumer preferences must be homothetic before consumer behaviour can be rigorously and consistently aggregated. Also, utilities must be independent.

[13] Pesaran, op. cit. citing Popper points out that neoclassical economics is a perfect example of *ad hoc* theory, although Popper uses the term differently from economists. Neoclassical economics treats tastes, technologies and endowments as exogenous and within this framework attempts to explain prices and quantities. But tastes and technologies are endogenous in the real world, determined by incomes, prices and quantities. This, by Popper's definition is *ad hoc* theory, explaining events in terms of variables that are determined by the events to be explained.

For within the economics profession there is now a polarization of beliefs about the nature of inflation and unemployment which can only generate confusion and contradiction. On the one hand, some macro-economists have opted for the neoclassical method of analysis or paradigm in their attempt to understand inflation and stagnation, while a smaller group has strongly rejected this approach as hopelessly simplistic. In its place, this latter group has tried, often in bits and pieces, to put together a workable, insightful, alternative framework, one that attempts to include modern institutions, complex organizations with market power and a realistic set of assumptions about the workings of markets, the price mechanism and, in general, a modern capitalist economy. The divisions are sharp and run deep and the positions largely irreconcilable.

The expressions 'new classical macroeconomics' or 'great monetarism' are terms used by economists to describe the modern application of the neoclassical principles to the problems of inflation and unemployment and stagnation.[14] What monetarism has done is to adopt the time-honoured view that product and labour markets operate in such a way that changes in prices and wages reflect shifting demand and supply curves. Using the modern terminology, most markets are assumed to be 'flex-price', operating much the same way as stock and bond markets. Labour markets, for example, are described in the simplest of ways, descriptions that deny that institutional developments are of relevance in influencing outcomes. The interdependence of wage settlements is barely considered, unions hardly matter either in wage setting in individual markets or in the inflationary performance of the economy, etc. As in general equilibrium theory, market transactions are assumed to always take place at intersection points. Why this must be the case is explained on *a priori* grounds, not by an appeal to facts. Unless prices adjust to clear markets, 'perceived gains from trade are foregone' and traders are alleged to be behaving irrationally.

On the basis of this flex-price edifice, the traditional demand–pull theory of inflation emerges with special emphasis on the role of the money supply. Inflation in the modern, monetarist world is essentially the same theory of inflation that completely dominated economic thinking until the 1950s. The presentation is more technical but the theoretical basis is hardly changed. New slogans have been invented to be sure. Instead of referring to inflation as 'too many

---

[14] The term 'great monetarism' has been used by R. Solow (1976) 'Comments on Stein' in *Monetarism*, Vol. 1, (Ed. J. Stein), North-Holland, Amsterdam.

dollars chasing too few goods', the expression is 'inflation is always and everywhere a monetary phenomenon'. But, in essence, the explanation of inflation is not appreciably changed from that popular 150 years ago. Variations in aggregate demand due to variations in the rate of growth of the money supply work through flex-price markets causing variations in the rate of inflation.

Since the money supply is treated as an exogenous variable by monetarists, albeit something under the control of the monetary authorities, an exogenous 'explanation' of inflation emerges to complement the neoclassical exogenous theory of growth and a newly arrived exogenous theory of the business cycle. Forces from outside explain inflation as well as growth and cycles. Ultimately, since output gravitates towards full employment, the inflation rate will converge on whatever (unexplained) rate of growth of the money supply (adjusted for the trend in real output) the authorities choose.

A POST-KEYNESIAN VIEW OF STAGFLATION

The view offered in these chapters is at odds with the monetarist view at every step along the way. The basic assumptions of neoclassical, monetarist analysis are challenged, as is the monetarist prescription for recovery. Tastes and technologies are considered to be endogenous variables whose behaviour is very much conditioned by economic events. Such a treatment of technology, for example, allows a clearer picture to emerge of the underlying causes of the low productivity growth. Stagnation is largely traced to depressed aggregate demand conditions. Investment, innovation and productivity growth in this view will never recover as long as the authorities persist in depressing aggregate demand in the interests of fighting inflation.

Going further, the position adopted here is that almost all labour markets and most product markets are 'fix-price' markets. In these markets prices and wages are largely fixed with respect to excess demand and supply conditions, but change with costs. For example, wages respond to changes in the cost of living and wage settlements in other labour markets. Price changes in product markets reflect changes in unit costs, only by accident will prevailing prices clear markets. This means that while prices are determined by economic events, to be sure, they are not the solution to a set of simultaneous equations portraying the standard demand and supply conditions in markets. And to say this is not to attribute irrationality on the part of the traders. Non-market clearing prices and wages can be seen as the outgrowth of rational, optimizing behaviour once the analysis moves beyond the overly simple modelling of neoclassical economics. Thus, the analysis offered below, like neoclassical analysis, employs models that relate means to ends subject to constraints, but it sees the world as more complex. As institutions evolve and societies become more structured and complicated, ends become more varied while constraints arise that involve non-economic as well as economic considerations.

From this view of markets emerges an understanding of inflation that is distinctly non-monetarist. Some commodity markets do operate like the stock market. To the extent that markets are flex-price, to that extent does the traditional demand–pull explanation of inflation hold. But the position adopted here is that inflation is essentially a cost–push phenomenon, sustained and driven by wage–wage and wage–price mechanisms. Both of these mechanisms are seen to be the outgrowth of institutional changes that have been evolving for some time. In particular, it is argued that the development of powerful unions and oligopolies operating in a full employment context have altered the nature of the inflationary process greatly since the days before unions, but markedly so ever since the beginnings of the postwar period.

Another point of importance becomes apparent. Many societies will not tolerate continuous, high unemployment and sooner or later the money supply and aggregate demand targets will be adjusted to stabilize unemployment. In this case some of the underlying causes of inflation must be seen as non-economic forces that drive the cost–push mechanisms. For example, strong trade unions generate strong political as well as market power. If unemployment rates cannot be allowed to rise without limit for political reasons, then whatever inflation is still left when the constraint is reached must be validated. The strength of inflationary pressures at this point is determined to a large extent by institutional, political and sociological as well as by economic phenomena. For example, if the unions have confidence in the political forces in power, wage and price restraint may be forthcoming. This is most clearly seen in the case of countries ruled by social democratic governments. These countries, with strong union movements, have not been the most inflation prone nor the most subject to disruption. On the contrary, economies that have malfunctioned the most obviously, e.g. strike-prone economies with high unemployment and low productivity growth, as well as high inflation, have tended to be those with weak union movements such as

Canada and the USA. This is not to argue that unions make no difference but to argue that the manner in which unions influence inflation is very much tied up with political and sociological factors.

The reader will soon be aware that this study places unions centre stage. There are good reasons why unions are singled out for special discussion. Partly it is because their existence, along with powerful oligopolies, has fundamentally transformed the nature of the inflationary process as well as the nature of the solution to the current stagflation. Unions and large corporations more than anything else have lead to cost–push inflation, a situation in which decreases in aggregate demand and rising unemployment are accompanied by continued inflation. To say this is but to repeat the earlier point that institutional changes do matter and do influence economic events dramatically. But unions also deserve special attention because their cooperation is absolutely essential if inflation is to be brought under control.

One of the central messages of the text is that restrictive aggregate demand policies, aimed at bringing down inflation by weakening the power of unions, will at best be successful in the short-run. They will be self-defeating in the long-run because any eventual restimulation of the economy will lead to inflation accelerating again, as unions (and business) attempt to recapture previous losses. Thus, such policies not only antagonize labour, they are costly and fruitless as well.

Neither will policies of deliberately engineered recession succeed in eliminating stagnation. Long drawn-out restrictive policies are hardly likely to revive investment, innovation and productivity growth. This means that even if unemployment rates are pushed high enough to greatly lessen union power and recreate conditions in labour markets resembling the late nineteenth century, neither stagnation or inflation will be defeated.

The message to be developed is that a different solution to stagflation is required, one that is based on increased cooperation between all the potential antagonists, a policy specifically aimed at gaining the cooperation of the unions because the most feasible policy to fight inflation, incomes policy, makes special demands upon workers. A solution to stagflation requires union cooperation, not union bashing.

A FAILED PERSPECTIVE

The initial but critical task in the pages ahead is to convince the reader that the application of the neoclassical precepts to macroeconomic problems, i.e. monetarism, results not only in a seriously flawed picture of today's economic problems but is a blueprint for disastrous policy measures. The difficulty is that neoclassical theory is, to recoin a phrase, *ad hoc* theory, an attempt to explain real-world events with little recourse to systematic observation of the real world.[15] To seek constant refuge and support in the notions of invisible hands, natural rates, price mechanisms and the inexorable workings of the forces of competition is incantation and exorcism not science. As a result the macro policies flowing from such theories have an air of unreality about them and when implemented in their extreme form, e.g. Thatcherism and large elements of Reaganomics, have disastrous effects. But even if pursued 'half-heartedly' in a manner advocated by a recent OECD report, they are wasteful, divisive and fruitless.[16]

To understand the flaws of monetarism, and indeed to understand the shortcomings of any anti-inflation policy based on restrictive aggregate demand policies, it is necessary to first understand the shortcomings of the neoclassical views of markets, technologies and tastes, conflict and power and the role of government. On these matters of importance, the neoclassical-monetarist position is found to be factually incorrect on every count. In its place an alternative view of how advanced capitalist economies work is offered. Basically this view argues that it makes little sense to pretend 'as if' markets operate according to some introductory economics textbook. We live in a world of strong organizations with enough market power to have a pronounced impact on economic outcomes and their influence cannot be ignored. The institutional developments will be pushed to the forefront in an attempt to suggest micro theories of behaviour that make understandable the macro events taking place. If you like, this alternative approach seeks a micro basis to explain the macro events rather than altering macro theory to conform to some assumed, but inappropriate, micro theory. Such restructuring of the problem is naturally only preliminary to the important task of formulating a policy response.

---

[15] This criticism is attenuated only slightly by the recognition of a vast amount of econometric work using highly aggregative, secondary data purporting to prove the monetarist case. Graduate students at computer terminals stand a much better chance of coming up soon with the New Testament, given the wealth of programmes for 'mining the data', than do the monkeys at typewriters in the British Museum.

[16] See *Towards Full Employment and Price Stability,* OECD, Paris 1978.

Much of what is to follow is highly speculative. Given the uniqueness of events in the post-war period, it could not be otherwise. Until the post-war period, the existence of trade unions operating under conditions of prolonged full employment was unheard of. This alone should have suggested that something novel might have been evolving in the OECD countries. For full employment redistributes economic and political power and intensifies aspirations and demands for equality. It also helps to fulfill those aspirations and demands. This appeared most clearly in the developments of the late 1960s and early 1970s. The only reasonable conclusion I could draw when I studied these dismal events was that fundamental institutional and structural changes had by then taken place. These changes, I concluded, had greatly altered our ability to contain inflation, unless we were prepared to recreate an industrial order like that of the late nineteenth century (or adopt the programme advocated here). To assume on the contrary, as do the monetarist and neoclassical writers, an unchanging economic structure so dominating performance that solutions to today's economic problems are no different from those of 50 to 100 years ago seems at best question begging. At worst it is a retreat into scholaticism.

CHAPTER 1

Closing Time in the Gardens
of the West

INTRODUCTION

1. Stagnation

A main concern of this book is to gain an understanding of the nature of the current stagflation. The simultaneous occurrence of high levels of unemployment, low rates of growth of productivity and output, together with high rates of inflation, has now plagued capitalist economies for a decade. The intensity of the problem has varied between the different capitalist countries, but in every OECD economy these symptoms of economic malfunction have persisted long enough to suggest serious economic problems may be endemic to modern capitalism.[1]

The period between the two World Wars was also characterized by slow growth and high rates of unemployment in many countries, suggesting that current difficulties may not be unusual when viewed in a longer historical context. However, high and often accelerating rates of inflation have been experienced in most economies throughout most of the past decade and a half, compared to a more limited incidence between the wars. An even more pronounced contrast with the current period is provided by a comparison with the period comprising roughly the quarter century following the Second World War. In no other period of development did so many capitalist countries grow so rapidly for such an extended period of time as from the early 1950s until shortly before the mid-1970s. With inflation at tolerable rates, unemployment rates fell to historical lows and growth rates of productivity and per capita incomes reached historical highs during this 'golden age' of capitalism.[2]

---

[1] See various issues of *Economic Outlook,* OECD, Paris, for comparable data on a wide number of developed capitalist economies.

[2] See J. Cornwall (1977) *Modern Capitalism: Its Growth and Transformation,* Martin Robertson, London, and (1978) St Martin's Press, New York, chapter II.

By 1973 or 1974, most developed capitalist economies had ceased to grow and for the first time in the post-war period most economies experienced actual declines in real aggregate output beginning in the early 1970s. Table 1.1 documents this aspect of the current malaise by contrasting average rates of growth of real GNP or GDP for the seven major OECD economies and the total OECD economies from the early 1960s until 1973 (the last 'boom' year for most OECD economies) with the period since 1973.[3] Even when the 'boom years' of 1976–79 are included, the pronounced slowdown in growth rates after 1973 is most apparent.

TABLE 1.1   *Annual average rates of growth of real GDP or GNP for selected periods and years for the seven largest OECD economies and total OECD.*

	1963–73 (%)	1973–81 (%)	1982* (%)	1983* (%)
USA	4.0	2.6	− 1.7	2.0
Japan	9.8	4.3	2.5	3.5
Germany	4.4	2.4	− 1.2	−0.2
France	5.5	2.8	1.5	0.5
UK	3.3	1.1	0.5	1.0
Canada	5.7	3.5	− 5.0	1.2
Italy	5.0	3.0	0.7	0.2
Total for seven largest	4.9	2.8	− 0.5	1.7
Total for OECD	5.0	2.8	− 0.5	1.5

Source: Economic Outlook, OECD, Paris, December 1982, tables 1 and R1.
* Projections.

This slowdown in growth rates of total output was primarily a slowdown in productivity growth and not the rate of growth of employment as can be seen from table 1.2. Here the rate of growth of GNP or GDP, $\dot{Q}$, is broken down for the seven major economies into annual average rates of growth of total employment, $\dot{E}$, and productivity per employed worker, $\dot{\rho}$. In every country the rate of growth of GNP or GDP slowed down, comparing the period of relatively rapid growth 1963–73 with the period since 1973, primarily because of the decline in rates of growth of productivity. For example, comparing the 1963–73 period with 1974–81, growth of GNP in Japan declined from an annual average rate of 9.8 to 3.7 per cent. This decline of 6.1 per cent in the growth rate of GNP was due

[3] The seven major OECD economies are Canada, France, West Germany, Italy, Japan, the UK and the USA.

TABLE 1.2　*Annual average of growth of output (Q̇) and employment (Ė) and productivity (ṗ) and average rates of unemployment (U) for selected periods for the seven largest OECD economies.*

	$\dot{Q}$ (%)	$\dot{E}$ (%)	$\dot{p}$ (%)	U (%)
USA				
1963–73	4.1	2.2	1.9	4.3*
1974–81	2.0	2.0	0.0	6.8
France				
1963–73	5.5	0.9	4.6	2.3*
1974–81	2.3	0.0	2.3	5.1
Canada				
1963–73	5.7	3.3	2.4	4.8*
1974–81	2.0	1.9	0.1	7.2
Japan				
1963–73	10.1	1.4	8.7	1.2*
1974–81	4.2	0.9	3.3	1.9
UK				
1963–73	2.9	−0.1	3.0	3.2*
1974–81	−0.2	−1.0	0.8	6.2
Italy				
1963–73	4.8	−0.6	5.4	5.6*
1974–81	2.3	1.4	0.9	6.9
West Germany				
1963–73	4.6	0.0	4.6	0.8*
1974–81	2.0	−0.5	2.5	3.4

Sources: Economic Outlook: OECD, Paris, July 1976, Table 13; December 1976, Table 8; July 1980, Table 7; December 1981, Table 5 and Table R12; and December 1982, Table 14, Table R1 and Table R12.
* 1965–73.

to a decline of 0.8 per cent in employment growth and 5.4 per cent in the rate of growth of productivity. Since productivity growth is the chief source of rising per capita incomes, the marked decline of the latter during the 1970s was predictable.

Table 1.2 also gives average rates of unemployment for the seven large OECD countries during the 1963–73 and 1974–81 periods. While the data indicate fairly substantial differences in any period between countries, comparison of the two periods country by country reveal a marked increase in unemployment rates in the post-1973 period in every economy. The post-1973 period was one of rising unemployment as well as falling rates of growth of labour productivity, but this is to be expected. Low rates of employment and low capital utilization rates go together. When utilization rates are low there is little incentive to add to capacity through expansionary investment. As maintained in chapter 10, this kind of expansionary investment is the most important means of introducing new technology and modernizing production. When it dries up, low rates of productivity growth result. The impact of low capital utilization rates is shown in table 1.3. Annual average rates of growth of total fixed investment and equipment investment are shown for nine OECD countries for the periods before the implementation of policies of restraint and immediately after. The decline of growth rates of these fixed investment categories in the more immediate period is apparent.

TABLE 1.3   *Rates of growth of plant and equipment and equipment investment in constant prices.*

	1962–73		1974–78	
	Plant and equipment	*Equipment*	*Plant and equipment*	*Equipment*
	(%)	(%)	(%)	(%)
Austria[a]	6.24	6.15	3.09	4.48
Canada	6.06	8.99	2.99	− 1.05
Germany[b,d]	4.85	5.78	− 1.49	n.a.
Netherlands[d]	5.11	5.85	0.96	1.60
Norway	5.07	5.58	2.41	− 3.30
Sweden	4.25	4.98	− 1.62	− 0.93
Switzerland[d,e]	4.85	4.58	− 4.47	− 3.91
UK	4.49[c]	5.10[c]	− 0.64	0.94
USA	5.08	7.54	0.79	2.53

Source: National Accounts of OECD Countries, 1961–1978, OECD, Paris.
[a] 1965–73, 1974–77.   [b] 1962–73, 1974–76.   [c] 1963–73.
[d] Includes land improvements.   [e] Includes residential construction.

2. Inflation

The picture sketched so far is that of stagnation in the OECD economies beginning in the first half of the 1970s. But the experience of the last decade and a half has been inflation as well as stagnation, i.e. stagflation. Table 1.4 gives some details on price behaviour during

TABLE 1.4 Average rates of inflation of consumer prices for selected periods and years.

	1960–70 (%)	1971–73 (%)	1974 (%)	1975 (%)	1976 (%)	1977 (%)	1978 (%)	1979 (%)	1980 (%)	1981 (%)	1982* (%)
USA	2.7	4.6	11.0	9.1	5.8	6.5	7.7	11.3	13.5	10.4	5.0
Japan	5.8	7.4	24.5	11.8	9.3	8.1	3.8	3.6	8.0	4.9	3.2
Germany	2.7	5.9	7.0	6.0	4.5	3.9	2.6	4.1	5.5	5.9	4.9
France	4.0	6.3	13.7	11.8	9.6	9.4	9.1	10.8	13.6	13.4	10.1
UK	4.1	8.6	16.0	24.2	16.5	15.9	8.3	13.4	18.0	11.9	7.3
Italy	4.0	7.1	19.1	17.0	16.8	17.0	12.1	14.8	21.2	19.5	17.1
Canada	2.6	5.1	10.8	10.8	7.5	8.0	9.0	9.1	10.1	12.5	10.4
Total of above countries	4.2	5.7	13.3	10.9	7.9	8.1	7.0	9.3	12.2	10.0	6.5
Total for OECD	3.3	6.0	13.4	11.4	8.6	8.7	7.9	9.9	12.9	10.6	7.3

Sources: Economic Outlook, OECD, Paris, July 1979, Page 149 and December 1982, Table 22 and Table R 10.
* Twelve months to September 1982.

the post-war period and provides an explanation of the behaviour of
the authorities following the recession of the first half of the 1970s.
The acceleration of inflation rates up through 1974 (1975 in the UK),
stands out very clearly. What is also clear is that while inflation rates
have declined from the 1974–75 highs and show a noticeable
reduction very recently, they still remained substantially above the
1960–70 rates well into 1982 everywhere except Japan. Only by the
6-month period up to September, 1982 (not shown) do inflation rates
fall to something like the 1960–70 averages.[4]

The acceleration of the rates of price (and wage) inflation that had
begun in the late 1960s and continued up through the early 1970s led
the authorities in the OECD countries to respond to the recession of
the first part of the 1970s in an atypical way. During the 1950s and
1960s when aggregate demand showed signs of weakening, the rise in
unemployment rates and the decline in capital utilization rates
spurred the authorities to introduce stimulative fiscal and monetary
policy measures to combat the recessionary tendencies. The response
in the early part of the 1970s was to permit a more pronounced
recession to develop than would have resulted had stimulative measures been applied once it was clear that unemployment rates were
rising. By 1975 some stimulative action was taken but only 'a moderate but sustained expansion was implicit in the actions of policy
makers from the bottom of the recession onwards'.[5] The unemployment figures in table 1.5 clearly reflect the moderateness of the
expansionary actions. Unemployment rates in the ten OECD economies in the period from 1976 to the present typically have remained
higher than even in the years of recession of 1974–75. Forecasts for
late 1982 and 1983 indicate a worsening of the unemployment
picture everywhere with total unemployment in the OECD fore-
casted to rise from 31.75 million in the second half of 1982 to 34.75
million in the first half of 1984.[6]

3. The shifting Phillips curve

Putting together the unemployment and inflation data for the seven
large OECD countries is of interest. Thus, in table 1.6 annual
average rates of unemployment and inflation for three successive

[4] The latest figures for all the OECD countries are found in *Economic Outlook,*
OECD, Paris, December 1982, table 22. Consumer prices have been used to depict
inflation rather than the GNP deflator since the behaviour of money wages is
more influenced by the former than the latter.
[5] *Towards Full Employment and Price Stability,* op.cit., section (68).
[6] *Economic Outlook,* OECD, Paris, December 1982, table 15.

TABLE 1.5 *Standardized unemployment rates in seven major countries and fifteen OECD economies, 1974–82.*

Percent of total labour force

	1974 (%)	1975 (%)	1976 (%)	1977 (%)	1978 (%)	1979 (%)	1980 (%)	1981 (%)	1982* (%)
USA	5.4	8.3	7.5	6.9	5.9	5.7	7.0	7.5	9.2
Japan	1.4	1.9	2.0	2.0	2.2	2.1	2.0	2.2	2.3
Germany	1.6	3.7	3.7	3.7	3.5	3.2	3.1	4.4	6.2
France	2.8	4.1	4.4	4.7	5.2	5.9	6.3	7.3	8.1
UK†	2.9	3.9	5.5	6.2	6.1	5.7	7.4	11.4	12.8
Italy	5.3	5.8	6.6	7.0	7.1	7.5	7.4	8.3	8.9
Canada	5.3	6.9	7.1	8.0	8.3	7.4	7.5	7.5	10.2
Major seven countries†	3.7	5.5	5.5	5.4	5.1	5.0	5.6	6.5	7.8
Total fifteen OECD countries†	3.5	5.2	5.3	5.3	5.2	5.1	5.8	6.8	8.0

Source: Economic Outlook, OECD, Paris, December 1981, Table R12.
* First three quarters.
† Series adjusted by the OECD.

TABLE 1.6 *Annual average rates of inflation of consumer prices ($\dot{p}$) and unemployment rates ($\dot{U}$) for the seven largest OECD economies for selected periods.*

	1961–66		1966–73			1976–80		
	$\dot{p}$ (%)	$\dot{U}$*	$\dot{p}$ (%)	U*	U†	$\dot{p}$ (%)	U*	U†
USA	1.6	5.2	4.4	4.5	4.3	9.0	6.7	6.6
Japan	5.9	1.3	6.2	1.3	1.2	6.6	2.1	2.1
Germany	2.9	0.4	3.8	0.8	0.9	4.1	3.3	3.4
France	3.6	1.8	5.1	2.5	2.4	10.5	5.5	5.3
UK	3.4	2.7	6.1	3.4	3.3	14.4	6.3	6.2
Canada	2.0	5.1	4.3	5.2	4.9	8.7	7.7	7.7
Italy	4.5	3.5	4.5	3.7	5.7	16.7	3.7	7.1
Total for seven largest	2.4	n.a.	4.7	n.a.	3.1	8.9	n.a.	5.3
Total for OECD	2.6	n.a.	4.9	n.a.	n.a.	9.6	n.a.	n.a.

Sources: Economic Outlook, OECD, Paris, July 1979, December 1981, Tables R10 and R12; *Monthly Labor Review,* US Dept of Labor, June 1972, June 1975, May 1979, and December 1981.
* Adjusted to US concepts by US Dept of Labor.
† Standardized unemployment rate from OECD.

post-war periods are given, two covering the boom of the 1960s and early 1970s and one covering the period following the downturn of the early 1970s. Table 1.6 suggests that if such a thing as a Phillips curve exists (i.e. a negative relation between rates of inflation and unemployment), this 'trade-off' has worsened over time in the sense that a much less appetizing 'menu of choices' between inflation and unemployment is available in the post-1975 period. Rising rates of unemployment in successive periods in most countries were accompanied by rising or constant rates of inflation, comparing the first two periods with 1976–80. For example, unemployment rates in Canada remained a little over 5 per cent from 1960 until 1973 while inflation rates rose moderately between the 1960–66 and 1966–73 periods. However, by the 1976–80 period, unemployment rates had risen to an average of 7.7 per cent. Instead of declining, the rate of inflation in Canada accelerated to 8.7 per cent in 1976–80.[7]

Table 1.6 indicates that during the period 1976–80, any rate of unemployment was associated with a higher rate of inflation than in, say, the 1960s or early 1970s. How to improve upon this disagreeable set of unemployment–inflation choices has been the concern of government leaders in all countries for almost 10 years. Unfortunately, there is much disagreement in the economics profession today as to the proper policy response to stagflation. As later chapters will reveal, this disagreement has to do with such matters as whether inflation and unemployment rates are causally related and, if so, which is the cause and which is the effect. Alternatively, it may well be that changes in rates of inflation and unemployment are better explained in terms of separate causes so that what is required is a separate theory of inflation and unemployment.

But granting for the moment the more usual view that there is a causal relation between inflation and unemployment rates, two questions immediately arise. First, given a desire to improve the unemployment–inflation choices facing the policy makers, what means are available for achieving such an improvement? Second, of all the policy means available, which are the least costly in the sense that they minimize both the time taken to realize the policy goals (since inflation and unemployment involve costs) and the number and intensity of adverse side effects? The next section will attempt to elaborate on these issues in a rather preliminary way but with enough detail to give some indication of the issues that must be

---

[7] Because they were years of prosperity in many countries, 1966 and 1973 were used as end points.

analysed more carefully and critically in later chapters. It will do so by outlining the analysis and policy prescriptions flowing from a highly influential report published under the auspices of the OECD in 1978, *Towards Full Employment and Price Stability*.[8] This report hereafter referred to as the 'Report' attempted to explain the acceleration of inflation that began in the second half of the 1960s in so many capitalist economies and to prescribe a policy response believed to lead to a return of market capitalism to something like its 'golden age', i.e. the period from the early 1950s until the late 1960s. A summary of the Report is an especially useful means of outlining some of the important, and as yet, unresolved policy issues confronting the authorities in the capitalist economies today. It was written by a group of economists with the highest credentials, and also represents what must be considered the views of the (albeit dwindling) majority of the economics profession. The policy recommendations of the Report also coincide with the policies adopted by a large number of governments to combat the inflationary tendencies of the current period.

A 'MAINSTREAM' INTERPRETATION OF RECENT EVENTS
AND A SUGGESTED POLICY RESPONSE

It is fair to say that until the mid-1960s, most economists felt that the relationship between the rate of price inflation, $\dot{p}$, and unemployment, U was fairly stable. Allowing for the fact that other variables influence the relationship between $\dot{p}$ and U, the conventional wisdom held that they did not change too dramatically or often. Furthermore, it was thought that this relatively stable relationship implied a number of unemployment–inflation rate combinations that were politically tolerable. Such a relationship is depicted in Fig. 1.1 by the (short-run) Phillips curve labelled '$\dot{p}^e$ = pre-1965 rate'. Following convention, it and the other curves are drawn such as to depict a downward-sloping, convex relationship with the rate of price inflation on the vertical and the unemployment rate on the horizontal axis.

Also following convention, the unemployment rate is interpreted as a proxy for the state of excess demand (or supply) in the labour (and product) market and causation is assumed to run from the unemployment rate to inflation. By, say, increasing aggregate

---

[8] *Towards Full Employment*, op. cit.

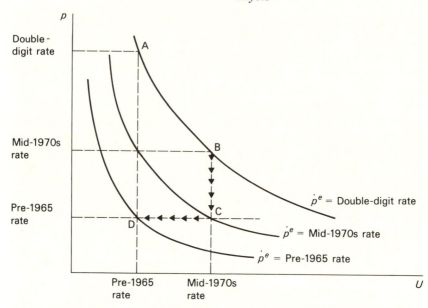

FIGURE 1.1   *Phillips curves and the recent inflation*

demand, the excess demand for labour rises (or the excess supply falls) in such a way that unemployment rates fall and this increased demand pressure in the labour market increases the rate of wage inflation. This, in turn, leads to an increase in the rate of price inflation, productivity growth being held constant.

As just mentioned, Phillips curve analysis does take into consideration other factors that affect the relationship between wage or price inflation rates and unemployment but assumes these other variables to be constant or to act as shift variables. For example, starting with the Phillips curve nearest the origin and moving outward to the right, the successive curves represent the new unemployment–inflation choices following an increase in some other variable(s) that positively affects the rate of inflation at any rate of unemployment.

Following the acceleration in inflation in the second half of the 1960s, almost every Phillips curve study included the expected rate of inflation, $\dot{p}^e$, as one of the additional variables explaining actual inflation rates. The higher is the expected rate of inflation, other things being equal, the higher will be the actual rate of inflation, a view adopted in the Report. Any change in $\dot{p}^e$ will, therefore, shift the curve. Graphically, with such an 'augmented Phillips curve' the actual rate of price inflation, $\dot{p}$, in figure 1.1 is related to the unemployment rate, U, but a separate Phillips curve is drawn for different expected rates of inflation, $\dot{p}^e$. No attempt has been made to scale either axis in figure 1.1. Qualitative measures of the Phillips curve trade-off are sufficient since the discussion need not be concerned with country-specific numerical properties of a Phillips curve.

The Report's interpretation of recent events can be described as follows. Up until, say, the second half of the 1960s, actual rates of inflation had remained relatively low. Under the circumstances those affected could ignore inflation in the sense that they expected inflation to continue more or less at the prevailing actual rate and were never proved to be too far wrong. In other words, the expected-rate of inflation, $\dot{p}^e$, by the mid-1960s was the rate that actually existed at that time. Let the relevant Phillips curve for any economy in mid-1960s be that labelled '$\dot{p}^e$ = pre-1965 rate' and assume that point D is the unemployment–inflation combination with which the economy initially finds itself. Note that at point D the expect rate of inflation is equal to the actual rate of inflation, i.e. the pre-1965 rate.

However, because of certain structural changes that were accumulating over the post-war period, (e.g. rising 'aspirations' and the expectation of guaranteed full employment), tight labour markets in the late 1960s and policy mistakes (e.g. stimulating demand just before election time even though the economy might be already 'overheated'), and 'shocks' beginning in the early 1970s (e.g. shortages and speculations in commodity markets, energy price increases and the demise of the adjustable-peg exchange-rate system), inflation began to accelerate in the late 1960s and continued into the 1970s. By 1973 in some countries and by 1974 and 1975 in most, double-digit rates of inflation had set in and this could be assumed to have caused an increase in the expected rate of inflation which would shift the Phillips curve outward to that denoted by '$\dot{p}^e$ = double digit rate'. If unemployment remains at its pre-1965 rate, the events described result in a movement to point A in figure 1.1. Again, point A like point D is assumed to describe a situation in which the actual and expected rates of inflation are equal.

Following the recession beginning in 1973 or 1974 (depending upon the country), most governments decided on a policy of curbing inflation by allowing unemployment rates to rise. By 1976 inflation rates had fallen below the double-digit level in most countries (see Table 1.4) but still remained very much above their pre-1965 rates (notable exceptions being the UK and Italy where inflation rates had hardly fallen at all), so that the situation at the end of the first half of the 1970s and the bottom of the recession could be depicted by point

B in figure 1.1. The actual causes behind the partial decline in the rate of inflation are still a matter of debate. The Report attributes the decline primarily to the induced effect of looser labour markets, along with the decline of prices in certain commodity markets following the lessening of the earlier speculative booms.

The 'game plan' envisaged by the fiscal and monetary authorities of the various countries who subscribed to the policies advocated in the Report was an eventual shift of the augmented Phillips curve to something like the Phillips curve relevant before the mid-1960s, i.e. the curve labelled '$\dot{p}^e$ = pre-1965 rate' by 1980. This was to be achieved by picking a point on successive Phillips curves that corresponded to a rate of actual inflation that was always less than the expected rate of inflation associated with that Phillips curve. Since B is such a point, this policy was supposed to lead initially to a shifting of the Phillips curve, downward to the left, say, to that labelled '$\dot{p}^e$ = mid-1970s rate'. In the event of such a shift actually taking place, the authorities could if they wished regulate aggregate demand in such a way that point C could be chosen, in which case they maintained the unemployment rate at the mid-1970s rate but obtained a decline in the actual rate of inflation to the pre-1965 rate. Since the actual rate of inflation associated with point C is less than the expected rate, i.e. $\dot{p}^e$ = mid-1970s rate, this, in turn, was to lead eventually to a further shift of the Phillips curve to that closest to the origin. Once that had happened unemployment could be reduced to the pre-1965 rate as the economy moved to point D. This particular unemployment–inflation strategy is traced out by the line with arrowheads. The policy was supposed to bring a return to the better days before the mid-1960s by 1980. In the meantime, depending upon how rapidly the Phillips curve shifts inward, high rates of unemployment and slow growth would have to be expected.

WHAT WENT WRONG?

It was the hope of many economists and political authorities that a policy-induced recession would soon cure the economy of high rates of inflation and lead shortly to a situation such as that indicated by point D. The targets set in the Report were actually less ambitious than a return to pre-1965 conditions. Rather they aimed at a recovery programme that was thought to be consistent with a non-accelerating rate of inflation but which did not target either an inflation or unemployment rate as low as the rates prevailing before

1965. The inflation and unemployment targets that were to be realized by 1980 were 5 and 4 per cent respectively. The actual rates of inflation and unemployment for the OECD as a whole were 12.9 and 5.8 per cent respectively in 1980.[9] Clearly targets of 4 per cent unemployment and 5 per cent inflation were overly ambitious.

As seen in table 1.5, unemployment rates never seemed to recover from the highs reached in the 1974–75 recession, except for the USA, and by 1980 or 1981 unemployment rates had begun to achieve new highs everywhere; and, as indicated in table 1.4, while inflation rates had begun to come down everywhere by 1982, up to the target date of 1980 the fight against inflation had gone very badly. Clearly something had gone very wrong with the 'game plan' of the Report. Inflation could not be brought down as quickly as was envisaged. More serious, in order to reduce inflation rates by the desired amounts, widespread, prolonged high unemployment rates were required. The use of restrictive aggregate demand policies (including restrictive growth of the money supply) to bring down inflation turned out to be much more costly than predicted.

As will be argued in the pages to come, much of the difficulty can be traced to certain structural changes that have been accumulating under market capitalism in the post-war period and continue to do so today. These structural changes will be seen to give rise to an inflationary bias which has much to do with the failure of current anti-inflationary policies. One manifestation of this bias is the great cost in terms of prolonged periods of high unemployment needed to reduce inflation rates. Another reflection of this bias would be revealed by the responses of wages and prices to a restimulation of the economy following a 'successful' anti-inflationary, restrictive demand policy. An inflationary bias is then revealed if there is widespread involuntary unemployment when the inflation rate starts to accelerate following the stimulation of demand. In the pages to follow it will be argued that this is very much the case today.

But it will also be argued below that these manifestations of an inflationary bias arise out of the existence of a basic asymmetry in the unemployment–inflation trade-off. This means that expansionary policies like those pursued in the period before the early 1970s lead to accelerating increases in prices, including money wages, as well as increases in output, while contractionary policies have their main impact on output and employment, up until unemployment rates reach double-digit figures and remain there.

[9] *Economic Outlook,* OECD, Paris, December, 1981, tables R10 and R12.

The possibility of an inflationary bias in this sense greatly restricts the effective use of aggregate demand policies *by themselves* for achieving unemployment–inflation goals. It limits the use of aggregate demand policy in reducing unemployment, as the early acceleration of inflation will restrain the authorities from pursuing a strong stimulative policy during a recovery programme. An inflationary bias also limits the effective use of aggregate demand policy in controlling inflation, as the increasing unemployment resulting from the anti-inflationary policies will restrain the authorities from further restricting demand when so little is achieved in reducing inflation.

CONCLUSIONS

The implications for policy of an inflationary bias are very great. It is popular today to speak of 'the death of Keynesian economics'. Presumably this is to be interpreted to mean that aggregate demand policy is an incorrect even harmful policy tool for attempting to stabilize the economy. What has just been said could be interpreted as support of this position. However, this would be incorrect. What will be quite clear in the second half of this study is that the announcement of the so-called death of Keynesian economics is somewhat premature. It will be argued that unless aggregate demand policies are accompanied by additional policy instruments, e.g. an incomes policy, they cannot play the stabilizing role that Keynes envisaged. However, when included as part of a policy package for relieving an economy of its stagnation and inflation problems, their necessary role is apparent.

One of Keynes' most important messages was that there was no invisible hand stabilizing demand at a level corresponding to full employment. Aggregate demand policies would be necessary periodically to maintain an economy at high levels of employment. But while the *General Theory* has done much to demolish the credibility of the invisible hand, Keynes' prescription for achieving macro stability was not comprehensive enough. Not only is there no natural tendency for unemployment rates to fluctuate ever so mildly around the full employment rate, there is no tendency for modern capitalist systems to experience non-accelerating rates of inflation at this unemployment rate. The result is that the healthy functioning of the modern-day capitalist system requires more, not less, intervention in an economy propelled by the private pursuit of private interests.

The inability of restrictive demand policies to reduce inflation rates noticeably without incurring long periods of high unemployment has given rise to alternative policies, some of which can only make matters worse. In general, in the English-speaking countries the alternative policies have stressed the need to have less government intervention with the workings of something called the 'price mechanism'. Indeed a whole new vocabulary and a whole new method of analysis has been developed (largely in the USA) to show that the current difficulties are but a temporary aberration from a natural state of economic grace, an aberration that would soon disappear if the free play of market forces were reinstated. The view adopted here is that such policies are disturbance amplifying and will lead to increased political and social as well as economic instability. Later chapters will present policies that place much less reliance on market forces, policies which play down conflict and stress the importance of cooperation.

These are matters that will be discussed at length presently. Before that, however, some rather preliminary work will be undertaken in chapters 2 to 4 which will trace some of the more significant developments in inflation and unemployment theory in the post-war period. Chapter 5 evaluates the various theories in terms of their micro underpinnings. Following that, the analysis proceeds in chapter 6 to outline a theory of inflation (and unemployment) that explains why inflation became such a serious problem in so many countries in the second half of 1960s, a matter discussed in detail in chapter 7. Chapter 8 concludes the first half of the study with a discussion of the involuntary nature of most unemployment during the past decade. The second half of the study is concerned with a policy response to the difficulties.

CHAPTER 2

Some Early Post-war Developments in Inflation Theory

INTRODUCTION

From the eighteenth century until the late 1950s demand or demand–pull explanations of inflation dominated the views of the profession and government leaders.[1] Just as conditions of demand in excess of supply at the current price was thought to generate price increases in individual markets, so in some aggregate sense would conditions of aggregate demand in excess of aggregate supply drive up some average of prices. Moreover, this process was thought to be symmetrical; conditions of excess supply would generate deflation.

During the early postwar period studies of the workings of labour and product markets, the relationship between the nature of these markets and the Phillips curve, and the dynamics of the inflationary process were widespread. From these efforts there emerged a running debate between those who felt inflation was a 'demand–pull' process, and those who viewed it as a 'cost–push' phenomenon and sought to replace the established view. This formulation of an alternative inflationary mechanism was one of the outstanding achievements of the period. Cost–push theories articulated the impact of large-scale organizations such as trade unions and giant corporations on inflation allowing the analysis to move beyond simple demand and supply analysis couched in a framework of atomistic competition. Unfortunately, recent discussion has lead to a down-grading of usefulness of this distinction between the two possible mechanisms of inflation. It will become clear that an understanding of the distinction between the sources and mechanisms of inflation is absolutely crucial if a correct policy response is to be formulated.

Chapter 2 is intended as a summary and evaluation of some of the

---

[1] See G. Ackley (1978) *Macroeconomics: Theory and Policy,* Macmillan, New York, p. 426.

more important developments in inflation theory during the post-war period up to the latter part of the 1960s.[2] During this period economists were very much preoccupied with developing theoretical underpinnings for the Phillips curve, along with refinements of what was thought to be a stable relationship of great theoretical and practical importance. Only later was the stability and, indeed, the very existence of a Phillips curve called into question. This scepticism is one of the chief interests of chapter 3.

A DEMAND–PULL BASIS FOR THE PHILLIPS CURVE

Implicitly, early demand–pull inflation models incorporated the assumption of market clearing prices. Trading in factor and product markets only took place at prices that equated amounts demanded and supplied.[3] An alternative version of demand–pull inflation was developed by Lipsey in order to provide a rationale for the Phillips curve.[4] Here, price movements, or more correctly wage movements, reflected the interplay of shifting demand and supply curves but disequilibrium trading was allowed, i.e. trading at prices that did not equate desired demands and supplies.

The Lipsey labour markets are markets of atomistic competition where excess demand leads firms to bid up wages while excess supply leads workers to undercut wages in order to obtain employment. Unlike the markets of a Walrasian general equilibrium world, exchange may take place at a wage at which the amount of labour demanded is not equal to the amount supplied, although the dynamics of the model lead to the eventual movement of wages upward or downward in response to disequilibria. As will be made clear later such things as 'auction' or 'flex-price' markets do exist (again to use the more up-to-date terminology) but in fact labour markets rarely function in this manner and such micro theory cannot be used to provide the basis of a Phillips curve.

---

[2] The publications of Professor Friedman's presidential address to the American Economics Association in December, 1967 provides a useful dividing line for developments in the postwar period. See M. Friedman (1968) The role of monetary policy, *American Economic Review*, March.

[3] Ackley, op. cit., pp. 430–4.

[4] See A. Phillips (1958) The relation between unemployment and the rate of change of money wage rates in the United Kingdom, 1861–1957, *Economica*, November; and R. O. Lipsey (1960) The relation between unemployment and the rate of change of money wage rates in the United Kingdom, 1862–1957: A further analysis, *Economica*, February.

Until the publication of Lipsey's article in 1960, there was little in the way of theory to explain the inverse relation Phillips found between the rate of change of money wages and unemployment. In its simplest form the Phillips curve can be written as:

$$\dot{w}_t = a_0 + a_1 U_t^{-1} \tag{1}$$

where $\dot{w}_t = (w_t - w_{t-1})/w_{t-1}$ is the overall rate of growth of money wages and U_t is the national unemployment rate in period t.

The original study by Phillips utilized other variables besides the unemployment rate to explain wage inflation. The rate of change of the unemployment rate was considered important and price behaviour was allowed to influence wage behaviour if price inflation was rapid enough. But in the early years of popularity of the Phillips curve it was felt (with some justification) that the relevant variables other than the unemployment rate, if they did vary, either would do so infrequently or insignificantly. As a result it was considered justified to assume that shifts in this curve would be infrequent or small. Furthermore, it was felt by policy-makers and economists alike that the position of the Phillips curve was such that a sizeable number of unemployment–wage inflation points were available that were politically acceptable even in the long-run. If inflation (unemployment) was thought to be too high, then policy could be altered in such a way as to reduce inflation (unemployment) and the cost or trade-off in terms of higher unemployment (inflation) would be relatively slight.

A COST–PUSH BASIS FOR THE PHILLIPS CURVE

An alternative explanation of the negative relation between wage inflation and unemployment gained popularity during this period, one firmly rooted in the institutional developments of the time. Cost–push theories differed from demand–pull explanations of inflation by allowing wages and prices to continue to rise even while involuntary unemployment was high or even rising. Unlike demand–pull theories, cost–push theories did not envisage an exchange process in which money wage or price changes were the outcome of individual firms and workers 'haggling' until a market clearing wage or price was found. Instead this new view saw wage and price movements as a response primarily to 'cost' influences. Underlying the traditional cost–push inflationary mechanism was a radically different view of how product and factor markets work from that described in the previous section. The so-called 'market forces', summarized by shifting demand or supply curves, were assigned a distinctly secondary role. Instead, product prices were adminstered by price-makers who mark-up prices over some measure of costs; e.g. unit costs or total unit costs 'normalized' to average out cyclical influences. Whatever formula was applied, the basic idea was the mark-up or profit margin and, therefore, prices were largely (if not completely) unaffected by fluctuations in demand. In labour markets prices (i.e. wages) were set as a mark-up of over the cost of living.

What has been termed the bargaining power version of cost–push inflation explains the downward-sloping Phillips curve along the following lines. At high rates of unemployment when strike funds are low and alternative job prospects poor, labour is more submissive and less demanding in its wage bargaining. Employers, on the other hand, are likely to be more assertive and less fearful of strikes if high wage demands are not met, since profits are relatively low and less is lost at this stage of the cycle by a strike. As unemployment rates decline, however, labour can be assumed to become more aggressive and show a greater willingness to strike. This partly reflects the realization on the part of labour that as unemployment falls and business conditions improve so do profits. Not only does business face greater losses should a strike occur, but since profits are pro-cyclical, business is in a better position to meet higher wage demands without cutting into 'normal' dividends and required retained earnings. The lower is the unemployment rate by this line of reasoning, the more readily will employers give in. The result once again is a negative relation between the rate of wage inflation and unemployment. But this 'trade-off' results because labour bargains less hard and management becomes more resistant to wage demands as labour markets loosen, and not to a more rapid bidding down of wages by employees the greater is the excess supply of labour, until markets clear.

A WAGE–PRICE INFLATIONARY MECHANISM

1. *The price–inflation Phillips Curve*

While the original Phillips curve was formulated in terms of a trade-off between wage inflation and unemployment, an alternative formulation in terms of price inflation and unemployment was often derived from the wage inflation–unemployment relation. An aggregate version of the mark-up pricing formula provided the means for doing this. Allow that product prices on average are a fixed percentage mark-up, α, over average costs, AC, or

$$p = (1 + \alpha)AC$$

and consider only labour and raw material costs, i.e.

$$AC = wN/Q + rm/Q$$

where w is the money wage rate, N is labour input, rm is total outlay on raw materials and Q is output. Then the rate of price inflation, $\dot{p}$, is equal to the rate of wage inflation, $\dot{w}$, minus the difference of the rates of growth of labour productivity $\dot{Q} - \dot{N} = \dot{p}$ and raw material costs, $\dot{rm}$, or

$$\dot{p}_t = \dot{w}_t - (\dot{p} - \dot{rm})_t \tag{2}$$

where the expression, $\dot{w}_t - \dot{p}_t$ is easily seen to be the rate of growth of labour cost. Substituting equation (1) into (2) gives:

$$\dot{p}_t = a_0 - (\dot{p} - \dot{rm})_t + a_1 U_t^{-1}. \tag{3}$$

Equation (2) depicts the passive response of business to wage inflation. If $\dot{w} > \dot{p}$ this increase in labour costs is simply 'passed through' to product prices. Underlying equation (2) is an assumption that profit margins are fixed. As a result, if for convenience it is assumed that $\dot{rm} = 0$, equation (3) graphs as equation (1) except it is vertically displaced downward by the rate of growth of labour productivity.[5]

2. *The dynamics of cost–push inflation*

The impact of labour market conditions on the degree of exertion of market power allows for changes in aggregate demand to affect the rate of wage and price inflation as described in the previous section. As such, however, the model described by equations (1) and (2) cannot be used to generate a cost–push inflationary process over time, but only two forms of the Phillips curve. There are no lags in the model so that the real-world, dynamic interaction between wages

---

[5] This type of derivation of a price inflation equation from a wage inflation equation, based on Lipsey's explanation, involves something of a contradiction. The labour market is seen as one where wage rates are a reflection of an interaction between demand and supply schedules while the price inflation equation is based on a pricing procedure that is simply a mark-up over costs and is insensitive to any direct influence of demand pressures.

and prices does not develop. Moreover, the essence of an inflationary mechanism that depicts the influence of market power on the rate of wage and price inflation is that it permits wages and prices to rise in the presence of rising unemployment rates.[6] This is not possible since equations (1) and (2) only allow a decline in the rate of wage or price inflation when unemployment rates rise.

Both shortcomings are easily corrected by introducing a basic tenet of cost–push inflation theories; that wages are a mark up over the cost of living, as workers strive to attain some target real wage. Thus, utilizing the simplest kind of lag structure, instead of equation (1) write;

$$\dot{w}_t = c_0 + c_1 \dot{p}_{t-1} + c_2 U_t^{-1} \tag{4}$$

where $\dot{p}_{t-1}$ is the rate of price inflation lagged one period and the other variables have their previous meaning.[7] Equation (4) describes a situation where wages respond to changes in the degree of tightness in labour markets for reasons given in the last section. The introduction of the lagged price variable implies a 'feedback effect', by which the past behaviour of prices affects current wage increases as labour attempts to protect (or even increase) its real wages. Moreover, equation (4) allows the rate of wage inflation to accelerate at the same time that unemployment is rising if a rising cost of living pushes up wages. For example, unemployment rates may have risen in the current period compared to period $t - 1$. However, if the rate of price inflation accelerated sufficiently from period $t - 2$ to period $t - 1$ the overall effect will be an increase in the rate of wage inflation.

THE LONG-RUN AND SHORT-RUN PHILLIPS CURVES

As will be detailed in chapter 6, the institutional changes that give rise to feedback and pass through effects critically alter the nature of inflation in capitalist economies. These two effects also make it necessary to distinguish between short-run and long-run Phillips curves. If equation (4) is substituted into equation (2) the result is:

$$\dot{p}_t = (c_0 - \dot{\rho}) + c_1 \dot{p}_{t-1} + c_2 U_t^{-1} \tag{5}$$

---

[6] See Ackley, op. cit., pp. 434–45.

[7] Both Phillips and Lipsey argued that cost of living changes could affect wage settlements as workers attempt to protect their real wage. See Phillips op. cit. and Lipsey, op. cit.

where the rate of growth of labour productivity, $\dot{\rho}$, is assumed given and $\dot{rm} = 0$. Equations (4) and (5) can be interpreted as short-run Phillips curves. Given some value for $\dot{p}_{t-1}$, they show the trade off between the unemployment rate and the rates of wage and price inflation, respectively, with

$$\partial \dot{p}_t/\partial U_t = \partial \dot{w}_t/\partial U_t = -c_2/U_t^2 .$$

Equation (5) is easily seen graphically as a vertical displacement downward of equation (4), the displacement being equal to the rate of growth of productivity, $\dot{\rho}$.

The long-run Phillips curves depict the trade-off between unemployment rates and price or wage inflation, when the interactions between wages and prices; i.e. the feedback effects of price inflation on wage inflation and the pass-through effects of wage inflation on price inflation, have worked themselves out.

Assuming $0 < c_1 < 1$, the long-run trade-offs between wage and price inflation can be written:

$$\dot{w}^* = (c_0 - c_1 \dot{\rho})/(1 - c_1) + [c_2/(1 - c_1)]U^{-1} \tag{4'}$$

and

$$\dot{p}^* = (c_0 - \dot{\rho})/(1 - c_1) + [c_2/(1 - c_1)]U^{-1} \tag{5'}$$

respectively.[8] Since $c_2/(1 - c_1) > c_2$ the long-run Phillips curves are steeper than the short-run curves. Comparing equations (4') and (5'), it is clear that for any given unemployment rate, the long-run rates of wage and price inflation differ only by $\dot{\rho}$, the rate of growth of labour productivity. To put the matter somewhat differently, a comparison of equations (4') and (5') reveals that the long-run effect of a once-over change in the unemployment rate on the rates of wage and price inflation are identical. The feedback effects of price inflation on wages and the pass through effects of wage inflation on prices ensure

---

[8] These long-run curves are found by assuming $\dot{w}_t = \dot{w}_{t-1} = \dot{w}^*$ and $\dot{p}_t = \dot{p}_{t-1} = \dot{p}^*$ and substituting $\dot{w}^*$ and $\dot{p}^*$ into equations

$$\dot{w}_t = (c_0 - c_1 \dot{\rho}) + c_1 \dot{w}_{t-1} + c_2 U_t^{-1} \tag{5''}$$

and (6), respectively and collecting terms. Mathematically, the long-run trade-offs are no more than parts of the analytical solutions of the system of first-order difference equations (5) and (6). By the standard treatment the solutions are: $\dot{w}_t = A(x)^t + \dot{w}^*$; and $\dot{p}_t = B(x)^t + \dot{p}^*$ where A and B are arbitrary constants dependent upon the initial conditions, $x = c_1$ is the root of the characteristic equation and $\dot{p}^*$ and $\dot{w}^*$ are particular solutions of equations (5) and (6), respectively.

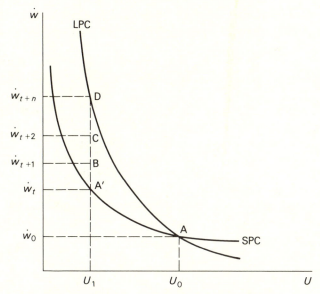

FIGURE 2.1   *The short-run and long-run Phillips curve*

that changing long-run as well as short-run rates of price inflation are accompanied by changing rates of wage inflation and vice versa.

Graphically, the distinction between a short-run Phillips curve (SPC) and a long-run Phillips curve (LPC) is shown in figure 2.1 for wage inflation. Assume initially that the unemployment and inflation rates in period $t - 1$ are U_0 and $\dot{w}_0$, respectively, and that by means of a more stimulative policy the unemployment rate is reduced to U_1 and remains there permanently. Since the lagged value for the price inflation variable, $\dot{p}_{t-1}$ is a datum in period t, the short-run impact on wage inflation is given from equation (4) as:

$$\partial \dot{w}_t / \partial U_t = -c_2/U_t^2 \, .$$

As a result the rate of wage inflation increases from period $t - 1$ to period t from $\dot{w}_0$ to $\dot{w}_t$ in figure 2.1. However this cannot be the end of the matter since from equation (2)

$$\dot{p}_t = \dot{w}_t - \dot{\rho},$$

as the increase in the rate of wage inflation in period t passes through to prices in the same period. As a result in period $t + 1$, the rate of wage inflation is given by:

$$\dot{w}_{t+1} = c_0 + c_1 \dot{p}_t + c_2 U_{t+1}^{-1} \tag{4}$$

which is greater than $\dot{w}_t$ since $\dot{p}_t > \dot{p}_{t-1}$. Let the rate of wage inflation and unemployment in period $t + 1$ be denoted by point B in
figure 2.1. Again, the increase in wage inflation in period $t + 1$ passes
through to prices in the same period with $\dot{p}_{t+1} > \dot{p}_t$, causing an even
higher rate of wage inflation in period $t + 2$, say, than that denoted
by point C, etc.

If it is assumed that eventually the interactions between wage and
price inflation lead to wages and prices converging to some constant
rate by, say, period $t + n$ then a line drawn through point A and D
can be said to trace out a long-run Phillips curve.[9] When all the
feedbacks or interactions between wages and prices have worked
themselves out, the long-run Phillips curve is steeper than in the
short-run, becoming vertical as U approaches some low value. With
$0 < c_1 < 1$ both a long-run and short-run trade-off between and
inflation exist.

THE INCLUSION OF ADDITIONAL (PREDETERMINED) VARIABLES

A vast empirical and theoretical literature was spawned by Phillips'
study of the late 1950s. Reasonable and often convincing arguments
were advanced in favour of the inclusion of other explanatory variables to explain wage and price inflation. More refined and sophisticated econometric techniques were utilized in testing the models,
using different time periods, different countries and various sectors of
the economy. The basic points already discussed, the interaction
between wage and price inflation, the distinction between long-run
and short-run Phillips curves, the need to model the inflationary
process as a macrodynamic process, all these essential points were
widely accepted among economists until the late 1960s.

A summary of a representative study brings this out. Consider the
following equation of wage inflation:

$$\dot{w}_t = d'_0 + d_1 \dot{p}_{t-1} + d_2 U_t^{-1} + d_3 R_t + d_4 \Delta R_t \tag{6}$$

where R is the current rate of return on capital, ΔR is the change in
this rate in the current period t over last period, $t - 1$, and all other
variables have their previous meanings.[10] As before, the rate of price

---

[9] This will be true provided $0 < c_1 < 1$. The intervening points along the curve
between A and D are points on the long-run Phillips curve corresponding to
different maintained rates of unemployment between U_0 and U_1.

[10] G. L. Perry (1967) Wages and guideposts, *American Economic Review*, September.

inflation (lagged one period) is introduced in the wage equation indicating that when the cost of living rises, this pushes up money wages.

Suppose that the rate of return on capital and changes in this rate are given. Equation (6) then can be written;

$$\dot{w}_t = d_0 + d_1 \dot{p}_{t-1} + d_2 U_t^{-1} \qquad (6')$$

where

$$d_0 = d'_0 + d_3 R_t + d \, \Delta R_t.$$

Treating equations (6') and (2) together and again assuming the rate of growth of labour productivity, $\dot{\rho}$ to be constant and rim = 0 gives a pair of simultaneous difference equations in the variables $\dot{w}_t$ and $\dot{p}_t$.

Once more, a distinction must be made between the short-run and long-run Phillips curves. Long-run and short-run trade-offs exist (the long-run curve is steeper) as long as the parameter measuring the impact of changes in the lagged price variable, d_1, satisfies the inequality, $0 < d_1 < 1$. Finally, as in the last model developed here, the behaviour of wages and prices is very similar, because of the pass-through effect of wage inflation on price inflation and the feedback effect of price inflation on wage inflation. In the long-run the rates of wage and price inflation are constant, and differ by the rate of growth of productivity. This remains true whether or not the other explanatory variables in the wage and price inflation equations are the same. As long as the pass-through and feedback effects are present, wages and prices will have similar movements.

INFLATION AWARENESS AND THE TRADE-OFF

1. *The 'two track' model*

An important conclusion must be noted at this point. Once the dynamic interactions between wages and prices are recognized, once-over changes in the other explanatory variables; e.g. the unemployment rate or the rate of return on capital, do not lead simply to once-over changes of the wage and price level. Instead they set in motion dynamic processes that result in permanent changes in rates of wage and price inflation. The permanent reduction of unemployment rates in figure 2.1 from U_0 to U_1 illustrates all too well that inflation rates are unstable upwards over an indeterminate range of unemployment rates.

These dynamic processes suggest an element of instability at work today. A related and more ominous possibility is found in a study that helps explain the acceleration of inflation during the second half of the post-war period; the 'two track' model of inflation.[11]

Write:

$$\dot{w}_t = e_0 + e_1\dot{p}_t + e_2[(\dot{p}_t + \dot{p}_{t-1})/2 - e_3] + e_4U_t^{-1} \tag{7}$$

and

$$\dot{p}_t = g_1\dot{w}_t + g_2\dot{w}_{t-1} - g_3\dot{\rho} \tag{8}$$

where (1) $0 < e_1 < 1$
     (2) $e_1 + e_2 = 1$
     (3) $e_2 = 0$ if $(\dot{p}_t + \dot{p}_{t-1})/2 \leq e_3$, otherwise $0 < e_2 < 1$
     (4) $e_3 = 2.5$
     (5) $e_4 > 0$
     (6) $g_1 + g_2 = g_3$
     (7) $g_1 + g_2 = 1$

Assumptions (1) to (7) are given the following interpretations:

(1) to (3) There is incomplete sensitivity of money wages to moderate inflation, i.e. when $(\dot{p}_t + \dot{p}_{t-1})/2 \leq e_3$; but when inflation is severe, i.e. $(\dot{p}_t + \dot{p}_{t-1})/2 > e_3$, there is complete sensitivity of money wages to severe inflation in the sense that any change in the rate of price inflation is completely transmitted to wage inflation.

(4) An average rate of price inflation of 2.5 per cent over the current and past year is the threshold separating a conscious concern and reaction by labour from a lack of concern and reaction.

(5) The relationship between wage inflation and unemployment is negative.

(6) The impact on the rate of price inflation is the same whatever the source of cost inflation.

(7) There is a lagged but complete pass through of changes in labour costs to prices.

By the usual statistical criteria the test of the model using post-war data on the USA was a success.

---

[11] O. Eckstein and R. Brinner (1972) The inflation process in the United States, *A Study Prepared for the Use of the Joint Economic Committee*, US Congress, February. See also R. J. Gordon (1972) Wage–price controls and the shifting Phillips curve, *Brookings Papers on Economic Activity*, No. 2.

The two-track model of inflation contains all the features of the model explained on pp. 41–4 plus an extension. Besides describing a dynamic wage–price inflationary mechanism, the model emphasizes that a qualitative change takes place in the nature of inflation when it exceeds some threshold rate; i.e. $(\dot{p}_t + \dot{p}_{t-1})/2 > 2.5$ per cent. The nature of the long-run trade-off between wage or price inflation and unemployment changes when inflation becomes 'severe'. Until that time, price inflation is not completely built into wage demands since $\partial \dot{w}_t / \partial \dot{p}_t = e_1 < 1$. Without stretching a point, as long as inflation does not exceed an average of 2.5 per cent per annum, it is not expected.

To see this it is necessary to solve the model for the long-run 'equilibrium', i.e. the non-accelerating–non-decelerating rate of inflation associated with some given rate of unemployment and productivity growth. Since the equilibrium rate of wage inflation differs from the equilibrium rate of price inflation by the known rate of growth of productivity, only one rate need be determined.

The long-run equilibrium rate when inflation is moderate implies that $e_2 = 0$. In this case the long-run Phillips curve for price inflation can be written:

$$\dot{p}^* = (g_0 + e_4 U^{-1})/[1 - (g_1 + g_2)e_1] = (g_0 + e_4 U^{-1})/(1 - e_1)$$

$$(8')$$

where $g_0 = (e_0 - g_3 \dot{p})$.

Since $0 < e_1 < 1$ by assumption, $1 - e_1 > 0$ and the division of the right-hand side of equation $(8')$ is appropriate. There is, thus, a trade-off between unemployment and inflation over that range of unemployment rates corresponding to rates of price inflation less than 2.5 per cent.[13]

Assume now that the average rate of inflation this period and the last exceeds 2.5 per cent and, therefore, $0 < e_2 < 1$. As equation (7)

---

[12] Equation $(8')$ is found by writing equation (7) as:

$$\dot{w}_t = e_0 + e_1 \dot{p}_{t-1} + e_4 U_t^{-1}.$$

If this expression and a similar expression for $\dot{w}_{t-1}$ are substituted into equation (8), the resulting expression is:

$$\dot{p}_t = g_0 + g_1 e_1 \dot{p}_t + g_2 e_1 \dot{p}_{t-1} + e_4 U^{-1}$$

where $g_0 = (e_0 - g_3 \dot{p})$ and U^{-1} is some fixed rate of unemployment. Then, assuming $\dot{p}_t = \dot{p}_{t-1} = \dot{p}^*$, substitute $\dot{p}^*$ into this last equation and collect terms giving $(8')$. The procedure for deriving equation $(8'')$ is the same.

[13] Eckstein's and Brinner's econometric estimates indicate that for $U = 4.2$ per cent, $\dot{p} = 2.5$ per cent.

includes the inflation severity factor, $[(\dot{p}_t + \dot{p}_{t-1})/2 - e_3]$, the long-run equilibrium rate of price inflation must now be written

$$\dot{p}^* = (g_0' + e_4\,U^{-1})/[1 - (g_1 + g_2)(e_1 + e_2)] \tag{8''}$$

where $g_0' = e_0 - g_3\dot{p} - e_2e_3$.

However, the numerator of this expression cannot be divided by the denominator since $1 - (g_1 + g_2)(e_1 + e_2) = 0$ by assumptions (2) and (7). There is no longer a trade-off between the rates of price (and wage) inflation and unemployment.

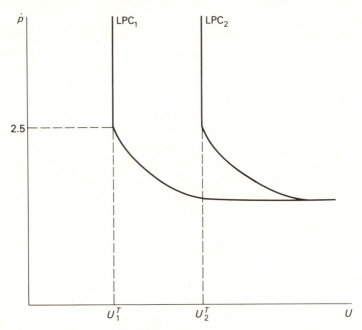

FIGURE 2.2   *Long-run Phillips curves for track I and II*

Figure 2.2 illustrates these results. Starting from a rate of unemployment greater than U_1^T, introduce stimulative demand policies to reduce the rate of unemployment. The long-run Phillips curve denoted LPC$_1$ indicates that as long as unemployment rates remain in excess of U_1^T, the associated rate of price inflation does not exceed the threshold rate of 2.5 per cent. In addition the Phillips curve has some curvature allowing reduced unemployment to be 'bought' at the cost of some increase in inflation. However, if an attempt is made to push unemployment rates below U_1^T, given the nature of the trade off, this shifts the economy to the second track. At this point, inflation is seen to be severe and labour, concerned lest its real wage should decline, responds by building price inflation completely into wage demands. This causes wage inflation to accelerate so rapidly that, taking account of the pass-through effects on price inflation and subsequent feedbacks on wage demands etc., wage and price inflation rates accelerate without limit. The trade-off ceases to exist at unemployment rates less than $U_1^T = e_4/(g_3\dot{p} + e_2 e_3 - e_0)$.

2. *Do workers get fooled?*

The segment of the Phillips curves in figure 2.2 which is not vertical corresponds to a range of inflation rates over which inflation is largely ignored by workers. Over this range, the response of wages to price increases in the current and previous period was 'incompletely sensitive' as $0 < e_1 < 1$. It has often been said in cases such as this that workers suffer from a money illusion or are fooled, since the money wage response to price increases is not sufficient to maintain real wages, the latter response seeming to require $e_1 = 1$. However, it is easily shown that if pricing is on a mark-up basis as in equation (8), the behaviour of real wages is completely independent of the size of e_1. Although not essential, if all costs other than labour are ignored, as in equation (8), and assuming $\dot{w}_t = \dot{w}_{t-1}$, then from equation (8) $\dot{p}_t = \dot{w}_t - \dot{p}$ or $\dot{w}_t - \dot{p}_t = \dot{p}$. Real wages, far from declining if $e_1 < 1$ actually rise in step with the growth of labour productivity. What is critical is the behaviour of employers not employees. If the former are content to maintain profit margins and merely pass though labour cost increases, nobody 'gets fooled'.[14]

3. *Accelerating inflation at any rate of unemployment*

Two final points in concluding this section. The two-track model, even more than the cost–push models shown above, suggests the danger of even moderate inflation; it becomes unstable upwards when the unemployment rate falls below some critical level, which then pushes inflation rates above some threshold. There is thus the ever-present danger that during the course of a boom, inflation can become serious. Alternatively, a general loss of faith by unions in the likelihood of a maintenance or rise in their real wages can lead to a decline in e_3, so that even very low rates of inflation can lead to a

[14] See W. Smith (1970) On some current issues in monetary economics: an interpretation, *Journal of Economic Literature,* September.

continuous acceleration in the rate of inflation. Moreover any shock which merely pushes the rate of inflation above the threshold can set off accelerating inflation rates in the not so short-run.

Second, it is important to note that in the discussion of threshold effects and workers losing faith in the ability of the market system to generate rising per capita real incomes, nothing was said about the nature of unemployment when the threshold is exceeded. Solving the two-track model reveals that the Phillips curve becomes vertical at the unemployment rate

$$U^T = e_4/(g_3\dot{\rho} + e_2 e_3 - e_0).$$

Thus, a decrease in the rate of growth of productivity, $\dot{\rho}$, shifts the long-run Phillips curve to the right, say, from LPC_1 to LPC_2 in figure 2.2. A decrease in the threshold inflation rate, e_3 has a similar effect, but such parameter changes have nothing to do with the reasons for being unemployed. Yet, as will be seen in chapter 3, theories have been expounded that assume that all unemployment is voluntary at an aggregate unemployment rate at which the Phillips curve becomes vertical. The two-track model reveals that any number of rates of unemployment can be associated with accelerating inflation.

CONCLUSIONS

The belief that one of the most important events in inflation theory is the development and refinement of the cost–push approach to inflation will be a recurring theme throughout this study. It has allowed the analysis to proceed beyond demand–pull theories of inflation, largely based as they were on overly simplistic notions of how markets work. Virtually devoid of institutional considerations, the demand–pull theories see the world in highly competitive terms with shifting demand and supply curves leading to rapid, predictable price adjustments. Cost–push theories recognize that the modern world is composed of large-scale, complex organizations, a world of price-makers and not price-takers, often of bilateral monopoly and always of power relations.

Underlying these theories is an assumption of non-competitive market behaviour in a world in which monopoly, oligopoly and other market imperfections are rampant. Pricing and wage decisions are not seen as the outcomes of the simple maximizing rules applicable in a world of pure competition under certainty, but of something that appeared to the investigators as more like 'rules of thumb'. Attempts to interpret such pricing and market behaviour as rational, optimizing forms of behaviour have been slower to develop.

One consequence of cost–push analysis was the development and formalization of the cost–push mechanism in dynamic models of wage–price interactions. This helped to clarify the distinction between long-run and short-run Phillips curves, and to emphasize new destabilizing influences. Another consequence was to polarize thinking within the profession, leading to the widely held view that inflation had to be either a cost–push or a demand–pull phenomenon.[15]

Chapters 3 and 4 discuss more recent developments in inflation theory. These developments, most unfortunately, have lead to an even further polarization within the profession along demand–pull or cost–push lines. Chapters 5–7 will attempt to establish the soundness of the analysis that allows both demand–pull and cost–push forces to interact.

[15] C. Schultze (1959) Demand–pull versus cost–push inflation, *Recent Inflation in the United States,* Study Paper No. 1, Joint Economic Committee, Washington, D.C.

CHAPTER 3

Some Recent Developments in Inflation and Unemployment Theory – I

INTRODUCTION

During the 1950s and 1960s, theorizing about inflation tended to divide along two lines. Either the inflationary process was thought to be generated by demand–pull forces that continuously reasserted themselves, or it was felt to be based on pass-through and feedback effects that led to a cost–push, wage–price spiral. Underlying these two alternative mechanisms were distinctly different assumptions about the functioning of labour and product markets. Demand–pull models assume that when excess demand or supply conditions arise in factor or product markets, prices adjust to clear markets. The economy is either one of atomistic competition with a large numbers of well-informed (often perfectly informed) buyers and sellers in every market or else performs 'as if' it is such an economy.

Underlying the cost–push inflationary mechanism was the view that prices in the real world do not adjust when excess demand or supply develops. Rather product prices are a mark-up over unit costs and wages are a 'mark-up' over the cost of living. While wages may rise as unemployment falls, thereby passing through to higher prices, the rise in inflation rates should not be interpreted as an upward bidding of prices and wages until excess demands are eliminated. Rather the cost–push inflationary process takes place in a world of organizations with market power. When labour markets tighten, unions exert a greater amount of bargaining power while oligopolistic enterprises tend to accede to these greater demands and adjust their prices in such a way as to maintain or increase their mark-ups.

This distinction between the nature of markets and the degree of competitiveness of the economy has had and continues to have very definite implications for modelling economic behaviour, including the inflationary process. When it is assumed that something called the 'impersonal market forces of competition' or the 'discipline of the market' provides an automatic regulatory mechanism, there is little reason to proceed beyond this to an analysis of the institutional setting within which these competitive forces operate and are shaped. The result is a form of modelling of economic behaviour that proceeds first by simply assuming some single target or objective of economic behaviour, e.g. the maximizing of utility or profits. Then, and more importantly, the analysis continues with little consideration of how such activities may be constrained (other than the 'discipline of the market') by institutional forces.

Conversely, a world of oligopolies, unions and big government is not a world of impersonal market forces but one of very distinct power centers. The fact that these forces are countervailing in various degrees, i.e. that power on one side of the market is met by power on the other, means only that economic activities are always highly constrained. Moreover, the development of large-scale, complex organizations has given rise to concerns over 'goodwill', 'fairness' and a desire to cultivate and maintain long-run attachments, even if only in the interests of long-run profit or income maximization. All of these influences channel and constrain the pursuit of economic activities. As a result optimizing activities can only be understood or 'modelled' when such institutional and cultural forces are explicitly treated as constraints on these activities.

Developments in the past decade or so, if anything, have led to a polarization of views as to the basic causes of inflation, the functioning of markets, the nature of the Phillips curve and the manner of modelling economic activities. Chapters 3 and 4 outline some recent developments in inflation and unemployment theory that illustrate this polarization. Chapter 3 does so by first discussing a form of theorizing which places great stress on the 'natural rate of unemployment hypothesis' (NRH)[1]. This is followed by a brief discussion of theories of inflation and unemployment that join the NRH with the rational expectations hypothesis (REH).[2]

The NRH and the REH, indeed the whole monetarist framework within which they are couched, are seen to arise out of very extreme

---

[1] See M. Friedman (1968) The role of monetary policy, *American Economic Review*, March; and E. S. Phelps *et al.* (1970) *Microeconomics Foundations of Employment and Inflation Theory*, Norton, New York.

[2] The REH has by now spawned an incredible amount of literature. One of the early writings outlining the general ideas in simple terms is T. J. Sargent and N. Wallace (1975) Rational expectations and the theory of economic policy, *Studies in Monetary Economics*, Federal Reserve Bank of Minneapolis, Minneapolis.

assumptions about the workings of markets. Especially by adherants to REH, the economy is held to be composed not only of highly competitive markets, but Walrasian-type markets of continuous and instantaneous (or at least 'within the period') market clearing. As might be expected, modelling of such markets and economies requires only the slightest deference to institutional and organizational contexts, and the complexities of motivations and behaviour. Before turning to a description of some of the new developments in demand–pull inflation theory, a brief discussion of monetarism will be undertaken.

MONETARISM

Monetarism comes in many forms, ranging from what has been referred to as 'little monetarism' to 'great monetarism'. Beginning with a position that says that 'money is what really matters' through one involving acceptance of the NRH and then the REH, the term monetarism has even been extended to cover certain political programmes, e.g. 'Thatcherism', and a rather radical conservative ideology.[3] The concern here is with a middle position. Of interest are those aspects of monetarism that contribute to the view that the main impact of aggregate demand policies is on prices (and wages) and not the real sector, thereby necessitating a separate explanation of the level of activity of the real sector, e.g. output and unemployment. To put the matter differently, this chapter considers some of the essential components of monetarism as distinguished from views that tend to be held by economists who are monetarists.[4] Six elements are singled out.

First, an acceptance of the quantity theory of money, in which changes in the money stock dominate in affecting changes in money

[3] The distinction between 'little' and 'great monetarism' is given in R. Solow (1976) Comments on Stein, in *Monetarism,* Vol. 1 (Ed. J. Stein) North-Holland, Amsterdam. See also J. Tobin (1980) Stabilization policy ten years after, *Brookings Papers on Economic Activity,* No. 1, and (1980) *Assets Accumulation and Economic Activity: Reflections on Contemporary Macroeconomic Theory,* Yrjo Jahnsson Lectures, Basil Blackwell, Oxford. Tobin uses the expressions mark I and mark II in this latter study to cover a distinction similar to that made in the text. The terms 'new classical economics' and 'new classical macroeconomics' are also found in the literature and are terms used to represent much the same areas of analysis as great monetarism mark I and mark II. See G. A. Akerlof (1979) The case against conservative macroeconomics: An inaugural lecture, *Economica,* August.

[4] See T. Mayer (Ed.) (1978) *The Structure of Monetarism,* Norton, New York.

income, is a basic component of monetarism. A transmission mechanism whereby changes in the money stock lead directly to changes in expenditures on both consumer and capital goods as well as securities is another distinguishing characteristic. Critical here, according to monetarists, is not only the wide range of assets that are exchanged following, say, a disturbance of the equality between the supply of real cash balances and the demand for them, but also the assumed stability of the income velocity of money or, at least, the demand for money function.

Together these two components suggest a general policy rule as an integral part of monetarism. The monetary authorities should adhere whenever possible to a fixed rate of growth of the money supply, the so-called money growth rule of monetarism.

A fourth widely accepted (and related) monetarist assumption, is that the private sector is, 'if left to itself', inherently stable. This has been given various interpretations.[5] But in the final analysis they amount to an assumption that the rate of growth of real output will be equal to the rate of growth of maximum output. Hence the desirability of the monetary rule and its advocacy by monetarists.

A fifth critical plank in the monetarist platform focuses on the alleged convergence properties of the economy. Most monetarists assume that the unemployment rate resulting if a monetary rule is followed would be a rate at which there is no (or little) involuntary unemployment.[6] Little effort has been given to justifying this assumption of full employment or at least full-employment tendencies but the analysis of those who have accepted the full-employment properties of the NRH tend to formulate their justification in terms of markets with flexible wages and prices. For present purposes this need not be interpreted to mean Walrasian markets with equilibrium trading. That interpretation will be reserved for the extreme brand of monetarism that accepts the REH. This, in turn, suggests the competitive model with its heavy emphasis on large numbers of buyers and sellers. It seems essential, therefore, to include the neoclassical, competitive model with its tendency towards full employment as a basic assumption underlying monetarism.[7]

---

[5] See for example ibid., pp. 14–5, 38; and R. Gordon (1981) *Macroeconomics,* 2nd edn, Little Brown, Boston, pp. 364–71.
[6] ibid.
[7] This is the view adopted in H. Frisch (1977) Inflation theory, 1963–1975: a 'second generation' survey, *Journal of Economic Literature,* December.

Finally, while capitalist economies are assumed to have strong full-employment tendencies, these tendencies can be thwarted by fiscal and monetary mismanagement and 'rigidities'. Efforts to correct past errors should work through regulation of the money supply. A money supply, not an interest rate or exchange rate target, is the appropriate policy response.

While some non-monetarists and monetarists would dispute the emphasis on certain of the items cited here (and some omissions as well), the list nevertheless includes the important elements underpinning the theory of employment and inflation espoused by monetarists. In chapter 9 a discussion of policies advocated by those who subscribe to a radical, conservative ideology will be taken up.

Recent developments in monetarism will be grouped together under two headings; great monetarism – mark I and mark II or simply GM-I and GM-II. GM-I is a view of an economy that incorporates all the basic tenets and beliefs just singled out; GM-II includes these beliefs but in addition incorporates what will be termed the strong REH. Both versions of monetarism can be thought of as the application of neoclassical precepts to the important macroeconomic problems of inflation and unemployment.

THE CORNERSTONE OF THE MONETARIST REVIVAL

1. The 'expectations augmented' Phillips Curve

The acceleration in inflation rates beginning in the late 1960s and the inability to reduce inflation in the 1970s and early 1980s to rates comparable to those of the 1950s generated a view that 'inflation had taken on a life of its own'. Predictably, economists caught up with trying to formalize these new developments, took to including expectations explicitly in their models of inflation. Figure 1.1 in chapter 1 illustrated a manner in which expectations could be introduced; the rate of price (or wage) inflation is made a positive function of the expected rate of inflation and a negative function of the unemployment rate. An increase in the expected rate of inflation results in a shift in the short-run 'expectations augmented' Phillips curve upward to the right. One use of expectations in the theory of inflation is the main concern of this section.

Figure 3.1 contains three short-run Phillips curves for price inflation which differ from one another according to the assumed expected rate of inflation. Allow that the economy is initially at point A with $U = U_0$ and $\dot{p} = \dot{p}^e = 0$; i.e. the actual and expected rates of

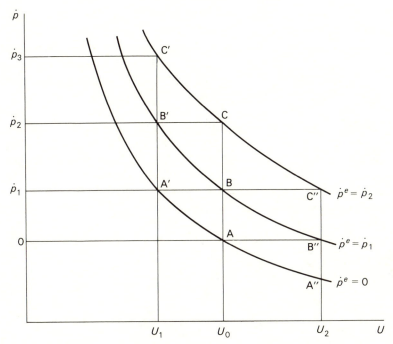

FIGURE 3.1   *Expectations augmented Phillips curves*

inflation are equal and the actual rate of inflation is non-accelerating, i.e. zero.

Introduce an increase in aggregate demand that pushes the unemployment rate down to U_1 and increases the rate of inflation to $\dot{p}_1 > 0$; i.e. a movement from A to A'. If the rate of price inflation associated with $U = U_1$ is severe enough, individuals will revise upwards their expectations about future rates of inflation to more closely correspond with the new realities. Let this revised rate of expected inflation be equal to $\dot{p}_1$, the new actual rate. Figure 3.1 is drawn in such a way that if aggregate demand is sufficient to maintain the unemployment rate at U_1, the short-run Phillips curve then shifts upward to that denoted by $\dot{p}^e = \dot{p}_1$. The economy then moves to point B' with an even higher rate of inflation, $\dot{p}_2$, the result of people acting on the basis of their expectations. Because at point B, $\dot{p}_2 > \dot{p}^e = \dot{p}_1$, it is reasonable to expect the short-run Phillips curve to eventually shift out further, as indicated by $\dot{p}^e = \dot{p}_2$.

The belief that the short-run Phillips curve might shift if expectations about the future course of inflation changes would find wide acceptance, even among many non-monetarists. A matter of contro-

versy is just how the curve shifts. In particular, the basic issue is
whether or not there exists some short-run Phillips curve passing
through a vertical line drawn through U_1 (or any other unemployment rate less than U_0) which is associated with an expected
rate of inflation equal to the actual rate of inflation at the point of
intersection. If there is, then the economy can move permanently
from point A to some point on the vertical line through unemployment rate U_1 without continuously accelerating inflation.[8] If, on
the other hand, an intersection point on such a short-run curve to
the left of $U = U_0$ is always associated with an expected rate of
inflation less than the actual inflation rate (as in figure 3.1), the above
line of reasoning suggests an inflationary process that feeds on itself
and accelerates over time.

2. *The natural rate of unemployment hypothesis* (*NRH*)

This controversy has been studied by advocates of the NRH. They
make very strong assumptions about the workings of modern capitalist economy in formulating their modern-day, polar version of the
demand–pull model of inflation. Among other things, this allows
them to derive very special results concerning shifts in the Phillips
curve.

In the original Friedman formulation and in textbook summaries
of the NRH, it is usually assumed that the rate of growth of productivity is zero (a not so innocent assumption) and the marginal
product of labour is a declining function of employment.[9] A simple
textbook model is then postulated which incorporates the law of
diminishing marginal product and the usual competitive assumptions. In particular, it is assumed that firms will only expand job
offers if the real wage declines. Given this and an additional assumption to be recognized presently, it is possible to derive the way the
Phillips curve *must* shift from the explanation of the supply response
of labour to an increase in aggregate demand.

One explanation of labour's response is that those workers unemployed at $U = U_0$ were not at the margin of indifference between
unemployment and employment but were unemployed because of a
lack of sufficient demand. Thus, demand stimulation increases
labour supplied and reduces unemployment, in spite of the decline in
the real wage (brought about by price inflation accelerating more
than wage inflation), because of the existence of involuntary unemployment in Keynes' sense.

[8] See figure 2.1 for similar results. There convergence is assured by $0 < c_1 < 1$.
[9] Frisch, op. cit.

This possibility is disallowed in NRH literature, as all unemployment is assumed voluntary. An alternative, monetarist explanation of the decrease in unemployment below U_0 is that someone was surprised or fooled. Assume employers always know the current rate of inflation in any period in the sense that the actual rate of price inflation is always equal to what they expect. On the other hand, allow that workers always expect the current rate of price inflation to be equal to the actual rate of inflation in the previous period, but assume that they correctly anticipate the current rate of wage inflation. Then, the actual rate of price inflation in the current period may exceed that of the previous period, in which case workers are fooled (by the increase in money wages) into thinking real wages have risen. A situation thereby arises where unemployment may fall even though all those unemployed at $U = U_0$ are voluntarily unemployed.[10] What is necessary is that money wages rise by less than prices as the economy moves from A to A', allowing some of the unemployed to be fooled into thinking that the real wage has risen.

However, assume that workers learn with a lag and that there is no further increase in the rate of growth of the money supply so that the rate of price inflation stabilizes at $\dot{p}_1$. Then, the knowledge that real wages have declined will lead to the newly employed workers withdrawing their services in the absence of further 'surprises' induced by the authorities stimulating demand. In this case, the movement is to point B where actual and expected rates of inflation are equal as at point A but at a higher rate. Such a withdrawal will cause the marginal product of labour to rise and therefore, given the competitive assumptions, the real wage.

Alternatively, starting from point A', a further demand stimulus can be injected through a higher rate of growth of the money supply thereby pushing up the rate of inflation again as the economy moves to point B'. As before, workers are fooled into thinking their real wages have risen and unemployment remains at U_1 while price inflation accelerates to $\dot{p}_2$. This process can be repeated but only at the cost of ever-accelerating inflation brought about by an acceleration in the growth rate of the money supply. By similar reasoning, only by refraining from an acceleration in the rate of growth of the money supply and aggregate money demand can the acceleration of infla-

---

[10] Actually the Friedman model has been widely interpreted as allowing a work–leisure rather a work–unemployment choice. Strictly speaking, then, additional employment implied by the movement from unemployment rate U_0 to U_1 comes from new entrants to the labour force. This raises some minor problems but a reasonable change that allows the analysis to keep sight of the really critical issues is to assume that Friedman allowed for frictional or search unemployment.

tion be brought to a halt. All non-accelerating rates of inflation lie along a vertical line through U_0, a locus of all points where the actual and expected rates of inflation are equal.

If accelerating inflation is ruled out, the only policy solution of long-run merit is to stop 'fooling around with Mother Nature' and to eventually move the economy to unemployment rate, U_0, the so-called 'natural' rate of unemployment. The GM-I theory of the natural rate is symmetrical in the sense that regulation of aggregate demand so as to push the unemployment rate above U_0 leads to decelerating rates of inflation. In the long run the Phillips curve is vertical since an ever-accelerating or decelerating rate of inflation is not an acceptable long-run policy.[11]

---

[11] Write:

$$\dot{p}_t = \alpha \dot{p}_t^e - \beta U_t \tag{1}$$

and;

$$\dot{p}_t = \sigma \dot{p}_t^e - \lambda(U_t - U_t^n) \tag{2}$$

where U^n is the natural rate of unemployment and all variables have their previous meanings. Equations (1) and (2) are linear versions of augmented Phillips curves, with equation (2) differing from the usual Phillips curve in that the rate of price inflation is made to depend on the difference between the actual and natural rates of unemployment. Next assume $\alpha = \sigma = 1$, the natural rate, monetarist hypothesis, and solve equations (1) and (2) for the unemployment variables giving:

$$U_t = (1/\beta) \cdot (\dot{p}_t^e - \dot{p}_t) \tag{1'}$$

and

$$U_t - U_t^n = (1/\lambda) \cdot (\dot{p}_t^e - \dot{p}_t). \tag{2'}$$

Equations (1') and (2') illustrate the GM-I assumption that the causation runs from changes in inflation to change in unemployment. Assume initially that the expected and actual rates of inflation are equal (i.e. $\dot{p}_t^e = \dot{p}_t$), giving $U_t = 0$ in equation (1') and $U_t - U_t^n = 0$ in equation (2'). In GM-I analysis this supposedly reveals the non-existence of involuntary unemployment when $\dot{p}_t^e = \dot{p}_t$.

Next allow for the actual rate of inflation to exceed the expected rate because, say, of an increase in the rate of growth of the money supply and aggregate demand. Equations (1') and (2') indicate that in this case the unemployment rate becomes negative or is reduced below the natural rate, respectively. This will result in an increase in aggregate output or supply to a level above the 'natural rate of output'. The causation runs from changes in inflation to changes in unemployment in GM.

The question naturally arises as to why the supply of aggregate output should depend upon inflation or price surprises. A surprise supply function clearly is a most unusual production function. Output, employment and unemployment can only deviate from their 'natural' rates if workers are fooled (i.e. $\dot{p}_t^e \neq \dot{p}_t$) because by assumption when $\dot{p}_t^e = \dot{p}_t$ all unemployment is voluntary. Related to this is the assumed channels of policy. If changes in the money supply are to have any impact on the real sector, including unemployment, they can only do so to the extent that they affect the rate of inflation.

3. *Some extensions*

There is no end to the ways in which the NRH can and has been embellished and refined. Various assumptions are made about who is fooled or misinformed. Alternative assumptions are made about how the voluntarily unemployed spend their time.[12] Two slightly different models have been developed, largely distinguished by the choices assumed open to workers. In the model just discussed workers are seen as choosing, on the basis of the expected real wage, whether to work or withdraw from the labour force. In other models, the choice is between working or leaving work to search for a better job.[13] Both types of models assume that the process of exchange in a labour market is the result of highly individualistic bargaining in which the participants 'haggle' over a wage until an acceptable one is found. In both models changes in unemployment result from those involved mistaking a change in the general price level for a change in relative prices. Most of the extensions have been but minor alterations made to fit within a zero involuntary unemployment framework.

However, attention has been drawn to a critical assumption of the NRH which illustrates an additional source of arbitrariness. This is the common assumption of the models of 'asymmetrical incomplete information'.[14] Demanders or buyers in markets are assumed to have complete or perfect information about prices and wages while sellers are less-well informed. This is essential if accelerating inflation is to lead to reduced unemployment and increased output, and decelerating inflation is to generate higher unemployment and lower output. By merely reversing the relative information endowments, for example assuming that employers underestimate price inflation following an increase in aggregate demand while workers have correctly foreseen events, the (incorrectly) expected decline in real wages seen by employers leads to a reduction of employment and output and a rise in unemployment. No justification for the information asymmetry is offered by the model builders.

---

[12] See, for example, R. J. Gordon (1976) Recent developments in the theory of inflation and unemployment, *Journal of Monetary Economics,* No. 2; Frisch, op. cit.; and A. M. Santomero and J. J. Seater (1978) The inflation–unemployment trade-off; A critique of the literature, *Journal of Economic Literature,* June.

[13] These are summarized in Santomero and Seater, op. cit.

[14] See J. Tobin (1980) Are new classical models plausible enough to guide policy?, *Journal of Money, Credit, and Banking,* November, Part 2.

INFORMATIONAL DISEQUILIBRIUM ANALYSIS (IDA)

1. *Continuous market clearing*

The NRH is both a distinct view as to the nature and causes of inflation and unemployment and a revival of the neoclassical analysis of markets that might best be termed informational disequilibrium analysis (IDA).[15] This is to be contrasted with non-market clearing disequilibrium analysis discussed in chapter 5. Informational disequilibrium analysis illustrates a common neo-classical research strategy. It is based on the desire to relax one of the obviously unrealistic assumptions of competitive analysis, and to then study the impact of this on the behaviour of the economic actors involved. In this case it is no longer assumed that the economic actors have complete and correct information of all past and current events. With incomplete information, expectations of the likely unfolding of economic events must be formed to provide a basis for current action and these expectations may or may not be realized. When they are not, those involved must adapt as best they can to the unforeseen events. Under certain conditions people learn from their mistakes so that eventually a situation in which expected and actual outcomes are identical is achieved.

The framework of IDA is really that of perfect competition with one change; information about current and future prices and wages is not perfect but incomplete.[16] By implication, information about all other events currently developing is available and costless. Moreover, the assumption of continuous and instantaneous market clearing is retained but with an obvious amendment. Demand and supply curves for labour are still drawn as though amounts demanded and supplied are functions of the real wage but allowance is made for the possibility that with incomplete information the expected real wage determines labour supply.

In any period employment is always found at the intersection of the downward-sloping demand curve for labour (a function of the actual real wage) and the upward-sloping supply curve of labour (a function of the expected real wage). Markets always clear but may be in disequilibrium in the sense that desired amounts supplied are based on incorrect information. Complete or 'full' equilibrium is reserved for those situations in which all expectations or expecta-

[15] See P. Korliras (1980) Disequilibrium theories and their policy implications: towards a synthetic disequilibrium approach, *Kyklos,* No. 3.
[16] See Phelps op. cit. who allows for price-makers in his model.

tions on the average are realized, e.g. any point along the vertical Phillips curve of figure 3.1.[17]

2. *Why full employment?*

It is fair to characterize the GM-I position as asserting that any deviations from full employment, i.e. the natural rate of unemployment, will be short-lived and insubstantial. The economy is always 'in the neighbourhood' of the natural rate, (always provided, of course, that the authorities have not caused a malfunctioning of the economy through their activist policies). It is this assumed tendency for a capitalist system to gravitate towards zero involuntary unemployment that allows the monetarist position on inflation and unemployment to be characterized as 'separatist'. In the long-run, the rate of inflation is explained by the rate of growth of demand. The rate of unemployment, i.e. the natural rate, must be explained by other factors.

The basis of the belief that an economy moves towards a situation where unemployment is voluntary unless disturbed by shocks is a born-again version of Adam Smith's invisible hand, if not quite Walras' auctioneer. Thus, the Walrasian world is one of perfect competition and perfect knowledge either on the part of the auctioneer or the economic agents operating in markets. It is also a world in which prices are flexible in both directions and where trading does not take place except at prices which clear markets, i.e. at prices at which excess demands or supplies are always zero. If the world of GM-I differs from that of Walras, it does so to the extent that surprises or mistaken expectations are allowed, such as those experienced by workers in the earlier example. Such mistakes or surprises allow for the unemployment rate to deviate from the long-run equilibrium, but such deviations are assumed to be short-lived.

WHAT IF UNEMPLOYMENT IS INVOLUNTARY?

The central message of the NRH is the automatic full-employment tendencies of capitalism in the absence of 'surprises'. The NRH has

---

[17] Any number of textbooks now include a chapter incorporating these notions in a study of 'the' labour market. See, for example, W. Branson (1979) *Macroeconomic Theory and Policy*, 2nd edn, Harper, New York, chapter 6. It should be noted that contrary to the text, some economists assume that only in 'full' equilibrium can one speak of continuous market clearing transactions. See Tobin, *Assets Accumulation*, op. cit.

been the cornerstone of the monetarist revival, in spite of the fact that it is based on unproved monetarist assertions, such as an automatic tendency towards full employment, and the most simplistic assumptions about the workings of capitalism, e.g. a highly complex world of unions, multinationals and big government can be modelled in terms of the theory of atomistic competition.

The full-employment assumption is critical for obtaining a vertical long-run Phillips curve and for the conclusion that the natural rate of unemployment can be alternatively defined as the unemployment rate at which there is no involuntary unemployment, at which the expected rate of inflation is equal to the actual, and at which the rate of inflation is constant. If the arbitrary assumption of automatic full employment is dropped, a long-run Phillips curve is still possible.

To see this consider figure 3.1, and once again assume an economy at point A initially with a zero rate of inflation. As before, suppose there is an increase in aggregate demand but assume the existence of involuntary unemployment in the Keynesian sense, i.e. a fall in the real wage due to prices rising more than money wages leads to an increase in labour supplied (and demanded). Again there will be a movement from point A to A' accompanied by an increase in money wages less than prices. But in this case there is nothing any longer in the logic of the situation that generates a movement to point B (as shown on pp. 58–60) once workers are aware that the real wage associated with point A' is less than that associated with A. Involuntarily unemployed workers are not at the margin of indifference between work and leisure by definition. Moreover, the case is strengthened if there is productivity growth, as is very likely when aggregate demand picks up. In this case a movement from point A to A' will likely increase labour's marginal product and real wage. The most that can be said about the larger labour input in this case is that a less rapid rise in real wages might result than if employment had remained constant.

But it is also possible that at point A' the expected rate of inflation may rise in which case the short-run Phillips curve shifts outward (although not along lines described by figure 3.1). It may even be possible that these expectations get built into wage demands, in which case if unemployment remains at U_1, the economy can be seen as moving upward vertically along a line such as that drawn through unemployment rate U_1. The monetary authorities will be accommodating the inflation.

The process ends if and when some shift in the short-run Phillips curve gives rise to an expected rate of inflation equal to the actual at

$U = U_1$. The likelihood of such a sequence is enhanced by the assumption of involuntary unemployment. A new point on the long-run Phillips curve is then determined, that corresponding to $U = U_1$.[18] Whether or not U_1 implies zero or positive involuntary unemployment cannot be known *a priori*. But the original unemployment rate, U_0, while corresponding to a non-accelerating rate of inflation (and a situation in which the expected and actual rates of inflation are assumed equal) is not an unemployment rate with zero involuntary unemployment. Furthermore, given the assumption of convergence at $U = U_1$, the expected and actual rates of inflation will eventually also be equal and constant just as at $U = U_0$. Thus, whether or not inflation rates are accelerating or the expected rate of inflation is equal to the actual need not reveal anything about the nature of unemployment.[19] Once involuntary unemployment is admitted, the natural rate of unemployment is no more than a synonym for the non-accelerating inflation rate of unemployment (NAIRU).

MINIMALIST ECONOMIES OR GREAT MONETARISM-MARK II

1. *Some long-run dynamics*

On pp. 58–60 a short-run Phillips curve was obtained within the monetarist framework by assuming that someone makes mistakes. By assuming that the expected rate of inflation in the current period was equal to the actual rate of inflation in the previous period, i.e. $\dot{p}_t^e = \dot{p}_{t-1}$, changes in aggregate demand in the current period could lead to deviations of the unemployment rate from the so-called natural rate of unemployment. However, once the information of what had taken place became known, workers would demand an adjustment in money wages in period $t + 1$ or would withdraw their labour services.

---

[18] Again, the analysis of convergence given in figure 2.1 is very similar to that discussed in the text.

[19] Unfortunately, the newer textbooks, when accounting for the rise in the natural rate of unemployment in recent times due to demographic changes, do not emphasize that this allows involuntary unemployment at the natural rate. See Gordon, op. cit., chapter 10.

Other more complicated formulations of expectations can be cited. Thus, write:

$$\dot{p}_t^e = \dot{p}_{t-1} + b(\dot{p}_{t-1} - \dot{p}_{t-2}) \tag{1}$$

$$\dot{p}_t^e = \dot{p}_{t-1}^e + c(\dot{p}_{t-1} - \dot{p}_{t-1}^e) \tag{2}$$

$$\dot{p}_t^e = \sum_{i=0}^{n} \lambda_i \dot{p}_{t-i-1}; \ \lambda_i \geq 0, \ \sum \lambda_i = 1. \tag{3}$$

Equation (1) states that expectations are generated in an extra-politive manner with a correction for past trends. Equation (2) describes an error learning or adaptive expectations function. Equation (3) is a general autoregressive or distributive lag function of past rates of inflation.

If it is assumed that $c = 1$, equation (2) reduces to

$$\dot{p}_t^e = \dot{p}_{t-1} \tag{2'}$$

the expectations generating formula on pp. 58–60. If in fact $c < 1$, the unemployment rate can deviate from the natural rate of unemployment for extended periods of time following a change in aggregate demand that displaces the system, even within the GM-I framework. Prices and wages become 'sticky' or rigid because of a slow adaptation of expectations. In chapter 2, the discussion of the feedback and pass-through effects of cost–push models of inflation distinguished between the long-run and short-run inflationary processes. The former process suggested how inertia can be built into inflation without even considering expectations. Models of the demand–pull variety discussed in this chapter, in incorporating relations like those described in equations (1)–(3), indicate an alternative (and complementary) means of generating long-run dynamic adjustment processes. Unemployment rates may rise, for example, and inflation persist; i.e. stagflation takes place, because of the slow adaptation of inflationary expectations.

2. A rational expectations model

Equations (1)–(3) share one important feature, all assume that expectations are generated from information about past events. In none of the functions is it assumed that information currently available, including the behaviour of the monetary and fiscal authorities, influences the formation of inflationary expectations. One implication of ignoring current events is that the unemployment rate (and other real variables) can be changed through policy because people are fooled. When, say, workers' expectations are generated according to an adaptive expectations process such as that described in equation (2), policy can alter the actual rate of inflation while the expected rate of inflation adjusts only after a lag. Inflation in this case is unanticipated and unemployment may deviate from the natural rate.

More generally, expectations generated according to processes described by equations (1)–(3) may very well lead to forecasts that are systematically biased or 'irrational' to use the current terminology. Thus, if the actual rate of change of the rate of inflation is a positive (negative) constant, then an expectations-generating process such as described by equations (1)–(3) will systematically underestimate (overestimate) the actual rate of inflation. Referring to figure 3.1, in the case where the authorities were determined to maintain an unemployment rate less (greater) than U_0, workers continuously underestimate (overestimate) the current rate of price inflation.

In an effort to handle problems such as this, models of rational expectations have been constructed. These models allow current events to play a role in generating inflation expectations. What is meant by the rational expectations hypothesis (REH) is rather ambiguous, however.[20] In what has been termed the weak REH, the hypothesis asserts no more than the non-controversial assumption that the economic actors use optimally whatever current as well as past information is available to them, balancing marginal costs and benefits, in formulating expectations.[21]

However, a strong REH has been used in most macroeconomic models that goes much beyond this and is the basis for what has been termed the new classical macroeconomics. The strong REH assumes that actors form their expectations on the basis of a knowledge of the process which will ultimately generate the realized outcomes that are being predicted. To put the matter somewhat differently, people are assumed to base their expectations on an information set which leads them to individually conceptualize the same model of the economy, which moreover depicts its true structure. Full knowledge of objective reality (except for a random term) is assumed.[22] As a result, predictions of future events differ only from

---

[20] See W. Fellner (1980) The valid core of rationality hypotheses in the theory of expectations, *Journal of Money, Credit and Banking*, November, Part 2.

[21] See J. Handra (1982) Rational expectations: What do they mean? – Another view, *Journal of Post Keynesian Economics*, Summer.

[22] To put the matter yet another way, expectations are based on a model of the economy which, when solved, predicts values for the economic variables (especially prices, wages and the money supply) that differ from actual outcomes by a random term at most. If the random term is suppressed, the models are seen to incorporate the assumption of perfect foresight.

the realized outcomes by a random term. For the most part GM-II
models of the economy incorporate the various basic elements of
GM-I but include some additional features.

To see the operation of the strong REH and to bring out some of
the important implications of the omniscience assumption, consider
the following simple model of the economy.[23]

$$\dot{p}_t = e_1 \dot{p}_t^e - e_2(U_t - U_t^n) + \varepsilon_{1t} \tag{4}$$

$$\dot{p}_t = \dot{M}_t + \varepsilon_{2t} \tag{5}$$

$$\dot{p}_t^e = \dot{M}_t^e \tag{6}$$

$$\dot{M}_t = h_0 + h_1(U_{t-1} - U_{t-1}^n) + \varepsilon_{3t} \tag{7}$$

$$\dot{M}_t^e = h_0 + h_1(U_{t-1} - U_{t-1}^n) \tag{8}$$

where $\dot{M}_t$ and M_t^e are the actual and expected rates of growth of the
money supply in period t, respectively, the ε's are random error
terms and all other variables have their previous meanings. Equation
(4) is an augmented Phillips curve introduced earlier, altered slightly
to allow the difference between the actual and natural rates of unemployment to influence inflation rates. Equations (5) and (7) depict the
structure of the economy. Equation (5) reveals that rates of inflation
always proceed at the same rate as the rate of growth of the money
supply and the relationship is symmetrical. Decreases in the rate of
growth of prices can be achieved as readily as increases through the
appropriate manipulation of the rate of growth of the money supply.
In REH literature this assumption finds its micro basis in the
assumption of flex-price markets in which prices (including wages)
always adjust within the period to clear markets; i.e. Walrasian
markets are assumed. Equation (7) describes the monetary authorities policy response to economic events. Any deviation of the actual
rate of unemployment from the natural rate in period $t - 1$ affects
the rate of growth of the money supply in period t in a systematic
way, a proportional feedback response.

Equations (6) and (8) describe the generation of rational expectations. They take account of current information, i.e. the expected
behaviour of the monetary authorities with regards to the money
supply and the expected behaviour of prices in period t. In addition,
and critical, the processes which generate expected rates of growth of
the money supply and prices are identical to the processes generating
the actual rate of growth of the money supply and prices. Everyone
knows the 'true' inflationary process as can be seen by comparing

[23] The model is that used by Gordon in his survey. See Gordon, Recent Developments, op. cit., pp. 199–200.

equations (5) and (6) and everyone knows what the authorities are doing currently, as can be seen by comparing equations (7) and (8). Finally, note that in the absence of the random terms the analysis assumes perfect foresight on the part of all concerned.

Rewriting equation (4) with $e_1 = 1$ gives:

$$U_t - U_t^n = -1/c_2(\dot{p}_t - \dot{p}_t^e - \varepsilon_{1t}),\tag{4'}$$

But since

$$\dot{M}_t - \dot{M}_t^e = \varepsilon_{3t}$$

and

$$\dot{p}_t - \dot{p}_t^e = \dot{M}_t - \dot{M}_t^e + \varepsilon_{2t},\ \dot{p}_t - \dot{p}_t^e = \varepsilon_{2t} + \varepsilon_{3t}$$

Equation (4') can then be written

$$U_t - U_t^n = -1/e_2(\varepsilon_{2t} + \varepsilon_{3t} - \varepsilon_{1t})$$

the actual rate of unemployment can differ from one period to the next from the natural rate only by a random component. Thus, there is not even a 'short-run' Phillip's curve. As can be seen by inspection of equation (4'), only if the authorities can affect $\dot{p}_t$ without similarly affecting $\dot{p}_t^e$ can U_t and U_t^n ever diverge (other than because of ε_{1t}). Since everyone knows the way the economy operates, including the behaviour of the monetary authorities, this is no longer possible.

While GM-I allowed for informational disequilibrium, GM-II does not. The economy, remains (in the absence of disturbances) in a perpetual state of (Walrasian) full employment equilibrium. Perfect foresight robs the authorities of any use for discretionary policy to regulate unemployment and output, since policy cannot affect the real sector, i.e. the 'superneutrality' result.[24] Proponents of GM-II, instead, advocate a monetarist money growth rule as the most appropriate policy stance. Both in the long-run and short-run, separate theories of inflation and unemployment are required.

THE CREDIBILITY HYPOTHESIS

In the mark I version of great monetarism changes in aggregate demand could temporarily affect the unemployment rate but in the long-run this option was ruled out. In the mark II version (strong REH assumption), aggregate demand cannot affect the unem-

[24] As pointed out, the results of the strong REH are almost too good to be true in the sense that they generate a kind of macro stability absent in the real world. For a discussion see Tobin, Stabilization policy, op. cit., and A. Okun, Rational expectations with misperceptions as a theory of the business cycle, (1980) *Brookings Papers on Economic Activity*, No. 1.

ployment rate even in the short-run. The difference in results does not lie in any difference in assumptions about the workings of markets. GM-II analysis is based on a micro view of markets identical with that of GM-I; markets are flex-price in the sense that prices adjust within the period to clear. At the aggregate level this generates a rate of inflation equal to the rate of growth of the money supply (disregarding random terms) in both versions. Related, both versions incorporate the NRH with its critical assumption of self-correcting, full-employment tendencies. Moreover, both versions introduce a separatist element in inflation and unemployment theory in the sense that separate forces are assumed to determine the unemployment and inflation rates in the long-run.

What differs between the two versions of the new monetarism can be put several ways. In GM-I the supply curve of labour is a function of the expected real wage which may systematically deviate from the actual real wage. This is not the case in GM-II. Alternatively, while unemployment in both versions may only deviate from the natural rate because of discrepancy between the actual and expected rates of inflation, a systematic discrepency is impossible in GM-II. This comes about not simply because price expectations under the GM-II regime take into account developments in the current period. In addition the true structure of the economy is assumed to be known by all in GM-II. As a result, systematic forecasting errors never develop.

In chapter 5 the relevance of any theory based upon an assumption of continuous market clearing is seriously questioned when the discussion centers on the way real-world markets operate. As a result little faith can be placed in any of the findings of GM-I, e.g. the short-run Phillips curve is based upon price surprises, the long-run Phillips curve is vertical and involuntary unemployment is non-existent. The relevance of the strong REH and GM-II for our understanding of inflation and unemployment and for formulating policy is even more questionable. The perfect foresight assumption can only be considered a set back in the development of economic theory.

What has become known as the credibility hypothesis (CH) can be viewed as an attempt to salvage some of the policy prescriptions of great monetarism, in particular the belief that restrictive aggregate demand policies are efficient and effective methods for reducing inflation.[25] The CH shares with the strong REH and GM-II the view

---

[25] See Fellner, op. cit., and (1979) The credibility effect and rational expectations: Implications of the gramlich study, *Brookings Papers on Economic Activity*, No. 1. More generally, the credibility hypothesis can be thought of as an attempt to re-establish the effectiveness of restrictive aggregate demand policies.

that the rate of price (and wage) inflation is very sensitive to current policies. It differs from GM-II in several important respects. For one thing, the CH allows for sizeable lage in the adjustment of current inflation rates to anti-inflation policy. The rate of price or wage inflation in the current period is a function of past rates of wage and price inflation as well as other variables including the unemployment rates. For another, the public is not assumed to know the monetary (and fiscal) aims of policy, such as depicted in equation (7), unless such goals of policy have been clearly and convincingly articulated by the authorities. Finally, unlike GM-I or GM-II, under the CH it need not be presumed that real-world markets continuously clear (although the more this is the case, the easier is the task for policy).

According to the CH, a determined attempt to reduce inflation by reducing the rate of growth of the money supply can, under certain conditions, be successful and at a minimum cost in terms of output and employment. This view suggests a policy response to inflation that would not differ substantially from that of GM-I. However, the CH need not be restricted to neoclassical economies. Indeed, such policies are often thought to have a chance of success in a world of fix-price markets, dominated by unions and oligopolies. A successful scenario would go something like this. The monetary authorities chose a target of reduced growth of the money supply in order to reduce inflation to some desired rate. It will then convince the public that: (1) it will adhere to this policy until price and wage stability is achieved; and (2) there is no alternative method to reducing inflation other than restrictive aggregate demand policies. By so convincing powerful economic groups of its resolve and insight, wage demands will be tempered and high wage settlements will be resisted by business. Because of pass-through and feedback effects this will set in motion a downward adjustment of wages and prices until inflation is under control. At that point, a restimulation of demand becomes feasible. In short, the CH is easily seen as a form of the policy recommendation of the OECD experts discussed in chapter 1.

Chapters 6 and 12 will evaluate the credibility of the CH. To anticipate, resoluteness in the application of depressed aggregate demand policies may succeed in reducing inflation, particularly if the authorities are not constrained in the extent to which they can be allowed to increase unemployment rates. Unfortunately for the CH, the authorities of a large number of developed capitalist countries can only allow limited increases in unemployment rates because of political, social and moral considerations. However, even if anti-inflation policies do succeed in bringing down inflation, the CH loses credibility because an eventual reflation merely leads to an acceleration of inflation while substantial amounts of involuntary unemployment still exist.

CONCLUSIONS

The recent period has been characterized by a polarization of beliefs about the nature of inflation and unemployment. The revival of monetarism should be seen as an attempt to re-establish an extreme version of demand–pull theories of inflation and the automatic full-employment properties of modern capitalist economies. It should be clear that the NRH raises a serious challenge to the inflation theorizing of the non-monetarists. Until the formulation of the NRH, both the demand–pull and cost–push versions of the inflation process discussed in chapter 2 took the view that there was both a short-run and long-run Phillips curve. This the NRH clearly denies whether it is treated as part of GM-I or GM-II. In the mark I version of the great monetarism changes in aggregate demand can temporarily affect the unemployment rate, but in the long-run this option is ruled out as changes in aggregate demand affect only prices. In GM-II models aggregate demand cannot affect the unemployment rate even in the short run. Other forces explain the unemployment rate. With the revival of monetarism, a separatist element in inflation and unemployment theory is introduced; separate forces are assumed to affect the unemployment and inflation rates.

Great monetarists of both persuasions come down hard against activist, interventionist policies, opting instead for rules such as a steady rate of growth of the money supply. It must be stressed, however, that both versions of great monetarism derive their conclusions from very special assumptions about the workings of modern economies. And oddly enough, the revival of monetarism in the recent period has not been accompanied or preceded by any new insights into the way markets operate and transactors behave that would support the GM theory of unemployment and inflation. Its increased popularity must be traced to other causes. Most of the remaining chapters of this study will consider one way or another the lack of realism of the basic assumptions behind the monetarist, neoclassical view.

CHAPTER 4

Some Recent Developments in Inflation and Unemployment Theory – II

INTRODUCTION

Chapter 3 summarized the monetarist-neoclassical theory of inflation and unemployment, a mode of analysis that stressed three important elements. First, monetarist-neoclassical theory is cast within a framework of atomistic competition, a world devoid of large-scale organizations, power relations and price-makers. Second, it is also a world of strong, if not instantaneous, tendencies towards full employment as exemplified by the NRH. Market-clearing prices prevail. Trading is always carried out at prices corresponding to the intersection of demand and supply curves. This economy is very similar to the Walrasian model popular with general equilibrium theorists. When the extreme assumptions of the rationale expectations models, including that of continuous market clearing, are combined with the natural rate hypothesis, the model is distinctly Walrasian. This should suggest that the assumptions about the manner in which markets function might be critical in determining the nature of the Phillips curve.

Finally, in the models of chapter 3 expectations played a critical role. Given the acceleration of actual inflation rates in the second half of the 1960s, monetarists and non-monetarists alike took to including expectations variables in their analysis.

The monetarist analysis of inflation and unemployment marks a resurgence in economics of a particular mode of analysis, neoclassical. Economics has been marked with a persistent tendency to revert to the model of atomistic competition at both the theoretical and applied levels. For reasons stated in the Introduction this is not to be confused with scientific progress. In the present context of inflation and unemployment theory, the monetarist application of neoclassicalism has merely modified and refined the textbook versions of the automatic full employment macro model.

The discussion in this chapter concerns an entirely different kind of theorizing about inflation and an entirely different view of how economies work. In the studies to be described it is assumed that there are markets which never clear in the sense that situations of excess demand and supply do not generate wage and price changes of any kind. On the basis of this assumption about markets (which although strong is less extreme than continuous market clearing), it is possible to develop a pure cost–push theory of inflation as a polar counterpart to extreme GM-I and GM-II pure demand–pull theories. This theory gives rise to horizontal short- and long-run Phillips curves in contrast to the vertical curves of GM. This difference results largely from the fact that cost–push models are based on a world of large–scale organizations engaged in rather intricate and continuous bargaining arrangements, while demand–pull models are derived from a world of atomistic competition.

While a detailed discussion of why market-clearing prices are not to be expected in any real economy will be taken up in chapter 5, chapter 4 discusses one reason for non-market clearing prices, in this case wages. Wage settlements (as well as product price settings) have been dominated increasingly during the past half century by non-market or 'fairness' considerations. Fairness in wage settlements has two dimensions, a fair real wage and a fair relative wage. Suffice it to say here that in a full employment context, it is the strength of trade unionism that largely determines the importance of fairness considerations in wage bargaining within a country. The result has been that wages have become relatively unresponsive to 'market forces'.

These fairness considerations will be seen as a kind of institutional constraint that is often binding upon market participants and leads to wage rigidity as well as to cost–push inflation. Chapter 4 also discusses further how fairness considerations give rise to another form of inertia, other than the influence of expectations. This again makes it difficult to eliminate inflation from any economy once it has become established.

The main purpose of the next three sections is to develop a number of pure cost–push models of inflation and to trace out certain of their implications, especially with regard to the impact of aggregate demand policies. These models are then modified in the concluding sections to take account of important demand–pull forces that very much shape the nature of the inflationary process.

PURE WAGE–PRICE INFLATION

It is customary to use the unemployment rate as a proxy for the state of excess demand or supply in the economy. For example, an increase in the rate of unemployment is interpreted as an indication of a general loosening of labour and product markets arising from a generalized increase of excess supply or decrease in excess demand in individual markets. When the world is one of atomistic competition or when the monopoly power exercised by workers or employers varies with the state of demand, inflation rates vary with unemployment rates. If, in contrast, wages and prices are completely insensitive to changes in excess demand and supply for whatever reason, then the aggregate level of the rate of unemployment will be unrelated to the rate of inflation of either wages or prices.

A version of this 'pure' cost–push thesis can be expressed as follows:

$$\dot{w}_t = a_0 + \sum_{i=1}^{n} a_i \dot{p}_{t-1} \qquad a_i > 0 \tag{1}$$

and

$$\dot{p}_t = b_0 + \sum_{i=1}^{m} b_i \dot{w}_{t-i+1} - \dot{\rho} \qquad \sum b_i = 1 \text{ and } b_i > 0 \tag{2}$$

where $\dot{w}$, $\dot{p}$ and $\dot{\rho}$ refer to the rates of money wage and price inflation and productivity growth (assumed for convenience independent of time), respectively, as before.[1] Equation (1) states that the rate of

---

[1] A belief in pure cost inflation with respect to wage inflation is well illustrated by the following:

The conventional view that there is a functional relationship between unemployment and inflation is based, at root, on the notion that the wage is set by supply and demand in a market process. Inflation is generated when demand exceeds supply, and the demanders drive up wages. . . . When (unemployment) is very high, supply exceeds demand and wages are stable or falling. . . . Those who hold the alternative view challenge this basic notion. They assert that wage determination and unemployment are two essentially distinct processes which must be understood independently of each other and can be attacked through separate policies.

See M. Piore (1979) Unemployment and Inflation: An Alternative View, in *Unemployment and Inflation: Institutionalist and Structuralist Views,* (Ed. M. Piore), M. E. Sharpe, White Plains, New York.

wage inflation depends not on 'market forces' but only upon the rate of price inflation in the previous n periods, as workers react to past inflation rates in order to protect their current real wages. There is a feedback effect from changes in the cost of living to wages, but the adjustment may be spread over several periods. Equation (2) is derived from a mark-up theory of pricing as outlined in chapter 2 and implies that the profit margin is fixed. As can be seen, business is 'neutral' in the wage–price inflation process in the sense that it merely passes through (with a distributed lag) wage increases in excess of productivity growth since $\sum b_i = 1$ by assumption.[2] On the other hand, the larger is the wage response to some past rate of price inflation, i.e. the larger are the a's, the larger is the feedback effect from price to wage inflation, which is then passed through to prices, etc. Given values for the parameters and some assumed values for the rates of price inflation in the previous periods, equations (1) and (2) can be described as short-run, horizontal Phillips curves.

Because of the feedback and pass through effects, there is an internal dynamic to the workings of the inflation process in this class of models like those of chapter 2. Wage inflation affects the rate of increase of prices when labour costs rise and price inflation affects the rate of increase in wages as the former feeds back into wages. Because of these interactions, it is possible as in chapter 2 to distinguish between the short- and long-run Phillips curves.

Both the short-run and the long-run Phillips curves for wage and price inflation are horizontal. These results can be generalized. More complicated lag patterns can be introduced along with the inclusion of additional explanatory variables. Provided that none of the latter vary systematically with the unemployment rate, the Phillips curves remain horizontal. In addition, the long-run behaviour of wages and prices follows a similar time path, the rate of wage and price inflation differing only by a constant.[3]

It is worth emphasizing that in order to obtain horizontal Phillips curves, it is necessary to make two strong assumptions. First, it must be assumed that the usual textbook competitive elements are missing in markets so that if a vector of prices is somehow established that generates excess demands or supplies, this does not lead to market

---

[2] Business could only permanently act in a non-neutral way by permanently altering its profit margins.

[3] This is generally true for linear difference equations systems that do not 'decompose'. See A. Goldberger (1959) *Impact Multipliers and Dynamic Properties of the Klein–Goldberger Model,* North-Holland, Amsterdam, pp. 133–34.

clearing prices through competition between buyers and sellers. Equally important, even if competition of the type just described is lacking, it is still necessary to assume that whatever monopoly power exists in markets, the extent to which it is exerted does not vary with the state of excess demand and supply.

In chapter 3, when the natural rate hypothesis was combined with the rational expectations hypothesis, vertical short and long-run Phillips curves resulted. Changes in aggregate demand could influence the rate of inflation but could have no effect on unemployment, as separate forces were at work determining the rates of inflation and unemployment. Conventional economic forces such as the rate of growth of the money supply determined the inflation rate. The unemployment rate, on the other hand, depended upon whatever unexplained factors determined the natural rate, e.g. 'imperfections' in the labour market. From a policy point of view, aggregate demand policies could only affect the rate of inflation.

The policy implications of the pure cost–push inflationary mechanism are no less dramatic than those of the pure demand–pull models. If Phillips curves are horizontal, changes in aggregate demand can only affect unemployment rates but can have no effect on rates of inflation. As with the pure demand–pull inflationary mechanism, separate forces are determining the rates of inflation and unemployment. But in the pure cost–push version, economic forces (i.e. aggregate demand) determine the unemployment rate. When Phillips curves are horizontal, anti-inflation policies must be designed to shift the curve downward. This involves seeking out the omitted variables from equations (1) and (2). Chapter 11 indicates that these are likely to be non-economic influences.

While these models seem at first sight to be unduly restrictive, models of inflation that repress the role of aggregate demand in determining inflationary outcomes have had a long and respectable tradition. The 'Scandinavian' model of inflation will be considered in the next section.

WAGE–WAGE INFLATION

1. *Wage setting in an institutional framework*

The horizontal Phillips curve arises when the inflationary process results from a wage–price interaction. Wages respond to nothing but changes in the cost of living; e.g. price inflation, and the latter merely reflects the underlying wage inflation. More recent developments in cost–push inflation theory can allow for this wage–price interaction but introduce additional adjustments which are consistent with a view that inflation rates are insensitive to changes in aggregate demand. The influence at work here is that of a 'relative wage' or 'spillover' effect, whereby changes in the wages of one group of workers lead to wage demands and settlements in other labour markets in the interest of 'fairness' and ultimately, morale or industrial harmony.[4]

Labour markets that are interrelated in this sense give rise to an additional pure cost–push inflationary mechanism, one of wage–wage inflation. Such interrelatedness also illustrates the importance of organizational and institutional forces in intermediating in the inflationary process, as these forces constrain (and even restrain) individual wage settlements at the same time as they lead to an important source of inertia.

Recognition of this influence is not new, having been stressed by institutionally minded labour economists for some time. A special formulation can be found in the general theory.[5] Its explicit recognition constitutes one of the more important recent developments in inflation theory, one with significant policy implications. At issue again is the relative importance of market and non-market forces in wage determination, of whether changes in wages reflect changes in excess demand and supply conditions or depend upon considerations of fairness, this time a fair relative wage. For if wages seldom reflect the interplay of market forces, then clearly inflationary impulses will not be transmitted throughout the economy in anything like the manner outlined in chapter 3.

Various explanations have been offered to explain why wage settlements in some labour markets are influenced by settlements elsewhere rather than the usual demand and supply influences. At the basis of all these explanations lie two determinants, one on the employee and the other on the employer side of the labour market. From the point of view of employees, it is in the first instance the interdependence of workers' utilities that generates a demand for 'comparability' in wage settlements. To alter the terminology, if wages rise in certain labour markets, workers elsewhere develop feelings of 'relative deprivation' if their wages do not rise to a new 'fair'

---

[4] Various theories of this interdependence are summarized in J. Addison and W. Siebert (1979) *The Market for Labor: An Analytical Treatment,* Goodyear, Santa Monica, chapter 13.

[5] J. M. Keynes (1936) *The General Theory of Employment, Interest and Money,* Macmillan London, pp. 14.

level. In unionized firms, the threat of rank and file revolt is a spur to union leaders to comply. In turn, employers respond to such pressures partly to earn the reputation as that of a 'good' employer, but even more basically in order to maintain morale and thereby, worker performance.[6] In non-unionized companies, the threat of unionization supports such a response.

Specifying the nature of the interrelations between wage groups, which sectors interact with which other sectors, whether this interaction involves a mutual dependence or one in which one or more groups are a key or leading labour group in setting the pace for others, whether the interrelations generate simultaneous determination of wage settlements or lagged relations, how and why the participants in this 'pattern bargaining' change, these and other important empirical points have been stressed in models of interdependent wage settlements. Formalizing the underlying events into a coherent, general theory has been slow, a difficulty accentuated by the need to develop primary sources of data.[7]

2. Wage interdependence and inflation

The general form of the spillover mechanism by which wage changes and inflation are transmitted throughout the economy can be written;

$$\dot{w}_j = \sum_{r=1}^{n} c_{jr} \dot{w}_r \qquad c_{jr} > 0 \tag{3}$$

where $\dot{w}_j$ is the rate of wage inflation induced in the jth sector by the growth of money wages in the sectors initiating the impulse, $\dot{w}_r$ (where $r = 1, 2, \ldots, n$) and c_{jr} is the coefficient measuring the size of the induced response.[8] For simplicity, all lags are ignored and the time subscript dropped.

In equation (3) wages in the jth sector are determined by wage increases in n other markets. If $n = 1$, the model is often termed a wage leadership model of wage determination. Thus, write

$$\dot{w}_i = c_i \dot{w}_k \qquad c_i > 0 \tag{3'}$$

---

[6] For example, dissatisfaction on the shop floor can lead to 'work to rule'.

[7] The point here is that economists increasingly turn to secondary data to bolster their theories because such data is so readily at hand. Access to a computer and a research assistant are almost sufficient for a successful research career. Primary data is needed but lacking in the area under discussion.

[8] This is the formulation found in Addison and Siebert, op. cit., pp. 466.

where c_i is a spillover coefficient indicating the size of the response in the ith sector to wage movements in the key sector. Models have been developed and tested in which the key sector is a group of industries where wages are determined simultaneously within some time period or 'wage round'. In its own bargaining, each member of the key group takes due account of the recent and current wage settlements reached by the remaining members of the key group. These settlements then determine wage demands and settlements in non-key sectors whose reference set is the key group.[9]

As just mentioned models of wage interdependence based on consideration of fairness have taken many forms reflecting the complexity of the real world. Consequently, models of wage–wage inflation incorporating this process of wage determination are numerous. A simple version of the wage leadership hypothesis can be used to illustrate a formal model of wage–wage inflation.

3. The 'Scandinavian model'

In the Scandinavian model of inflation, the key sector is referred to as the competitive sector, indicating that in addition to providing leadership in wage settlements, this sector also competes for sales in foreign markets and is subject to import competition at home.[10] The remaining sectors are grouped together into one sector termed the 'sheltered' sector indicating that these industries are not subject to foreign competition (nor do they compete abroad).

Such a model may be written

$$\dot{w}_k = \dot{\rho}_k + \dot{p}_f \tag{4}$$

$$\dot{w}_s = \dot{w}_k \tag{5}$$

$$\dot{p}_k = \dot{w}_k - \dot{\rho}_k \tag{6}$$

$$\dot{p}_s = \dot{w}_s - \dot{\rho}_s \tag{7}$$

---

[9] See O. Eckstein and T. A. Wilson (1962), The determination of money wages in American industry, *Quarterly Journal of Economics,* August. For a study that allows both market and non-market spillover influences to operate see L. Christofides, R. Swidinsky, and D. Wilton, A microeconometric analysis of spillovers within the Canadian wage determination process, *Review of Economics and Statistics.* See also A. Wood (1978), *A Theory of Pay,* Cambridge, pp. 217.

[10] For an early example of the Scandinavian model see L. Jacobson and A. Lindbeck (1971) On the transmission mechanism of wage change, *Swedish Journal of Economics,* September.

$$\dot{w} = \lambda\dot{w}_k + (1 - \lambda)\dot{w}_s \tag{8}$$

$$\dot{p} = \lambda\dot{p}_k + (1 - \lambda)\dot{p}_s \tag{9}$$

where $\dot{w}$, $\dot{p}$ and $\dot{\rho}$ refer to the rate of growth of money wages, prices and labour productivity, respectively, and the subscripts k and s refer to the 'key' and 'sheltered' sectors of the economy, respectively and λ and $(1 - \lambda)$ are weights $(0 < \lambda < 1)$ reflecting their relative importance. The variable $\dot{p}_f$ designates the rate of growth of prices of foreign goods that compete with domestically produced, tradeable goods.

The sense of equation (4) is that under a system of fixed exchange rates, only if wage inflation proceeds at a rate equal to the combined rates of growth of productivity in the competitive sector plus the increase in prices of foreign goods will the competitive sector remain price competitive. Thus, substitution of equation (4) into (6) gives: $\dot{p}_k = \dot{p}_f$. Equation (5) describes the spillover effects of wage inflation in the key sector to the sheltered sector. An increase in $\dot{w}_k$, for example, leads to an equal increase in $\dot{w}_s$, as wage increases in one sector are always generalized throughout the economy.

The overall rate of wage and price is found by substitutions to be

$$\dot{w} = \dot{\rho}_k + \dot{p}_f \tag{8'}$$

$$\dot{p} = (\dot{\rho}_k - \dot{\rho}_s)(1 - \lambda) + \dot{p}_f \tag{9'}$$

Equation (9') reveals why domestic inflation can proceed at a substantial rate and a country still remain competitive; it is only necessary that the rate of inflation of traded goods not exceed 'world' inflation rates. Equation (9') also indicates that rapid growth in productivity in the key sector will accelerate price inflation (as well as growth in real wages) when labour markets are highly integrated as they are in Scandinavia. Most important, given the sectoral rates of productivity, the overall rate of inflation as expressed in equation (9') is independent of aggregate demand, being determined outside the system by $\dot{p}_f$. The Phillips curve for price (and wage) inflation is horizontal.

CYCLICAL VARIATIONS IN THE WAGE STRUCTURE

1. *Disturbances of the wage structure*

The pure cost–push inflationary mechanism (either wage–price or wage–wage) strains credibility in its assumption that the state of aggregate demand does not influence the rate of inflation. As already indicated in chapter 2, even if flexprice markets are disallowed, such an assumption cannot be maintained. This and the next section introduce additional aggregate demand effects.

An important implication of interdependence of wage settlements is a stable structure of wages. For example, in the Scandinavian model, wages in the sheltered sector always grow at the same rate as those in the key, competitive sector thereby ensuring that relative wages remain constant over time.[11] However, it is necessary to recognize that in the short-run, the stability of wage structure is being disturbed constantly by labour groups, especially unions, attempting to improve their position. This leads, alternatively, to a narrowing and widening of the dispersion and often a leap-frogging of groups higher in the rankings thereby altering the rankings. The wage structure may have an equilibrium in some long-run sense but it resembles a constantly disturbed equilibrium whereby a disturbance of the dispersion or rankings sets in motion reactions and counter-reactions that take time to sort themselves out. The rate of wage (and price) inflation is then strongly influenced by the rate and size of these disturbances and reactions.

But there are other forces at work leading to disturbances of customary wage structures which are systematic in nature. And it is a consideration of these forces that show; (1) the need to distinguish between the cyclical behaviour of wage structures and their long-run behaviour and; (2) the need to recognize that changes in aggregate demand can effect the overall rate of wage inflation once the cyclical impact of aggregate demand on wage structures is taken into account. The second point suggests another shortcoming of the models on pp. 75–81 in addition to that cited in chapter 2. It does not, however, lend support to the sort of competitive model discussed in chapter 3.

Consider first the following example of a long-run equilibrium wage structure. From one cyclical peak to the next during the

---

[11] For some relevant empirical studies see T. A. Papola and V. P. Bharadwaj (1970) Dynamics of industrial wage structure: An inter-country analysis, *Economic Journal,* March; H. A. Turner and D. A. S. Jackson (1969) On the stability of wage differences and productivity based wage policies: An international analysis, *British Journal of Industrial Relations,* No. 1; W. Godley (1977) Inflation in the United Kingdom, in *Worldwide Inflation: Theory and Recent Experience* (Eds L. Krause and W. Salant) The Brookings Institution, Washington, D. C., pp. 461; and J. Eatwell *et al.* (1974) Money wage inflation in industrial countries, *Review of Economic Studies,* October.

postwar period, the relative dispersions of wages in manufacturing industries has tended to change only slightly, approximately 5 per cent upward or downward, in all but one of seven economies for which there exists comparable data.[12] In addition, over approximately the same period, industry rankings within manufacturing changed little in the vast majority of a larger sample of market economies.[13] Yet, the tendency for the relative dispersion of wages to move counter-cyclically is indicated in regressions where the coefficient of variation of industrial earnings is regressed upon current and past values of the unemployment rate and other variables.[14] The reciprocals of the unemployment variables take a negative sign and are highly significant indicating the counter-cyclical behaviour of the relative dispersion of the earnings structure.

2. Some explanations of cyclical variations

During a boom a general 'bumping up' of the labour force takes place in the sense that there is a relative and absolute expansion of job opportunities in the high-wage industries.[15] This means that firms in low-wage sectors of the economy will most likely have to raise wages relatively, as labour markets tighten, if only to retain workers. This is reinforced by the fact that firms in high-wage sectors tend to be firms with exceptional non-pecuniary benefits as well. Expansion of employment becomes possible for these latter firms by merely advertising additional job vacancies. The overall rate of wage inflation rises as unemployment falls if for no other reason than the bidding up of low wages.

Various explanations have been offered as to why high-wage firms 'permit' lower-paying firms to raise their wages relatively (but not necessarily allowing a disturbance of the rankings). First, high-paying firms tend to be unionized and are often locked into a con-

---

[12] See J. Cornwall (1977), op. cit., Table 5.7.

[13] See references in footnote 11.

[14] See M. Wachter (1974) The wage process: An analysis of the early 1970s, *Brookings Papers on Economic Activity*, No. 2; G. L. Perry (1978) Slowing the wage–price spiral: The macroeconomic view; *Brookings Papers on Economic Activity*, No. 2; and W. Polland (1980) Wage rigidity and the structure of the Austrian manufacturing industries: An econometric analysis of relative wages, *Weltwirtschaftliches Archiv*, No. 4.

[15] See A. Okun (1973) Upward mobility in a high pressure economy, *Brookings Papers on Economic Activity*, No. 1; and W. Vroman (1977) Worker upgrading and the business cycle, *Brookings Papers on Economic Activity*, No. 1.

tract during the boom. This is especially true in North America where a three-year contract is very common. The result may be that it is legally impossible to restore the wage structure existing at the beginning of the boom and bargainers must wait until the subsequent recession to do so. Second, it has been suggested that labour leaders in high-wage firms are willing to sacrifice part of a potential increase in wages during the boom if they feel this can be recaptured in the ensuing slump. Third, labour leaders in high-wage firms may be gearing their wage demands at least partially to what workers in other high-wage firms and industries have recently gotten or will obtain shortly. The relevant spill-over effect that generates a call for fairness is from one or more members of a 'key' group to the others. As a result a relative improvement in the wages of low-paid workers outside the key group may be of little concern.[16]

During the subsequent recession the wage dispersion again widens, as high-wage groups press for a restoration of the earlier structure. Since money wages seldom if ever fall absolutely, the widening of the dispersion arises from relatively large wage increases among high-paying compared to low-paying sectors. Wages in the latter are more influenced by labour-market conditions and low-paying firms can now obtain all the labour they need while still falling behind relatively in the pay structure. This desire to widen the wage dispersion will be reinforced if inflation exceeds some threshold during the previous boom as the evidence indicates that the impact of inflation on wage rates is greatest in the high-wage industries.[17]

Finally, it should be noted that because of lags in the adjustment of the wage structure, an important source of inertia is also built into the inflationary process. Disturbances of the wage structure in the past, just like past rates of inflation of prices, give rise to strongly felt inequities which must be corrected in the present and near future. In chapter 6, this inertia is shown to lead to an inflationary bias.

INFLATION AND THE UNEMPLOYMENT RATE

The cyclical variation in the wage structure generates important inflationary influences. A fall in unemployment rates during a boom

[16] See M. Wachter (1970) Cyclical variation in the interindustry wage structure, *The American Economic Review*, March.
[17] See G. L. Perry (1978) Slowing the wage–price spiral: the macroeconomic view, *Brookings Papers on Economic Activity*, No. 2; and S. A. Ross and M. L. Wachter (1973) Wage determination, inflation, and the industrial structure, *The American Economic Review*, September.

leads to a narrowing of the dispersion of the wage structure as wage inflation in low-wage sectors rises. But since this latter development leads to subsequent efforts (and some current efforts, surely) by the high-wage groups to restore their position, another influence of unemployment rates on wage inflation is introduced.[18]

The matter can be put more generally. In chapter 2 it was argued that labour is bound to be more aggressive and successful in its wage demands, other things being equal, the lower is the unemployment rate. But not only is the wage–price mechanism more likely to be activated and operative the lower is the rate of unemployment, the same is true of the wage–wage mechanism. Thus, in an economy with a fragmented union movement in which individual unions enter into collective bargaining separately, it can be expected that a larger number of unions will successfully press for higher wages as unemployment rates fall throughout the economy. The likelihood of such settlements upsetting the wage structure thereby setting off the wage–wage mechanism is therefore increased. Wage–wage and wage–price inflation will increase as unemployment rates fall whereas only the latter mechanism would come into play under centralized bargaining.[19]

The cyclical response of the wage structure also points up the need to drop the assumption that all labour markets are fix-price. The narrowing of the relative dispersion of the wage structure during the boom, for example, arises because of a bidding up of wages following an increase in excess demand for workers in low-wage sectors. Markets may not be Walrasian but shifting demand and supply curves do influence wages in this case.

In chapter 5 it is recognized that prices in some product markets also reflect the interplay of shifting demand and supply curves even though reactions to conditions of excess demand or supply are unlikely to be instantaneous. Prime candidates for this category are those markets in which homogeneous commodities such as industrial and agricultural raw materials are traded.

By allowing for the existence of some 'flex-price' markets as well as 'fix-price' markets, the inflationary mechanism becomes more complicated than the process described up to this point. An increase in aggregate demand activates both cost–push mechanisms, but in

[18] Wachter, Cyclical variation, op. cit., p. 83. One study found that this cyclical variation in the wage structure was attenuated when foreign labour could be imported during boom conditions as in Austria and Germany. See Pollan, op. cit.

[19] In chapter 12 an argument is made that under certain conditions inflation rates are lower at any unemployment rate under coordinated collective bargaining.

addition periods of boom are accompanied by a bidding up of wages in low-wage sectors and of raw materials prices in commodity markets which are then passed through to product prices to reflect the rising cost of these inputs.[20]

In formal, but general, terms this hybrid model of demand–pull, cost–push inflation can be written as:

$$\dot{w}_t = c_0 + \sum_{i=1}^{v} c_i \dot{p}_{t-1} + \sum_{i=1}^{w} d_i U_{t-i+1}^{-1} \qquad c_i > 0 \qquad (9)$$

$$\dot{p}_t = d_0 + \sum_{i=1}^{r} d_i \dot{w}_{t-i+1} - \dot{\rho} + \sum_{i=1}^{s} \beta_i U_{t-i+1}^{-1}$$

$$\sum d_i = 1 \text{ and } d_i > 0. \qquad (10)$$

Both wage and price inflation are to be seen as complicated, distributed lag functions of prices and wages, respectively, and of unemployment rates. Inflation is no longer a simple cost–push process as described by equations (1) and (2). The unemployment variable is included to pick up the several influences of aggregate demand conditions on inflation: the increased aggressiveness of labour and decreased resistance of employers; the greater likelihood of disturbances to the wage structure; the bidding up of wages in low-wage sectors and prices in commodity markets, all when unemployment rates fall, and the lagged response by workers in high-wage industries to earlier (cyclically induced) changes in the wage structure.

CONCLUSIONS

In the 1950s and 1960s a subject of much debate was whether inflation was a cost–push or demand–pull phenomenon. Chapter 2 attempted to give some of the flavour of this debate. In this earlier period, both the demand–pull and cost–push versions of the inflation process were thought to be consistent with a trade-off between price or wage inflation and unemployment. Chapters 3 and 4 strove to show that more recent developments have led to a further divergence of views concerning the nature of the Phillips curve. Separate and quite distinct explanations of unemployment and inflation have been developed.

[20] The first such study of this kind of interaction was J. Duesenberry (1950) The mechanics of inflation, *Review of Economics and Statistics,* May.

The polar models of chapters 3 and 4 challenge the traditional Phillips curve analysis in which changes in demand pressures determine simultaneously the rates of inflation and unemployment. In the pure cost–push models on pp. 75–81, conventional economic forces, i.e. changes in aggregate demand, determine the unemployment rate. The rate of inflation is uninfluenced by changes in excess demand and supply. As a result, Phillips curves are horizontal both in the short and long-run.

The alternative position that changes in demand pressure do not simultaneously determine the rate of wage and price inflation and unemployment stresses the impact of changes in aggregate demand on prices and wages, but denies the ability of changes in aggregate demand to influence the unemployment rate in the long run (without accelerating or decelerating inflation) and even in the short-run. In both cases, the Phillips curve is vertical in the long-run; in the latter, the Phillips curve is vertical in the short-run as well.

In the final analysis, not only must the extreme demand–pull and cost–push models of inflation be rejected, so must be the either/or models of chapter 2. Inflation is the result of both types of influences, although in chapter 6 it will be argued that it is cost–push forces that make inflation so much of a problem today.

Chapter 5 evaluates the importance of demand–pull and cost–push forces in an understanding of inflation by considering the manner in which markets, especially for labour, operate. It seeks to discredit the monetarist position about markets, and instead argues that most markets are fix-price, although the existence of flex-price markets is recognized. Once that is done, it becomes clearer why inflation has been so persistent in spite of large amounts of involuntary unemployment, a matter discussed in chapters 6 and 7 and why unemployment today is such a serious problem, a matter discussed in chapter 8.

CHAPTER 5

Equilibrium and Disequilibrium Economics

INTRODUCTION

Chapters 3 and 4 indicated how diverse are the explanations today of unemployment and inflation. The polar positions that the Phillips curve is vertical, on the one hand, and horizontal, on the other, naturally have profoundly different implications for policy. Furthermore, advocates of both views are strongly convinced that the acceleration of inflation in the late 1960s and early 1970s and its persistence into the 1980s can be explained quite adequately within their respective frameworks. But clearly two such diametrically opposed explanations of the current inflation and unemployment difficulties cannot both be correct.

At various points throughout chapters 2–4 it was stated that both extreme positions are seriously flawed. A more systematic effort to get at the basis of the inflation–unemployment difficulties is in order. Since aggregate rates of inflation and unemployment are weighted averages of rates in individual markets, a strategy suggests itself; a detailed analysis of the way in which product and labour markets work.

Thus, aside from a recognition that wages in the low-wage sectors of the economy are flex-price, at least upwards, and prices in some commodity markets flex-price in both directions, there has been little discussion of the question of whether markets are flex-price or fix-price. But assume that all markets are flex-price, as Walrasian general equilibrium theory would have us believe. Then, not only do changes in prices, including wages, reflect shifting demand and supply curves but adjustments to excess demand and supply are in the right direction and rapid enough that transactions always take place at prices that clear markets. In such a case, the economy would always attain an equilibrium position in which excess demands and supplies were non-existent in all markets, including those for labour.

Automatic full employment is always realized in this Walrasian world. No recourse is needed to rational expectations, for that matter.[1] Changes in aggregate demand can only affect the price level thereby giving rise to vertical Phillips curves, at least in the long-run. In this case the control of inflation is a simple manner; control aggregate demand through control of the money supply.

Consider, on the other hand, a world in which all or nearly all markets are fix-price, a world in which price movements are unrelated to changes in excess demands or supplies. Here, it would only be an accident if such an economy settled down to a full employment equilibrium (in the absence of policy) as Keynes indicated a half-century ago. Changes in aggregate demand may have some impact on inflation even if markets are fix-price as indicated in chapters 2 and 4. It was also argued in those chapters that if fairness considerations are important in wage settlements, then an on-going inflation may be difficult if not impossible to eliminate, at least within a democratic framework, through repressing aggregate demand. Some other kind of policy is called for when markets are fix-price.

All of this suggests that the relevance of any theory of inflation and unemployment may be judged to a large extent by the realism of its description of markets. Chapter 5 questions the relevance of GM on the basis of a profound discrepancy between its micro foundations and real-world markets. It is argued that Keynes in the *General Theory* was not sweeping enough in his partial rejection of flex-price markets. Most markets, it will be concluded, are fix-price and, therefore, the appropriate form of modelling market behaviour is neither Walrasian or Marshallian but what will be termed 'non-market clearing disequilibrium analysis' (NDA). Within this context, chapter 5 discusses the importance of constraints on economic behaviour with an aim towards discrediting on *a priori* grounds the GM explanation of inflation and unemployment.

DO THE TEXTBOOKS LIE?

1. *Equilibrium trading as a special case*

The important point that emerged from the discussion of information disequilibrium analysis (IDA) in chapter 3 was that GM-I (and

---

[1] See G. A. Akerloff (1979) The case against conservative macroeconomics: An inaugural lecture, *Economica,* August, p. 230.

its micro basis, the 'new microeconomics of employment') involves only an unimportant alteration of the competitive, automatic full-employment framework. IDA merely makes clear that it is not necessary that everyone possess perfect knowledge in order that full employment be established. Workers may be missing one important bit of information, temporarily at least, but based upon the information currently available, the amount of labour exchanged corresponds to full employment. When new information becomes available indicating that a mistake may have been made, appropriate adjustments again lead to market clearing.

This model of automatic full employment assumes something very similar to perfect competition.[2] In this world, workers and firms alike are price-takers, not price-makers. But the model must make the more critical assumption of continuous and instantaneous price adjustments such that transactions always occur at prices that just clear markets. Thus, the models of GM-I and GM-II represent macro counterparts to Walrasian general equilibrium models of equilibrium trading. They incorporate a special case of a more general theory of trading in which transactions are not necessarily limited to trading at market clearing, equilibrium prices.

The analysis turns now to a quite different kind of disequilibrium analysis, explained by a failure of the price system to equate demand and supply. Alternatively, interest shifts from a form of theorizing in which incomplete information causes traders to perceive potential gains from trade incorrectly, to that in which it is alleged by critics that traders forego perceived gains from trade.[3] The radical nature of this change will soon be apparent.

The ability or inability of prices to adjust in such a special manner that markets always clear has far-reaching consequences. Among other things, instantaneous price adjustments prevent the occurrence of quantity adjustments should any temporary set of disequilibrium prices arise. The Keynesian case of rigid money wages downward is an example, not merely of the absence of instantaneous adjustments

---

[2] The words are deliberately chosen. In Friedman's presidential address, he spoke of the natural rate as something that emerges when an equilibrium in the structure of real wages has been ground out by a system of general equilibrium equations, provided that account is taken of some vaguely defined market imperfections. In spite of this deference to market imperfections, the workings out of the NRH require the competitive assumptions, e.g. price takers. See M. Friedman, p. 8.

[3] See P. Korliras op. cit., p. 457; and H. Grossman (1979) Why Does Aggregate Employment Fluctuate?, *American Economic Review*, May.

but, at best, very sluggish adjustments of wages. If such rigidities exist, involuntary unemployment, a quantity adjustment results. An important question is what is required if these kinds of adjustments are to be avoided and trading is to be carried out always at equilibrium prices. To put the matter differently, what is required if markets for labour and output are to function like the stock or bond markets?

2. The conditions for equilibrium trading

Starting from a position of equilibrium introduce a disturbance that leads to a price that does not clear some market. Continuous and instantaneous market clearing necessitates that a price instantly be found to eliminate excess demand and supply so that no 'false trading', i.e. trading at a price other than that which clears the market, takes place. It might be thought that equilibrium prices would result if markets are characterized by atomistic competition. This is usually taken to mean that there are such a large number of buyers and sellers that collusive activities can be ruled out, and that all traders always face infinitely elastic demand and supply curves at some given price.

However, much more is required for equilibrium prices than the assumption of atomistic decision making. What is critical is the nature of information flowing to traders. Thus if all traders have perfect knowledge of the equilibrium prices and if this information is costless, then any disturbance of the equilibrium would be of the shortest duration and trading would, after an infinitely short lapse of time, proceed to take place at equilibrium prices. IDA alters this only slightly. Given workers' expected price level of output and perfect, costless information about other prices, a vector of prices that clears markets is assumed to be known. In both cases the velocity of price adjustments correcting any disturbance is infinite.

An alternative condition for equilibrium trading is the existence of some mechanism *'unrelated to the trading process itself* that would supply the needed information *costlessly'*.[4] Such a procedure is followed by Walras who assumed no trading could take place in any market until the vector of prices that clears all markets had been established. This vector of prices was to be obtained, in turn, not by

---

[4] See A. Leijonhufvud (1968) *On Keynesian Economics and the Economics of Keynes,* Oxford University Press, New York, p. 69.

participants to the exchange searching and experimenting in the market but by an auctioneer soliciting information from the potential participants about their desired (or 'notional') demand and supply responses to various hypothetical prices. Once the correct equilibrium set of prices was determined, these prices were announced and trading allowed to take place. Alternatively, Edgeworth's recontracting assumption could be invoked.

3. *Atomistic trading without an auctioneer*

Unfortunately there is not and never was such an auctioneer and information is not costless in the sense that traders must take time in fact to search and must pay for useful information.[5] Traders would have to experiment in order to find the equilibrium vector of prices and such experimentation necessitates dropping the assumption of infinitely rapid price adjustments. In fact such trial and error search processes suggest a very lengthy adjustment process would be required.

This is even more apparent when account is taken of the fact that real economies are constantly undergoing structural changes, are constantly being subjected to shocks and are characterized by economic actors woefully lacking in relevant information. All things considered on *a priori* grounds there is no reason to believe that the prevailing prices in most markets are market-clearing prices except by accident. The exceptions might be markets for some monetary assets and for standardized goods such as raw materials where cartel arrangements are absent. In such markets as these, mechanisms could exist allowing a market-clearing vector of prices to be obtained at a very low cost. But for other markets, very unrealistic assumptions are needed in order to generate the kinds of behaviour required to prevent quantity adjustments. If disequilibrium prices are the rule of the day, a study of the workings of markets that do not clear is in order. Keynes' labour market with downward rigidity of money wages is the obvious first step.

---

[5] In a world of competitive markets without an auctioneer, it is not even legitimate to treat sellers as price takers following upon some disturbance because there is then 'no one left over whose job it is to make a decision on price'. See K. Arrow (1959) Towards a theory of price adjustments, in *The Allocation of Economic Resources* (Eds M. Abramovitz *et al.*), Stanford, quoted in Leijonhufvud, ibid., p. 67.

FIX-PRICE LABOUR MARKETS AND UNEMPLOYMENT

The characteristics of fix-price markets can now be studied more carefully. The concern is not just with non-market clearing prices, but trading at prices that show little or no tendency to respond to conditions of excess demand and supply. With Keynes the analysis was limited to a fix-price labour market with wages rigid in one direction only, downward. Thus, a decline in aggregate demand for labour lead to a decline in employment because of a failure of money wages to adjust downward to clear the labour market.

Clearly, in the absence of discretionary policy, involuntary unemployment was now a distinct possibility. But Keynes assumed prices and wages were flex-price upwards. As a result, a stimulative fiscal or monetary policy or both could return the economy to full employment. Provided the stimulative policy leads to a larger increase in the price level than in wages, additional labour would be demanded. From this condition, Keynes' definition of involuntary unemployment, i.e. more labour is supplied (and demanded) following a reduction of the real wage in this manner, evolved.

Expectedly this definition or condition for the existence of involuntary unemployment generated considerable controversy, since if only labour would allow money wages to fall, the labour market would clear and policy would be unnecessary. The assumption of rigid money wages downward was, according to Keynes' critics, obviously a very special case based on a 'money illusion' and irrational behaviour on the part of workers. An identical response to decreases in the real wage induced by a falling money wage, price-level constant, and a rising price level, money-wage constant, was considered by them to be the only form of rational behaviour. The discussion will return to this asymmetric response by labour of the *General Theory* (see pp. 98–107). There it will be argued that Keynes' critics were at best engaging in moral philosophy, not sound economic analysis. The neoclassical supply of labour function, in which only the real wage enters as a determinant, is seen as a special case of a more general supply function.

It is important at this juncture to acknowledge that automatic full employment is no longer ensured once wage rigidity is introduced. The next section is concerned with work that extends the domain of inflexibilities. It has been argued that Keynes did not go far enough in his rejection of universal price flexibility and continuous and instantaneous market clearing. If true, the belief in automatic full employment in particular and a self-regulating economy in general is seriously challenged.

QUANTITY CONSTRAINT MODELS

1. *Interdependence of markets – Clower*

Although Keynes in the *General Theory* limited his analysis to rigid money wages downward, some of his interpreters (rightly or wrongly) have argued that 'the revolutionary impact of Keynesian Economics on contemporary thought [stems] . . . from Keynes' reversal of the conventional ranking of price and quantity velo- cities'.[6] According to these economists, a 'true' reading of the *General Theory* reveals that Keynes felt most trading would be at non- market clearing prices and corrections would be slow or non- existent. As a result when a disturbance leads to either excess demand or supply in some market, the response is not a relatively rapid adjustment of price in order to clear markets, but a relatively rapid adjustment of output. By interpreting Keynes in this light, post-Keynesian macroeconomics was thought to finally free itself from the unfruitful attempts 'to coax Keynesian results out of a framework of general market equilibrium'.[7]

Non-market clearing disequilibrium analysis (NDA) was first con- cerned with generalizing the idea of price rigidities to include product as well as labour markets and the interdependence of markets arising from rigidities. Later developments explained why these rigidities arose from rational, optimizing behaviour. The anal- ysis has been extensive and highly technical but the central ideas are easily summarized.

Consider the case again, where the labour market is initially in equilibrium with a real wage that equates amounts demanded and supplied, but a disturbance leads to a decrease in the price level. If the money wage is assumed rigid downward, the real wage rises leading to excess supply in the labour market. Employment is now determined by the demand for labour, the short side of the market. Disequilibrium in the labour market has repercussions in the product market. With the real wage permanently higher and employ-

---

[6] Leijonhufvud, op. cit., p. 67.
[7] R. Barro and H. Grossman (1971) A general disequilibrium model of income and employment, *American Economic Review*, p. 82.

ment, income and output lower, the demand for goods will fall relative to the quantity produced and demanded before the disturbance. This generates an excess supply of goods. As in the labour market, the short side of the market determines sales while the long side of the goods market, supply, is said to be 'rationed' as firms cannot sell all they would like at the new fixed price. Note that in this example, first developed by Clower, actual sales of output can be said to be constrained by actual quantities traded in the labour market where the disturbance originated.[8]

2. *Interdependence of markets – Patinkin*

The causation can go the other way as in the Patinkin example where the initial disturbance takes place in the goods market.[9] Again starting from an equilibrium in which the price level and real wage are such as to clear both markets, let a disturbance lead to an increase in the price level creating an excess supply of goods. This new higher price level remains fixed by assumption. Since the short side of the market determines sales or the amount traded, i.e. demand determines output, supply is rationed. This leads firms to reduce their derived demand for labour compared to the original equilibrium. Employment is demand-determined once again, but this time because transactions in the labour market have been constrained by sales in the goods market.

By viewing the interdependence of the labour and product markets in the Clower and Patinkin manner, Keynes' multiplier sequence was seen more clearly and a sounder basis for his consumption function was formulated.

3. *Disequilibrium prices and optimizing behaviour*

According to Clower the effective demand for output was determined or derived from some given (demand-determined) level of employment. With Patinkin the effective demand for labour was derived from a given (demand-determined) level of output. Subsequent efforts explained the demand for labour in the Clower model and the demand for output in the Patinkin model in such a way as to allow output and employment to be simultaneously determined.

---

[8] See R. W. Clower (1965) The Keynesian counter-revolution: A theoretical appraisal, *The Theory of Interest Rates* (Eds F. Hahn and F. Brechling), Macmillan, London.

[9] See D. Patinkin (1965) *Money, Interest and Prices,* 2nd edn, Harper & Row, London.

Most of the attention has been devoted to what was referred to as the Keynesian case, i.e. excess supply in the labour and product markets. Quantity constraint models have been developed that allow for excess demand in both product and labour markets, as well as excess demand (supply) in one market and excess supply (demand) in the other.[10] In order to concentrate on one of the important conclusions flowing from the quantity constraint models, the remainder of this section will use the Keynesian case.

Flex-price models with equilibrium trading and fix-price models with disequilibrium trading can be distinguished by the constraints assumed. In a Walrasian world of equilibrium trading, output and employment can be considered to be choice variables, the result of optimizing behaviour on the part of firms and households (workers). Firms choose a level of output that maximizes profits, subject only to a technology constraint. Households (workers) maximize utilities constrained by their preference maps and budgets. Income does not appear as an independent variable in household consumption functions as it is a choice variable dependent upon work effort which is maximized out.[11]

Under disequilibrium trading in the Keynesian case, output and employment are independently given to the firm and household, being determined by demand, and can be treated as parameters. Labour is rationed since demand determines employment just as sales and output are demand determined. What advocates of NDA have shown is that given the (unexplained) rigidity of prices and wages, norms of behaviour that are optimizing within this fix-price context can be derived rigorously.

4. *Information flows*

Disequilibrium situations can be described in terms of the information being transmitted between market participants. In a fix-price, quantity constraint world, the market-clearing vector of prices is not supplied by the market. When the rankings of price and quantity velocities are reversed, the price system is supplying something else. For example, involuntary unemployment always leads to an effective

[10] These are now summarized in the textbooks. See W. Branson (1979) *Macroeconomic Theory and Policy,* 2nd edn, Harper, New York, chapter 16.

[11] See Barro and Grossman, op. cit., p. 87; and T. Negishi (1979) *Microeconomic Foundations of Keynesian Macroeconomics,* North Holland, Amsterdam, chapter 5.

demand constraint in the product market as already indicated. This lower demand (lower than the full-employment level) is the market signal transmitted to firms as they draw up their production plans. The notional demands for output at prevailing prices, that is the demand for output that would be forthcoming if all labour that wanted to work was employed (and which would justify that amount of employment), is information that is never transmitted to the market. What is transmitted is information regarding the level of output that can be sold.

But even if prices are not rigid in some long-run sense and allowed to adjust later after trading has taken place, there is no reason to assume that they will have an equilibrating, market-clearing effect. For if in the meantime, traders have received and reacted to the effects of quantity rationing leading to the multiplier rounds, market-clearing price adjustments would be even more difficult to ascertain should traders desire to make these adjustments.

Finally, the informational problem when trading is allowed before a market-clearing vector of prices has been determined can be cast in terminology favoured by the monetarists. Assume workers quit jobs because of faulty information about real wages, i.e. they think the real wage is lower than it actually is. Assume that this results in a reduction of expenditures because of reduced income causing the supply side of the goods market to be rationed. Allow further that through their search activities these workers are actually able to determine that their estimate of the real wage was incorrect at which point they may wish re-employment. Unfortunately, because of a decline in their incomes and expenditures, the information that they wish to be re-employed and increase their expenditures to levels prevailing before they quit is never transmitted to producers. The stage is set for a multiplier contraction.[12]

Both of the two informational examples illustrate important implications of the 'reversal of the conventional ranking of price and quantity velocities' mentioned at the beginning of the section. The next two sections discuss why demanders and suppliers have little interest in even attempting to make price adjustments in the hopes of clearing markets.

---

[12] See A. Hines (1976) The 'micro-economic foundations of employment and inflation theory'; bad old wine in elegant new bottles in *The Concept and Measurement of Involuntary Unemployment* (Ed. G. Worswick), George Allen & Unwin, London.

WHY ARE WAGES RIGID?

1. *Introduction*

If wages and prices are rigid, the Keynesian case suggests that periods of involuntary unemployment will be a permanent feature of a capitalist economy. In contrast, great monetarism (GM) and information disequilibrium analysis (IDA) have no explanation of layoffs and involuntary unemployment, disallowing any kind of unemployment except that which is voluntary and frictional. Equally important, to the extent that wages and prices are rigid in the face of fluctuating demand, to that extent must inflation be seen as a cost–push phenomenon.

Critics of quantity-constraint modelling have taken exception to any conclusions based on this kind of analysis arguing that market behaviour that involves trading at false prices is not optimal. Allegedly buyers and sellers act 'irrationally' since they forego perceived gains from trade.[13] The conclusion is then drawn that NDA is suspect since it requires behaviour that is clearly irrational. Unfortunately, this view was given support inadvertently by the failure of the early advocates of quantity-constraint models to provide an explanation of rigid wages and prices. The remaining task of chapter 5 is to indicate that critics of NDA have become at best victims of the neoclassical tendency to oversimplify.

Frequent reference has been made in earlier chapters to the propensity of neoclassical and monetarist model builders to ignore the institutional framework within which their economic actors are (presumably) to operate. This allows them to formulate extremely simple notions about motivation, ends and the required consistent means to the realization of economic goals. The neoclassical assumption about the supply curve of labour is a case in point. In neoclassical and monetarist analysis the supply of labour is assumed to be a simple function of the real wage.[14] But the earlier discussion in chapter 4 of the determinants of wage settlements suggests that

---

[13] As pointed out in the Introduction, these same critics have a predilection for assuming some kind of goals to be maximized, then deducing consistent, i.e. rational, behaviour in terms of these goals. Unfortunately, little effort is made to determine whether the assumptions correspond to the real world behaviour, e.g. whether the supply of labour is simply a function of the real wage, and if wages and prices actually are rigid.

[14] Matters are a little different if the expected real wage is substituted for the real wage and allowance is made for 'endowments'.

matters are nowhere near this simple. When account is taken of additional important determinants of labour supply, it is no longer necessarily true that perceived gains from trade are foregone when trading takes place at non-market clearing prices.

In general what is to be argued is that behaviour which might be considered irrational or non-optimal will be seen to be optimal in the sense of consistently bringing the means to bear in order to achieve some specified end(s) once two amendments are made; more realistic assumptions about ends are adopted and the institutional forces which constrain behaviour are more properly specified.[15] This section seeks to establish why wage rigidity in the face of fluctuating demand and supply curves exists on such a broad scale. The next section poses the same question in the context of product markets. Once this is done, the analysis can centre on the forces that have over the past century become increasingly important in explaining wage and price movements. These influences were referred to as fairness considerations in chapter 4 and do much to explain why wages and prices are largely 'cost determined' and why inflation is largely cost–push today.

Some terminology first. When the expressions 'spot', 'auction' or 'flex-price' markets are used, it is to indicate a market for labour or goods where prices adjust 'very quickly' to disequilibrium so that amounts exchanged are the desired amounts or nearly so. A market-clearing mechanism is said to exist in such markets. In contrast, the terms 'career', 'customer', 'administered' or 'fix-price' market are used to indicate a market in which prices do not adjust to clear the market. Prices are rigid or inflexible with respect to excess demand or supply and, instead, depend first upon cost factors, either unit costs in the case of product markets or the cost of living in the case of labour markets, and second upon wages paid elsewhere, i.e. relative wage effects in the case of labour markets.

2. Why are money wages inflexible downward – the relative wage effect

When discussing wage settlements, IDA envisages a world of atomistic competition with individual buyers and sellers haggling over an acceptable wage. In some versions, wages fluctuate with changes in the relationship between the actual going wage and workers' expec-

---

[15] See, for example, R. M. Solow (1979) Alternative approaches to macroeconomic theory: A partial view, *Canadian Journal of Economics*, August, p. 345.

tations of what the market will bear. This view is at variance with the actual workings of large sections of North American labour markets and with practically all labour markets in the heavily unionized European economies. Even in non-unionized labour markets this analysis is inappropriate.[16]

Not only is the real world one in which collective agreements dominate wage settlements, it is one in which most labour markets are fix-price. Keynes argued that involuntary unemployment exists if a decline in the real wage brought about by a rise in the price level (money wages remaining fixed) would elicit an increase in both the amount of labour supplied and demanded. As just pointed out, Keynes' critics argued that workers suffered from a money illusion or irrationality in this case. Keynes, according to his early critics, must surely have written a very peculiar general theory. However, a more careful reading of the *General Theory* revealed that the labour supply function Keynes had in mind was: (1) more complicated than what had earlier been ascribed to him; and (2) more in tune with what practically-minded labour economists had believed for some time.[17] For what the *General Theory* makes clear is Keynes' belief that the supply of labour to any market was not just a function of the real wage but something just as real to workers, the relative wage received. To put the matter differently, optimizing behaviour on the part of workers is constrained by the wages received by other workers. Thus write:

$$N_i = f_i(w_i/p_1 \, w_1/w_i, \ldots, 1, \ldots, w_n/w_i) \tag{1}$$

where N_i is the amount of labour supplied to the ith market, w_i/p is the real wage earned in that market and the various wage ratio terms are the money wages paid in the other $n - 1$ labour markets relative to that paid in the ith market.[18]

As indicated in chapter 4, a solid, well-articulated theory explaining what determines the boundaries of interdependence of different occupational, regional or industrial groups has yet to be developed, but this does not refute the fact that relative earnings are of the utmost importance to the workers themselves. Because of this, the

[16] See R. Lester (1969) Wage–price dynamics, inflation, and unemployment – Discussion, *American Economic Review,* May.

[17] J. Tobin (1972) Inflation and unemployment, *American Economic Review,* March; and J. A. Trevithick (1976) Money wage inflexibility and the Keynesian labour supply function, *Economic Journal,* June.

[18] This is to be compared with the inverse of the neoclassical supply function $w/p = F(N)$ or $N = F^{-1}(w/p)$.

unwillingness of some groups of workers to take a cut in money wages in exchange for employment but to accept employment if real wages are reduced through inflation becomes both understandable and 'rational'. After all, they cannot be sure that by accepting a cut in their money wages all other groups in their 'orbit of comparison' will follow suit (and rightly so, since this is not a practical possibility). A general rise in the price level serves as the only means of preserving the existing wage structure while at the same time reducing the real wage.

This modification of the supply curve of labour, to take account of an influence of the greatest importance to labour, points out quite well the danger of ignoring the institutional structure of an economy when theorizing. An unwillingness to chance a possible decline in its relative wage is a very real concern to labour groups. The resistance of a labour group to a cut in its money wage does not signal a willingness to forego perceived gains in this case, but an effort to maintain gains. Resistance to money wage cuts under the circumstances described is a rational optimal response once it is acknowledged that relative wages enter into a worker's utility function.

3. Worker-job heterogeneity

Additional explanations of downward rigidity of money wages are not hard to find, which compliment the relative wage explanation. One such explanation runs in terms of the inelasticity of expectations.[19] Another, that stresses relative attitudes of employers and employees towards risk, is based on a version of implicit contract theory and attempts to provide an explanation of layoffs. It is not without its difficulties.[20]

A more fruitful use of a contract theory explanation develops along lines that recognizes that in a modern organization hired labour must be treated as a long-term investment in human capital.[21] Basic to this explanation is the importance of training and

---

[19] See A. Hines (1971) *On the Reappraisal of Keynesian Economics*, Martin Robertson, London, chapter II.

[20] R. Gordon (1981) *Macroeconomics*, 2nd edn, Little Brown, Boston, p. 208 and references cited.

[21] 'Wages are insensitive to current economic conditions because they are effectively installment payments on the employer's obligation to transfer a certain amount of wealth to the worker over the duration of the employment arrangement.' See R. Hall (1980) Employment fluctuations and wage rigidity, *Brookings Papers on Economic Activity*, No. 1.

acquired skills, seniority and a distinction between workers already employed and those on the outside.[22] These issues are best seen by way of contrast. For example, in labour markets where skills required for the job are minimal, where promotion prospects are limited and where little has been invested by either the employer or employee in training, workers and jobs are more or less interchangeable. In such labour markets, seniority does little to improve the job status of the employee and turnover may be little more than a nuisance for the employer. The result is that a sense of continuity and attachment fails to develop between the participants to the exchange. If some particular labour market is 'loose' in the sense that there is a surplus of applicants available for a limited number of slots, a process of competitive underbidding of wage rates could possibly be initiated. If so, then it could be said that there exist flex-price labour markets where wages reflect the interplay of demand and supply forces *and* where money wages may be flexible downwards.[23] However, even in this case it is unlikely that money wages would actually fall. Only in such unusual circumstances as the imminent bankruptcy of a firm is there evidence that this happens. Employers simply do not want the reputation of being bad employers.[24]

It is when the analysis turns to what has been alternatively referred to as career or 'primary' labour markets that the reasons for the non-existence of a market-clearing mechanism when excess supply develops in labour markets become most apparent. In most general terms, the distinction that must be made was that made almost 50 years ago by Hicks and updated more recently.[25]

(The basis of the theory of money wage changes lies in) the distinction between casual employment, the single job implying no durable relationship, and regular employment, in which people work together and go on working together. . . . Now it is necessary, purely on grounds of efficiency, in regular employment that both parties, employer and employed, should be able to look forward to some

[22] See P. Doeringer and M. Piore (1971) *Internal Labour Markets and Manpower Analysis,* Heath, Lexington; A. M. Okun (1975) Inflation: Its mechanics and welfare costs, *Brookings Papers on Economic Activity,* No. 2, and (1981) *Prices and quantities: A macroeconomic analysis,* The Brookings Institution, chapters 2 and 3; M. Wachter and O. Williamson (1978) Obligational markets and the mechanics of inflation, *Bell Journal of Economics,* Autumn; and Akerloff, op. cit.

[23] See Doeringer and Piore, op. cit.

[24] This was not always true. See T. Scitovsky (1978) Market power and inflation, *Economica,* August.

[25] J. R. Hicks (1974) *The Crisis in Keynesian Economics,* Basic Books, New York.

durability in their relationship . . . so it is necessary for efficiency that the wage-contract should be felt, by both parties but especially the worker, to be *fair*.

As Hicks and others have pointed out this gives rise to 'stickiness' in money wages whenever excess supplies of labour develop because of the bad effect on labour morale of money wage cuts by employers.[26]

Low morale, in turn, leads to high rates of turnover which becomes a matter of real concern if jobs involve skills, especially skills learned on the job and financed by the employer. And even if job dissatisfaction induced by wage cutting does not result in turn-over, there are problems. Most often, acquiring job-skills is primarily a matter of on-the-job training, usually involving the assistance of workers currently employed. If competition for jobs takes the form of wage competition (as in the earlier auction market example) then any attempt to cut money wages when excess supplies of labour arise will lead to situations of non-cooperation between new workers and the currently employed labour force. The marginal product of labour is not some immutable datum that depends purely on economic variables (e.g. the amount of capital employed). It is something very much dependent upon morale.[27]

What has been discussed is a species of 'implicit contract' theory which was originally formulated to account for wage rigidity down-ward but has more recently been extended to wage rigidity upward and price rigidity in both directions. These latter occurrences are discussed in the next part of this section and the following section. In the present case, the fact that very often jobs do differ in skill requirements and workers must be trained to perform these different tasks leads to processes that preserve and promote the ongoing employer–employee relation. These processes may result in an explicit contract such as a collective bargaining agreement or merely an implicit, unwritten agreement, either of which act to maintain a long-run relation. However, contracts will be incomplete in the sense that some of the terms will be vague and not all contingencies will be covered. In fact, a certain flexibility is allowed and felt desirable in the contract to handle unforeseen contingencies, the most being fluc-

---

[26] See also A. Okun (1973) Upward mobility in a high pressure economy, *Brookings Papers on Economic Activity,* No. 1; and Solow, op. cit.

[27] See L. Thurow (1975) *On Generating Inequality,* Basic Books, New York. This idea has been formalized by Solow 'by the unconventional device of including the wage as an argument in the firm's production function to represent the morale, productivity, and quality effects in a summary way'. Solow, op. cit., p. 348.

tuations in the demand for labour caused by changes in the demand for output. Adjustments must be made by management in wages or employment when a decline in demand for output leads to a decline demand for labour.

When workers are heterogeneous along skill and experience dimensions, management is forced to choose a response that minimizes the risk of alienating its experienced labour force. After all, economic conditions are bound to improve. Lowering wages, when no written collective arrangement prevents it, is generally considered to be taking advantage of the weakened bargaining position of labour. It is unfair and invites retaliation. In contrast, laying off and rehiring workers at an unchanged wage does not incur hostility to nearly the same extent since the decline in demand for output was clearly something outside the control of the firm. As a result of these contracts, even in the absence of labour unions, if there is worker–job heterogeneity and on-the-job training, downward rigidity of money wages is to be expected. Introducing labour unions would only strengthen the case for rigidity. If there appear to be some gaps remaining, then perhaps one final point can be made. In situations of excess supply of labour, employers can be expected to opt for a fixed money wage and redundancies rather than allow wages to decline (assuming they could) simply because of the desire of employers to be able to control the size of the wage bill.[28]

What has just been discussed will be seen in later chapters to have an important bearing on the overall productivity and inflation record of an economy. A key part of the industrial relations framework of a country is the nature of the attachment between employers and employees; simply put, in whether there is an adversarial or cooperative arrangement between the two groups. The kinds of implicit contracts under discussion strengthen the cooperative ties between management and workers. Going further, developments discussed in the next two chapters reveal that the notion of implicit contracts has been extended, largely due to the rise of unions, to include other aspects of fairness. These also lead to stronger cooperation between labour and management.

4. *Do money wages respond to excess demand?*

What has just been said may seem to be belabouring the obvious. However, it seems necessary to repeat arguments that are now famil-

[28] See R. J. Gordon (1976) Recent developments in the theory of inflation and unemployment, *Journal of Monetary Economies*.

iar to the profession because GM, both mark I and II versions, adopts the view that markets always clear in the short run even if this requires a decline in wages (or prices). In contrast to the flex-price world, the view accepted here is that 'virtually no wages are set in auction markets'.[29] This holds true in many markets for excess demand as well as excess supply conditions. To complete the analysis of money wages, then, it is necessary to ask whether excess demand in some labour market is likely to generate a rise in wage rates (always assuming average costs and the relative wage structure unchanged). Since much of the groundwork has already been laid in the previous part the discussion can be appreciably condensed.

Thus, the worker–job heterogeneity model is useful in analysing the response of employers to shortages as well as surpluses of labour. In jobs that involve firm-specific, on-the-job training, the cost of such training is borne by the firm. This investment in human capital naturally gives the employer an incentive to reduce turnover as already discussed. Various contractual arrangements are employed to accomplish this end. Some work to make wages rigid upwards. Thus, promotion from within to jobs involving higher firm-specific skills and greater supervisory roles, as well as higher pay, serves to generate greater monopoly rents for those already employed in a firm which are lost to the worker if he quits. As a result, 'closed internal labour markets' develop. In these markets a distinction is made between those already employed and workers on the outside (i.e. in the 'external labour market'). Workers in one internal market, already one or more rungs up the promotion ladder, are to a large extent frozen into their job if 'ports of entry' into other internal markets are the low-wage, low-skilled jobs. They too develop an incentive for reducing turnover. In the event of labour shortages it is entirely unnecessary to raise wages in order to retain workers in these situations.

There are additional considerations that bear on both the means adopted for the retention of existing workers and the expansion of employment. They suggest that employers do not wish to raise wages to increase supply. Within a firm there tends to develop internal wage structures that are considered fair to the workers. If labour shortages develop in one particular job classification, an increase in wages in this job raises equity problems throughout the firm. In this case a restoration of the previous internal wage structure is often

[29] G. L. Perry (1978) Slowing the wage–price Spiral: The macroeconomic view; *Brookings Papers on Economic Activity,* No. 2, p. 263; and Okun, op. cit.

required. This can only be achieved with wage increases in the other job classifications. The marginal cost of the newly hired worker is greater than his supply price if the latter implies a higher market clearing wage. Finally, there is the relative wage or spillover effect at work in labour markets. Individual employers soon become aware of the interdependence of their actions when they respond to labour shortages by raising wages. The result is that even in a world of moderately tight labour markets, there will be a tendency to try to expand employment by intensifying recruitment efforts. Thus, rather than fruitlessly raising wages in order to attract new job applicants, job vacancies will be created since employers learn to anticipate that any wage increases will be matched by other employers who recruit from the same labour market. Anti-pirating schemes can be seen as a confirmation of this likely chain of events. As before, the pervasiveness and intensity of the rigidity is reinforced by the presence of unions.

The previous remarks may seem to be somewhat question-begging. They assume that by merely advertising vacancies, labour shortages in individual markets can be overcome. While this is certainly true for 'good' job openings, it cannot be assumed to be true for what the dual labour market economists refer to as unrewarding jobs in the 'secondary labour market'.[30] There is conflicting information on this matter. Case studies suggest an upward rigidity in money wages, other things being equal, while econometric work gives some support for upward wage flexibility when excess demand for labour arises in low-paying, unpleasant jobs.[31] These results were cited in chapter 4 when discussing the narrowing of the dispersion of the industrial wage structure during the boom. The fact that ports of entry into other firms and industries may be the low-paying, low-skilled jobs does not act to reduce labour mobility for workers already employed in low-paying unpleasant jobs. Nor is turnover such an important concern with employers in these jobs as investment in firm-specific training is likely to be minimal. The result, not unexpectedly, is that the contractural processes and arrangements

[30] The division of labour markets into only two types should be looked upon as a metaphor. In reality, there exists a continuum of jobs from the 'worst' to the 'best' whatever criteria is chosen to grade jobs.

[31] See M. J. Piore (1979) Wage determination in low-wage labour markets and the role of minimum-wage legislation, in *Unemployment and Inflation, Institutionalist and Structuralist Views* (Ed. M. Piore), Sharpe, White Plains, New York; M. Wachter (1970) Cyclical variations in the interindustry wage structure, *The American Economic Review*, March; and (1965) *Wages and Labour Mobility*, OECD, Paris.

that make for continuity do not develop. When labour markets tighten, workers in these inferior jobs experience a relative rise in their wages since the wage is the only instrument available to management to reduce attrition of their work force. Such labour markets qualify as flex-price markets at least when excess demand for labour develops.

WHY ARE PRICES RIGID?

1. *Intermediate products*

Non-market clearing disequilibrium analysis is not limited to labour markets, as most product markets must also be considered fix-price. Price rigidity in product markets for intermediate as well as final goods has also been explained as rational, optimal behaviour when account is taken of important constraints on behaviour. Much that has been said about labour markets carries over to product markets. Much of the current work undertaken in support of fix-price market analysis can really be thought of as an amplification of explanations of price rigidities put forth by businessmen, economists and teachers in business schools for some time.

The downward rigidity of product prices in the face of depressed demand is most apparent from the experience of the 1930s. Various econometric studies provide support for the view that, rather than demand conditions, variations in product prices can be quite well explained in terms of a mark-up over unit costs (variously defined) especially when the latter have been 'normalized' so as to eliminate transitory seasonal and cyclical influences. In other words, product prices are set in fix-price markets.[32]

Early attempts to explain this lack of response to market conditions ran in terms of kinked demand curves in oligopolistic industries.[33] More recently contract theory has been utilized to explain rigidity of product prices in an upward direction in the presence of excess demand. As with most labour markets, it is often in the interests of the buyer or seller or both to promote an ongoing exchange relation or continuity because termination of an agreement or contract would involve large costs. In the case of intermediate

---

[32] See K. Coutts, W. Godley and W. Nordhaus (1978) *Industrial Pricing in the United Kingdom,* Cambridge University Press, Cambridge, and P. Sylos-Labini (1979) Industrial pricing in the United Kingdon, *Cambridge Journal of Economics,* No. 3, and the bibliography therein.

[33] See Negishi, op. cit., chapters 7 and 8.

products, if sellers have been required to undertake substantial investment outlays in order to meet a demand for non-standardized goods, a long-term relation with the buyer becomes essential if capital costs are to be covered and long-run profits maximized.[34] In this respect the motivation of management is very similar to that governing its attitude towards investment in human capital in the form of firm-specific training. The buyer of intermediate products, in turn, will want to maintain continuity, especially when non-standardized goods are being exchanged, since he will be concerned with having a continuous readily accessible source of supply and in reducing the various costs involved in finding another seller. He will likely be willing to pay a premium to ensure this. Note that this suggests under what circumstances, flex-price or spot-product markets are likely to develop: in those cases where the good exchanged is homogeneous, with little or no extra investment required for developing the product into something that is non-standardized (analogous to the unskilled labour case) and where a steady source of supply is little more than a matter of accumulating buffer stocks, ongoing relations acquire less importance.

As in the case of implicit labour contracts, these contracts will be incomplete in the sense that some of the terms of the contract remain vague and some contingencies ignored. Such incompleteness again has the benefit of allowing for flexibility; i.e. adjustments of some of the terms of the contract following the occurrence of unforeseen circumstances. For example, an unanticipated shortage of raw materials forces a would-be supplier of an intermediate product to adjust price or quantity terms of a contract which can no longer be fulfilled as initially agreed upon. As with labour markets, flexibility in product markets will manifest itself primarily in quantity adjustments. In the example just cited, the adjustment will be a lengthening in delivery dates, not an increase in the price of the product. Once again, quantity adjustments will be seen by buyers as a response to exogenous circumstances beyond the control of sellers.

2. Final goods

Implicit contracts between buyers and sellers are even more likely to be established in the case of non-standardized final goods.[35] These

---

[34] See M. Wachter and O. Williamson, Obligational markets, op. cit.; and Okun, op. cit.

[35] ibid.

contracts are both implicit and incomplete to an even greater extent than in labour and intermediate product markets. When such contracts cannot be filled immediately, e.g. demand for some product is temporarily outstripping supply, a price or quantity adjustment is required. As before, quantity response in the form of temporary rationing is the likely response. Raising price to take advantage of excess demand gives rise to a charge of unfairness, of 'gouging' the market. The latter induces customers to undertake a search process in an effort to find a 'fair' supplier. Thus, once again, maintaining prices (assuming unit costs unchanged) is a means of obtaining long-run customer satisfaction and reducing search activity. Such continuity helps ensure that the capital costs incurred in processing and marketing the good can be recovered, solvency maintained and long-run profits maximized.

Rigidity of product prices in the face of excess demand does not imply rigidity of prices in general. The discussion in earlier chapters of mark-up pricing is supported by implicit contract theory. If average costs rise, prices can be raised since such adjustments do not reveal unfair behaviour. Cost increases are seen to be beyond the control of the firm.

3. Excess supply in product markets

What evidence there is suggests that when excess supply develops in product markets, prices tend to hold firm, at least in comparison to what would be predicted in flex-price markets. To a large extent this can be explained in terms of what was just concluded about the behaviour of money wages. Money wages seldom decline in real life, they tend to rise in line with other wages and the cost of living.

As detailed in chapter 6, in earlier times, employers could adapt a 'take it or leave it' attitude with their work force because of their superior bargaining strength. This in effect gave employers control of wages and therefore a greater control over their costs compared to modern times. Today, with employers unable to arbitrarily lower wages to offset a decline in price, conditions of excess supply are less likely to result in price cuts.[36] This conclusion does not hold true for markets in which homogeneous goods are traded, a matter considered in the next section. In chapter 6, when the analysis focuses on

[36] Phelps in his review of Okun's book assumes that if firms reduce prices following a decline in demand they will (somehow) reduce money wages. The real world is rather different unfortunately. See E. Phelps (1981) Okun's micro–macro system: A review, *Journal of Economic Literature,* September, p. 1067.

fix-price markets, the likelihood of asymmetrical responses of wages and prices to changes in their cost determinants is considered.

FLEX-PRICE PRODUCT MARKETS

In all types of markets considered so far, labour, intermediate and final product markets, the units exchanged shared one important quality in common; they were non-standardized. Labour units displayed varying degrees of skill and employed workers were recognized by their employer as different than others; i.e. the 'ins' versus the 'outs'. Goods supplied in both kinds of markets also shared this quality; they were something differentiated by the buyer and seller from similar competing goods. In all three cases the desire for continuity constrains the use of price changes as an instrument for clearing markets. As a result fluctuations in demand and supply give rise to false trading. Most importantly, given the desire for continuity, to be seen as a fair trader, such responses to excess demand and supply should be seen as straightforward optimizing behaviour.

The candidates for the flex-price market designation considered so far were the markets for low-payed, low-skilled workers who shared one important characteristic; they were hardly distinguishable from one another. It was suggested above that homogeneous products would very likely be sold in flex-price markets also. Industrial and agricultural raw materials and many foodstuffs, goods often traded on international markets, are notable examples of flex-price product markets. Some of these commodities obviously do not trade on flex-price markets, the most notable fix-price commodity market being the OPEC producers' cartel. It seems useful, therefore, to think of a continuum of commodity markets starting with cartels where most of the commodity is sold at a contract price fixed by the cartel. This continuum then stretches over to commodity markets where a large percentage of the good traded is sold in markets where variations in price reflect day-to-day shifts in demand and supply for the good. For example, it is often argued that traded industrial raw materials other than oil tend to move either with the general level of final demand or industrial production in the developed economies.[37] In markets for agricultural raw materials, the impact of supply shifts on prices is usually given more stress. Somewhere in between will be markets for internationally traded goods where this spot market may

---

[37] *Economic Outlook*, OECD, Paris, July 1974, p. 27 and December 1979, p. 40.

be thin but where prices in the spot market influence individual contract prices. In these markets price adjustments may often predominate over quantity adjustments. Related to this, changes in aggregate demand can be expected to have an influence on prices in these markets. As pointed out in chapter 4 this will activate a wage-price mechanism in fix-price product and labour markets. In chapter 6 it will be argued that upward trends in markets for food and energy are likely at full employment. The upward trend in food prices arises because of a tendency for international demand to grow more rapidly than supply. The latter trend can be expected if demand and (cartel) supply arrangements lead to a situation in which the price of oil in the spot market is pushed above the OPEC contract price for any length of time. This suggests that in a strong boom oil prices will henceforth act more like industrial and agricultural raw materials prices.

CONCLUSIONS

The main conclusion to be drawn after this lengthy discussion of markets is that the neoclassical, monetarist view of an economy as one predominantly of flex-price markets, in which market clearing prices always prevail, is not sustainable. Rather the presumption that the real world is comprised largely of fix-price markets has far greater merit. This conclusion will be of no surprise to economists at business schools, businessmen and labour leaders who have been involved in real markets for some time. Only in the cases of labour markets for unskilled workers and product markets for standardized products do actual markets even begin to approximate the notion of a flex-price market. The assumption that money wages do not rise to eliminate excess demand in fix-price markets is a more controversial assumption than wage rigidity downward. But in real economies not only do wages not have to rise in most markets to allow employment to be expanded, there are good reasons for management to resist such adjustments.

The debate over whether markets are flex-price or fix-price illustrates all too well the recurring tendency for economists to reinvent the wheel. Participants in real-life markets have long been aware that quantity, not price, adjustments are the expected response to excess demand and supply conditions. Yet economists have been forced to reaffirm these truths, thereby diverting their attention from 'getting on with the job'. In this very important sense, neoclassical analysis has been a real impediment to scientific progress.

Two important points come out of this discussion. First, with most markets fix-price, changes in aggregate demand induce quantity not price responses, including changes in employment. Second, the existence of some flex-price markets, including the response by wage bargainers to changes in aggregate demand, ensures that there is some price response, however. And these responses, by activating the cost–push mechanisms discussed in chapters 2 and 4, will set in motion inflationary movements that may be prolonged and accelerating. Chapter 6 discusses the impact on inflation of this interaction between flex-price and flex-price markets. In addition, an analysis of asymmetries in the response of wages and prices to changes in their 'cost' determinants, in fix-price markets, and their market determinants, in flex-price markets, is undertaken. Even in a comparative static sense, these asymmetries lead to an inflationary bias; wages and prices are less likely to fall than rise. When the dynamics of inflation are considered, i.e. the feedback and pass-through effects that generate cost–push inflation, these same asymmetries lead to an inflationary bias in a more pernicious sense. Rates of growth of prices and wages are less likely to fall than rise in response to changes in cost determinants and aggregate demand. Chapter 6 discusses in some detail other types of asymmetries and as well as the existence of an inflationary bias in modern capitalism.

CHAPTER 6

Asymmetries, Biases and the Inflationary Mechanism

THE BASIC QUESTIONS

Chapter 1 outlined the mainstream policy response to inflation and its rationale. Much of what was discussed in chapters 2 to 5 can now be brought together in order to evaluate this and other policies. Recall that the main policy recommendation of the Report was to allow unemployment rates to rise in some short-run sense until inflation had been reduced and then to reduce unemployment slowly until something like full employment was re-established.

There are two critical questions to be asked about this kind of policy, a policy so widely adopted and still adhered to today in many countries:

Assuming that there is some political limit to how high and how long the unemployment rate can be allowed to rise in an effort to fight inflation, can a policy of restrictive aggregate demand succeed in bringing down inflation rates if constrained to operate within this unemployment range and for a limited period of time?

Assuming that inflation rates can be brought down to the desired rate even while unemployment rates are so constrained, will any attempt to then restimulate the economy lead to an acceleration of inflation rates while involuntary unemployment still remains high?

If the answer to the first question is no, then the burden of proof is on advocates of current restrictive demand policies to show that a failure to fight inflation has worse costs than unemployment. If they cannot, adopted policies must be judged a failure. But even if the answer to the first question is 'yes' and inflation rates can be brought down, a negative answer to question two evokes a similar adverse judgement. Note that both questions are framed in such a way as to take account of an unemployment constraint. The monetarists, especially, are guilty of overlooking this point. In forever blaming the monetary authorities for causing inflation and failing to bring it under control, monetarists fail to take account that in modern democracies even the most 'independent' central bank must eventually be aware of the costs of unemployment.

What needs to be shown is that the forces giving rise to an unemployment constraint also; (1) increase the likelihood that the answer to the first question is no; and (2) very greatly increase the likelihood that the answer to the second question is yes. These developments, some of which have been discussed earlier, are the rise in the importance and power of labour in the bargaining process, the increased complexity of processes and products used and produced by the modern corporation, the increased influence of fairness considerations in labour and product market transactions and Keynes' rigid money wage effect and other asymmetries. In addition, account must be taken of threshold effects and the likely upward trend at full employment of prices in two important markets, those for food and energy. Beginning in the next section these various elements are brought together to formulate a theory of inflation that allows an understanding of; (1) why the inflation in the postwar period has been so different from that experienced in other times; and (2) why the inflationary process is fundamentally changed under conditions of sustained high employment, affluent unions and powerful oligopolies. This will eventually lead to answers to the two questions just posed.

In order to keep the discussion focused on the essentials, important related issues have been assigned to appendices. Appendices B and C discuss the importance of unions and the money supply in explaining inflation and the results are easily incorporated into the ideas developed in the text. Before getting on with the main issues dealt with in the chapter, a brief recapitulation of some earlier findings is undertaken.

TAKING STOCK

1. *Fairness and price and wage adjustments*

Much of chapter 5 was taken up with the question of why shifting demand and supply curves do not lead to wage and price adjustments. In modern economies the desire to maintain long-term, ongoing market relationships ruled out as unfair some types of wage and price adjustments. The attachment or continuity of the relationship between buyer and seller would be terminated if prices or wages were adjusted in response to excess demand or supply conditions. Quantity adjustments to excess demands and supplies were more usual since these were considered to be reasonable and fair responses by participants. Most markets are fix-price, not flex-price.

To recapitulate, wages in fix-price labour markets are determined by the cost of living and wages paid elsewhere. Changes in the cost of maintaining or increasing real living standards give rise to wage demands in the interests of 'fairness'. It is not enough that employers refrain from cutting money wages. For good profit maximizing reasons, employers are attentive to wage demands based on this kind of fairness argument, demands which are not highly sensitive to the state of the labour market.

But fairness has another dimension and that has to do with the fairness of one's relative wage. In chapter 4 it was argued that in developed capitalist economies labour markets have become highly integrated in the sense that an increase in wages on one sector 'spills over' to other sectors as fairness or equity demands that others receive similar (usually percentage) increases. These considerations are repeatedly invoked in wage disputes and are also largely independent of demand conditions in labour markets.

In product markets also, it is often in the interests of the buyer or seller or both to promote continuity of the exchange relation because termination of an agreement or contract would involve large costs. When such contracts, usually implicit, cannot be filled immediately, e.g. demand for some product is temporarily outstripping supply, a price or quantity adjustment is required. Raising prices to take advantage of excess demand leads to a charge of unfairness, of 'gouging' the market. But raising price to cover an increase in costs does not evoke such a response since costs are beyond the control of the seller.

2. The cost–push mechanisms and their activation

The emphasis on what is a fair wage or price increase helps in understanding the nature of the inflationary process. Thus, in an economy composed of nothing but fix-price markets, two inter-related cost–push inflation mechanisms are at work, wage–price and wage–wage. They interact and are capable of generating a strong inflationary process when activated. For example, let wages in some industry increase to such an extent that they temporarily 'leap-frog' wages in several other industries. This disturbance can then activate a wage–wage mechanism as different labour groups attempt to restore the original wage structure which could well involve a sequence of leap-froggings. In the meantime, this wage–wage mechanism activates the wage–price mechanism as higher labour costs in the industries concerned are passed through to product prices.

For reasons discussed earlier, either or both of the cost–push mechanisms can be activated by changes in the unemployment rate. When labour markets tighten labour bargains more aggressively and employers become increasingly less resistant even to accelerating wage demands. In addition, it is likely that disturbances of the relative wage structure increase as labour markets tighten largely because of this increased aggressiveness.

3. The interaction of flex-price and fix-price markets

There are other examples of such systematic disturbances. Thus, while most markets are fix-price, the real world contains flex-price labour and product markets. Markets for casual labour involving little firm specific training tend to be flex-price upwards. Typically during a boom wages in these sectors tend to rise relatively, leading to a decrease in the relative dispersion of the wage structure. Just the opposite occurs during a recession. In countries with piece rates, variation in the amount of wage drift over the cycle also introduces a flex-price dimension to labour markets. Markets for goods that are undifferentiated, such as industrial and agricultural raw materials, have shown a tendency to be flex-price in both directions. In the course of a boom rising prices in these markets activate the cost–push mechanisms just discussed. Higher raw material prices are passed through to finished goods prices and higher relative wages in low-wage sectors will eventually activate the wage–wage and wage–price mechanisms.

4. Asymmetries

The inflation mechanism just outlined describes reasonably well the basic inflationary process at work in capitalist economies under conditions of high employment. The disturbances coming from sources such as OPEC, upward trends in prices in markets due to a long-run imbalance between demand and supply and movements in the exchange rate are easily grafted on to it. In addition, inflationary expectations can be introduced by means of a threshold effect first discussed in chapter 2.

There is one other basic element that needs to be considered before it is possible to understand the inflationary mechanism at work today. The major oversight so far has been a consideration of various asymmetries at work in a modern economy. Keynes had stressed the asymmetrical response of money wages to increases and decreases in aggregate demand. Labour markets were rigid or fix-price downward in the *General Theory*. Chapter 5 argued that, if anything, Keynes did not go far enough. Both wages and product prices are unresponsive to changes in excess demands and supplies in most markets, although support was found for Keynes' asymmetry; i.e. excess demands are more likely to push up wages than excess supplies will lead to declines. But having argued that most markets are fix-price and that wages and prices are cost determined, it must now be argued that wages and prices respond in an asymmetrical way to changes in costs. Money wages respond less in a downward direction than an upward direction to changes in their cost determinants; i.e. the changes in the real wage and the wage structure. Furthermore, an asymmetry in the behaviour of price to its cost determinant, i.e. average unit cost, is quite possible.

What will be argued is that these asymmetries are sources of inflationary bias in modern capitalist economies and result primarily from structural changes in the labour market that have been accumulating for some time and from sustained full employment.

To see how these asymmetries operate and give rise to inflationary biases, the following strategy is adopted. In the next section a brief summary of the historical developments that have led to cost-determined wages and, to a lesser extent prices, is undertaken. These same developments will be seen as the source of asymmetries that bias the movements of prices and wages upward. These asymmetries are then discussed on pp. 121–3. On pp. 123–30 the dynamic effects of the asymmetries are developed by combining them with the other features of the inflationary mechanism just summarized. An explanation of the current stagflation follows from this, one very much at odds with that offered by the monetarists.

THE HISTORICAL BACKGROUND

It is often stated that structural changes have been taking place leading to a rise in the importance of fix-price and a corresponding decline in flex-price markets. A common argument centres on the declining importance of a traditionally flex-price sector, agriculture. Of more relevance have been developments in product and labour markets in the industrial sector. These historical changes have been pinpointed rather well by several writers and this section will rely heavily on their views.

Scitovsky divides the economic history of modern capitalism into three phases; first, the period encompassing the development of the factory system in the late nineteenth century; second, the period encompassing the development of the trade union movement; and third, roughly the post-war period up to the early 1970s.[1] In the first phase, employers had the upper hand in both product and labour markets. They were price-makers in the former and wage-makers in the latter. Because of a vastly superior bargaining strength, wages were very often set by employers on a take-it-or-leave-it basis. While there is evidence that wages even before unions were often inflexible downward, such superior employer power tended to stabilize prices in an upward direction because employees were in no position to exert an upward pressure on wages.[2]

With the rise of the trade union movement, the bargaining power of employees greatly increased. This change, according to Scitovsky, greatly reduced the downward flexibility of money wages and, assuming mark-up pricing, the downward flexibility of product prices also. The upward flexibility of wages and prices was enhanced, naturally. Lewis also attributes this asymmetry to the rise of unions, choosing the 1880s as the date when a continual upward movement of money wages began in Britain, somewhat later in the nineteenth century for France and Germany, and the recession of 1949 for the USA.[3] The rate of growth of money wages, on the other hand, continued to respond to the trade cycle rising during booms and falling during recessions.

While the rise of trade unionism strengthened the downward rigidity of money wages, labour still lacked 'staying power'; i.e. the ability

---

[1] T. Scitovsky (1978) Market power and inflation, *Economica,* August.

[2] This suggests that flex-price labour markets were not particularly widespread even in the nineteenth century. However, particular wages did move in both directions in response to changes in the prices of goods produced by these workers, which is something different from market determination of wages. See R. Tarling and F. Wilkinson (1982) The movement of real wages and the development of collective bargaining in the U.S.: 1955–1920, *Contributions to Political Economy,* No. 1.

[3] A. Lewis (1980) Rising prices: 1899–1913 and 1950–1979, *Scandinavian Journal of Economics,* No. 4.

to absorb the costs of industrial warfare. During the post-war period changes occurred that increased the ability of labour to absorb the costs of, say, a prolonged strike. These developments included the widespread adoption of social and welfare services and payments and the accumulation of assets by workers and their unions as a result of increased affluence. It is also clear that underlying this development of increased power for labour was the commitment to full employment by governments. This period was associated with a profound change in the inflationary process as seen below.

This evolution in the relative powers of employers and employees had three main results.[4] First, concurrent with these developments in the labour market was an increasing superiority of employers (sellers) in the product market manifesting itself in a secular decline in the price elasticity of demand for goods. This product market development was attributed to the increased number and complexity of consumer goods, affluence and increased industrial concentration. More important, the declining price elasticity of demand meant that employers had an increasingly smaller stake in the outcome of wage bargaining; wage increases could be passed along with increased impunity. The historical trend in labour market interrelatedness reinforced this tendency, as will be seen shortly. This decrease in employer interest in bargaining outcomes, together with the other influences just noted, accentuated an important asymmetry, the downward stickiness of money wages and the upward flexibility of money wages and ultimately prices. Together, these influences gave rise to what will be considered in this study as structural changes leading to an inflationary bias in the weak sense, an upward bias in the levels of wages and prices.

The second result of developments in the labour markets was that the principle of fairness came to dominate wage bargaining. As labour became more nearly an equal of employers in the bargaining process, the arbitrary use of power, which characterized employers bargaining in an earlier era, declined. Demands, offers and settlements had to seem fair and reasonable, i.e. related to changes in the cost of living and wage settlements elsewhere. In short, labour markets showed increasingly the characteristics of the fix-price labour markets (of the previous section). Lewis dates the beginning of this development as 1939. Before that Adam Smith's remarks were thought to hold true:

---

[4] Scitovsky, op. cit.

The wages of labour do not in Great Britain fluctuate with the price of provisions. These vary everywhere from year to year, frequently from month to month. But in many places the money price of labour remains uniformly the same sometimes for half a century together.[5]

As already seen, fairness considerations altered the nature of price and wage adjustments. As indicated on pp. 121–130 below, fairness considerations introduce a number of important asymmetries and profoundly alter the nature of inflation which, in turn, greatly magnifies the impact of these asymmetries. The importance of the changes in the cost of living on wage settlements is the second important structural change contributing to an inflationary bias. It leads to what will be called an inflationary bias in the strong sense, an upward bias in the rates of wage and price inflation.

The final result was that the acceptance of the principal of fairness in bargaining allowed workers to extend their horizons beyond their own industry and craft resulting in comparisons with an ever-widening number of labour groups. Labour markets become increasingly more integrated to use the terminology of chapter 4.

The greater integration of wage settlements strengthened the inflationary bias, certainly in the weak sense. Thus, when workers' horizons were limited, say, to the firm or even the industry within which they work, the employer's argument that 'exorbitant' wage increases would price their products out of market had a great deal of force.[6] In such a situation, workers would not assume that any contemplated wage increase would be part of a general economy-wide wage increase. Such narrow perspectives characterized the period before the Second World War and reinforced a compliance of labour with a take it or leave it wage offer by employers. During the period following the Second World War, the period in which Scitovsky saw the development of staying power and widened worker horizons, and Lewis in his study cited the influence of the cost of living on wage settlements, labour developed a consensus that wage increases sought within their own group constituted part of a general movement of wages. The result was the individual bargaining groups were less constrained in their wage demands and there developed a more extensive interrelatedness of wage settlements throughout the

---

[5] Lewis' finding is found in Lewis, op. cit., p. 430. The quotation is from A. Smith, *The Wealth of Nations, Book I,* chapter 8, p. 76 of Cannan's edition, quoted by Lewis, ibid., p. 427.

[6] See E. Phelps Brown (1971) The analysis of wage movements under full employment, *Scottish Journal of Political Economy,* November.

economy, this at a time when reduced price elasticities of demand would ensure employers' complicity.

Just as in the case of cost of living considerations, largely enforced by the presence of unions, the interrelatedness of wage settlements introduced another factor making wage settlements more independent of the state of demand. Such feelings were encouraged by a wider dissemination of information through mass communication systems and a rising tide of egalitarianism. But the underlying force behind these developments was the growing power of labour under full employment. To this could be added a complementary factor, the rising concern of employers with worker cooperation. Thus, Scitovsky attributed the growing price inelasticity of demand of consumer goods to the increased complexity of these goods. If increased complexity is interpreted (quite reasonably) as increased fabrication, a greater need for quality control and subsequent servicing, together with increased skill requirements for producing high-quality goods, then a growing desire for continuity in employer–employee relations follows quite simply. Fix-price labour markets with wages influenced by fairness considerations are a manifestation of this desire.

ASYMMETRIES IN A STATIC CONTEXT

1. *The money wage*

This rising power of labour in bargaining has important implications for understanding the nature of inflation today and efforts to control it. Because of this change, not only have cost factors come to influence wage settlements, but asymmetries permeate the entire pricing mechanism in modern times and lead to an upward bias in prices and wages. At the most basic level are the asymmetries arising from fairness consideration in labour market, enforceable at high or full employment levels because of labour's enhanced power. Thus, in chapter 5 it was allowed that some labour markets may be flex-price in response to changes in excess demand or supply but only in an upward direction. Money wages seldom fall unless the firm is on the verge of bankruptcy.[7] A wage floor is a basic fact of life ignored by economists but not by businessmen and workers.

---

[7] See R. Solow (1979) Alternative approaches to macroeconomic theory: A partial view, *Canadian Journal of Economics,* August. Solow speaks of the reputation of being a bad employer. Studies cited in footnote 2 suggest that this concern goes back to the nineteenth century.

More relevant to the modern period, wage settlements are increasingly influenced by settlements in other markets as just pointed out. As a result a wage increase in one sector is viewed as a reason for at least a comparable wage adjustment elsewhere. But a wage decline in some sector, should it ever occur, is not likely to set in motion a series of equal downward adjustments by other labour groups. Unlike an upward disturbance in the wage structure, workers who might contemplate a cut in wages in response to an initiating cut elsewhere have nothing to gain and very likely something to lose by doing so. The same kind of reasoning applies to rates of change of wages, moreover. A rise in the rate of increase in wages in some sector is more likely to generate increases in rates of increase elsewhere than a comparable decline will induce other reductions. All of this is but to rephrase the explanation Keynes gave 50 years ago of rigid money wages downward. Rates of growth of money wages may also be rigid downward.

2. The real wage

Wage settlements are also strongly influenced today by the cost of living as workers have a strong interest in maintaining and increasing their real wages. Of interest here is whether a rise in the real wage, either absolutely or relative to trend, tends to dampen money wage demands to the same extent that an actual or potential fall in the real wage accelerates money wage demands. For example, if some trend behaviour of real wages has become standard, then employers have a case in arguing for reduced money wage demands by workers, following an abnormal rise in real wages. However, as before, workers have much to gain and nothing to lose by increasing money wage demands when real wages or their trend rate of growth decline, and little to gain by reducing such demands when real wages move unexpectedly upward. As a result, another asymmetry is introduced. Considering both aspects of fairness, as well as those cases where changes in excess demand does have an influence on wages, a case can be made for marked asymmetries in the response of wages to changes in their determinants. The effect, naturally, is an upward bias in wages and, therefore, prices.

3. Average costs

As prices are cost determined in fix-price markets, an asymmetrical behaviour of prices in fix-price markets results if there exists a differential response of prices to increases and decreases in average costs. Here the evidence is mixed.[8] However, a bias is still present because of the asymmetrical behaviour of money wages. Since the latter show a greater tendency to move upward than downward in response to their determinants, to that extent will average costs and prices be biased upwards.

Taken together, the overall impact of these asymmetries is a pronounced inflationary bias in the weak sense. Wages and prices in the modern era can be expected to drift upward even when certain dynamic considerations are not taken into account.[9] When they are, the force of this bias is greatly increased, a matter to be discussed in the next section.

ASYMMETRIES AND THE INFLATIONARY PROCESS

1. *From statics to dynamics*

Naturally with asymmetrical wage and price behaviour so firmly established in labour and product markets, an inflationary bias results. But the full intensity of this bias cannot be modelled within a comparative static framework, since it reveals itself as a dynamic process under high employment conditions. In particular, the ways in which the asymmetries and the inflationary bias accelerate the *rate* of inflation would be obscured.

Recall the discussion on pp. 117–21 above in which the Second World War was seen as ushering in an era of profound structural change in labour markets. Changes in the cost of living became an important influence on wage settlements. This formalization of fairness considerations on wage settlements was very much related to the rising importance of trade unions and full employment policies.

---

[8] P. Sylos-Labini (1979) Prices and income distribution in manufacturing industry, *Journal of Post Keynesian Economics*, Fall. For a contrary view see F. Ripley and L. Segal (1973) Price determination in 395 manufacturing industries, *Review of Economics and Statistics*, August; and J. Tobin (1972) The wage–price mechanism: Overview of the conference in *The Econometrics of Price Determination: Conference* (Ed. O. Eckstein), Board of Governors of the Federal Reserve System and Social Science Research Council, p. 7.

[9] In a study of the American economy it was discovered that by comparing cycles over nearly 100 years, a pronounced inflationary bias was apparent. This took the form of prices falling during recessions in earlier times but actually rising in recent downturns. See P. Cagan (1974) *The Hydra-Headed Monster*, American Enterprise Institute.

Hitherto, wages trended upward as unionization, even in its early stages, reinforced a downward money wage rigidity. As a result, a disturbance led to an upward drift in money wages which would, in turn, lead to an increase in the price level when not offset sufficiently by productivity growth.

But in this earlier era, a comparative static form of modelling could still be used to explain inflation, supplemented by the kind of simple dynamic theorizing suggested by the quantity theory of money. Continuous inflation could be modelled in terms of continuous increases in aggregate demand, as the inflation process was merely a sequence of comparative static changes. In the more recent period, disturbances set in motion different dynamic processes which are generated and shaped by powerful bargaining units. As discussed throughout chapter 2, a lagged price inflation influence on the rate of wage inflation introduces a feedback effect from price to wage inflation which generates a cost–push or, more particularly, a wage–price inflationary mechanism. As a result it is necessary to distinguish between a short- and long-run Phillips curve. It is also necessary to recognize that; (1) disturbances may activate dynamic cost–push mechanisms that take time to work themselves out; and (2) changes in the unemployment rate can generate permanent changes in the rate of inflation.[10]

However, because of the static asymmetries, anything that leads to an increase in aggregate demand, a decline in real wages or a wage increase that disturbs the wage structure is much more likely to activate the wage–price and wage–wage mechanisms upwards than disturbances leading to a decrease in aggregate demand, a rise in real wages or a relative wage decline in some sector will set off cumulative movements downward. In this sense the economy is clearly unstable upwards and subject to an inflationary bias in the strong sense.

2. *Asymmetries over the cycle*

The existence of asymmetries has further dynamic implications for wage (and price) inflation, this time over the cycle. Consider a cycle with a boom and recession of more or less the same amplitude and duration, with unemployment rates falling during the boom by as much as they rise during the recession. Then during the course of the

[10] See chapter 2, pp. 41–4.

boom, the rate of wage and price inflation can be expected to accelerate as labour bargains more aggressively and disturbances of the wage structure became more frequent. However during the subsequent recession, while it is true that labour's bargaining position is weakened, the desire by labour in general to maintain real wages and the desire by each individual group to at least maintain its rankings in the wage structure will lead to a smaller decline in inflation than the earlier rise.

The impact of this can be phrased several ways; (1) it takes longer through restrictive aggregate demand policies to reduce the rates of inflation than it does to increase inflation rates by the same amount through expansionary policies; (2) from one cycle to the next, inflation rates accelerate unless policy-induced periods of high unemployment are increasingly substituted for those of low unemployment; and (3) high and accelerating rates of inflation are easier to get into a system than they are to get out. However it is phrased, the transformation of static asymmetries into dynamic ones through the cost–push mechanisms is very destabilizing. In a second sense inflation rates are unstable upwards and modern economies are subject to an inflationary bias in the strong sense.

The asymmetrical response of inflation rates over the cycle is shown in figure 6.1 where the rate of wage inflation $\dot{w}$ is measured on

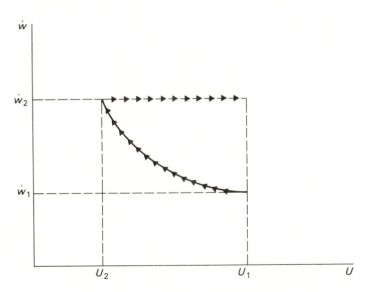

FIGURE 6.1   *The inflation ratchet*

the vertical axis and the unemployment rate, U, on the horizontal.[11] The direction of the arrows is meant to convey the movements of aggregate demand and unemployment over time. Starting from a rate of unemployment, U_1, aggregate demand increases until unemployment rates have been reduced to U_2 and the rate of wage inflation increased from $\dot{w}_1$ to $\dot{w}_2$. A similar time path would be traced out for price inflation given the pass-through effects from wages to prices and the feedback effects from prices to wages. As drawn, the unemployment rate of U_2 is the minimum rate of unemployment achieved during the boom. Having reached that low point the arrows then follow the path of unemployment during the ensuing recession. The asymmetric response of inflation rates to the direction of changes in aggregate demand is indicated by the failure of inflation rates to decline as unemployment rates rise again to U_1.

3. *Inflation during the boom*

The acceleration of inflation rates during the boom can be explained in terms of some of the earlier findings. Starting from an unemployment rate of U_1, declines in unemployment and increases in output will lead to price rises in flex-price labour and raw materials markets. Thus, even in the early stages of the boom some wages and prices can be expected to rise. This will lead to rising prices in fix-price product markets that utilized either or both of the inputs traded in flex-price markets.

Before the Second World War this pass-through effect from raw material and labour costs to prices would mark the end of the inflationary process since a feedback effect from the cost of living to wages was much less apparent. Product prices in a largely fix-price world would be pushed up only to the extent that cost increases induced by excess demand conditions in flex-price markets were at work. The inflationary mechanism could be quite adequately explained within a comparative static framework. Alternatively, a growing money supply could be called upon to produce a continuous source of disturbance constantly opening up some kind of inflationary gap.

However, once the feedback effects are recognized, wage–price and wage–wage mechanisms are activated in which the inflationary

---

[11] The axes are not scaled because, while the pattern of wage inflation and unemployment have been quite similar across countries, average rates of inflation and unemployment over the cycle have varied considerably between countries.

process becomes 'stretched out' and takes on a life of its own. As price inflation picks up, and unemployment rates fall, labour reacts by stepping up wage demands for at least three reasons. First, fairness dictates that real wages be protected. While the existence of widespread involuntary unemployment may attenuate demands initially, further decreases in unemployment will soon be an influence of some consequence. Thus, a second reason for accelerated wage demands is the greater aggressiveness of unions and the greater compliance of employers to their demands whatever the behaviour of real wages, a point emphasized in the early developments of cost–push inflation theory. Third, with labour becoming more aggressive in the aggregate, a larger number of individual bargaining units will be jockeying for a better position in the wage structure, the number depending upon the extent to which the union movement is fragmented. This means that disturbances of the wage structure (in addition to that coming from the flex-price labour markets) will increase as unemployment rates fall thereby activating the wage–wage inflationary mechanism. This inevitably intensifies the wage–price process. The entire process is represented by the arrows moving from right to left in figure 6.1 along a line very much resembling an ordinary Phillips curve.

4. *Inflation during the recession – symmetry*

What happens in the slump depends upon what has happened to wages and prices in the previous boom especially towards its end. If in the closing periods of the boom price and wage inflation had been proceeding at similar rates with the two differing approximately by the rate of growth of productivity, then the early stages of the down swing could be characterized by an immediate decline in the rates of wage and price inflation. Other things being equal, a rise in unemployment rates leads to less aggressive union behaviour, excess supplies in flex-price labour and product markets and fewer (upward) disturbances of the wage structure. With most product pricing on a mark-up basis this should soon feed through to prices thereby reducing the rate of price inflation, and alleviating somewhat the concern labour might have about reduced wage settlements.

The inflationary process just outlined makes several very critical assumptions. Of these, the assumption about the behaviour of wage inflation in the early stages of the down swing can be singled out. The assumed response of wage inflation to rising unemployment allows a slow down in the rate of price inflation which feeds back to wage inflation etc., allowing a convergence of wages and prices to a lower rate of inflation. It is possible in a case like this that the behaviour of inflation during the recession could reverse the time path of inflation of the boom. In figure 6.1 this means going up and coming back down the same curved line, i.e. symmetrical inflation behaviour over the phases of the cycle.

5. *Relative wages and a dynamic asymmetry*

However, if for whatever reason the rate of wage inflation does not adjust downward to rising unemployment rates in the period immediately following the peak in real activity, an entirely different time path for wage and price inflation during the recession is likely. Other things being equal it is certainly true that wage inflation and unemployment are negatively related for reasons already noted. The other things subsume a number of items including labour's attitudes with respect to the wage structure and real wage prevailing when the economy turns down.

Chapter 4 discussed the cyclical behaviour of the wage structure whereby the relative dispersion of the wage structure narrows during the boom as low-wage workers experience a rise in money wages both absolutely and relatively. Now in some countries high-wage workers have shown an ability to restore their relative position in the wage structure during the slump.[12] Assume that this happens and let rates of wage inflation in the low-wage sectors be maintained at their boom rates in the slump or abate only moderately. Meanwhile, high-wage workers in their effort to restore wage relatives, will be demanding a higher rate of growth of their money wages, at any given rate of unemployment, in the slump that they did in the boom. Since the rate of overall wage inflation at any rate of unemployment will be a weighted average of the rates of wage inflation in the low-wage and high-wage sectors, the overall rate of growth of wages will be higher in the slump than the boom. The result is an asymmetrical response to changes in aggregate demand giving rise to the kind of cyclical movements of prices and wages depicted by following the arrows in figure 6.1 back to the slump rate of unemployment, U_1.[13]

---

[12] See M. Wachter, Cyclical variations . . . op. cit.
[13] Appendix A illustrates this and the following asymmetry in more detail.

6. *Real wages and a dynamic asymmetry*

Such relative wage influences on wage bargaining are more likely in economies with fragmented labour movements, in which centralized bargaining is unheard of, and where long-term wage contracts are common. Even so, there are other forces at work in all economies leading to similar results. Thus, consider the case where the rate of growth of money wages has not kept enough ahead of the rate of growth of prices shortly before and after the peak in the boom to maintain the accustomed growth in real wages or, worse, has not kept even. This could arise for several reasons; a sudden spurt in food and energy prices, a reduction in productivity growth, adverse movements of the terms of trade or simply a lag in the adjustment of money wages to current inflation due, say, to labour being tied into long-term contracts. Consider, now, an implication of the asymmetrical response of money wage demands to changes in the real wage, i.e. 'real wage resistance'.[14]

Following the peak in economic activity unemployment rates again rise. However, unlike the symmetry case just discussed, the example here allows for the fact that the growth of real wages has been reduced for any one or more of the reasons just mentioned and this is assumed to influence labour's money wage demands rather strongly. If caused by a spurt in food and energy prices, this naturally tends to increase the rate of price inflation experienced at the peak of the boom compared to the earlier example. This likely means a reduction in real wages which, in turn, feeds back on money wage demands, reducing and possibly eliminating any tendency for wage inflation to abate because of rising unemployment rates.[15]

A rapid increase in the rate of growth of productivity soon after the peak in activity could offset this unfortunate chain of events. Unfortunately, the rate of growth of productivity has a strong pro-cyclical component and actually declines during recessions. A decline in productivity acts to reduce the real wages, as does an adverse

---

[14] See J. Hicks (1975) What is wrong with monetarism, *Lloyds Bank Review*, October. Also, see M. Artes and M. Miller (1979) Inflation, real wages and the terms of trade, *Inflation, Development and Integration: Essays in Honour of A. J. Brown* (Ed. J. Bowers), Leeds. The notion of a real-wage resistance was formalized and its importance was estimated econometrically in the following type of model. Write: $\dot{w}_t = f[U_t, (w/p)_{t-1}]$ where $(w/p)_{t-1}$ is the real wage lagged one period and U_t the current rate of unemployment. The expected sign of both independent variables is negative.

[15] An appreciation of the exchange rate would work to offset this chain of events.

movement of the terms of trade. If workers again resist real wage reductions by stepping up their money wage demands, all cases lead to accelerated wage demands as the slump develops, thereby preventing a downward adjustment in rates of price inflation. Furthermore, if because of a fear of inflation the authorities persist in a contractionary policy into the slump, the negative impact of depressed demand on productivity growth and, therefore, real wages does not bode well for bringing inflation under control through depressed aggregate demand policies. There arises the distinct possibility of wage and price inflation continuing during the recession at rates similar to those experienced at the peak in the boom. This could be true even in the absence of the relative wage effect discussed above. The presence of the latter merely strengthens the case for asymmetry.

ADDITIONAL ADAPTATIONS

Neither the real wage or relative wage effect would be operative without affluent unions. Whether or not this asymmetry and the resulting inflationary bias can be eliminated by prolonged and increasing rates of unemployment today is one of the questions raised at the beginning of the chapter. This will be considered below. The issue is largely whether the kinds of fairness considerations, associated with the rise of unions and full employment, are attenuated before an unemployment constraint becomes binding.

Real wage resistance raises the issue of adaptations to the ongoing inflation and their impact on inflation. Such adaptations are formally equivalent to a variable coefficient model in which the coefficient(s) of the lagged price variable(s) in the wage equation increases whenever real wages fail or are expected to fail to grow at some accustomed rate. In general, the more pronounced and extended is the acceleration of inflation in the boom, the more forceful and pronounced will be the efforts by labour groups to maintain their relative wage position and protect their real wages.

Other institutional adaptations can be expected, their intensity also related to the seriousness of inflation. The earlier discussion of implicit contracts emphasized the desire on the part of transactors to maintain continuity in the exchange relationship. Furthermore, since every conceivable contingency can hardly be spelled out, contracts are incomplete. General rules of fair play emerge when certain terms of the contract cannot be fulfilled, and usually entail quantity adjustments rather than price.

However, markets in which implicit contracting is important are markets that function best in a non-inflationary milieu. When inflation exceeds some threshold, transactors tend to 'change the rules'. Labour groups seek means by which to hedge against inflation, e.g. cost-of-living clauses and shorter contracts. Firms attempt to widen their mark-ups and pass through cost increases more rapidly. In determining mark-ups, firms increasingly focus on replacement rather than original costs of capital, and future deliveries of goods do not carry a definite price.[16] All of these factors increase the rate of inflation associated with any rate of unemployment. They also increase the likelihood of an asymmetric response of the economy to changes in aggregate demand, as the adaptations to inflation during the boom will carry over to the recession. This is but to say that once inflation gets into an economy, it is difficult to get it out. The extent to which inflation itself will generate adaptations to inflation, which have the effect of making it even more persistent, depends very much on the extent of its acceleration.

This concept of adaptations can be pursued further. The discussion up to this point has centred on the description of mechanisms that give rise to an inflationary 'ratchet' effect in which increases in aggregate demand have a larger impact on the rate of price and wage inflation than decreases in aggregate demand. It is the view taken here that this asymmetry or ratchet does much to explain the acceleration in inflation rates in the 1970s compared with the half of the postwar period before the late 1960s.

But consider the discussion of the 'two-track' models of inflation in chapter 2 which indicated how unstable upwards the inflationary process has become. Disturbances or a reduction of the unemployment rates during the boom that push the inflation rate above some threshold create adaptations to inflation that make the inflation process decidedly explosive. They also make it difficult to eliminate inflation through restrictive demand policies.

Assume that the threshold rate of inflation (which will vary between countries) has been exceeded during the boom because of a number of coincidental shocks interacting with the cost–push mechanisms or simply because unemployment rates have fallen. This threshold effect will greatly accelerate the rate of inflation, leading to exceptionally high rates as a more explosive cost–push process will be at work. Sooner or later the authorities will intervene. But unless the rate of price inflation can be brought down below this threshold

---

[16] See A. Okun (1973), Upward mobility in a high pressure economy, *Brookings Papers on Economic Activity*, No. 1.

by policy measures, the accelerated wage demands and settlements will likely continue despite rising unemployment, thereby sustaining price inflation. As before, the asymmetries work to maintain these high wage demands. Higher unemployment rates work to reduce the rate of wage inflation but the task has now been increased by the workings of the inflation severity factor which, by accelerating inflation rates in the boom, generates increased wage resistance during the slump.

If at the same time productivity growth declines sharply and the terms of trade turn against a country, the growth of real wages may decline dramatically. This will confirm workers' worse fears and intensify wage resistance through accelerated wage demands.

This is but to say that the inflationary mechanism is stable downwards. And this holds true whether the present interpretation of inflation is accepted or some other. For example, monetarists are given to 'explain' the persistence of inflation in spite of high unemployment in terms of slowly adapting inflationary expectations. This brings the analysis back to the two questions raised at the outset.

ARE THESE HARDSHIPS SUFFICIENT?

1. *The first question*

Obviously, rising unemployment rates will have an impact on inflation rates if increased far enough. However, the first basic question asked in the introductory section was whether restrictive aggregate demand policies could reduce inflation rates if subject to an unemployment constraint. This constraint has at least two dimensions, one of duration and the other of magnitude. High rates of unemployment might be tolerable for short, but not long, periods of time, e.g. some part but not all of a 5-year parliamentary election period, while lower rates of unemployment might be acceptable for extended periods of time. Naturally, this constraint will vary across countries and over time, reflecting differences between countries in their demand for and supply of employment as a counterpart to their demands for and supply of inflation. Countries with strong trade union movements are more limited in how far they can push their restrictive demand policies than, say, the two North American economies.

Proponents of the credibility hypothesis (CH) emphasize the importance of labour (and management) believing that they will suffer now and in the future if they do not restrain their wage and price demands.[17] If this belief is widespread, they argue, restrictive policies will bring down inflation quickly. With this in mind, it is necessary to ask what kinds of labour market conditions would have to be created to bring about the required reduction of wage and price inflation rates, if the authorities rely entirely on restrictive policies to accomplish their goals.[18] An answer to this question helps to answer the second basic question; what happens when stimulative policies are again implemented?

Consider what must be done to offset the forces acting to sustain the rate of wage inflation into the recession. Given a desire on the part of workers to maintain past trends in real wages and their position in the wage structure, the policy goal must be to so increase workers' fear of possible unemployment that wage demands are no longer formulated in terms of realizing these targets. In other words, the aim of policy must be to create a situation in which labour no longer demands that wage settlements be framed in terms of fairness. This means the creation of conditions in labour markets similar to those before unions, when employers could adopt a take it or leave it attitude in their wage offers.[19]

Naturally, if there are no limits to how high unemployment rates can be pushed, it is reasonable to assume that sooner or later labour will be willing to settle for whatever employers have to offer. After all, even money wage levels fell in many countries from 1929–33.[20] Restrictive policies have a real ring of credibility with these kinds of policy options available and a rapid reduction in inflation might be possible. But in a number of economies, especially those with strong trade unions, political (and ethical) considerations will not allow the authorities to increase unemployment without limit, thereby creating nineteenth-century labour markets. In these situations the CH may be of little relevance.

The experience of the recent past is only of partial help in testing the CH. It is clear now that unemployment rates can rise to levels

---

[17] See chapter 3, pp. 69–72.

[18] It is important to emphasize at this point that the sole policy instrument being considered is restrictive demand. Later chapters will consider the use of incomes policies as well.

[19] To change the terminology, it is a matter of putting in place Kalecki's political business cycle, a condition under which greater job security is exchanged for reduced wage demands. See M. Kalecki (1977) Political Aspects of Full Employment, in *Selected Essays on the Dynamics of the Capitalist Economy 1933–1970,* Cambridge.

[20] See E. Phelps Brown (1968) *A Century of Pay,* Macmillan, London, figure 33.

previously thought to be politically intolerable without the drastic repercussions once predicted. It is also true that inflation rates had begun to decline rather sharply by 1982 as detailed in Table 1.5 in chapter 1. However, this last finding is not as informative as might be thought. A large number of countries pursuing restrictive policies over the past decade are countries in which both employer and employee organizations have traditionally conducted collective bargaining negotiations in a way that was consistent with macroeconomic goals such as wage and price stability. In other words voluntary incomes policies have been pursued at the same time as restrictive policies. For reasons which will be made clear in chapters 11 and 12, only in the English-speaking economies might it be said that there has been any sort of test of the efficacy of restrictive policies. Here the recent experience indicates restrictive policies do reduce inflation rates noticeably before an unemployment constraint becomes binding, but only after prolonged periods of high unemployment.[21] While restraint eventually 'works', it is not clear that the recent experience supports what the advocates of CH had in mind. On the other hand, believers in the CH can and have argued that restrictive policies were never made credible.

2. *The second question*

However, the question of whether or not recent events provide any kind of test of this part of the CH can be finessed. Even if current policies could substantially reduce inflation rapidly without creating political and economic instability, there is the second question posed earlier that must be resolved. The issue now becomes what happens when governments feel that the inflation problem is under control (or that a balance of payment constraint is no longer an impediment to expansionary policies, or both), and policies are implemented to reduce unemployment. To frame the question in its bluntest, will labour (and management) have learned its lesson or will wages (and prices) begin to rise as they did in 1934 following the 'lesson' of 1929–33? It is not enough for proponents of the CH to maintain that correctly formulated and implemented restrictive policies will lead to a sharp decrease in wage demands. To be of relevance this doctrine must maintain that such policies will lead to wage restraint once the economies have been restimulated.

---

[21] In terms of figure 6.1, as unemployment rates increase beyond U_1, wage inflation declines from $\dot{w}_2$.

There are two possibilities worth considering. In economies with a strong trade union movement, and possibly pro-labour parties in power, the previous restrictive policies may have been undertaken only after consultation with the trade unions. Consultation prior to restimulating the economy would then also be likely, with an aim to obtaining cooperation in keeping down wages if unemployment rates are allowed to fall. This possibility very much resembles the kind of voluntary incomes policies tried with varying success in several continental European countries in the past and will be discussed further in chapter 11.

Here a reasonable case can be made for labour restraint as unemployment falls, i.e. when the previous restrictive policies were not viewed by labour as a means of reducing their power. But it is essential to note that if policy succeeds, its success does not depend solely or even mainly upon labour learning its lesson through the threat and the experience of prolonged unemployment spells. As argued in chapter 11, post-war experience indicates that success would be due to cooperation and the government's ability to convince labour (and other groups) that cooperation and sharing the costs of restraint is in everybody's long-run best interests. A voluntary incomes policy is not the same thing as a 'market solution' to the inflation problem, a distinction that will loom large in later chapters.

The second possibility leads to a different conclusion. This is the case in which restrictive policies were seen to be undertaken for the purpose of reducing union power and to have costs that are unequally distributed. In this case restrictive policies will certainly teach labour a lesson but it will not likely be the lesson that the credibility policy advocates had in mind. The lesson labour will have learned is that they have been deliberately made the victims of the earlier restrictive policies, suffering hardships not borne equally by other groups in the society. As unemployment rates begin to fall, efforts will be made to restore real and relative wages to their 'rightful' place, as rapidly as possible. This will be done in the only way possible, through accelerated wage demands. After all, no individual labour group can be sure that other groups will not be doing the same. As a result inflation rates will begin to accelerate while unemployment rates are still quite high. If this leads governments to once again return to restrictive policies, the result is a fulfilment of Kalecki's vision of the political business cycle, one that leads to continued stagnation if not stagflation.[22]

---

[22] See footnote 19.

3. *Wage restraint and legitimacy*

What has just been said has certain similarities to arguments that posit an inflationary bias today because economic groups, especially labour, have increasingly called into question the distributional fairness of modern capitalist systems. Following Hirsch, two kinds of economic power are recognized; 'acquisitive power' measured by the economic rewards attained through the market and (potentially) 'disruptive power' resulting from collective organization and extended through political and quasi-political means, e.g. parliament and collective bargaining.[23] The main source of disruptive power is found in the trade unions. When market-determined outcomes are called into question, disruptive power is exerted through the normal political channels and collective bargaining. The relative importance of the two channels depends upon the receptivity of government to demands for equity by labour and other, usually, low income groups. If the government is unreceptive, then labour will seek redress through collective bargaining. Other things being equal this leads to less restraint in wage demands.

   This general mood of dissatisfaction and its alleged acceleration in the post-war period has several explanations. On the one hand, writers of a conservative persuasion see the questioning of the market system as a manifestation of rising aspirations or, less kindly, of unconstrained hedonism of the general population. Furthermore, efforts to accommodate inflation are not seen as a lesser of two evils, the greater evil being more unemployment, but often as part of a short-sighted effort by politicians to court public favour and remain in office. This idea was formalized in the 1970s in another model of the political business cycle which saw governments prepared to maintain high levels of employment at almost any cost, the direct opposite of the Kalecki political business cycle.[24] The conservative view sees accommodation of inflation not as a means of legitimizing government but as an irresponsible, irrational form of behaviour leading to another source of inflationary bias.

   On the other hand, there are writers who attribute this dissatisfaction and questioning to an increasing commercialization and secularization of life, in which distributional results that would have

---

[23] See F. Hirsch (1976) *The Social Limits to Growth*. Harvard University Press, Cambridge, Mass., chapter 77.

[24] An early example of this version of the political business cycle is W. Nordhaus (1975) The political business cycle, *Review of Economic Studies*.

been accepted in an earlier era are no longer thought justified or tolerable.[25] Purely market determined outcomes are considered to be unfair, resulting from accident or unequal opportunities. Furthermore, industry in an age of affluence inadvertently encourages this challenge to the market system by encouraging unconstrained and conspicuous consumption. These writers also see this development as a source of inflationary bias. But rather than describe government action as irresponsible and even criminal, this view associates such actions as necessary to maintain the legitimacy of government.

While no 'hard evidence' is available to support the view that capitalism is losing its 'legitimacy' (a view largely adopted here), its relevance for the question of wage constraint following restimulation is obvious. Thus, if a case can be made for increased dissatisfaction with market outcomes during an age of rapid rise in real wages, then an overwhelming argument can be made for a rapid increase in wage demands following a period of felt unfairness.

CONCLUSIONS

When it is recognized that important structural and institutional changes are constantly taking place that affect economic outcomes in a significant way with no eternal truths to guide the investigator, many 'inductive leaps' are required. Throughout this chapter it has been maintained that such changes have taken place during the post-war period and they resulted primarily from the rising power of trade unions and industrial oligopolies, together with a commitment until the early 1970s to full employment. Underlying this have been egalitarian trends leading to a questioning of market-determined distributional outcomes.

The rising power of unions and large-scale firms was responsible for the development of the two kinds of cost–push inflationary mechanisms first discussed in chapters 2 and 4. These influences made inflationary developments both widespread and pervasive. Together they cause inflation rates to be unstable upwards.

---

[25] See J. Goldthorpe (1974) Social inequality and social integration in modern Britain, in *Poverty, Inequality and Class Structure* (Ed. D. Wedderburn), Cambridge University Press, Cambridge, and (1978) The current inflation: Towards a sociological account, in *The Political Economy of Inflation* (Eds F. Hirsch and J. Goldthorpe), Harvard University Press, Cambridge, Mass. and F. Hirsch, op. cit.

But equally ominous is the finding that in the modern age, inflation may be stable downward. Governments may be able to drive up
unemployment rates high enough to have an impact on rates of
inflation, but any subsequent restimulation of the economy will lead
to an acceleration of inflation long before involuntary unemployment has been eliminated. If governments feel required to
periodically restimulate the economy, inflation rates will tend to
ratchet upwards. In this case, the hardship of high unemployment is
not sufficient to cure inflation and allow an eventual return to full
employment. Much of the second half of this study is given to
arguing that the present hardships may not even be necessary in
order to realize price stability and eventually full employment.

APPENDIX A: A TWO-SECTOR MODEL OF INFLATION

1. *Fairness and the wage structure*

An understanding of the influences of the wage structure, real-wage
resistance and, ultimately, considerations of fairness on inflation as
described in the chapter is facilitated by figure 6.2. For the sake of
simplicity, suppose that there are only two labour groups, one high
wage and the other low wage. Although not essential, it is useful to

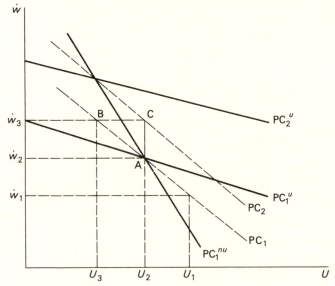

FIGURE 6.2   *Asymmetries and the Phillips curve*

think of the former being made up on unionized, skilled workers while the latter includes those workers that are thought of as comprising the 'secondary labour market'.[26] Suppose that the rate of increase in money wages for the high wage groups depends strongly upon the rate of price inflation in the past, weakly on the degree of tightness of labour markets and upon the difference between wage levels of the two groups, i.e. a consideration comparable to the impact of the relative dispersion of the wage structure, but again with a lag. On the other hand, assume that the rate of growth of money wages in the low-wage sector depends only, and very strongly, upon the degree of tightness of the labour market.[27] Then, for some given past behaviour of price inflation and some given wage structure, (linear) Phillips curves PC_1^u, and PC_1^{nu}, are drawn in figure 6.2 to represent the initial 'trade-offs' for the high-wage and low-wage groups, respectively. For simplicity assume that unemployment rates are identical for each group and, therefore, equal to the aggregate unemployment rate. The resulting aggregate Phillips curve relation for the whole economy is drawn as a dashed line in figure 6.2 and labelled PC_1.

Starting from unemployment rate U_1 assume a boom sets in leading to a decline in unemployment rates. As unemployment rates decline from U_1 to U_2, the rate of wage inflation rises in both markets but more rapidly in the secondary labour market than in the high-wage market. Naturally the overall rate of wage inflation rises in this case from $\dot{w}_1$ to $\dot{w}_2$. At unemployment rates less than U_2 the rate of wage inflation in the secondary labour market exceeds that in the high-wage sector. From this point onward the relative difference in levels of money wages between the two sectors narrows and continues to do so as long as unemployment rates remains below U_2.

Suppose the unemployment rate U_3 to be the rate at the peak of the boom and let this boom be such that at the peak the relative difference in money wage rates between the two sectors is less than it was at the unemployment rate U_1 at the beginning of the boom. Finally, suppose that high-wage workers, for whatever reasons, do not succeed in adjusting their wages to the narrowing of relative wage differences that took place during the boom until the recession. Let this recession adjustment be reflected in the shift of their short-

---

[26] See Doeringer and Piore, op. cit.

[27] G. L. Perry, Slowing the Wage–Price Spiral: The macroeconomic view, *Brookings Papers on Economic Activity*, No. 2.

run Phillips curve to PC_2^u. With an unchanged Phillips curve for the low-wage sector, the new aggregate unemployment wage inflation trade-off is then given by dashed line PC_2. If at some point the recession leads to an unemployment rate of U_2 and no further shifts of the high-wage Phillips curve take place in the interim, then a recession unemployment rate of U_2 is associated with a rate of wage inflation of $\dot{w}_3$ compared with a rate of wage inflation of $\dot{w}_2$ midway through the previous boom. A similar outcome is evident for other recession unemployment rates compared to their boom counterparts, leading to the kind of asymmetry discussed in the chapter and the resulting inflationary bias.

2. Fairness and real wages

Figure 6.2 can also be used to illustrate a second, more general, fairness consideration, a reaction to a failure of real wages to rise sufficiently. Allow as before a fall in unemployment rates from U_1 to U_3 during the course of the boom. Again, let U_3 be the minimum rate of unemployment during the boom, at which point unemployment rates begin to increase towards U_2. Disallowing any relative wage effect, this loosening of labour markets in the recession can be expected to lead to less aggressive activity by labour and a reduction in the rate of wage inflation towards $\dot{w}_2$. However, suppose that just before the recession commences there is a rapid run up of the cost of living that does not generate higher compensating money wage increases at the time. Alternatively, let the rate of price inflation during the boom accelerate enough that workers become so concerned with protecting their real wages that they accelerate their money wage demands immediately following the boom. In other words, the 'inflation severity factor' of chapter 2 comes into play for the high wage group. Then, in either case an upward shift of the Phillips curve for high-wage workers from PC_1^u to PC_2^u can be expected during the recession as these workers attempt to protect their real wages. The expression 'real wage resistance' has been used to describe this reaction.[28] As before, when unemployment rates rise to U_2 the new aggregate Phillips curve, PC_2, reveals an overall rate of wage inflation of $\dot{w}_3$. This will feed through to price inflation maintaining the inflationary process.

---

[28] See J. Hicks, What's wrong . . . , op. cit.

3. Fairness and stagflation

Several points are worth noting. First, during the recession when unemployment rates are rising from U_3 to U_2, rates of wage and price inflation need not decline. This is the essence of stagflation. Second, there is an asymmetrical relation between increases and subsequent decreases in aggregate demand, especially when inflation rates are pushed to historical highs during the boom. Increases in aggregate demand will lead to an increase in rates of inflation but if (short-run) Phillips curves respond to changes in the wage structure or the cost of living strongly enough, decreases in aggregate demand may have little or no effect on the rate of overall inflation, at least until unemployment rates have been increased appreciably. If the shift of the Phillips curve of the unionized sector is sharply upward and to the right and if the relevant points on the new Phillips curve lead to such rapid rates of wage inflation that, when passed through to prices, they sustain the rate of price inflation that induced the shift, this becomes a real possibility. Naturally, if the Phillips curve for the non-unionized sector also shifts, this intensifies the inflationary pressures. Third, both examples of asymmetries show that unions make a difference. It is difficult to think of these results in a non-unionized world.

APPENDIX B: DO UNIONS CAUSE INFLATION?

1. Union militancy and inflation

The discussion in chapter 6 is relevant to the issue of whether 'unions cause inflation'. Fortunately, what has just been said on pp. 121–32 allows a somewhat different and more fruitful method of analysing this important issue than in earlier studies.

The views of economists on the impact of unions on inflation vary widely. One of the better-known asserts that unions are more like a thermostat than a furnace, doing little more than acting as intermediaries between the underlying market forces of demand and supply and price and wage behaviour.[29]

[29] See M. Freidman (1951) Some comments on the significance of labour unions for economic policy, in *The Impact of the Union* (Ed. D. Wright), Harcourt, Brace, New York, p. 222.

A common method adopted to determine the impact of unions has been to find a measure of union market power or militancy and to determine whether it correlates with the rate of wage inflation. The two most popular measures of union militancy have been some measure of union density, i.e. the proportion of the labour force organized or the rate of change of this proportion, and some measure of strike activity.[30] Matters have tended to become somewhat confused because a comparative static framework is usually used to test for union power and because the measures of union militancy are often ambiguous and rather limited. As a result, the empirical results are not conclusive and subject to differing interpretations.

Consider the matter of how union militancy is defined and measured first. Most of the studies limit themselves to one (often ambiguous) measure of militancy; e.g. number of strikes. In contrast, the evidence reveals that how much militancy unions exert in bargaining is a function of a wide number of forces, some non-economic and others economic in nature.[31] Union rivalries, political infighting in some union, rank and file attitudes and political strategies at the national level are non-economic forces constantly influencing the degree of militancy and exertion of union power. Examples of economic influences on militancy are reductions in real wages caused by a supply shock and disturbances of the wage structure for whatever reason. Disturbances of the wage structure generate efforts by individual unions to restore 'relativities'. Before the advent of unions, changes in the cost of living that reduced real wages and relative wage considerations had little influence on wages. Today they are important determinants of labour unrest, militancy and wage demands.

Consider next the impact of general economic conditions. In earlier chapters, it was argued that labour militancy also increases as unemployment rates fall, if for no other reason than the fact that employer resistance to higher wage demands lessens during prosperous times. Labour-management bargaining is a situation of bilateral monopoly. The behaviour of labour is very much conditioned by the probable behaviour of management, hence the positive association between militancy and employment.

---

[30] See C. Mulvey and J. Trevithick (1973) Trade unions and wage inflation, *Economic and Social Review*, January, for a useful summary.

[31] See L. Ulman (1980) Union behavior and incomes policy, unpublished paper, McGill University.

Whatever the measure of union militancy adopted, the various studies have other serious shortcomings. The usual test of the impact of unions is based on how closely changes in militancy are correlated with wage changes. But the comparative statistics of this kind of testing inevitably omits what is the most important influence of unions on inflation, one stressed throughout the study. An increase in wage settlements due to increased union militancy is passed through to prices which feeds back onto wages, etc. It is this wage–price (together with the wage–wage) mechanism that promulgates inflation and this development can be traced to the development of unions in recent times. These cost–push effects measure the impact of unions on inflation and not simply the effects resulting from some once-over change in union militancy however measured. To draw the latter conclusion is to think in a comparative static manner about what is an essentially dynamic process. It should be noted in passing that the popular notion that 'inflation is always and every-where a monetary phenomenon' affects these conclusions little if at all. This matter is discussed further in Appendix C.

All of these influences and more are at work putting pressure on wages that would be absent in the competitive world. Determining their exact impact is extremely complicated. What can be said unequivocably, however, is that it is difficult to think of a relative wage and cost of living influences affecting wage settlements in the absence of unions. Unions are not merely a conduit for the under-lying competitive market forces, but a powerful force in their own right.

2. The impact on the Phillips curve

The simplest way of summarizing the impact of unions is to contrast models describing the inflationary process in the absence and pre-sence of unions. The former situation involves an economy in which the wage–price and wage–wage mechanism is absent. The rate of growth of wages is influenced only by the unemployment rate; an assertion supported in chapters 6 and 7. This relationship can then be combined with the assumption of mark-up pricing leading to the equations:

$$\dot{w}_t = a_0 + a_1 U_t^{-1} \tag{1}$$

$$\dot{p}_t = \dot{w}_t - \dot{\rho} \tag{2}$$

where all variables have their previous meaning. This is shown

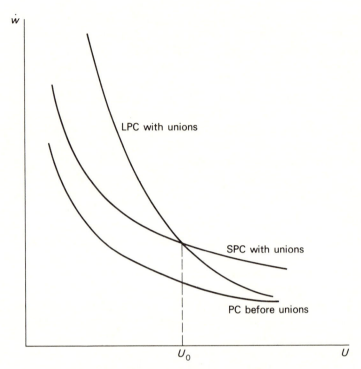

FIGURE 6.3   *The impact of unions on the Phillips curve*

graphically in figure 6.3 as the relatively flat Phillips curve for wage inflation, 'PC before unions', as would be expected when there is no feedback effect.

Next, let cost-of-living considerations influence wage settlements so that the equation for wage inflation is written as:

$$\dot{w}_t = c_0 + c_1 \dot{p}_{t-1} + c_2 U_t^{-1}   0 < c_1 < 1. \tag{3}$$

Equation (3) combined with equation (2) is the basis of the textbook, cost–push model of inflation first described in chapter 2, and leads to the distinction between the long-run and short-run Phillips curve shown earlier in figure 2.1. The short-run Phillips curve, equation (3), is shown as 'SPC with unions' in figure 6.3 and drawn parallel but above the Phillips curve before unions for convenience.

Finally, a long-run Phillips curve, 'LPC with unions', is drawn in figure 6.3 incorporating the feedback and pass-through effects that were described earlier in chapter 2. It is steeper than either of the other two curves for reasons already discussed in that chapter and this is the critical point. Thus, at any unemployment rate less than U_0, declines in unemployment lead to a greater increase in the rate of wage inflation with unions than without. Shifting the long-run and short-run curves for a unionized economy about would not affect the nature of the results since the conclusion depends only upon the long-run curve being steeper than the Phillips curve relevant before feedback effects were influential. In this sense alone unions cause inflation.

APPENDIX C: INFLATION IS ALWAYS
AND EVERYWHERE A MONETARY PHENOMENON

1. *The long run is for undergraduates*[32]

If trade unions are the prime movers behind cost–push inflation, central banks are the ultimate determinants of inflation in the monetarist, demand–pull world. As the monetarists are constantly reminding the profession, 'inflation is always and everywhere a monetary phenomenon'. The following points are helpful here.

Write the equation of exchange $MV = pQ$ where M, V, p and Q denote the money supply, the income velocity of money, the price level and output, respectively. Transforming the equation into growth rates gives; $\dot{M} + \dot{V} = \dot{p} + \dot{Q}$ where a dot over a variable indicates the rate of growth of the previously defined variable.

Now if the 'always and everywhere' dictum means anything at all it means that there is a strong, positive correlation between $\dot{M}$ and $\dot{p}$. Inflation cannot persist indefinitely, monetarists argue, unless validated by growth in the money supply. A great deal of ambiguity remains as to what time intervals are appropriate in devising a test to establish this correlation. For example, it is often acknowledged that velocity, in a statistical sense, can vary in some kind of short-run thereby disallowing any correlation. But supposedly given enough time for this kind of 'noise' to work itself out, the dictum asserts that not only is there a strong correlation between $\dot{M}$ and $\dot{p} + \dot{Q}$, i.e. the rate of growth of money output and incomes, but also between $\dot{M}$ and $\dot{p}$. The latter assertion is based ultimately on the inherent full employment tendencies of an economy so that the growth of the economy, $\dot{Q}$, will take place at its 'historical trend' rate determined by supply factors. Clearly there is a basic disagreement here between this monetarist view of the driving force behind infla-

---

[32] Attributed to Keynes by J. E. Meade.

tion and that discussed throughout chapter 6. Fortunately, what has been said on pp. 121–30 can help resolve this difference.

In particular, consider the interpretation of events summarized graphically in figure 6.1. The arrows were drawn to trace out a period of growing aggregate demand followed by a decline. For present purposes this can be thought of as being generated by an increase in the rate of growth of the money supply until unemployment is reduced to U_2 followed by a contraction of the growth rate of the money supply.

The asymmetrical response of wage and, ultimately, price inflation to changes in aggregate demand and the resulting inflationary bias means that decreases in the rate of growth of the money supply (and aggregate demand) will not be associated with a reduction in inflation, only reductions in employment rates and $\dot{Q}$. In this case, the rates of growth of the money supply and prices are not correlated just because inflation is generated by a cost–push mechanism. However, there will be a correlation if the central bank is not constrained in its restrictive policies, since sooner or later such policies should reduce inflation by creating a depression; i.e. should reduce both $\dot{p}$ and $\dot{Q}$.

On the other hand, if the authorities feel that unemployment rates have been pushed high enough and should be stabilized, e.g. $U = U_1$ in figure 6.1, then, assuming no change in the velocity of money, whatever rate of inflation prevails at U_1 will determine the validating rate of growth of the money supply as $\dot{Q} \simeq 0$. The rates of growth of the money supply and prices are now correlated but the causation runs from the rate of inflation to the rate of growth of the money supply.

The correlation between $\dot{M}$ and $\dot{p}$ will be strengthened by the typical pattern of rates of growth of prices and the money supply during a boom, both increase. Again, however, the direction of causation can go either way depending upon whether the banking system responds to credit demands and upon the reactions of the central bank.

Quite possibly taking the whole of the business cycle and comparing price and money supply movements averaged over this whole period with movements of the same variables averaged over some other cycle, a long-run correlation would emerge (even though velocity in reality is pro-cyclical). But this should be of little value to policy makers or anyone else for that matter.

Basically the notion that inflation is always and everywhere a monetary phenomenon arises from the monetarist's neglect of the unemployment problem and their concentration on the long-run. In some long-run, steady-state sense everything gets sorted out in the monetarist world. Velocity is constant or has a predictable trend and the economy grows at the full employment, unemployment rate. Unfortunately this concentration on the long-run has lead even non-monetarist economists to believe that reducing the rate of growth of the money supply will permanently cure inflation. With $\dot{V} = 0$ and $\dot{Q}$ fixed by assumption, a decline in $\dot{M}$ must be associated with a decline in $\dot{p}$ and one need never worry about the nature of real-world economies in drawing this conclusion. Once, however, it is recognized that a constant rate of growth of output and a constant velocity of money are only true to some reasonable degree of approximation in some long-run sense, e.g. from one cycle to the next, while subject to pronounced variability in the 'here and now', the monetarist dictum becomes at best a vacuous statement.

Something else of importance develops out of this. Governments of modern democracies are limited in how far unemployment can be allowed to rise and for how long a period. This limit will differ across countries depending upon such factors as the strength of the trade union movement and the independence of the central bank.[33] Nevertheless, in explaining the desire of the authorities to accommodate inflation rather than allow unemployment rates to rise further, it is not necessary to invoke myopic or irrational leadership. Such accommodation is likely to reflect a view that the harm caused by a further rise in unemployment rates is greater than that due to the on-going inflation. Unfortunately, monetarists are given to interpret this inclination of central bankers to eventually validate inflation as a kind of betrayal of principles. Officials responsible for running real economies are more prone to feel that high and persistent rates of unemployment are a distinct sign of a failure of the economy to work properly, if not an omen of impending political upheaval.

2. *Cost–push versus demand–pull inflation*

Even more important, when some consideration is given to the not-so-short-run effects on unemployment of attempts to reduce inflation through demand restraint, then the way is cleared for a more fruitful analysis of the underlying inflationary mechanisms. Thus:

---

[33] See D. Hibbs, Inflation political support and macroeconomic policy, *The Politics of Inflation and Recession*, The Brookings Institution, forthcoming.

Even if the control of the monetary supply is politically feasible, and technically so, the costs of its use far outweigh the benefits, and since the costs are borne particularly by a group which is largely not responsible for the problem, to a government which accepts some duty to protect the needs of the weak against the claims of the strong, it is not an exogenous variable in the relevant sense.

. . . The money supply is socially endogenous and a search for a cure for inflation must start from an analysis of its causes.[34]

The realization that politically unemployment rates do have some upper bound in most economies, and that cost–push forces do lead to asymmetrical responses and a bias leads straight to the conclusion that inflation may often have to be (and has often been) accommodated in the interests of political and economic stability. Thus, the monetarist dictum and correlation of rates of growth of money and prices from one cycle to the next in no way refutes the conclusion that inflation is to a very great extent the result of cost–push forces.

Note further that the distinction drawn by economists during the first half of the post-war period between cost–push and demand–pull inflation still remains a very useful one. To be sure the model of inflation outlined here contains elements of demand–pull inflation to supplement the basic cost–push mechanisms. And forward looking expectations, a favourite 'monetarist' explanation of persistent inflation, are easily grafted onto the model. But their effect is merely to strengthen the case for asymmetry based on lagged adjustments. The initiating cause and the forces leading to the persistence of inflation are cost–push. The wage–wage and wage–price mechanisms are essentially lagged adjustments to disequilibrium in the wage structure and the distribution of income and would be operative even in the absence of forward-looking expectations.[35] The fact that inflation persists as the economy moves from left to right along the horizontal portion of figure 6.1 with rising unemployment reflects this underlying cost–push process.

---

[34] J. Bowers, The theory of the cost of inflation, in *Inflation, Development and Integration . . . ,* op. cit., p. 41.

[35] See J. Tobin (1980) Stabilization policy ten years after, *Brookings Papers on Economic Activity,* No. 1, and (1980) *Assets Accumulation and Economic Activity: Reflections on Contemporary Macroeconomic Theory,* Yrjo Jahnsson Lectures, Basil Blackwell, Oxford; and W. Poole (1980) Comments, in *Brookings Papers on Economic Activity,* No. 1.

CHAPTER 7

Some of the 'Stylized Facts' of Inflation

INTRODUCTION

Inflation has been a recurring phenomenon throughout the history of capitalism. This does not mean, however, that the forces making for the very rapid rise in prices in the present period have been the same as influences at work during past epochs of inflation. The contrary view that inflation is 'everywhere and always a monetary phenomenon' is little more than a long-run truism and detracts from efforts to get at its root causes. In contrast, the emphasis in chapter 6 on the importance of the rise of trade unions and fairness in wage and price settlements, the cost–push mechanisms and the asymmetries and biases, was meant to suggest that the inflationary mechanism at work today is of a quite different nature from that of earlier times.

A stress on structural change can be pushed too far, however. For example, the rapid acceleration of inflation rates beginning in the second half of the 1960s could lead observers to conclude that a new mechanism was at work. The position presented in this chapter is that while it is true that different inflationary mechanisms have been at work at different times, the same mechanism generating the double-digit inflation of the last decade and a half has been operative throughout most of the post-war period. Important structural and institutional changes influencing the nature of inflation have been at work for over a century, and these have greatly altered the nature of the inflationary process today compared, say, to the period before the First World War. But the structural and institutional prerequisites for the kind of inflation outlined in chapter 6 were more or less in place by the beginning of the post-war period. Once the economies had gone through a conversion period from the war and full employment policies were implemented, the inflationary process described in chapter 6 began to operate. What did change during the post-war period was the extent to which the various forces underlying the modified cost–push mechanism spread through the market system and the increased intensity with which demanders and suppliers in markets, especially labour markets, reacted to changing circumstances.

In chapter 6, it was argued that with the development of trade unions and oligopolies, the increased affluence associated with a prolonged period of full employment gives rise to an inflationary mechanism that is potentially very unstable upwards. These developments were common to all the developed capitalist economies in the post-war period. They are seen in this chapter to be the main explanation of the acceleration of wage and price inflation rates in the 1950s and 1960s compared with earlier periods.

Furthermore, these same changes account for the explosion of wages and prices beginning in the late 1960s. Not only do similar institutional developments in the different economies explain the emergence of an inflationary bias in the strong sense, i.e. a tendency for inflation rates to drift upwards over time, they also illustrate how very unstable upward is this inflationary mechanism in a high-employment setting. The world-wide nature of the accelerated inflation in the post-war period can, therefore, be largely attributed to similar internal developments within each country. This pervasiveness would naturally be reinforced by the increased economic and political interdependence of the economies considered. The matter can be put otherwise. Rather than attributing the inflationary difficulties of the post-war period to spineless central bankers (especially American ones), the argument is made in this chapter that accelerated inflation throughout the capitalist world can be attributed to the workings of the cost–push mechanisms discussed in chapter 6.

Why the potentially destabilizing properties of the wage–price fixing mechanisms lead to higher rates of inflation in some countries than others will be taken up in chapters 11 and 12. It is argued that unconstrained collective bargaining that is not somehow coordinated with macroeconomic policy objectives gives rise to a greater inflationary bias and greater potential instability. Fortunately, in some countries coordination of collective bargaining with national economic goals has developed at the same time as affluent unions, thereby constraining the potential unstable inflationary situation.

The next section records some of the more important developments in labour and product markets over an extended period ending in the 1930s that bear on the nature of the inflationary process at work during that particular period. Special attention is given to the impact of these developments on the relative importance of demand–pull versus cost–push forces, the shape of the Phillips curve, and the presence of inertia and asymmetries. Following that the analysis turns to the post-war period from the early 1950s to the present.

THE RISE OF UNIONS: THE EARLY YEARS

1. *Wages*

Phelps Brown's study of trends and cycles in money wage earnings (hereafter money wages) in France, Germany, Sweden, the UK and the USA during the period 1860–1913 revealed several important patterns. First, sensitivity of money wages to the business cycle is most apparent; the rate of wage inflation increases during boom periods and declines during recessions. Second, aside from the serious depression of the 1870s, there is an asymmetric response of wage inflation to changes in aggregate demand. During booms the rate of wage inflation increases more than it declines during recessions. Third, except for the great depression of the 1870s there is a tendency for money wage levels to increase during recessions, at least outside of the two English-speaking countries. A floor to wage levels is apparent and this seems to be true even before unions had attained political and economic power on a wide scale. The asymmetric behaviour of wages naturally results in a ratchet effect leading to an upward trend in money wages throughout the period. For example, the strong secular trend in money wages in countries like Sweden and Germany can be traced to sharper rises of wages during booms and smaller declines during recessions than in other countries.[1]

There is some dispute over the trends in wages since the great depression of the 1870s. Lewis found a great deal of steadiness in the rate at which money wages grew from 1883 to 1913, while Phelps

---

[1] See E. Phelps Brown (1968) *A Century of Pay*, Macmillan, London, p. 77. The wage figures are aggregates and conceal wage reductions in some sectors. What appears to be happening from the 1870s onward is that wages in fewer and fewer sectors are flex-price downwards. See Tarling and Wilkinson (1982) The movement of real wages and the development of collective bargaining in the U.S.: 1955–1920, *Contributions to Political Economy*, No. 1.

Brown found a distinct acceleration in the rate of wage inflation in the 1890s, at least for Germany, Sweden and the USA.[2]

The behaviour of money wages in the same countries during the interwar period reveals a rapid deflation everywhere following the First World War, a rapid decline in wages during the early part of the 1930s in Germany and the USA, and the rapid increase in wages everywhere following the trough of the Great Depression. The German deflation in the early 1930s can be attributed to legislation specifically enacted to reduce wages. The behaviour of wages in the USA during this period reflects the severity of the depression. Looking at the entire period up to the Second World War, the responsiveness of money wages to economic conditions and their downward rigidity stands out.

Taking a longer view, before the advent of the trade cycle, roughly up until the mid-nineteenth century, wage rates showed signs of inertia, neither moving up or down. Once a stage of capitalist development had been reached in which investment (and savings) was sizeable, the multiplier effects of fluctuations in investment resulted in pro-cyclical movements of wages.[3] The depressions of the 1870s and 1930s did see a decline in wage rates but the resumption of the upward trend in wages early in the 1930s when unemployment was still appreciable attests to the resistance to declines. In the USA, unemployment exceeded 20 per cent in 1934 when money wages again moved upward. Moreover, this movement of wages was widespread across industries and occupations.[4] This says much about the likely consequences of a restimulation of an economy today.

2.   Labour Costs and Prices

The years just before the turn of the century marked the beginning of a period in which two pronounced trends were reversed. Starting in

[2] See Phelps Brown, op. cit., pp. 93–5; and W. Lewis (1978) *Growth and Fluctuations: 1870–1913*, George Allen & Unwin, London, p. 83.

[3] 'In one way, indeed, the cycle acted like a war; it unclenched the dead hand of use and wont, overturned the judgement-seat of custom, and threw the wage question open. Thereby it gave men more opportunity to try to better their condition.' Phelps Brown, op. cit., p. 75.

[4] See R. Gordon (1976) Recent developments in the theory of inflation and unemployment, *Journal of Monetary Economics,* No. 2, pp. 194–5. Of great significance was the upward movement of wages of farm labourers as early as 1934. Thus, there was a net migration into agriculture in the USA in the 1930s suggesting the existence of surplus labour at a time when wages began to rise. Between 1934 and 1940, unemployment never fell below 14.3 per cent yet money wage rates of farm workers rose 28–30 per cent.

the late 1870s and continuing in the early 1880s, average labour costs fell as productivity growth out-stripped wage increases. Sometime in the 1890s, however, the rate of growth of money wages began to exceed the growth of productivity. As a result, average labour costs rose persistently until the First World War. The 1890s also marked the reversal of a downward price trend that had originated in the depression of the 1870s, with both the cost of living and GNP deflators moving upward until the outbreak of the First World War.

Thus, the years when average labour costs were falling (along with prices), roughly from the early 1880s to the mid-1890s, was a period of rising real, and to lesser extent, money wages. As rising labour productivity would be the main force behind rising real wages, this productivity growth was translated into rising real wages through falling prices. Just the opposite took place beginning shortly before the turn of the century. Real wages continued to rise in Sweden, USA, Germany and France, but at a slower rate, after the mid-1890s.[5] But since prices also started to rise, productivity growth had to be translated into rising real wages through money wages rising more rapidly than prices (disregarding terms of trade effects). This kind of relative wage and price movement, whereby workers receive the benefits of productivity growth through growth of money wages rather than a decline in the price of goods they produce, is something that would be associated with superior bargaining power on the part of labour, a matter discussed shortly.

3. *A monetarist explanation of price trends*

Lewis considers several alternative explanations of the reversal of price trends in several countries around the turn of the century.[6] Among these were the monetarist explanation as offered by Friedman and Schwartz.[7] Choosing the period from 1879 to 1897 and comparing it with that from 1897 to 1914, Friedman and Schwartz found a positive correlation between the rate of growth of the money supply and price inflation in the USA. The inference to be drawn is that differences in the rate of price inflation in the USA were caused by differences in the rate of growth of the money supply. In contrast, Lewis did not find an obvious association between the growth of the money supply and price inflation. Any association was found to be

---

[5] See Phelps Brown, op. cit., pp. 157–73.
[6] ibid., Chapter 3.
[7] See the discussion in Lewis, op. cit., pp. 87–93.

critically dependent upon the dates chosen, in some cases yielding no correlation whatsoever.[8] Lewis chose what he considered to be a more appropriate dating scheme for understanding the period, peak dates for production, yielding the following growth rates for each of the components of the quantity equation.

TABLE 7.1 *Average annual rates of growth*

	Money supply (%)	Velocity (%)	Real GNP (%)	Price (%)
1882–1892	5.6	−4.0	3.7	−2.0
1892–1906	6.5	−1.4	4.3	0.8
Difference	0.9	2.6	0.7	2.8

Source: Lewis, op. cit. p. 91.

Table 7.1 reveals a positive correlation between the rate of growth of the money supply and price inflation but tells nothing about the direction of causation. Now from one period to the next, the rate of growth of money GNP increased by 2.8 + 0.7 = 3.5 per cent. Only about one-quarter of this increase, 0.9/3.5, was financed by an increase in the rate of growth of the money supply, the rest by velocity adjustments. During a period when the banking system and the use of checking accounts was expanding rapidly, when the relationship between the stock of gold and the money supply varied widely, Lewis concluded that variables on the right-hand side induced changes on the left-hand side with velocity doing most of the required adjusting. This is the interpretation that is adopted here.

4. *An alternative explanation of price trends*

Another stylized fact of some importance was that unit labour costs and prices showed fairly similar trends in France, Germany, the UK and the USA from 1883 to 1913. Lewis' explanation, largely supported by Phelps Brown, relied on the workings of the Scandinavian model of inflation discussed in chapter 4.[9] Both writers saw the behaviour of money wages within a country as determined by the rate of growth of productivity within that country plus the rate of growth of prices of internationally traded (German for Lewis)

[8] ibid., pp. 90–1.
[9] ibid., pp. 109–11; and Phelps Brown, op. cit., pp. 130–1.

goods.[10] Given the 'law of one price', under this kind of wage and price setting arrangements unit labour costs (and prices) grow at the same rate in every (competing) country.

However, even if it is accepted that the workings of the law of one price explains the similar movements of unit labour costs and prices between countries, there still remains the question of why price and unit costs started to rise around the turn of the century. Lewis' explanation emphasizes the behaviour of agricultural prices and ultimately the growth of demand relative to supply of agricultural output. In particular, American agricultural output and exports decelerated at this time, forcing up agricultural prices which, in turn, pushed up the general price level.[11]

But there is another explanation that is consistent with and complements Lewis, and that is the rising strength of the trade unions around the turn of the century. Union membership grew rapidly at the time that unit labour cost and price trends reversed themselves suggesting that unions did influence price and cost trends through their influence on money wage trends. An acceleration in money wage increases, which took place in several countries at this time, could be attributed simply to a reduction in the proportion of labour markets that are flex-price downward, something that Scitovsky attributed to the rise in unions and something borne out by case studies.[12] In addition, using the kind of (limited) statistical tests described in chapter 6, appendix B, for measuring the impact of unions on wages, Phelps Brown found some support that unions were an additional force pushing up wages.[13] Greater support was found for the belief that unions improved the non-pecuniary conditions of work.

---

[10] Thus, $\dot{w}_i = \dot{\rho}_i + \dot{p}_f$ where $\dot{w}_i$, $\dot{\rho}_i$ and $\dot{p}_f$ denote the rate of growth of money wages and productivity in the ith country and the rate of growth of prices of traded goods. The rate of growth of unit labour costs is then: $\dot{p}_f = \dot{w}_i - \dot{\rho}_i$.

[11] ibid., p. 80.

[12] See the comments in chapter 6 (pp. 117–21) and Tarling and Wilkinson, op. cit., especially p. 14. Lewis in one study denies an acceleration of money wages outside the USA at this time while Phelps Brown found a reversal of trends in Germany, Sweden and the USA. However, Lewis's more-recent study sees unions having a more pronounced impact on prices. See Lewis, 'Growth and Fluctuations . . .', op. cit., p. 83, Phelps Brown, op. cit., pp. 93–4 and Lewis (1980) Rising Prices, 1899–1913 and 1950–1979, *Scandinavian Journal of Economics*, No. 4, p. 427. The failure of labour productivity to grow in Britain beginning around the turn of the century would work to keep average money wages from growing while the union influence would keep them from falling.

[13] op. cit., pp. 92–104.

THE TRANSITIONAL PERIOD

The rise in unionization at the time when unit labour costs and prices reversed downward trends and began to rise (the mid 1890s) suggests that unions did have an effect on wages, costs and prices that was not as strong as that in the current period, but none the less important. This impact, in which downward rigidity of money wages throughout the economy became so apparent, and in which productivity growth was translated into rising real wages through money wage increases exceeding price increases, was referred to in chapter 6 as the emergence of an inflationary bias in a weak sense.

However, in the period of industrialization up to 1914, there was little evidence that the cost of living had any impact on wage settlements.[14] Changes in living costs were not generally measured before the First World War. Thus, even during the quarter-century before the First World War, a period of rising union strength, fairness considerations were not a dominant issue in wage settlements. This finding indicates an intermediate stage in the evolution of wage determination (and the inflationary mechanism) between the period

TABLE 7.2   *Average annual rate of growth of wage earnings and cost of living, 1886–1913*

	USA (%)	UK (%)	Sweden (%)	Germany (%)	France (%)
Wage earnings	1.59	1.04	2.57	2.32	0.88
Cost of living	0.26	0.50	0.99	1.04	0.31

Source: Calculated from E. Phelps Brown and Margaret H. Brown, *A Century of Pay,* op. cit., Appendix 3.

when unions were largely absent and the current period. Table 7.2 summarizes the relevant trends in money wages (in manufacturing) and the cost of living for five countries.[15] For each country the rate of growth of money wages exceeds that of consumer prices, largely reflecting rising labour productivity. However, unlike the period before the 1880s, rising real wages were accompanied by rising prices.

---

[14] See Lewis, *Growth and Fluctuations* . . . , op. cit., pp. 83, 107; and Phelps Brown, op. cit., p. 112.
[15] The end points, if anything, exaggerate the growth rates.

THE POST-WAR PERIOD

1. *1955–1965*

Wage and price data in the period since the Second World War is available for a wider sample of countries. Figures 7.1 and 7.2 show annual rates of wage inflation for the large OECD countries and Austria. Table 7.3 reveals most of the same information in tabular form. The first row gives average annual rates of wage inflation from 1955–65 disregarding the years of conversion from the Second World War and the years of wage (and price) explosion of the second half of the 1960s. It encompasses a period of sustained growth in the OECD countries.

Figure 7.1 reveals that in four of the larger OECD economies there was little evidence that rates of wage inflation showed any tendency to accelerate. However, the pattern of wage inflation depicted for four other economies in figure 7.2 is more typical of the

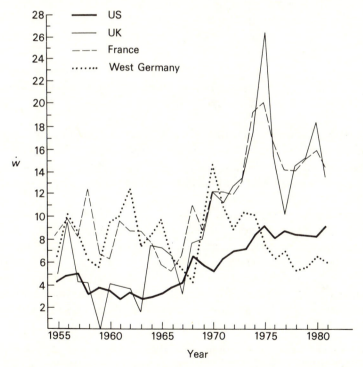

FIGURE 7.1   *Annual rates of wage inflation in selected countries; 1955–81*
Source: *Economic Outlook*, July 1981, OECD, Paris, Chart H

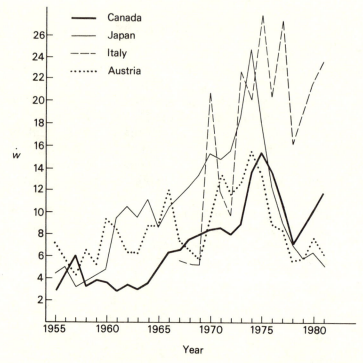

FIGURE 7.2 *Annual rates of wage inflation in selected countries; 1955–81*
Source: as figure 7.1

developed capitalist economies during the period. Thus not only did inflation rates accelerate between 1955 and 1965 in Austria, Canada and Japan, acceleration tendencies were equally if not more marked in Belgium, Denmark, Netherlands, Norway, Sweden and Switzerland.

But what stands out and illustrates the impact of the structural changes during a period of development of strong, affluent trade unions is the pronounced acceleration in the rates of inflation in the period 1955–65 compared with the period before the First World War.[16]

Comparing the 1955–65 with the 1886–1913 period, the acceleration of rates of wage inflation must be attributed to the generalized

[16] The interwar period does not invite comparison with any other period (the possible exception being the USA in the 1920s) and is not considered. IMF data is used because comparable data is available for a longer period than from other sources.

TABLE 7.3   *Annual and annual average rates of growth of wages in selected countries 1955–81*

Year	USA (%)	Canada (%)	Japan (%)	France (%)	West Germany (%)	Italy (%)	UK (%)	Austria (%)
1955–65	3.5	3.7	6.8	8.4	8.6	n.a.	4.6	6.9
1966	3.9	6.2	10.5	5.3	6.6	n.a.	6.7	12.0
1967	4.1	6.5	11.4	6.3	3.2	5.6	3.4	7.5
1968	6.7	7.6	12.3	11.0	4.3	5.3	7.8	6.5
1969	5.9	8.0	13.4	8.4	8.9	5.3	8.0	5.9
1970	5.2	8.4	15.3	12.1	14.9	20.9	12.1	9.4
1971	6.5	8.5	14.9	12.1	11.0	11.8	11.3	13.5
1972	7.0	8.0	15.6	12.0	9.0	9.3	12.8	11.6
1973	7.1	9.0	18.7	13.3	10.4	22.9	13.5	12.9
1974	8.3	13.5	24.9	19.2	10.3	20.2	17.7	15.7
1975	9.1	15.5	18.1	20.3	7.8	28.0	26.6	13.4
1976	8.1	13.8	12.5	16.5	6.4	20.9	15.5	9.0
1977	8.8	10.8	9.2	14.2	7.0	27.6	10.3	8.6
1978	8.6	7.2	7.1	14.2	5.4	16.2	14.6	5.7
1979	8.6	8.7	5.9	15.3	5.8	19.3	15.3	5.8
1980	8.5	10.1	6.4	16.0	6.6	21.9	18.7	7.9
1981	9.9	12.0	5.2	14.4	5.6	23.9	13.4	6.2

Source: IMF, International Financial Statistics Yearbook, 1981 and 1982.

nature of wage increases throughout the economy due to fairness considerations in wage settlements in the more recent period. Wage increases in one sector induced wage increases elsewhere, as groups sought to maintain relativities and cost of living increases generated wage increases throughout the economy.[17] Given mark-up pricing, generalized wage increases caused by wage imitation or previous cost-of-living increases passed through to prices permitting inflation to take on a life of its own. This separate life was nurtured throughout the period by an unemployment constraint; i.e. an unwillingness of the authorities to push up unemployment without limit in an effort to reduce inflation, caution on the part of the monetary authorities to tighten credit too rapidly and induced adjustments in

[17] Cagan has argued that in the recent period, price increases tend to be more generalized, at least in concentrated industries, due to a tendency for businesses to coordinate price increases. See P. Cagan (1974) *The Hydra-Headed Monster*, American Enterprise Institute, Washington, p. 34.

the payments system that allowed for sizeable cyclical swings in velocity.

As a result of these fairness considerations (ultimately traced to the rising power of unions, the increased inelasticity of demand for output and egalitarian tendencies), the feedback and pass through effects transmitted inflationary impulses throughout the economy in a manner quite different from earlier times when wage (and price) increases were not so generalized. Given the static asymmetries discussed in chapter 6, this transmission process generated dynamic asymmetries.

This change in the inflationary mechanism that has emerged in all the developed capitalist economies is the explanation offered not only for the acceleration in inflation rates between the period prior to the First World War and 1955–65 period, but for the acceleration of rates within the 1955–65 period, as well as the marked acceleration to follow.[18]

2. The world-wide nature of the inflation

The analysis of this and the previous chapter indicates that even in the absence of international linkages, the structural changes in labour and product markets just referred to would lead to accelerated inflation rates in the post-war period in all the developed capitalist economies. None the less the greater openness of the economies in the post-war period would increase the possibility of external impulses activating the inflationary mechanisms within any country. Thus, the discussion on pp. 154–5 showed that because of the law of one price, inflation rates were linked in different countries as early as the turn of the century. These links were certainly strengthened during the post-war period.

The rapid acceleration of inflation rates in so many countries in the late 1960s and early 1970s intensified an interest by economists

---

[18] It is interesting to note that this interpretation agrees substantially with a recent study of the USA. This study attempted to explain why inflation had become so much more of a problem after the Second World War than before. A distinction was made between the proximate sources or initiating forces behind inflation and the transmission mechanism. The former focussed on changes in aggregate demand due to fiscal and monetary impulses. See ibid., p. 34.

It must be emphasized that when discussing the acceleration of inflation rates over time the analysis is confined to the developed market economies and to periods of 'normal' economic development. Periods such as the conversion from the First World War and the Great Depression are therefore not considered for comparative purposes.

in the international linkages or the international inflation transmissions mechanisms. In their least controversial forms, these theories stressed price, income and liquidity effects whereby inflationary movements in one country are then transmitted to the rest of the world. In this manner inflation becomes a world-wide phenomenon. Furthermore, given the kinds of static asymmetries discussed in chapter 6, the downward rigidity of wages and prices in each country engaged in trade would lead to a world-wide inflationary bias under the fixed exchange rate system that prevailed before the early 1970s.

There is no need to dispute the contention that a greater openness of economies exposes them to more inflationary impulses or 'shocks' coming from abroad. Unfortunately, people who place so much reliance on the international transmission of inflationary impulses as an explanation of world-wide post-war inflation are usually guilty of errors of omission and commission. First, this kind of modelling of inflation tends to ignore the powerful domestic inflationary mechanisms that intensify and prolong inflation even in a closed economy. Second, these kinds of models of world-wide inflation are full employment models that make very special kinds of assumptions about the workings of labour, product and financial markets in the home and foreign countries. For example, the earlier chapters argued that most markets for labour and products were fix-price markets. A higher rate of growth of demand set off by, say, an increase in the rate of growth of the money supply need not have any domestic price effect, especially if unemployment is high. A demand for more imports may result, which turns the payments position towards a deficit and may put pressure on prices in foreign countries. But again unless costs are raised in the process, prices in fix-price markets abroad need not rise.

A higher level of imports in the initiating country may well lead to a rise in international reserves in the surplus country, which gives rise to an increase in the money supply. Given the assumptions of constant velocity of money and full employment, this must generate more inflation. However, even granted the constant velocity–full employment assumptions, even if capital markets in the surplus countries are not sufficiently developed to allow central bank actions to neutralize the higher level of bank reserves, other measures can and have been taken to control credit expansion.[19]

[19] See J. Duesenberry (1975) Worldwide inflation: A fiscalist view, in *The Phenomenon of Worldwide Inflation* (Eds. D. Meiselman and A. Laffer), American Enterprise Institute, Washington; and R. Gordon (1977) World inflation and monetary accommodations in eight countries, *Brookings Papers on Economic Activity*, No. 2.

WHAT HAPPENED IN THE SECOND HALF OF THE 1960s?

1. *The monetary approach to the balance of payments*

None the less, in spite of all these necessary qualifications, a very rigid doctrinaire version of the international transmission mechanism of inflation has been developed that purports to explain not only the world-wide nature of the post-war inflation and its acceleration over rates experienced in earlier years but also the timing of the acceleration of inflation rates in the late 1960s and early 1970s period. Moreover, this theory has found a culprit, the American monetary authorities. It is usually referred to as international monetarism or the monetary approach to the balance of payment (MAB) when applied to fixed exchange-rate systems.

For example, inflation will be world-wide, will be at a higher rate than in some earlier period and will accelerate markedly if monetary expansion occurs simultaneously in most countries, at a higher rate than in some earlier period and greatly accelerates, respectively. However, the historical experience that advocates of MAB wish to explain has different features. Thus, MAB argues that persistent, world-wide inflation can also be generated if growth in the money supply occurs in a large country which through trade links is in a position to have a substantial impact on the rest of the world and if this same large country does not have to worry about running out of reserves.[20] This version of the theory is then used to explain the worsening world-wide inflationary condition beginning in the late 1960s.

In the studies undertaken to test this version of MAB the key relationships are between: (1) the rate of growth of the money supply in the USA, assumed to be the causal factor driving the world-wide inflationary process, and the rates of growth of the money supply in countries tied to the USA through trade and capital markets; and (2) the rate of growth of the money supply in some country (other than the USA) and the rate of growth of prices in that country. Alternatively, the rate of growth of prices in any country can be linked directly to the rate of growth of the money supply in the USA. The first relationship is meant to indicate the impossibility of any country linked to the USA having a monetary policy independent of that in the USA. The second, coupled with the first, reveals the dominant

[20] See A. Swoboda (1977) Monetary approaches to worldwide inflation, in *World Wide Inflation: Theory and Recent Experience* (Eds. L. Krause and W. Salant), The Brookings Institution, Washington.

role played by the USA in the determination of world-wide inflation. The equation expressing this second linkage can be treated as a reduced-form equation that summarizes the various structural relations within an economy; the impacts of wages on prices, unemployment and price expectations on wage and price formation and changes in the money supply on unemployment, etc.

A good deal of empirical work was undertaken to establish these linkages and although proponents of the MAB view felt the evidence supported their view, others have had serious difficulties in accepting the results. More important, more powerful econometric techniques have been employed in a recent study to test these linkages and the conclusion was quite unequivocal; the primary factor responsible for monetary growth and inflation in other countries during the period 1964–71 was not monetary growth in the USA.[21]

2. The wage explosion

In understanding why the MAB theory of world-wide inflation is not able to withstand such econometric tests, it will do well to look closely at events of the beginning in the second half of the 1960s. First, Table 7.4 indicates clearly that a wage explosion occurred in many European economies in the second half of the 1960s, according to both IMF and OECD data. For example, the rate of wage inflation more than doubles in France (OECD) and in the UK (IMF) between 1967 and 1968, in West Germany between 1968 and 1969 (IMF) and more than doubles in Italy (IMF and OECD) from 1969 to 1970.[22] According to international monetarism, these developments would be explainable along the lines suggested on pp. 160–1. A prior stimulating demand impulse originating in the USA would lead to a payments deficit there and payments surpluses in countries such as the UK, West Germany and France. Under a fixed exchange regime this leads to an accumulation of dollar assets by foreigners which end up in the hands of the central banks of their

---

[21] See E. Feige and J. Johannes (1982) Was the United States responsible for worldwide inflation under the regime of fixed exchange rates? *Kyklos,* No. 2. Their study covered the years 1964–71 because this period corresponded to a period of fixed exchange rates and full employment.

[22] Soskice dates the high wage settlements in France, Italy and West Germany as June, 1968, December 1969 and September 1969, respectively. See D. Soskice (1978) Strike waves and wage explosions, 1968–1970: An economic interpretation, in *The Resurgence of Class Conflict in Western Europe Since 1968* (Eds. C. Crouch and A. Pizzorno), Holmes and Meir, New York, p. 229.

TABLE 7.4 Annual rate of growth of wage inflation as measured by the IMF and OECD

	USA		Canada		Japan		France		West Germany		Italy		UK		Austria	
	IMF (%)	OECD (%)	IMF (%)	OECD (%)	IMF (%)	OECD (%)	IMF (%)	OECD (%)	IMF (%)	OECD (%)	IMF (%)	OECD (%)	IMF (%)	OECD (%)	IMF (%)	OECD (%)
1967	4.1	4.2	6.5	5.7	11.4	11.7	6.8	5.8	3.2	6.1	5.6	5.4	3.4	3.9	7.5	n.a.
1968	6.7	6.3	7.6	6.8	12.3	14.9	11.0	12.4	4.3	6.0	5.3	3.6	7.8	8.6	6.5	n.a.
1969	5.9	5.9	8.0	10.8	13.4	16.4	8.4	11.2	8.9	9.7	5.3	7.5	8.0	7.8	5.9	n.a.
1970	5.2	5.1	8.4	5.5	15.3	17.7	12.1	10.6	14.9	16.7	20.9	21.6	12.1	12.7	9.4	n.a.
1971	6.5	6.7	8.5	7.5	14.9	13.7	12.1	11.1	11.0	13.7	11.8	13.6	11.3	11.4	13.5	n.a.
1972	7.0	6.7	8.0	7.3	15.6	15.6	12.0	11.3	9.0	8.7	9.3	10.4	12.8	12.8	11.6	11.6
1973	7.1	6.8	9.0	9.2	18.7	20.7	13.3	12.7	10.4	11.9	22.9	19.9	13.5	12.4	12.9	15.8

Sources: IMF, International Financial Statistics, Yearbook 1981; OECD, Economic Outlook, December 1967, July 1971, December 1972 and December 1974.

countries, as the latter seeks to stabilize the exchange rate. As exports rise in the surplus countries, the demand for money rises and is automatically accommodated by the central bank. This increase in aggregate demand leads to a (temporary) reduction in unemployment because of price 'surprises', i.e. a discrepancy between the expected rate of inflation and the now higher rate of inflation.[23]

Unfortunately for this theory, the wage explosion in several European countries preceded a large increase in the payments deficit in the USA.[24] Neither wage nor price inflation within the European economies can be adequately 'tracked' by standard, international monetarist models.[25] The standard MAB model has been extended by assuming that the imported price inflation generated price surprises. These then resulted in a decline in real wages, labour frustration and finally strikes and accelerated wage settlements.[26] Again, there are difficulties since the rate of price inflation in the different countries preceding the wage explosion was not of a magnitude to warrant this conclusion.

The use of dummy variables in regression studies revealed that after the impact of the usual economic variables is taken into account, some other influence(s) at work during this period lead to an acceleration of the rate of wage inflation.[27] Statistically significant dummy variables only indicate the omission of some other influence(s), not what the other influence(s) might be. A study employing analytical techniques along with a good deal of historical detail traced the developments in labour markets during this period and attributed the wage explosions in Europe together with increased strikes and labour unrest to 'frustration' factors. Instead of price surprises, however, the intensified labour unrest was attributed to such factors as a previous shift in the distribution of income to profits and a slowdown in the growth of real wages, a marked disturbance of the wage structure and a reorganization of production forced upon workers by their employers (depending upon the country). This took place over a period from early 1968 until late

---

[23] See chapter 3, pp. 56–61.

[24] Soskice, op. cit., p. 229; R. Gordon, 'World Inflation . . .', op. cit., p. 441. Gordon cites 1971 as the first year in which money and international reserves exploded while Soskice cites 1970.

[25] Soskice, op. cit., pp. 226–9, and references.

[26] Soskice, op. cit., pp. 229–30 cites a study by Ward and Zis as an example of this kind of theorizing.

[27] See the two studies cited by Gordon, op. cit., fn. 19.

1969, triggering off large increases in wages in an effort to bring industrial peace.[28]

If it is true as maintained here that the wage explosion must be explained in more mundane 'sociological' terms which were particular to the country, then each instance of wage explosion can be treated as an independent example of an inflationary situation that was about to prove itself very unstable upwards. Thus, it must be emphasized that such sociological explanations of the initiating forces behind accelerated inflation cannot be interpreted simply as mere 'after the fact' theorizing. One of the central conclusions of chapter 6 was that in an age of sustained full employment, rates of inflation tend to drift upward as a natural outcome of alternating periods of excess and shortfalls of demand. But the inflationary mechanism is unstable upwards in an additional sense. At any rate of unemployment disturbances are much more likely to activate the inflationary mechanism upwards than downwards because of certain asymmetries. The 'frustration' factors just cited merely illustrate this last point; i.e. the instability upwards of inflation rates in full (or near full) employment economies when social and economic factors activate the inflationary mechanism.

3. *The lull before the storm*

The acceleration in wage and price inflation rates by 1970–71 compared to, say, 1955–65, illustrates the impact of what the OECD Report described as the accumulation of structural changes, e.g. rising aspirations and the expectation of guaranteed full employment by a labour force that was increasingly composed of workers who had never experienced the Great Depression.[29] As just described these impulses would activate the cost–push mechanisms causing wage and price increases to become generalized throughout the economy.

Figures 7.1 and 7.2 reveal that by 1970 wage inflation rates had accelerated in most of the countries and in spite of restrictive policies in 1968 and 1969. This was true for the other capitalist economies as well. Moreover, while unemployment rates rose in many countries in

---

[28] See Soskice, op. cit.; and G. Perry (1975) Determinants of wage inflation around the world, *Brookings Papers on Economic Activity*, No. 2. Perry offers evidence that it was a struggle over income shares triggered by efforts of unions to restore an earlier distribution.

[29] See the discussion in chapter 1, pp. 29–32.

TABLE 7.5   *Standardized unemployment rates, 1966–74 per cent of total labour force*

	1966 (%)	1967 (%)	1968 (%)	1969 (%)	1970 (%)	1971 (%)	1972 (%)	1973 (%)	1974 (%)
USA	3.6	3.7	3.4	3.4	4.8	5.8	5.5	4.8	5.5
Japan	1.3	1.3	1.2	1.1	1.1	1.2	1.4	1.3	1.4
West Germany[a]	0.2	1.3	1.5	0.9	0.8	0.9	0.8	0.8	1.6
France[a]	1.8	1.9	2.6	2.3	2.4	2.6	2.7	2.6	2.8
UK[a]	2.2	3.3	3.2	3.0	3.1	4.0	4.2	3.2	3.1
Italy	5.7	5.3	5.6	5.6	5.3	5.3	6.3	6.2	5.3
Canada	5.3	3.8	4.4	4.4	5.6	6.1	6.2	5.5	5.3
Austria	1.8	1.9	2.0	2.0	1.4	1.3	1.2	1.1	1.4
Major seven countries[a,b]	2.6	2.8	2.9	2.7	3.2	3.8	3.8	3.4	3.7
Total (in fifteen OECD countries)[a,c]	2.5	2.7	2.8	2.6	3.0	3.6	3.6	3.2	3.5

Source: OECD, *Economic Outlook,* July 1982 and December 1982, Table R.12.
[a] Series adjusted by the OECD.
[b] USA, Japan, West Germany, France, UK, Italy and Canada.
c Major seven countries and Austria, Australia, Belgium, Finland, Netherlands, Norway, Spain and Sweden.

1970–71 as shown in table 7.5, rates of wage inflation in 1971 responded only slightly if at all leading to an upward ratcheting of inflation rates over the 'cycle'. The breakdown of the Bretton Woods fixed exchange rate system also began in 1971. Table 7.6 summarizes the cumulative impact of all these events on rates of price inflation for eight countries. As is clear by the end of the 1960s and through 1971 rates of price inflation had accelerated noticeably above their 1955–65 average outside of Canada. Equally important, outside of

TABLE 7.6   *Annual average rate of growth of consumer prices 1955–71*

Year	USA (%)	Canada (%)	Japan (%)	France (%)	West Germany (%)	Italy (%)	UK (%)	Austria (%)
1955–65	1.5	1.6	3.3	4.4	2.3	3.3	2.9	2.8
1966	3.1	3.8	4.9	2.7	3.5	2.4	3.9	2.2
1967	2.6	3.6	4.1	2.8	1.6	3.7	2.7	3.9
1968	4.2	4.0	5.3	4.5	1.7	1.5	4.8	2.7
1969	5.4	4.5	5.3	6.2	1.8	2.6	5.4	3.2
1970	5.9	3.4	7.6	5.8	3.3	4.8	6.3	4.3
1971	4.3	2.8	6.2	5.5	5.3	5.0	9.4	4.7

Source: IMF, *International Financial Statistics,* Supplement in Price Adjustment, 1981.

North America rising unemployment rates had litle or no effect on inflation rates.[30] All this before the huge payments deficits in the USA, the rapid increase in food and raw materials prices in 1972–74, the simultaneous boom in aggregate economic activity in the OECD countries in 1972–73 and the quadrupling of oil prices in 1973–75.

THE LAST BOOM

The dismantling of the Bretton Woods fixed exchange-rate system was completed by 1973. During the dismantling period the large external deficits of the USA resulted in a dramatic increase in international liquidity. The most important impact of these deficits was, in the eyes of the OECD Report, to have 'effectively removed balance of payments constraints in other OECD countries, and facilitated a massive expansion of money supplies'.[31] But the Report also views the breakdown of the fixed (or pegged) exchange-rate system as a 'shock' to the system which in terms of the model of chapter 6 would have reinforced other pressures gathering force by 1972.

Thus, the rising unemployment rates in 1970 and 1971 had become a cause of concern in most of the OECD countries and, as a result, stimulative monetary and fiscal policies were intensified over this 2-year span and into 1972. What took place in 1972 was a boom that was synchronized throughout the OECD but in addition a boom that expanded at an unprecedented speed through 1972–73.[32] Moreover, it was a boom which was accompanied by a renewal of strong inflationary measures very soon after it was underway. Thus, table 7.7 indicates that inflation rates began to accelerate in several countries in 1972 and in all the countries in the table by 1973. Biannual data reveal that the acceleration for every country can be dated as early as the second half of 1972.[33]

To a large extent this rapid run up of prices (and wages) can be attributed to a rapid increase in food and raw materials' prices.[34] Both demand and supply factors were at work in food and agricul-

---

[30] The Nixon administration instituted wage and price controls in the USA beginning in August 1971.
[31] See *Towards Full Employment and Price Stability*, OECD, Paris (1978), Section (68), p. 56.
[32] ibid., p. 58.
[33] See *Economic Outlook*, December 1981, OECD, Paris, Table R11.
[34] The various influences at work are summarized in *Towards Full Employment* . . . , op. cit., p. 59.

TABLE 7.7   Annual rate of growth of consumer prices 1971–81

Year	USA (%)	Canada (%)	Japan (%)	France (%)	West Germany (%)	Italy (%)	UK (%)	Austria (%)
1971	4.3	2.8	6.2	5.5	5.3	5.0	9.4	4.7
1972	3.3	4.8	4.4	6.2	5.6	5.7	7.3	6.3
1973	6.3	7.5	11.8	7.4	6.9	10.8	9.1	7.7
1974	10.9	10.9	24.3	13.7	7.0	19.1	16.0	9.5
1975	9.2	10.7	11.9	11.7	5.9	17.0	24.2	8.5
1976	5.8	7.5	9.3	9.6	4.3	16.8	16.5	7.3
1977	6.5	8.0	8.1	9.4	3.6	17.0	15.9	5.5
1978	7.5	9.0	3.8	9.1	2.8	12.1	8.3	3.6
1979	11.3	9.2	3.6	10.7	4.1	14.7	13.4	3.7
1980	13.5	10.1	8.0	13.3	5.5	21.2	18.0	6.3
1981	10.4	12.4	4.9	13.3	5.9	17.8	11.9	6.8

Source: IMF, International Financial Statistics, Supplement in Price Adjustment 1981, and November 1982.

tural raw materials markets driving up prices. A marked acceleration in the increase in industrial raw materials (i.e. minerals and metals) prices followed soon after as seen in figure 7.3. What was unusual about the 1972–73 boom was the much greater increase in non-oil commodity prices compared to industrial production. Heretofore, both indices had moved together and some run-up of commodity prices would have been expected as a natural working of flex-price markets during a boom.

The unprecedented nature of the inflation of commodity prices has been attributed to 'imbalance' and a deliberate run-down of inventories of raw materials beginning as far back as the 1950s.[35] Naturally, the run-up of food, agricultural and industrial raw materials prices would feed into the ongoing inflationary processes in all the countries. This 'external' influence would link inflation rates world wide. The feedback effects of rising costs of living on wages would reinforce world wide the acceleration tendencies within each country.

The situation was viewed by the authors of the OECD Report as follows: 'In general, the prospects as seen in the latter part of 1973 were for a moderate policy-induced cooling-off period, with some modest reduction of inflation – in other words, a repeat performance, at higher rates of inflation, of the 1969–71 experience.'[36] What took place late in 1973 was the implementation of restrictive policies to

[35] ibid., p. 60.
[36] ibid., p. 66.

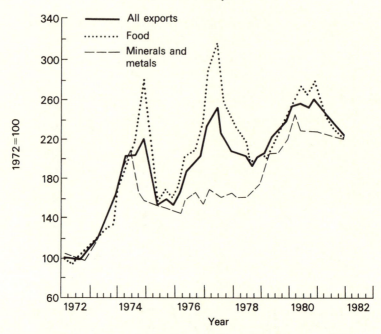

FIGURE 7.3　*Index of non-oil commodity prices in terms of SDR*
Source as figure 7.1

combat these worsening inflationary tendencies. Partly in response to policy and partly for reasons endogenous to the income gener- ating mechanism driving the real sector, in 1974 recessions began in most countries which were also internationally synchronized.

Tables 7.6 and 7.7 reveal that outside of Japan rates of wage and price inflation declined only slightly through 1975 and even acceler- ated in the UK. Yet a rapid increase in unemployment rates took place during this recessionary period. In addition, figure 7.3 indicates the deflationary impact of the recession on non-oil commodity prices beginning in early 1974. Even so, the quadrupling of oil prices in late 1973, together with strong and often accelerating rates of wage infla- tion, was enough to sustain the double-digit inflation rates in most countries through 1975.

BEFORE THE SECOND OIL PRICE RISE

Tables 7.7 and 7.8 summarize quite well the macroeconomic events of recent times; the simultaneous occurrence of stagnation and infla- tion. For the most part, the experience of the different countries has

TABLE 7.8   *Standardized unemployment rate in the seven large OECD economies*

	USA (%)	Japan (%)	West Germany† (%)	France (%)	UK† (%)	Italy (%)	Canada (%)
1973	4.8	1.3	0.8	2.6	3.2	6.2	5.5
1974	5.5	1.4	1.6	2.8	3.1	5.3	5.3
1975	8.3	1.9	3.6	4.1	4.7	5.8	6.9
1976	7.5	2.0	3.7	4.4	6.1	6.6	7.1
1977	6.9	2.0	3.6	4.7	6.5	7.0	8.0
1978	5.9	2.2	3.5	5.2	6.4	7.1	8.3
1979	5.7	2.1	3.2	5.9	5.7	7.5	7.4
1980	7.0	2.0	3.0	6.3	7.3	7.4	7.5
1981	7.5	2.2	4.4	7.3	11.4	8.3	7.5
1982*	9.2	2.3	6.2	8.1	12.8	8.9	10.2

Source: Economic Outlook, OECD, Paris, December 1982, Table R12.
* First three quarters.
† Series adjusted by the OECD.

been one of high and rising rates of unemployment so that by the early 1980s these rates have achieved double-digit level in many countries. Table 13.1 below summarizes the adverse effects of depressed demand conditions on productivity growth.

The outstanding characteristic of the period from 1976 to the present has been the slow descent of the OECD economies (and the rest of the world) towards a state of depression and possibly breakdown. Some temporary unemployment relief took place in the 1976–79 as some of the economies experienced a mini boom, as can be seen in the behaviour of the unemployment rates for the USA and West Germany shown in Table 7.8. And while the worst features of the wage and price explosion disappeared after 1975 (outside of Italy), rates of wage and price inflation settled at a plateau of high inflation in 1976 and remained there until very recently.

To be sure efforts to curb inflation were hampered to some extent by the run up in food and other non-oil prices in 1976–77, as seen in figure 7.3, due largely to supply problems and the mini booms in the USA and West Germany. But even so, what is most clear about the period is a failure of depressed labour market conditions, which generated sustained and high unemployment rates by post-war standards, to have a noticeable effect on wage inflation up through 1981.

The second explosion of oil prices occurred in 1979–80 and is reflected in the acceleration of consumer prices in table 7.7 in 1980.

Not only did the rise in oil prices feed through to the cost of living, it also created balance of payments difficulties in all of the non-oil exporting countries. Both effects intensified restrictive efforts by the authorities as reflected in the rising unemployment rates of all the countries in figure 7.7 and in the other OECD countries as well.

AT THE END OF THE TUNNEL

By 1982 the deceleration of wage inflation had become even more apparent, as unemployment rates continued to rise everywhere. After almost a decade, inflation rates are coming down. The question was raised at the end of chapter 6: What can be expected if, following the period when inflation has been brought under control, the authorities decide to stimulate the economies once again? It was concluded that if stimulative policies are in fact put into effect in the near future, inflation rates will again begin to accelerate. Chapter 8 considers some of the costs of restrictive policies.

CHAPTER 8

Free to Lose

Strange they don't lose hope altogether, always busy with
things that don't matter, digging greedily for treasure, and
happy when they come across an earthworm.
Goethe's Faust
Translated by Fairley Barker

INTRODUCTION

The concept of the natural rate of unemployment played a central
role in both the mark I and mark II versions of great monetarism in
chapter 3. In the mark I version a capitalist system has a natural
tendency to operate in the vicinity of the natural rate, a manifestation of the inherent stability properties of the private sector. Wide
and prolonged deviations from the natural rate might occur if the
authorities had been foolish enough in previous periods to try and
drive the unemployment below the natural rate. As discussed in
chapter 3, in order to bring down a high rate of inflation resulting
from such bad demand management, it then would be necessary to
maintain a rate of unemployment substantially above the natural
rate and for some time.[1] Other than this case, however, the economy
would not be experiencing any serious unemployment problems.

With the mark II version of GM, the economy is at the natural
rate from one period to the next (aside from a random component).
Fluctuations in the observed unemployment rate must therefore be

[1] In a recent study, it has been suggested that the current situation of rising unemployment and inflation indicates that structural and institutional changes have
taken place that may require decades before adjustments can be made, one of
which is to lower rates of inflation. See M. Friedman (1977) Nobel Lecture:
Inflation and Unemployment, *Journal of Political Economy,* June.

attributed to exogenous factors only; e.g. changes in tastes and technologies. However, the observed fluctuations of the unemployment rate in real life are not random but are (positively) serially correlated. This has led to some ingenious bits of reasoning among the GM-II theorists in their efforts to explain these fluctuating unemployment rates; efforts that have allowed them to minimize and even neglect any possible costs connected with unemployment.

A related monetarist view has it that the failure of restrictive policies to reduce inflation (until recently) has been because the rising unemployment rates of the 1970s are really reflecting high and rising rates of frictional, voluntary unemployment. Only if unemployment rates had been pushed above this rising natural rate, say, to double-digit rates, could it be expected that inflation rates would have come down.

Chapters 4–6 argued that none of these views could be taken seriously, since few labour markets operate in such a way that markets clear. As a result excess demand or supply for labour must be considered a natural tendency in labour markets. But it is at this point that the 'as if' doctrine discussed in the Introduction can be invoked. Thus, non-monetarists and perhaps even some monetarists might be prepared to accept the view that labour markets do not usually clear and are not flex-price downwards or even upwards. However, if most unemployment can be seen to be voluntary, then it could be said that the economy behaves 'as if' labour markets clear.

The central purpose of chapter 8 is to analyse in detail several dimensions of the unemployment problem; e.g. why workers become unemployed, what kinds of workers become unemployed, how often and for how long are workers unemployed and how these aspects of unemployment are affected by changes in the aggregate rate of unemployment. Answers to these questions should help determine to what extent unemployment in the 1970s and 1980s is voluntary or involuntary.

The conclusions reached in the earlier chapters already suggest what to expect. Labour markets with excess supply generate quantity (i.e. involuntary dismissals) not price adjustments. Therefore, involuntary layoffs will likely be a frequent cause of unemployment. However, the implications of the earlier analysis for policy can be given added force if unemployment is studied directly. Once this is done the study can proceed with the formulation of a policy response to unemployment and inflation. The analysis turns first to the natural rate of unemployment concept followed on pp. 176–8 by an evaluation of the use of the actual rate of inflation as an indicator of the nature of unemployment.

THE NATURAL RATE AND FULL-EMPLOYMENT RATE
OF UNEMPLOYMENT

According to Friedman, the natural rate of unemployment is defined as follows:

At any moment of time, there is some level of unemployment which has the property that it is consistent with equilibrium in the structure of *real* wage rates. . . . The 'natural rate of unemployment', in other words, is the level that would be ground out by the Walrasian system of general equilibrium equations, provided there is embedded in them the actual structural characteristics of the labour and commodity markets.[2]

As has been pointed out, the natural rate, so defined, little differs from the concept of the full employment rate of unemployment, a situation in which all labour markets clear.[3] Moreover, what it is that defines or determines full employment is the same in the *General Theory* as is implied by Friedman's statement, namely, conditions in the labour market.[4] What differs in the two approaches is the equilibrating mechanism that is available if the real wage is to adjust, equating quantities demanded and supplied should involuntary unemployment develop. With Keynes it is increases in the price level brought about by aggregate demand policies. With Friedman and the pre-Keynesian theorists flex-price labour (and product) markets lead to falling money wages relative to prices in such circumstances. If these equilibrating tendencies are rapid, vacancies will be quickly filled and workers temporarily unemployed in one market will soon find work in another. In an economy operating at the natural rate, any unemployment will be frictional and voluntary since at this highly aggregated level, the treatment of labour as homogeneous eliminates any possibility of 'structural' unemployment.[5]

---

[2] See M. Friedman (1968) The role of monetary policy, *American Economic Review,* p. 8, (March).

[3] J. Trevithick (1976) Inflation, the natural unemployment rate and the theory of economic policy, *Scottish Journal of Political Economy,* February 1976.

[4] ibid. In contrast, full employment could be defined in terms of preferences of policy makers, simply as the rate of unemployment at which inflation is non-accelerating or the rate at which the payments position is in some sort of equilibrium.

[5] Strictly speaking, in Friedman's version of the natural rate hypothesis, at $U = V$, $U = 0$. See chapter 3, fn. 10.

WHEN IS THE ECONOMY AT THE NATURAL RATE?

Difficulties begin when an attempt is made to determine at just what rate of aggregate unemployment all markets clear and all unemployment is voluntary. As has been remarked, it is not even clear whether a modified Walrasian general equilibrium that would grind out this rate of unemployment exists.[6] The position taken by proponents of the natural rate hypothesis, as discussed in chapter 3, pp. 56–61, is that two of the additional defining characteristics of the natural rate are the equality of the expected and actual rates of price (and wage) inflation, and the non-accelerating nature of inflation at that unemployment rate. Unemployment rates greater than (less than) the natural rate generate expected rates of inflation greater than (less than) the actual rates and lead to decelerating (accelerating) rates of inflation.

It will be recalled from chapter 3 that the ability to define the natural rate of unemployment as the rate of unemployment at which expected and actual inflation rates are identical and non-accelerating and all unemployment is voluntary required the competitive assumptions. Markets must be flex-price, atomistic competition must prevail, misinformation must be arbitrarily assumed to be limited to mistakes about prevailing prices, etc. When these assumptions are made, any attempt to reduce unemployment below the natural rate, can only succeed if some of the voluntarily unemployed took employment. This involved fooling workers by creating a discrepancy between actual and expected rates of inflation. Since a continuous process of fooling someone was not considered feasible, in the long-run the unemployment rate hovered around the natural rate at some non-accelerating rate of inflation; i.e. the Phillips curve was vertical in the long-run at the natural rate of unemployment.

Advocates of the natural rate hypothesis would have it that a 'test' of their theory of zero involuntary unemployment tendencies is whether inflation rates accelerated when aggregate demand is stimulated.[7] But it must be emphasized that the response of inflation rates

---

[6] See J. Tobin (1972) Inflation and unemployment, *American Economic Review,* March.

[7] Obviously, ascertaining whether a supposed equality between the actual and expected rates of inflation has been disturbed in order to test the zero involuntary unemployment tendencies is impractical.

to changes in aggregate demand is not a 'test' of whether the economy operates at zero involuntary unemployment or, ultimately, the competitive assumptions. The conditions of a correctly anticipated and non-accelerating rate of inflation (like that of zero involuntary unemployment) are simply deduced from the particular set of competitive assumptions used by natural rate theorists, assumptions that are known to be widely at variance with the important features of modern capitalist economies. Once this is realized, the important issue becomes whether the existence of correctly anticipated and non-accelerating rates of inflation are of any assistance for determining the nature of current unemployment.

Clearly, the natural rate theorists have shown that these conditions are consistent with a particular competitive world and, therefore, zero involuntary unemployment. But this is hardly the same thing as saying such conditions are necessary or sufficient conditions for an absence of involuntary unemployment.[8] For example, in chapter 3, pp. 63–5, an example was given in which an increase in aggregate demand led to a permanent reduction of involuntary unemployment at the same time as it caused an acceleration of inflation. This suggested, at best, that a state of non-accelerating inflation may be only a necessary condition for the absence of involuntary unemployment.[9]

This points up clearly the need to keep separate the two different definitions of the natural rate of unemployment; that unemployment rate at which all unemployment is voluntary and that unemployment rate at which inflation is correctly anticipated and non-accelerating or NAIRU. This difference in meanings is crucial because there is an

---

[8] The issue is somewhat related to the 'as if' problem discussed in the Introduction to Part I. The deductions from a set of hypotheses, if carried out according to logical principles correctly, reveal conditions or conclusions that are logically consistent with the assumptions. However, the relevant condition, in this case non-accelerating inflation, is consistent with a number of other assumptions as seen in chapter 3, pp. 63–5.

[9] As Trevithick points out, when wage determination is based on maintaining relative wages, the natural rate of unemployment derived from econometric work will merely be some average of unemployment rates during the sample period. See Trevithick, op. cit. But non-accelerating inflation need not even be a necessary condition for the absence of involuntary unemployment. In a world of fix-price labour markets and wage–wage and wage–price inflation, the behaviour of prices and wages with zero involuntary unemployment is indeterminate.

important welfare distinction to be made when contrasting voluntary with involuntary unemployment.[10]

The nature of unemployment at any unemployment rate must be determined on the basis of other factors than the actual rate of inflation.[11] The 'new' microeconomics of unemployment has been offered as one such determination.

UNEMPLOYMENT AS A PURPOSIVE QUEST
FOR SELF-IMPROVEMENT

1. *Two views*

In the original formulation of the natural rate of unemployment by Friedman (but not by Phelps) it was implicitly assumed that labour was homogeneous.[12] Barriers to entry into the various labour markets were unimportant and, as a result, the possibility of structural unemployment could be ignored. The unemployment (and vacancy) rate need not be assumed zero at the natural rate since the latter was compatible with a certain amount of voluntary unemployment generated by the presence of 'frictions' in the labour market. Prior to the development of the 'new' microeconomics of unemployment, the nature of such frictions were not well defined. Explanations ran in terms of information lags, the opening and closing of jobs as the result of shifting tastes and technologies, etc.

The development of the 'new' microeconomics of unemployment not only introduced a whole new vocabulary but sought to detail the nature of movements from employment to unemployment and vice versa in its description of how labour markets work. It was also responsible to a large extent in fostering the view that unemployment should not be viewed as a more or less permanent condition for a small proportion of the labour force who were left over after the stock of available jobs were filled. Rather unemployment in

---

[10] It has been argued that unemployment, even though it results from being permanently laid off a job that the worker found most satisfactory, is to some extent 'voluntary unemployment' since the newly unemployed worker can always find *some* other job. It is difficult to think of anyone other than a fully employed economist making this statement. See R. Lucas, jr (1978) Unemployment policy *The American Economic Review, Paper and Proceedings,* May.

Aside from the fact that it is not always true that unemployed economists can find jobs as hospital orderlies, this viewpoint downgrades the difference in personal welfare between an unemployed economist who might be forced to take a job as a hospital orderly and those who resign one university post in order to search for another.

[11] See chapter 3, pp. 000–000.

[12] See Friedman, The Role of . . . , op. cit.; and Phelps, op. cit.

the new view was the result of a quest for self-improvement in which the turnover of jobs was normal and widespread. A corollary of this was the notion that unemployment was a status widely shared but of short duration.

Another aspect of this kind of theorizing was the view that previously employed workers in their quest found it much more efficient to search for better jobs only after having quit their present job. Still another facet, already described in chapter 3, was the notion of workers being fooled or information disequilibrium. This led among other things to a prediction of counter-cyclical movements of the quit rate, a result clearly at variance with the facts. In any case, rather than look upon turnover as the result of shifting demand and supply curves for labour in separate markets, turnover came to be seen as the result of misconceptions about the real wage ruling in any period, misconceptions resulting from unanticipated changes in money wages and prices.

Tables 1.2 and 1.5 and figure 8.1 indicate a trend in unem-

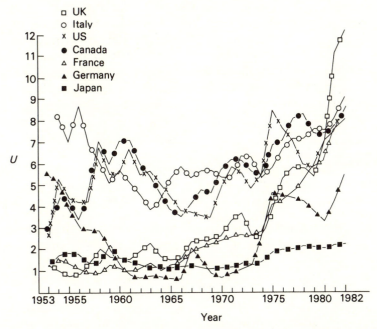

FIGURE 8.1   *Standard unemployment rates in seven major OECD countries;*
1953–82[a]

Sources: Main Economic Indicators, OECD, 1966 and 1980; *Labour Force Statistics,*
OECD, 1963, 1965, 1972 and 1981; and *Economic Outlook,* OECD, December 1981,
July 1982.

ployment rates in several economies with rates rising somewhat
gradually before the 1970s and then increasing quite dramatically in
the 1970s and 1980s. The view that this might be at least partly
attributed to higher rates of structural unemployment at any aggregate rate of unemployment will be discussed later in the chapter.
However, the new view of unemployment highlights frictional unemployment that is also voluntary. Indeed, in many versions all unemployment is voluntary. This suggests that two versions of the new
view might be formulated and evaluated. First, the position can be
taken that all unemployment is frictional and voluntary so that the
upward trend, and indeed any movement in unemployment rates,
reflects movements in the rate of frictional unemployment. This position coincides with Mark II version of Great Monetarism.

Second, a less extreme position argues that while the unemployment rate may have a cyclical, involuntary component, there has
been a marked secular increase in the rate of frictional unemployment associated with any aggregate rate of unemployment. In
the first interpretation, labour markets maintain a more or less constant degree of tightness whatever the aggregate rate of unemployment. In the second, since the share of any aggregate rate of
unemployment attributable to frictional unemployment rises over
time, labour markets are tighter at any rate of aggregate unemployment over time. Both views minimize the welfare implications of
rising unemployment rates. The second version is further discussed
on pp. 192–5.

2. Some difficulties

The first version of the new view ignores the heterogeneous nature of
labour and denies the existence of the Keynesian type of unemployment associated with a lack of effective demand. But the
assumption that all unemployment is frictional and voluntary
resulting from workers leaving their jobs and engaging in job-search
activities runs up against some well-known facts. For example,
unemployment rates among teenagers are higher than those of adults
of either sex. This, it could be argued, is because of a more prolonged
search for a decent job by the young, made possible by a lack of
family responsibilities, living at home, etc. However unemployment
rates for blacks of all ages and both sexes are higher than their white
counterparts of the same age-sex group. But 'why as compared to
whites should blacks be better neo-classical optimisers, better
informed, less subject to price or wage illusion, and hence making

better use of the labour market by engaging in a more optimal level of search?'[13]

Alternatively, the argument has been made that since women and minority groups are often shunted to secondary labour markets, leaving may be more frequent, searching for better jobs may be more prolonged and, therefore, unemployment rates higher for these groups. But this kind of labour market behaviour has serious welfare implications, as the resulting unemployment is 'the unproductive consequences of dissatisfaction rather than a rational quest for self-improvement'.[14]

Even if the labour force were comprised of nothing but white males with several years of work experience, there are difficulties with this version of the new view. Thus, everyday experience suggests that leaving in order to engage in off-the-job search will be less efficient than on-the-job search. This is primarily because past employment records are a useful screen for personnel officers to use in selecting job applicants. Leaving one or more previous jobs is very likely to be interpreted as an indication of an unstable character leading to future turnover problems. Moreover, leaving a job is very often not essential for either on-the-job or off-the-job search. A large amount of job information is conveyed through informal information networks such as social gatherings, lunch-hour conversations, professional associations and clubs, and the local pub, etc.[15]

However, even if leaving could be interpreted as a rational, purposive quest for self improvement, the new view just discussed has an air of unreality about it. Data are available that convincingly show most unemployment to be of a totally different nature than assumed in the new view. In the next three sections the analysis focuses on two key dimensions of the current unemployment problem; the reasons for being unemployed and the duration of unemployment spells. Evidence that most unemployment is the result of leaving a job, is of short duration, and within any period of time, say a year, spells are infrequent, would be considered by most economists as evidence supporting the new view that most unemployment is voluntary, even if rates are relatively high. If, on the contrary, most unemployment results from being fired or being unable to find a job,

[13] See A. Hines (1976) The micro-economic foundations of employment and inflation theory: Bad old wine in elegant new bottles, in *The Concept and Measurement of Unemployment* (Ed. G. Worswick), George Allen & Unwin, London, p. 76.

[14] This (unattributed) phrase is quoted by Hines, op. cit., p. 75.

[15] See references cited in Hines, ibid., pp. 72–3.

Part I   Analysis

is of a long-term nature, and if many of the unemployed suffer from multiple spells of unemployment, then a quite different interpretation of the current situation is necessary.

REASONS FOR BEING UNEMPLOYED

Consider the findings of an early study that incorporated the new view of unemployment. This study found that in 1971, a year of high aggregate unemployment, total accessions and separations in US manufacturing exceeded 4 per cent each month.[16] An additional finding was that in 1969 and 1971, 58 and 45 per cent respectively of those unemployed had been unemployed for less than 5 weeks. And those unemployed for more than 26 weeks comprised only 4.7 and 10.4 per cent of the unemployed in 1969 and 1971, respectively. Finally, with regards to causes of unemployment, in 1969 when aggregate unemployment was at a low of 3.5, only about one-third of these were unemployed because they lost their jobs. The remaining two-thirds either left their jobs, had just re-entered the labour force or were new entrants to the labour force.

All of this might seem to suggest that the overwhelming share of unemployment is the result of people moving into and out of the labour force or voluntarily leaving their jobs. Furthermore, with the average duration of unemployment so short, these findings suggest that those moving into unemployment or the labour force need wait but a short time before taking employment. In evaluating these arguments, it is helpful to first trace the unemployment figures over a longer period of time, one that encompasses at least a business cycle. Data in table 8.1 give the behaviour over time of the aggregate

TABLE 8.1   *Unemployment rates by reason, 1970–79*

	1970	*1971*	*1972*	*1973*	*1974*	*1975*	*1976*	*1977*	*1978*	*1979*
Total unemployment rate	4.9	5.9	5.6	4.9	5.6	8.5	7.7	7.0	6.0	5.8
Reasons unemployed:										
Lost last job	2.2	2.8	2.4	1.9	2.4	4.7	3.8	3.2	2.5	2.5
Left last job	0.7	0.7	0.7	0.8	0.8	0.9	0.9	0.9	0.8	0.8
Re-entered labour force	1.5	1.7	1.7	1.5	1.6	2.0	2.0	2.0	1.8	1.7
Never worked before	0.6	0.7	0.8	0.7	0.7	0.9	0.9	1.0	0.9	0.8

Source: Handbook of Labor Statistics, US Department of Labor, December 1980, Table 3.9.

[16] See M. Feldstein (1973) *Lowering the Permanent Rate of Unemployment,* Joint Economic Committee, US Congress, Washington, DC, pp. 11–12.

unemployment rate, and the unemployment rates according to the reason for being unemployed. Clearly the cyclical movements in the aggregate unemployment rate is dominated by the swings in unemployment rates of those losing their jobs. What also stands out is the lack of fluctuation in the rate of persons leaving their jobs. Contrary to the assumption of the new economics of unemployment, the leaving rate does not move counter-cyclically. But of more importance, the extreme version of the new view of unemployment asserts that the rise of unemployment rates from, say, 4.9 per cent in 1973 to 8.5 per cent in 1975 would have to be due to an increase in the rate of frictional unemployment of the same magnitude. Table 8.1 seriously challenges this view in revealing that the unemployment rate of workers leaving their jobs rose from 0.8 to 0.9 per cent during this period. In contrast, the rate of unemployment due to a worker losing his last job rose from 1.9 to 4.7 per cent from 1973 to 1975. This more than accounts for the overall rise in unemployment rates from 4.9 to 8.5 per cent.

MEASURING THE DURATION OF UNEMPLOYMENT

1. *Unemployment spells completed and in progress*

Even more revealing about the nature of unemployment are several recent detailed studies focusing on the duration of unemployment. The duration of unemployment is a dimension of unemployment that well describes the personal welfare loss of being without a job. The official government statistics on duration in the UK and the USA are based on monthly surveys in which persons without a job, but looking for work, are asked how long they have been looking for work. Thus, they measure the length of a spell of unemployment that is still in progress. A better measure of loss of welfare based on the duration of unemployment is obviously the length of a completed spell of unemployment. Various methods have been devised for estimating the latter from data obtained in monthly surveys. Depending upon the method of estimating, the average length of a completed spell has been found to differ substantially from the average length of an unemployment spell still in progress.[17] Table 8.2 gives an esti-

---

[17] See N. Bowers (1980) Probing the issues of unemployment duration, *Monthly Labor Review*, July; and K. Clark and L. Summers (1979) Labor market dynamics and unemployment: A reconsideration, *Brookings Papers on Economic Activity*, No. 1.

TABLE 8.2   *Estimated completed spells of unemployment by duration of unemployment, 1968–79*

		Number of weeks unemployed				Expected duration of a completed spell (weeks)
Year	Total spells	Less than 5	5–10	11–14	15–26	More than 26	
1968	21 587	12 372	4474	1272	1510	964	6.8
1969	21 841	13 718	4503	1371	1434	815	6.7
1970	27 323	16 445	5933	1711	2075	1159	7.7
1971	31 002	16 503	6962	2353	2945	2230	8.3
1972	31 023	16 755	6729	2024	2981	2534	8.0
1973	29 661	17 018	6267	1895	2520	1961	7.5
1974	32 854	19 330	7092	2017	2077	1738	8.0
1975	41 012	19 496	9110	3341	4908	4156	9.8
1976	39 613	18 926	8527	2760	4193	5207	9.5
1977	39 878	19 874	9091	2774	3998	4141	8.9
1978	37 480	20 183	8163	2601	3554	2979	8.3
1979	37 126	20 691	8321	2597	3288	2229	8.3

Source: N. Bowers (1980) Probing the issues of unemployment duration, *Monthly Labor Review,* July, Table 3.

mated distribution of completed unemployment spells by number of weeks unemployed, together with the estimated or expected average duration of all completed spells in any year from 1968 to 1979 in the USA. Taking the years 1969 and 1971, table 8.2 reveals that unemployment spells of less than 5 weeks comprise 63 and 53 per cent of all unemployment spells, respectively, while spells of those unemployed for more than 26 weeks comprised 4 and 7 per cent, respectively of all unemployment spells. Even when long-term unemployment is treated as any spell over 14 weeks, long-term spells comprise only 11 and 16 per cent of all spells in 1969 and 1971, respectively.[18]

According to the new view, data such as that in table 8.2 support the belief in 'an active labour market in which almost everyone who is out of work can find his usual type of job in relatively short time'.[19] In other words, benign neglect will do quite well.

[18] Feldstein in the study referred to in fn. 16 uses spells in progress, not completed spells, in arriving at his figures.

[19] See M. Feldstein, op. cit., p. 11.

TABLE 8.3   *Expected duration of a completed spell of unemployment (weeks)*

	1969	1971	1975	1978	1979
All workers	6.7	8.3	9.8	8.3	8.3
Persistent jobseekers	8.7	11.8	14.7	11.6	11.4

Source: N. Bowers (1980) Probing the issues of unemployment duration, *Monthly Labor Review*, July, Table 2.

2. *Persistent versus discouraged jobseekers*

However, such benign conclusions are decidedly unwarranted even if attention is focused on years of low-aggregate unemployment rates. First, it has been found that almost one-half of all unemployment spells end by withdrawal from the labour force.[20] Table 8.3 gives figures for the estimated average duration of unemployment of two kinds; first, the conventional measure which considers unemployment to be terminated either when a worker finds a job *or* leaves the labour force; and second, a calculation that considers unemployment to be terminated only when another job is found, the unemployment of the 'persistent' jobseekers. The differences in duration range from 2 years or $2/6.7 = 30$ per cent in a boom year such as 1969 to 4.9 years of $4.9/9.8 = 50$ per cent in a recession year such as 1975.

Table 8.3 suggests that, unless it can be argued that withdrawal from the labour force has nothing to do with the lack of prospect of finding a job (i.e. is truly voluntary), duration of completed spells is a misleading indicator of the difficulty of finding a job. A test suggested for determining whether withdrawals from the labour force of the unemployed are voluntary or not is to what extent their probability of withdrawing mirrors the probability of those employed withdrawing. It has been estimated that the probability of withdrawal from the labour force when unemployed is of the order of magnitude of six to seven times that of withdrawal when employed. This led to the conclusion that only a small share, roughly one-

[20] See Clark and Summers, op. cit. For a similar finding using British and Canadian data see B. Main (1981) The length of employment and unemployment in Great Britain, *Scottish Journal of Political Economy*, June; and A. Hasan and P. de Broucker (1982) Duration and concentration of unemployment, *The Canadian Journal of Economics*, November.

seventh to one-sixth, of the unemployed voluntarily withdrew from the labour force.[21]

3. *Multiple spells*

The arbitrariness in making a sharp distinction between the unemployed and discouraged workers is seen in another way. Not only are most withdrawals from the labour force involuntary, a recent study has found that this kind of withdrawal is shortly followed by re-entry into the labour force. All of this suggests that what is in fact one long spell of unemployment is picked up in the statistics as two relatively short spells.[22] Table 8.4 shows the results of an attempt to determine multiple spells of unemployment by questioning respondents to a survey on their work experience over the entire previous year. As is clear from the last column, a large percentage of those unemployed during any year experienced multiple spells of unemployment. The middle three columns indicate that the estimates of average duration of unemployment shown in table 8.2 underestimate the duration of being out of work. First, the multiplicity of spells is not picked up in the duration figures of table 8.2. Thus the total unemployment in any year of this multiple spell group is underestimated. Second, Table 8.4 reveals that for persons actually experiencing only one spell of unemployment over a calendar year, it is of longer duration than the average duration of a spell for those with multiple spells. Since table 8.2 figures are an average of those having single spells and those who have multiple spells, the duration of spells of the former are also underestimated.[23]

4. *The distribution of weighted unemployment spells*

But disallowing these types of problems, the use of such data as in table 8.2 to infer the difficulty of finding a job, the nature of turnover and the distribution of unemployment is still seriously misleading.

---

[21] See G. Perry (1972) Unemployment flows in the U.S. labor market, *Brookings Papers on Economic Activity,* No. 2, pp. 270–5.
    Some economists, unlike other social scientists, are able to discount any serious loss of personal welfare stemming from this sort of exit from the labour force. After all discouraged workers have 'free choice' in the matter. This argument springs from the same source as that which asserts that even if fired, a person can always find 'some' job.
[22] See Clark and Summers, op. cit., p. 31.
[23] This point is also made by G. Akerlof (1979) The case against conservative macroeconomics: An inaugural lecture, *Economica,* August, p. 229.

TABLE 8.4 Average duration of unemployment by spells of unemployment, for all persons with some work experience, 1967–78

Year	Total duration of unemployment (weeks) for people with:			Average spell length (weeks) for people with:			Total number of spells (thousands)†	Per cent unemployed with more than one spell
	1 spell	2 spells	3 spells or more*	1 spell	2 spells	3 spells or more		
1967	7.6	13.3	16.5	7.6	6.7	4.7	16 449	31.6
1968	7.2	13.3	16.5	7.2	6.7	4.7	15 681	31.0
1969	7.5	12.4	16.5	7.5	6.2	4.7	16 719	32.2
1970	10.0	15.4	19.1	10.0	7.7	5.5	20 489	33.6
1971	11.8	17.6	20.4	11.8	8.8	5.8	21 515	32.5
1972	11.2	16.4	19.4	11.2	8.2	5.5	20 855	32.6
1973	9.7	15.2	18.3	9.7	7.6	5.2	20 325	32.4
1974	9.8	15.7	18.0	9.8	7.9	5.1	25 569	36.0
1975	14.4	19.2	19.4	14.4	9.6	5.6	27 422	31.3
1976	13.8	18.4	20.3	13.8	9.2	5.8	27 405	32.7
1977	12.9	17.1	18.8	12.9	8.6	5.4	26 399	32.6
1978	12.0	16.1	18.1	12.0	8.1	5.2	24 400	32.5

Source: N. Bowers (1980) Probing the issues of unemployment duration, Monthly Labor Review, July, Table 5.
* Assumes average of 3.5 spells.
† Excludes persons who looked for work but did not work.

For example, it was already mentioned that in 1969, 63 per cent of all unemployment spells lasted less than 5 weeks while only 4 per cent continued beyond 26 weeks. From this it can be correctly inferred that most people experience short spells of unemployment. But the short spells may be so short and the long spells so long, that most of the total weeks of unemployment in any year may be experienced by a small minority of the unemployed. Thus, if the spells of unemployment are weighted by the average number of weeks of unemployment within each spell group and summed, a figure is obtained for the total weeks of unemployment experienced within a year. Let this form the denominator of a fraction, the numerator of which is the number of spells of some length multiplied by the average weeks of unemployment in that spell group. This ratio then express the percentage of all weeks of unemployment during the year experienced by each spell group.

Table 8.5 is relevant in this regard. Section A of the table reveals that in 1969, a year of prosperity, 8.5 million people experienced unemployment. This can be contrasted with 'All groups' in the recession years of 1974 and 1975 when 14.1 and 17.4 million workers experienced some unemployment. However, the numbers in the rows under sections B and C are of more interest. Beginning with 1969, and taking all groups of unemployed, the last two rows in section C indicate that 15.8 per cent of all the weighted unemployment spells were 40 weeks or more while $34.9 = 19.1 + 15.8$ per cent of these weighted spells lasted more than 26 weeks. In comparison, during the recession year of 1975, 32.5 per cent of such unemployment was due to spells lasting more than 40 weeks and 54.8 per cent was due to spells lasting more than 26 weeks. These results can be stated somewhat differently. In a year of relative prosperity, 1969, almost one-sixth of all unemployment experienced during the year resulted from people unemployed for over 40 weeks and about 35 per cent from people unemployed for over 6 months. In a recession year, 1975, almost one-third of the unemployment results from the experience of people out of work for 40 or more weeks and over one-half from people out of work at least 6 months.

The rows under section B of the table indicate how concentrated was the unemployment in another way. For example, in 1969 15.8 per cent of the unemployment that lasted more than 40 weeks was experienced by only 0.4 per cent of the labour force while about 35 per cent of the unemployment fell upon 1.1 per cent of the labour force, those unemployed for more than 26 weeks. The column figures for 1975 in section B reveal how small a percentage of the labour force had to bear the long-term unemployment of a recession year.[24]

Table 8.5 contains additional information that combines the unemployment spell with the duration of weeks outside the labour force for those listing 'unable to find work' or 'looking for work'. Thus the duration figures for 'non-employed' persons are the combined length of the search and spells of withdrawal due to discouragement. For example, in 1974 over 41 per cent of non-employment was non-employment of 40 weeks or more (section E) and this was experienced by just 2.5 per cent of the labour force (section D).

In sum:

The preceding tabulations suggest that most unemployment is the result of a relatively small part of the population suffering repeated, extended spells. The unemployment rate is high even at full employment because a few people are out of work for much of the year. The dominant theoretical views of unemployment fail to explain this concentration that characterizes actual experiences in labour markets.[25]

Rather than 'normal turnover' (short spells of unemployment followed by employment) characterizing unemployment, with unemployment being 'passed around' as the new microeconomics of unemployment would have us believe, in good years and bad most unemployment is of long duration, highly concentrated and hardly the result of a rational quest for self-improvement. This is especially true for recession years like 1975 as already seen. It is even more true today. Thus the duration data, like the data on reasons for being unemployed, indicate that the new view of unemployment is highly misleading. For:

if we stopped counting as unemployed all those persons with less than five weeks of unemployment during the year, the measured unemployment rate would fall only from 6 percent to 5.75 percent. By contrast, if we stopped counting those with six months or more, the unemployment rate would fall from 6 percent to 3.5 percent.[26]

What was true in the mid-1970s is even more true today and in more than one country. 'Thus, although there may be many short spells of

---

[24] Similar results are found in Bowers (1979) The theory of the cost of inflation, in *Inflation, Development and Integration: Essays in Honour of A. J. Brown* (Ed. J. Bowers), Leeds.

[25] Clark and Summers, op. cit., p. 46.

[26] ibid., pp. 71–2.

TABLE 8.5 Characteristics and distribution of unemployment and non-employment by demographic group, 1974, and for all groups, 1969 and 1975

| | 1974 | | | | | 1969 | 1975 |
| | Males | | Females | | | | |
Characteristics or distribution	16–19	20 and over	16–19	20 and over	All groups	All groups	All groups
A. Characteristic							
Persons with labour force experience (millions)	2.8	51.3	2.5	37.4	94.0	85.2	94.5
Unemployed persons (millions)	0.9	6.8	0.9	5.5	14.1	8.5	17.4
Average weeks of unemployment per unemployed person	18.6	15.8	14.8	13.9	15.0	12.4	18.8
Non-employed persons (millions)	0.9	6.8	0.9	5.6	14.2	8.7	—
Average weeks of non-employment per non-employed person	25.7	18.9	24.9	18.9	19.9	15.9	—
B. Distribution (percentage of labour force)							
Unemployed persons							
1–4 weeks	6.3	2.5	11.0	5.3	3.7	3.4	3.5
5–14 weeks	9.5	5.1	9.8	5.4	5.3	3.6	5.7
15–26 weeks	8.1	3.4	8.1	3.3	3.4	1.9	4.5
27–39 weeks	4.9	1.3	3.7	1.3	1.4	0.7	2.3
40 weeks or more	3.5	0.9	2.4	0.9	1.0	0.4	2.3

C. Weeks of unemployment (percentage of weeks)

1–4 weeks	2.6	4.4	5.3	5.5	4.2	5.7	2.6
5–14 weeks	16.2	22.6	18.3	31.1	22.4	27.8	15.6
15–26 weeks	27.4	32.7	32.6	27.3	31.7	31.6	27.0
27–39 weeks	26.3	21.0	22.2	17.4	21.1	19.1	22.3
40 weeks or more	27.5	19.3	21.6	18.7	20.7	15.8	32.5

D. Non-employed persons (percentage of labour force)

1–4 weeks	4.2	2.0	6.9	3.9	2.9	—	—
5–14 weeks	7.4	4.5	7.7	4.2	4.5	—	—
15–26 weeks	5.3	3.0	4.9	2.2	2.8	—	—
27–39 weeks	7.0	2.3	5.3	2.0	2.4	—	—
40 weeks or more	9.2	1.6	11.4	2.7	2.5	—	—

E. Weeks of non-employment (percentage of weeks)

1–4 weeks	1.4	2.5	1.8	3.4	2.6	—	—
5–14 weeks	7.5	15.1	7.6	13.7	13.0	—	—
15–26 weeks	11.8	22.8	10.2	15.0	17.7	—	—
27–39 weeks	26.7	29.2	18.3	23.2	25.6	—	—
40 weeks or more	52.2	30.4	62.1	44.6	41.1	—	—

Source: K. B. Clark and L. H. Summers (1979) Labor market dynamics and unemployment: A reconsideration, Brookings Papers on Economic Activity, No. 1, Table 4.

unemployment the majority of unemployment falls in very long spells with the typical week of unemployment falling in a spell of 80 weeks by the late 1970s'.[27]

THE INFLUENCE OF UNEMPLOYMENT BENEFITS

The evidence on duration of unemployment spells and the reasons for being unemployed cast serious doubt on explanations of unemployment framed wholly or even largely in terms of 'frictions in the labour market', 'voluntary search' or 'quests for self-improvement'. The same doubts, naturally, apply to such explanations of the spectacular rise in unemployment rates in the 1970s and 1980s. However, the matter cannot be laid to rest here. Arguments have been made suggesting that during the recent period important 'structural' changes have occurred that can explain the long duration of unemployment as a voluntary choice on the part of the unemployed.[28]

The structural change given most attention is the growth of unemployment benefit programmes. These, it is said, reduce the cost of being unemployed which supposedly lengthens the duration of job search and increases the flows from employment to unemployment. From this emerges an explanation of the recent rise of long-term unemployment (and aggregate unemployment); the increase in unemployment benefits in the late 1960s and 1970s.

Economists in their calculations of the 'costs' of being unemployed are given to emphasizing and often focusing entirely on the financial costs of unemployment, e.g. the difference in income before and during unemployment. The replacement ratio, which measures the ratio of the benefits received (variously defined) while unemployed to net income received from employment is meant to capture this financial burden. The fact that this ratio rose in the 1970s in many countries, thereby reducing the financial costs of unemployment, is seen by many economists as a cause of higher unemployment rates. Voluntary unemployment, at any aggregate rate of unemployment, supposedly rose during this period due to an increased flow of workers from employment to unemployment and a lengthening of the dura-

---

[27] Main, op. cit., p. 163.

[28] A useful comparative study of the Netherlands, Sweden, the UK and the USA is R. Haveman (1978) Unemployment in Western Europe and the United States: A problem of demand, structure, or measurement? *American Economic Review,* May.

tion of unemployment. The rate of unemployment at which all unemployment is voluntary increased as the monetarists would have it.

A vast amount of empirical work, especially in the UK and the USA, has sought to test this proposition.[29] Both microeconometric (cross section) and macroeconometric (time series) techniques have been employed to determine how strong is the influence (if any) of unemployment benefits on employment.

Little evidence has been found that unemployment compensation affects unemployment rates by increasing the flows from employment to unemployment. The results of studies attempting to pick up the impact of unemployment compensation on the duration of unemployment, i.e. whether greater benefits lengthened search, have been less conclusive. However, the microeconometric studies taken as a whole have shown that rising unemployment benefits have only a small (positive) impact on unemployment.[30] The duration of unemployment might be affected but the impact on aggregate unemployment rates slight.[31] What has emerged from these studies is a positive effect on labour force participation rates during a period when benefits rose.[32]

The results of macroeconometric studies have been mixed although some support emerges for a stronger positive impact of benefits on unemployment.[33] There has been wider agreement that structural changes of some kind took place in several countries during the 1970s, that might increase unemployment.[34]

---

[29] Some studies have concentrated on the impact of the maximum duration of unemployment benefits on unemployment. See G. Chaplin (1971) Unemployment insurance, job search and the demand for 'leisure', *Western Economic Journal.* Attempts have also been made to explain the impact on unemployment benefits on lay offs but the evidence is scarce. See B. Walsh (1981) *Unemployment insurance and the labour market: A review of research relating to policy.* Report to OECD, Manpower and Social Affairs, May, p. 26. This section has benefited greatly from Walsh's comprehensive survey.

[30] For a representative UK study see S. Nickell (1979) The effect of unemployment and related benefits on the duration of unemployment, *Economic Journal,* March. A well-known American study is R. Ehrenberg and R. Oaxaca (1976) Unemployment insurance, duration of unemployment and subsequent wage gain, *American Economic Review,* December.

[31] See S. Marston (1975) The impact of unemployment insurance on aggregate unemployment, *Brookings Papers on Economic Activity,* No. 1.

[32] See the various references in Walsh, op. cit.

[33] ibid.

[34] See Haveman, op. cit.

At most, what these studies suggest is that in some countries it is likely that at any rate of unemployment labour markets became tighter in the 1970s. This tightness, however, could have been due to several influences, only one of which supports a view that there was an increase in voluntary unemployment at any rate of total unemployment. The most reasonable conclusion to draw concerning the impact of unemployment benefits is best left to the concluding quotation of a comprehensive survey of many OECD countries.

Whatever conclusions emerge in the longer run from the continuing academic debate about the importance of insurance-induced unemployment, the evidence so far suggests that this phenomenon does exist and should be taken into account in policy evaluations of the rise in officially measured unemployment during the 1970s. However, the evidence lends no support to the more lurid views of the importance of this phenomenon that have gained some popular credence. Moreover, governments have been quick to respond to the spread of this view about unemployment and most of the more glaring loopholes and anomalies in the unemployment insurance systems have been closed. For this reason, the further rise in unemployment that have been recorded in many OECD countries since 1979 should not be regarded as induced by the unemployment insurance system.[35]

Taken together the various studies of the impact of unemployment benefits on unemployment leave little doubt that for most people, unemployment benefits are a safety net in the event of bad economic conditions, not an inducement to substitute leisure for work. Most of the real costs of unemployment, e.g. loss of self-respect and self-esteem, mental breakdowns, broken homes, suicides and battered wives and children, are ignored by economists. Other social scientists, more prone to working with primary data and more willing to deal with the unemployed, have not been so limited in their perspectives. Field workers have long recognized unemployment for what it is, a cause of all kinds of socio- and psychopathology that would only multiply without unemployment benefits.

But while one can be grateful that modern capitalism has seen fit to provide a safety net for the unemployed through unemployment benefits (and an important built-in stabilizer), two unfortunate side effects of this aspect of 'humane' capitalism must be noted. The lack of urgency in finding alternative methods of combating inflation is

[35] Walshe, op. cit., p. 57.

the more obvious. Using restrictive aggregate demand policies as the main instrument in the anti-inflation fight becomes more acceptable when unemployment has allegedly a lower 'cost' today. Less obvious, but not less important, is the likely long-run effects of unemployment benefits when combined with prolonged periods of stagnation. When prolonged and frequent spells of unemployment become common over an extended period of time, non-work becomes increasingly a 'normal' way of life for younger members of the labour force. As a result, if unemployment benefits have not proved to be an important factor contributing to the higher rates of unemployment of the 1970s and early 1980s, a continuation of the current stagnation will fulfil the wildest fantasies of many economists writing on the unemployment problem today.

CONCLUSIONS

There is no need to have unlimited faith in econometrics to draw the one sensible conclusion from what has been said. The studies of the impact of unemployment benefits on unemployment, the findings on long-term unemployment and its response to increased aggregate unemployment rates and the causes of unemployment, all lead to the conclusion that the spectacular rise in unemployment rates over the past decade have been due primarily to inadequate aggregate demand. All this is but in keeping with the more abstract arguments of chapter 5. Whatever is meant by the currently fashionable expression 'the failure of Keynesian economics', it cannot mean that Keynesian economics is incapable of explaining most of the fluctuations in unemployment rates in modern capitalist economies. Furthermore, even much of the so-called structural unemployment can be seen to have its origin in a lack of sufficient aggregate demand. Higher levels of aggregate demand induce technological changes and additional on-the-job training that bring the skills of the labour force more in line with skill requirements of the available jobs. There is no reason to believe that this would not have been the case over the past decade had aggregate demand pressures been greater.[36]

The latest OECD forecast predicts unemployment will reach almost 35 million by the middle of 1984.[37]

[36] It was a widely held view in the USA in the late 1950s and early 1960s that unemployment rates were unusually high (for that time) because of various structural factors. This view lost much of its popularity during the boom of the second half of the 1960s.

[37] See *Economic Outlook,* December 1982, Table 15.

PART II

Policy

Introduction

What part I has described is nothing less than economic breakdown in the developed capitalist countries. The last decade has seen growth grind to a halt, unemployment high and rising, while inflation continues to be a major concern. Keynes' *General Theory* was written in response to another major breakdown, revealed largely in terms of mass unemployment. The problem as he rightly saw it arose as part of the natural evolution of capitalism; a failure of industrialized capitalist economies to automatically generate enough aggregate demand to provide full employment. The solution as he also rightly saw it was for government intervention to correct the demand deficiencies of the private sector.

What the early chapters argued was that full employment, affluent capitalism generates new problems. What this more modern form of capitalism suffers from is a propensity to overspend, not just at full employment but even when the economy still has a good deal of slack. However, the notion of overspending must be interpreted with some care. The problem is not that prices are pulled up because of an excess of aggregate demand at or near full employment. Rather it is that as the economy moves towards full employment, different groups intensify their efforts to increase their share of income (through price and wage increases) in order to increase their demands on output.

As events of the early 1970s made clear, once this inflationary bias was revealed in a noticeable acceleration of inflation rates, governments responded with restrictive aggregate demand policies. This had one unambiguous effect; it led to an increase in unemployment rates and, as discussed in chapter 10, it was also largely responsible for a reduction in rates of growth of productivity. The additional restrictive measures undertaken almost everywhere in response to balance of payments difficulties, brought on by OPEC, only accentuated these policy-induced problems.

1. *Output symmetries – inflation asymmetries*

In the pages to follow it is argued that the correct policy response is not for governments to cut back aggregate demand, as such a policy will always generate adverse unemployment effects. This is due to a basic asymmetry in the manner in which modern capitalist systems work, a matter discussed in chapters 6 and 7. Increases in aggregate demand, other things being equal, have a greater impact on price and wage increases than comparable decreases in aggregate demand have on price and wage decreases. If an economy is to function at all well, the earlier message was that policy must be structured in such a way as to cope with this basic asymmetry, and this requires even more government intervention than Keynes envisaged if full employment is to be realized again.

The failure of restrictive demand policies to curb inflation without a painful, prolonged period of high unemployment has been partly responsible for the allegation that 'Keynesian economics has been proven wrong'. Supposedly if aggregate demand stimulation could solve unemployment problems, symmetry requires that restrictive policies should handle inflation difficulties. Since such a symmetry is clearly lacking today, this somehow 'proves' that the Keynesian emphasis on aggregate demand is incorrect. However, the existence of asymmetrical responses of wages and prices in no way disproves the Keynesian view of the output and employment effects of changes in aggregate demand. Increases and decreases in aggregate demand have symmetrical (Keynesian) output and employment impacts.

Because he wrote at the bottom of the Great Depression, Keynes was not concerned with all the implications of wage and price asymmetries. Thus, while he saw that downward money wage rigidity is and was an important fact of life that has much to do with the absence of any mechanism automatically generating full employment, he did not develop the implications of this asymmetry (or others discussed in chapters 5 and 6) for anti-inflationary policies. The correct inference to draw is not that stagflation indicates that demand management or 'activism' must be rejected. Changes in aggregate demand do affect the real sector. Rather the conclusion to be drawn is that demand management is a most unsuitable instrument for reducing inflation.

2. *The overloaded economy*

Policy-induced recessions have also been responsible for the increased popularity of another current view, that of an 'overloaded political economy'. In such an economy, the growing demands of the different economic groups outstrip the growing capacity of the economy to supply goods and services to satisfy these needs. Obviously, under stagnating conditions, actual output declines or at least shows slower growth. If demand is not cut back simultaneously, then just as obviously there is an overloading of the economy. However, those affirming the arrival of an overloaded political economy and the related notion of 'crowding out' have something more definite in mind than this. As some assert, especially those of monetarist persuasion, the advent of stagnation accentuates a problem that has been developing for some time. And this is, not only have demands upon the economy been outpacing its ability to satisfy all of them, but also the resulting overload can only be dealt with by reducing the size of the public sector. The government is the enemy according to this view. Nowhere has this been more evident than in the UK and the USA.

Now it may be true that the large defence budget of the USA goes some way in explaining its relative economic decline. Furthermore, it is not to be doubted that a 'zero-sum society', in which slow growth requires that the gains of one group be at the expense of another, raises fundamental problems for economic and political stability. In the secular world of today the very legitimacy of distribution outcomes has increasingly been questioned. Rising per capita incomes have until recently acted to attenuate this potential source of instability. With growth absent, potential distributional inequities can no longer be reconciled by allowing all to receive a share of the benefits of growth. However, it will be maintained here that cutting back on the welfare state, far from solving distributional conflict, will make matters worse. It will lead to more divisiveness, not less, and make cooperation in the interests of returning to some kind of growth situation near impossible.

1. *Alternative policies*

The remaining chapters of the book deal with programmes and policies aimed at attacking the stagflation problem. This involves a consideration of policies that not only aim to relieve an economy of an overload or stagnation but policies that are put forward with a view to curbing inflation. Chapter 9 begins with a brief discussion of some of the implications of an overloaded economy followed by an equally brief discussion of a rather defeatist 'solution' to the current difficulties: a policy of stagnation without inflation. Chapter 9 then considers the first of two types of programmes that have only one important point in common. Both programmes profess to offer a means of simultaneously resolving the inflation and the stagnation problems.

The chapter evaluates a programme for attacking stagflation that involves greater reliance on the 'market', together with a cutback on government expenditures and taxes as a means of combating both inflation and stagnation. Advocates of this class of policies see the stagnation of today not as the result of a lack of effective demand but more the result of a 'lack of market incentives', 'bad management', 'the encroachment of the welfare state', etc. As a result, these policies can rightly be considered part of 'supply-side economics' as they envisage an attack on the stagnation problem as the first step. Stimulate productivity growth first and that will be a means to bringing down inflation.

2. *The goal of full employment*

Chapter 10 outlines the beginnings of a policy package for attacking stagflation that is entirely different. It offers a programme for achieving full employment, price and wage stability and higher productivity growth based on an understanding of markets and the inflationary process found appropriate in the earlier chapters. This programme stresses less reliance on the market and greater government intervention as the only possible way out of stagflation. Far from having a beneficial effect on inflation and productivity, cutting back on the welfare state is seen as disturbance amplifying. Such reductions increase inflationary pressures at full employment and reduce long-run productivity growth at any level of employment. Instead, this programme charts a return to full employment through stimulative aggregate demand policies as a precondition of productivity growth and an end to an overload.

Clearly, productivity growth is the basis for rising per capita incomes, private and public consumption and an exit from the zero-sum society. A preliminary step in stimulating productivity is a return to full employment. In their concern with the resumption of growth, economists and politicians alike have overlooked a simple truth that would not be lost upon businessmen. Productivity growth depends upon investment, especially the innovative kind, but there is little incentive to invest when firms and economies are plagued, as today, with so much excess capacity and low profits. Only by the elimination of excess capacity will businessmen be made aware of the profitability of investment. In this important sense such policies can be thought of as examples of 'demand-side economics'.

3. *Price stability and full employment*

However, it is extremely unlikely that the governments of the OECD countries will implement full-employment policies unless inflationary pressures at full employment have been greatly reduced first. Because of this, the reduction of inflationary pressures is a precondition of productivity growth rather than (as under the 'market solution') its result. Since a restimulation of the economy will by itself only intensify inflationary pressures eventually, even if there is a sizeable productivity response to improved demand conditions and other policies, instruments of policy that lead to price and wage stability at full employment are required. Central banks, international financial institutions and the financial community in general must be convinced that full employment need not bring renewed inflation. In chapters 11 and 12 the consequences of wage and price asymmetries for the control of inflation at full employment are treated; a permanent incomes policy is advocated. The nature of this policy will necessarily vary from country to country because of the presence of vastly different institutions. However, in all cases a voluntary, long-run policy is put forward. Emphasis is on the permanent nature of an incomes policy (although initially temporary statutory incomes policies may be needed). This is in keeping with an earlier conclusion. The permanent structural changes that have overtaken modern economies and will not permit full employment and price stability to be realized simultaneously, given current collective bargaining arrangements in the various countries.

4. *Productivity growth*

However, there is no guarantee that the reduction of unemployment
and excess capacity will in itself ensure enough productivity growth
to attenuate distributional issues. What is also required is an industrial policy aimed at relieving economies of supply constraints. To
put it otherwise, there is a legitimate sense in which 'supply-side
policies' in contrast to 'supply-side economics' have an important
role to play. Unlike the versions put forward by the Thatcher and
Reagan administrations, the supply policy offered below does not
increase the degree of inequality in the distribution of incomes.
Rather it is an industrial policy that aims to increase the response of
an economy to demand pressures without reducing taxes for the rich
and benefits for the poor.

Chapter 13 is concerned with developing policies that stimulate
productivity and real-wage growth. Such industrial policies are
important because they enhance labour's support for an incomes
policy and help prevent the dismantling of the welfare state. Successful industrial policies are also required to handle balance of payments constraints, a matter also discussed in chapter 13.

Thus, policy must relieve not only supply constraints in the ordinary sense; i.e. allow a more rapid rate of growth of maximum
output. Policies must also be designed to raise any balance of payments ceiling or constraint that is likely to develop in the process of
moving to full employment. This task has been made extremely difficult by the heavy dependence upon foreign sources of energy. A
successful policy of energy independence is a critical part of any
complete anti-stagflation policy. Almost as important are commodity price stabilization and manpower policies. None of these has
been developed here. References are made, however, to other policy
studies in these areas which indicate the manner in which the programme outlined here may be easily supplemented.

5. *The end of the line*

Unfortunately, in order to obtain a favourable supply response, in
particular to stimulate a more rapid growth in productivity, the
entire industrial relations system may need revamping. This may be
and probably is an impossible task in some societies and, as a result,
they are most likely doomed to stagflation or, more likely, stagnation for some time to come. What the post-war record of the more

successful economies should have taught us is that the kind of adversarial industrial relations system found in the English-speaking countries is and has been a definite liability in their efforts to achieve a decent economic performance.

For example, until recently the USA has been considered a model of efficiency and an example to be imitated in formulating a policy for raising productivity and incomes. However, in a dynamic sense the evidence points to the relative inefficiency of the American economy. Rates of growth of productivity in the USA have been low enough to rank it at the bottom of the productivity growth league for over 30 years. This can be attributed in large part to its conflict-oriented industrial relations system. The relatively high levels of per capita income found today in the USA (and other English-speaking countries) can, in fact, be traced to relatively high initial per capita income levels during the early phases of its industrialization effort. This, in turn, can be attributed to such things as an abundance of good agricultural land and raw materials and a large and expanding domestic market. It is the contention of this study that without these 'gifts of nature', income levels would be relatively low in the USA today. Efforts to alter an industrial relations system towards the cooperative 'continental model' outlined in chapters 11 and 12 are an essential part of a policy to improve productivity in many countries.

THE POLITICAL ECONOMY OF STAGFLATION

The policy advocated in chapters 10 to 13 is framed around the desirability and importance of achieving full employment. From what has already been said it is clear that this programme must be one that can work within an institutional context of strong, affluent unions, and a reasonably generous welfare state. The policy package to be put forward is only an outline, however, with a deliberate neglect of much of the institutional detail that must be taken into consideration in individual economies if the programme is to work. This neglect is partly in the interest of brevity, but can be defended in more important ways. The case for the kinds of policies advocated here can be strengthened if the analysis proceeds at a level of generality that indicates their appropriateness in any developed capitalist economy. Furthermore, the correct policy response must be said clearly and simply, given the widespread acceptance today of policies to combat stagflation that are so perverse in their impact.

Moreover, a general policy recommendation can be valuable because of two important considerations, one already discussed. The earlier chapters argued that the inflationary mechanism at work in the different capitalist economies is in all essentials the same. The correct anti-inflation (and stagnation) policy will therefore be similar even though there are important institutional and political differences across countries and this point should be emphasized. Of equal importance is the belief that any policy of successfully combating stagflation requires wide acceptance of that policy and this involves strong, intelligent, conciliatory, political leadership. If this kind of political leadership is available, then given a limited number of institutional and political constraints that cannot be ignored and which are explicitly considered in outlining the policy, the correct detailed economic form of the anti-stagflation policy will be found by a trial-and-error process. But without that leadership, it is difficult to think of any policy that can bring us out of stagflation. In that one important sense alone stagflation is a political problem as much as it is an economic one.

AN ERA OF PERPETUAL STAGNATION

Admittedly, what has just been put forward involves a rather radical change in institutions and outlooks but consider the likely alternative. Assume that current restrictive policies eventually succeed in bringing down inflation. This will be accomplished primarily by increasing unemployment to double-digit rates and keeping them there for some time. Expectedly, union membership will fall off during the process and efforts will be (and have been) made to break down the system of wage bargaining based on 'fairness'. Arguments by labour that wage settlements be based on cost-of-living considerations and wage settlements elsewhere, i.e. relativities, will be downgraded and ignored and the weakened position of workers *vis-à-vis* employers will be reflected in reduced wage settlements. Meantime, productivity growth will have stagnated as the zero-sum condition persists.

If and when the rate of wage and price inflation is finally brought under control, two choices are available to the authorities. They can either keep unemployment rates high out of fear of renewed inflation or, related, a payments problem, in which case inflation will be cured but stagnation will continue. The performance of the British economy between the wars provides a useful comparison. On the other hand, feeling that labour has learned its lesson, and business as well for that matter, a policy of stimulative aggregate demand policy can then be undertaken. Unemployment and excess capacity rates will start to decline, profits will rise and a boom will get underway. Unfortunately very soon after this reversal of policy has been in force, labour will become more aggressive, not just because its market power will be enhanced but in order to recoup past losses and to 'get even'. Business will increasingly acquiesce to higher wage demands to keep profitable conditions going and accelerated inflation will set in. All this, it is maintained, will take place long before anything like full employment is achieved. At some point either a policy along the lines suggested in chapters 10 to 13 will have to be adopted or restrictive policies put in force once more. If the latter, a period of stagnation again results.

As already admitted, all this is speculative but certainly no more so than the belief that inflation can be permanently cured by restricting aggregate demand. For almost a decade now governments have been telling us that they could see the 'light at the end of the tunnel', that current restrictive policies were 'just about to make a difference' and that 'it would be a pity to give up now since the main costs have already been borne', etc. Ten years is long enough, surely, to 'test' policies now in effect. Working out a sensible, equitable solution to stagflation along the lines suggested will be difficult to be sure. It will certainly require much wider support than is now present for such a reorientation in policy. But one of the essential conditions for success in overcoming inflation is that we discard the ineffectual and divisive policies now being pursued. They are based on an erroneous view of the way real-world economies work and condemn us to economic decline.

Chapter 14 considers the likely possibility that policy makers in the USA will (perhaps inadvertently) adopt a policy of stagnation. This scenario closely resembles Kalecki's theory of the political business cycle in which out of fear of inflation and the power of unions at full employment, governments deliberately choose to run the economies at high enough rates of unemployment to permanently keep down inflation.[1] The result, expectedly, is long-run stagnation in the USA and a recreation there of conditions similar to those of the early stages of industrialization of the various OECD countries. It is also pointed out how such a policy greatly increases the difficulties of ending stagnation elsewhere. The concluding chapter contains some suggestions for dealing with the American response.

[1] This is Kalecki's theory of the 'Political Business Cycle'. See M. Kalecki (1971) Political aspects of full employment, *Selected Essays on the Dynamics of the Capitalist Economy*, Cambridge University Press, Cambridge.

CHAPTER 9

Supply-side Economics

CROWDING OUT AND OVERLOADING

1. *Introduction*

Often those emphasizing the 'overloading' of an economy, in which demands on output consistently exceed supplies, assume that a resumption of steady growth is no longer possible even if inflation is brought under control. Various reasons are given. A permanent shift in income away from profits is foreseen, leading to a drying up of investment funds and slowing productivity growth; a shift in output towards services supposedly leads to an additional source of decline in productivity and output growth; and rising energy prices intensify this general deterioration. Whatever the cause, an overload by definition can only be relieved if some claims are reduced. For example, what might be termed the 'defeatist market' view has it that in the modern commercial world of today, the average citizen will not tolerate a slowing down in the growth of his after-tax real income (let alone an actual decline in its level). In the face of a need and desire to maintain private consumption, non-military public expenditures must therefore be cut back. Modern economies can no longer afford the welfare state according to this view.

The notion of an overloaded political economy is often merged with the assertion that the large and growing government deficits or even simply large and growing government expenditures 'crowd out' private expenditures, especially investment. Since the latter is a prime source of productivity growth, increased government activities retard growth according to this view by crowding out investment. The defeatist market solution to the crowding out of investment is the same as its solution to an overload; reduce any deficit and cut back government spending and taxes. However, it must be made clear that the overloading of an economy is not necessarily the same as crowding out certain types of spending. This distinction is made clear below.

2. Budget deficits and crowding out

Consider first a recent course of events as outlined in table 9.1. Total government budgetary surpluses (in parentheses) and budgetary deficits as a percentage of total economic activity are shown for several OECD countries. Over time, the typical pattern in the different countries is one in which the budget either moves from surplus to deficit or moves to a greater deficit. Data for central government budgets reveal similar patterns. Also of interest are the relatively large deficits experienced by Japan and West Germany in the 1970s, by agreement two of the best-managed economies.

Much confusion has arisen over the causes of the rising government deficits throughout the OECD. In some circles, rising deficits were supposed to reflect fiscal 'looseness' and run-away government expenditures. As a matter of fact the rate of growth of government expenditures in most of the OECD economies slowed down in the

TABLE 9.1 *Deficits of government as percentage of GDP*[a] *1970–80*

Country	1970	1971	1972	1973	1974	1975	1976	1977	1978	1979	1980
USA	1.9	2.6	1.2	0.3	1.0	5.0	2.9	1.7	0.8	0.3	0.5
Japan	(1.4)[c]	(0.8)	0.3	(0.3)	0.1	2.3	4.3	4.2	6.5	5.0	4.5
West Germany	0.1	0.6	1.0	(0.7)	1.9	6.3	4.1	3.0	3.2	3.5	4.1
France	(0.1)	0	0.1	(0.1)	0.3	3.2	1.5	1.6	2.0	1.7	0.8
UK	(1.4)	(0.2)	3.0	4.8	5.1	6.2	6.3	4.7	5.5	4.5	4.2
Italy	3.8	5.5	7.7	7.4	7.3	12.0	9.3	8.2	10.1	9.8	8.1
Canada	0.5	1.3	1.3	0.4	(0.4)	3.9	3.1	4.0	4.6	3.2	3.6
Austria	(0.3)	(0.6)	(0.5)	0.6	0.3	3.6	4.4	4.1	n.a.	3.2	2.6
Belgium	1.3	2.3	3.3	2.7	1.8	4.1	4.8	5.0	5.4	6.2	8.4
Denmark	(1.5)	(2.4)	(3.1)	(5.2)	(3.9)	2.1	1.0	n.a.	n.a.	n.a.	n.a.
Netherlands	1.5	1.2	0.7	(0.5)	0.8	3.4	3.1	2.1	2.9	3.7	5.0
Norway	(2.5)	(3.6)	(3.8)	(5.2)	(3.9)	(3.0)	(2.4)	(0.8)	0.3	(0.9)	(4.9)
Sweden	(3.1)	(4.1)	(3.3)	(3.0)	(0.7)	(1.6)	(3.4)	(0.5)	1.7	8.2	8.6
Switzerland[b]	(5.2)	(4.3)	(4.5)	(4.6)	(4.2)	(3.4)	(3.6)	(3.3)	(3.7)	(2.9)	(3.2)

Source: *Economic Outlook*, OECD, December 1981 and July 1982.
[a] Deficit = Total outlays – Current receipts.
  Total outlays consist of current disbursements (final consumption expenditures, interest on the public debt, subsidies, and social security transfers to households) plus gross capital formation.
  Current receipts consist of direct and indirect taxes, and social security contributions paid by employers and employees.
[b] Only current disbursements.
[c] The figures shown in parentheses are surpluses.

1970s compared with the 1960s.[1] However, given the importance of direct taxes in the OECD countries, the stagnation of the 1970s and 1980s could be expected to result in a decline or at least less growth of tax receipts. With an unchanged tax structure this, other things equal, would act to increase the size of the deficit.

These events are illustrated in comparative static terms in figure 9.1. The IS curve shift from IS_0 to IS_1 along LM_0 can be interpreted

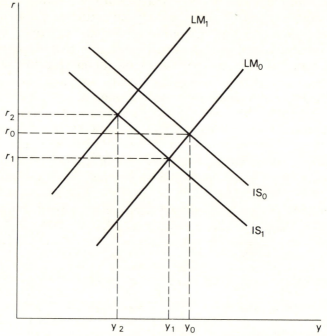

FIGURE 9.1   *Interest rates and budget deficits*

as the result of a leftward shift of the investment–demand curve in response to the stagnating demand conditions of the recent period. The result is a decline in income from y_0 to y_1, and a fall in interest rates from r_0 to r_1. Holding government spending constant, the decline in income will result in a fall in tax receipts and an increase in the government deficit. But a rise in the deficit because of depressed aggregate demand conditions can hardly be interpreted as fiscal looseness. Instead it reflects the built-in stabilizing properties of modern capitalist economies.

[1] See F. Gould (1982) The development of public expenditures in Sweden: A comparative view, *Skandinaviska Enskilda Banken Quarterly Review*, No. 3.

Moreover, tight monetary policies were followed in many of the OECD countries until late in 1982 partly because of an alleged looseness of fiscal policy, and this would act to increase the deficit further. This can be shown in figure 9.1 in the following way. Allow for a decrease in the nominal stock of money which leads to a shift in the LM curve from LM_0 to LM_1 along IS_1. The rise in interest rates from r_1 to r_2 will lead to a decline in investment and, therefore, income. The fall in income from y_1 to y_2 will then cut further into tax receipts thereby increasing the deficit further. Thus, to attribute large deficits (large, that is, in absolute size) to fiscal 'looseness' is to miss a few essential points. The deficits recently being experienced throughout the OECD were reflecting the poor performance of the private sector, partly induced by tight monetary policies (until recently). Related, the high interest rates should be seen as a cause of the large deficits and not vice versa.

Monetary policy eased in many countries by 1983 but the pre-occupation, particularly in North America, with the deficit continued. The concern with the absolute size of the deficit (rather than the deficit as a share of GNP) and a lack of understanding of the causes of current deficits have suggested a 'need' for fiscal restraint, which is usually interpreted as a cutback in government expenditures or an increase in tax rates.

Most unfortunately for those affected by these policies, attempts to balance the budget under present circumstances can only worsen the unemployment picture and lead to a further slump in investment from its present depressed state. Thus, if a realistic view is taken of the determinants of investment, allowing the level of aggregate demand to positively affect investment, then it is clear that deficits do not crowd out investment under current conditions. Furthermore, and even more seriously, attempts to reduce the size of the deficit will lead to further decreases in investment, not increases, as is alleged so often today. To use the alternative terminology, budget deficits are not necessarily a reflection of an overloaded economy. Very likely they reflect a situation with too little in the way of demands upon output.

3. *Financial versus physical crowding out*

Some further insights into the problem of overload and crowding out is provided with the help of figure 9.2. In figure 9.2 it is assumed that private spending, notably investment, is very interest elastic. Allow now for an increase in government expenditures financed by

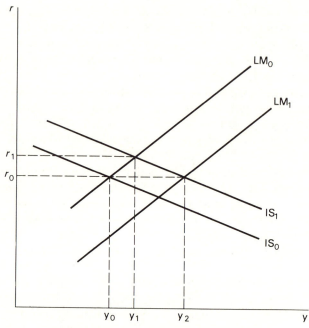

FIGURE 9.2   *Financial crowding out*

the sale of government bonds to the non-bank public. The resulting increase is seen as a shift in the IS curve from IS_0 to IS_1 along LM_0 with the equilibrium level of income rising from y_0 to y_1 and the equilibrium rate of interest rising from r_0 to r_1. The stimulating effect of an increase in government expenditures succeeds in driving up interest rates. As a result income rises not to y_2, the new equilibrium if the rate of interest remained at r_0, but only to y_1 since higher rates of interest depress investment.

It is often said, rather uncritically in this case, that higher government spending crowds out investment. There is a fiscal impact increasing aggregate demand but less than would be the case if interest rates did not rise. An obvious, but none the less frequently ignored, answer to all this is that if there are involuntarily unemployed resources, the money supply can be increased shifting the LM curve from LM_0 to LM_1 thereby, restoring interest rates and investment to their old level. This possibility indicates how essential it is to distinguish between a financial crowding out of investment, because of a rise in interest rates that is not offset by a loosening of monetary policy, and a government spending measure that leads to a decline in investment because of some physical limitation on the supply of output.

But matters do not end here. All of this assumes that given some interest-elasticity to the demand for money, fiscal policy does have an impact on aggregate demand. There has developed recently a fairly substantial volume of literature denying that fiscal policy *per se* can have any effect on aggregate demand, either in the short run or long run or both. For example, what has become known as the 'Ricardian equivalence theorem' (which is neither Ricardian nor a theorem) would have it that the increase in government expenditures just described, financed by selling bonds to the non-bank public, will have no impact on aggregate demand even in the short run. This is assumed to be the case because this kind of deficit financing is supposed to lead the holders of government bonds: (1) to recognize that the new debt must be eventually retired through higher taxes or serviced through higher interest payments of the same present value; and (2) to respond to these higher anticipated future tax liabilities by reducing consumption by an amount equal to the increased government expenditures and debt.[2]

If this sounds a bit contrived, and little evidence is offered in support of this so called '*ex ante* crowding out' effect, another argument has been advanced. This asserts that deficits financed without increasing the money supply have wealth effects that negate in the long run the initial stimulative effect. Thus, as government debt held by the non-bank public grows, the demand for money to hold as wealth rises. This leads to a shift of the LM curve upward and to the left forcing up interest rates until income has fallen back to its previous level or has even declined. The empirical significance of this wealth effect has also been disputed.[3]

The artificiality of these kinds of crowding out arguments is again seen when it is merely allowed that some of the deficit is financed through money creation. This leads to a final crowding out possibility. This is the popular monetarist argument that states that the relief to investment given by a loosening of monetary policy (following a stimulative fiscal impulse) and the subsequent shift of the LM curve in figure 9.2 from LM_0 to LM_1 is only temporary. Easy money policies, according to this view, may temporarily lower

[2] For a summary, see M. Feldstein (1982) Government deficits and aggregate demand, *Journal of Monetary Economics*, January.
[3] See J. Tobin (1979) Deficit spending and crowding out in shorter and longer runs, in *Theory of Economic Efficiency: Essays in Honor of Abba P. Lerner* (Eds H. Greenfield *et al.*), MIT, Cambridge.
  This kind of long-run consideration is very artificial. For example, no consideration is given to the possibility that a fiscal stimulus could set in motion other long-run dynamic processes such as an accelerator-multiplier interaction.

interest rates but after a lag, inevitably of indeterminate length, interest rates will again rise as inflation sets in. In terms of figure 9.2, the LM curve will eventually shift back from LM_1 to LM_0 as the rising level of prices reduces the real value of money balances. The real sector, i.e. output, is eventually unaffected.

This argument leads directly into the question of physical crowding out. In figure 9.3 an aggregate demand and two supply curves

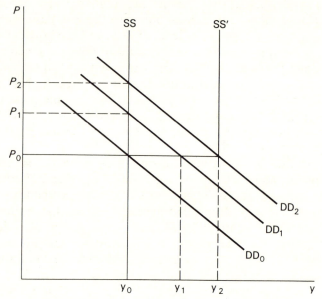

FIGURE 9.3   *Financial and physical crowding out*

are drawn, one of which is completely inelastic while the other is infinitely elastic up to full employment output, y_2. Vertical supply curves are based on the neoclassical assumption of automatic full employment, at least in some long-run sense, with all the auxiliary assumptions of the competitive model needed to derive this result, including continuous market clearing. In this kind of world, higher government spending, which would shift the DD curve from DD_0 to DD_1, must be offset by tighter money if the inflation is to be averted. On the other hand, easy-money policies to keep interest rates low would merely make inflationary matters worse, shifting the DD curve further to the right, say, to DD_2 and pushing the price level up further to P_2.

But once the assumptions of automatic full employment and flex-price markets are dropped and unemployment conditions such as those of today are recognized, any crowding out of private investment that might occur following an increase in government expenditures would have to be attributed to the tightened stance of monetary policy. To put it differently, there is no overloading of the economy in the sense that demands are greater than what can be produced. There can only be a financial crowding out of investment, no doubt because of fear of inflation.

For example, an increase in government spending in a world of fix-price markets and widespread unemployment will not generate price increases but only quantity adjustments. In the short run, inventories will be run down while the long-run adjustments will take the form of expansion of employment and capital, at least up to full employment. A likely result in this situation can be shown as a shift in the aggregate demand curve in figure 9.3 from DD_0 to DD_1 along the horizontal aggregate supply curve, SS'. Income increases from y_0 to y_1, as in figure 9.2. If, then, an expansionary monetary policy is introduced to keep interest rates at r_0 in figure 9.2, the additional stimulus to aggregate demand will shift the DD_1 curve to DD_2 in figure 9.3, increasing income to y_2. Only if aggregate demand increases further can it be said that there is physical crowding out, and this cannot be relieved by easier monetary policy.

CAN STAGNATION BE CURED?

This blurring of the distinction between crowding out in a financial and physical sense arises as in so many cases from the tendency to think in terms of an economy that is seldom if ever faced with problems of involuntary unemployment. Such confusion also serves to relieve the authorities of the criticism that they might be responsible for the high unemployment. Unfortunately, such thinking does absolutely nothing to help find a way out of stagnation and the zero-sum society.

The overload or conflict is usually framed in terms of private consumption versus social welfare expenditures. In contrast, during the 1960s and 1970s rapid economic growth provided a kind of social consensus and harmony in the capitalist economies because it allowed for rising per capita consumption at the same time as it permitted the expansion of social welfare measures; e.g. health care, unemployment and welfare benefits, free education and generous pension schemes. A kind of social justice was seen to prevail that permitted all to share in the benefits of capitalism thereby legitimatizing an increasingly commercial, secular society. With the end of growth these various social welfare measures have often taken on an aspect of charity rather than the sharing of an ever-increasing bounty with the less fortunate.

But while 'market defeatism' has been implicit in much of recent discussion, the zero-sum society as a permanent steady state has seldom been accepted in principle by any segment of the political spectrum. Politicians of all leanings are loath to accept retrenchment, at least publicly, as a permanent solution to the overloading of the economy.[4] It appears to be true that unemployment rates can rise and real incomes can even fall substantially without the political disruption that economists might have predicted even as late as five years ago. But in terms of political rhetoric, whatever the underlying ideology, few groups are willing to publicly accept a zero-sum society in which the problem of overload is resolved by simply imposing significant economic and social losses on certain groups. And since it is widely accepted that it is the lack of growth that intensifies conflict, pitting one economic group against another, the basic issue is whether an appreciable increase in the rate of growth of productivity is possible.

The analysis, therefore, now turns to the first of two kinds of programmes for ending stagflation, i.e. ending stagnation to break out of the zero-sum society and greatly reducing inflation. An evaluation is made of those programmes that stress a cutback in the size and influence of the public sector as a means of speeding up productivity growth and reducing inflation. Advocates of these programmes believe that a greater use of the market mechanism is required to solve current economic problems. They do not see the stagnation as the result of anti-inflation policies, but rather as a malfunction caused by 'bad government', 'over regulation', etc., and they envisage a strategy in which productivity growth is first accelerated as a means of reducing inflation. In terms of overall political and economic philosophy, more reliance on the private pursuit of self-interest is called for as it will lead to a higher public good.

SUPPLY-SIDE ECONOMICS

Caught today in a zero-sum game with little agreement among economists as to which way to turn, some economists and government leaders have found sympathy with programmes that promise a rejuvenation of the 'market'. As a result, there is increasing pressure

---

[4] This is not to say that over the next decade or so governments may not in fact (inadvertently) choose policies that lead to stagnation. This possibility is discussed in chapter 14.

to seek relief from stagnation through a cutback in the welfare state. As these groups would have it, the unemployed are really unemployed by choice, exploiting the generosity of a system that is finding it increasingly hard to be so generous; hence, reduce unemployment compensation, relief funds, etc. Similarly, the elderly must enrol in the fight against inflation. In this case an incomplete indexing of pensions is not too large a price to pay for preserving economic freedom. Related arguments are invoked to downgrade the need and even the desirability of maintaining standards in public health and education.

But there is more to this response to stagnation than retrenchment. In particular, the various versions of these programmes suggest that productivity and per capita income growth can be greatly increased without first reducing unemployment and excess capacity. Moreover, some versions suggest a costless 'quick-fix' way out of stagflation, which has very much to do with their popularity.

These programmes can be characterized in another way. In chapter 3 an attempt was made to distinguish between some of the essentials of monetarism, in contrast to views that happen to be held by monetarists. Here the discussion deals with the attitudes of many if not most monetarists towards the role of the central government. Thus, the neoclassical-monetarist assumption of flex-price markets fits well into the market solution framework, along with the monetarist desire to reduce the rate of growth of the money supply. But the views about government and its proper budgetary role are not derived from monetarist explanations of the role of money, etc. It is the budgetary aspects of different forms of these programmes that are central here. For want of a better expression, the different forms of these programmes will be lumped together under the heading of supply-side economics (SSE).[5]

---

[5] There is a certain amount of difficulty in detailing the proper references for assertions made in the text. Partly this is due to the lack of any relatively coherent body of theory to underpin what goes under the heading of supply-side economics. Also the programmes have evolved and even been altered rather drastically in the political process in the two countries in which they have been adopted. Most of the discussion has been in the popular press and in government circles. See, however, S. Danziger and R. Haveman (1981) The Reagan Budget: A sharp break with the past, *Challenge,* May–June 1981; President Reagan's economic policy, *Midland Bank Review,* Summer; J. Brooks (1982) Annals of finance, *The New Yorker,* April 1982; G. Gilder (1979) *Wealth and Poverty,* Basic Books, New York; C. Pratten (1982) Mrs Thatcher's Economic Experiment, *Lloyds Bank Review,* January; R. Heilbroner (1981) The demand for the supply side, *New York Review of Books,* June 11; and W. Buiter and M. Miller (1981) The Thatcher experiment: The first two years, *Brookings Papers on Economic Activity,* No. 2.

Several points of emphasis are common to these variants of SSE.[6] They include deregulation of industry, an anti-inflationary monetary policy in the form of reduced growth of the money supply, tax incentives for investors and savers (high-income groups) and cutbacks in non-military government spending. For present purposes, the important thrust behind SSE is that policies should at the very least increase the supply of aggregate output more than the demand. Since supply is seen primarily as a function of the amounts of labour and capital supplied in production, policies should provide incentives that increase the amount of savings, investment and work effort. Allegedly, this is most effectively accomplished by tax cuts for business and the wealthy and cutbacks in welfare programmes. Tax cuts are especially critical because they are required to increase the rate of savings which, it is argued, will drive down interest rates and increase investment. In addition, tax cuts spur work effort, but apparently only for some. Cuts in taxes for the rich unequivocably increase work effort but reducing income supplements for the poor who find work (in effect, an increase in their tax rate) has been deemed correct by the Reagan Administration.[7]

Together the impact of tax cuts on labour supply and investment and savings is to increase the supply of output of the economy. The increased investment is especially important as it is to give the boost to productivity needed to get supply to increase more than demand. This added excess supply is assumed to reduce inflationary pressures. How the increased supply leads to more demand in the absence of a market clearing mechanism is never made very clear. If it does not, then, of course, the policy must lead to more unemployment. To illustrate these policies, two North American versions of SSE economics together with Mrs Thatcher's programme can be distinguished.

REAGANOMICS

Reaganomics splits into two schools; one that insists that any cut in taxes be accompanied by an equal decrease in government spending

[6] These programmes could also be referred to as 'voodoo economics', for two reasons. First, in order to accept the main points of these programmes, it is necessary to believe that there are devils about causing harm to the economy that must be driven out by incantation and sacrifice. Second, the term voodoo economics was used by vice-president of the USA, George Bush, during the 1980 Republican presidential primary campaigns to describe the economic policies proposed by his rival at the time, Ronald Reagan.

[7] See L. Osberg (1983) *Economic Inequality in America*, Sharpe, Armonk, New York, chapter 13.

and one that does not.[8] The former view, which will be called Magic, argues that a tax reduction must be accompanied by a more or less equal reduction of government expenditures in order to balance the budget at the same time as the policy is seen to generate the desired redistribution of output towards investment; otherwise the latter will allegedly be crowded out by the continued large size of government. This seems to be true no matter what the extent of excess capacity and unemployment in the economy at the time of the expenditure cuts: but ignore this difficulty. The important belief is that a substantial spending cut by government is required to generate more savings which, it is alleged, automatically flow into investment and lead to a 'natural increase' in output and productivity. In addition, such cuts will be necessary to convince the general public that the authorities are serious in their efforts to fight inflation.

An alternative version of supply-side economics puts less emphasis on balancing the budget in the short-run and better describes the original programme knows as Reaganomics. This version stresses the need to reduce the size of government but sees great possibilities opened up by the 'Laffer curve', the notion that a cut in tax rates will so stimulate the economy that at the new higher level of output, more tax receipts will be generated.[9] Sceptics of the Laffer curve have been led to refer to this budgetary policy as 'reactionary Keynesianism'.[10]

The main thrust of this programme is to stimulate aggregate demand by increasing the deficit through large tax cuts and increased military spending, while cutting back non-military expenditures. In the short run the higher deficit is deemed essential if growth is to be re-established. In the 'long run' (by 1984 in the original estimates by the Reagan administration), the accelerated growth is assumed to generate additional tax receipts which together with restrained non-military government expenditures will bring the budget into balance. The initial stimulus to supply, provided by increased savings and work effort, is assumed as before to be greater than the stimulus given to demand, even though a higher budget deficit is targeted for the short run. The net impact is alleged to solve the inflationary problem but again raises the possibility of greater excess capacity and unemployment. On the other hand, there may be some intermediate and long-run considerations (never made explicit)

---

[8] This split reflects reactions in the legislative branch of government to Mr Reagan's proposals.
[9] For a favourable view see J. Wannicki (1975) The Mundell–Laffer hypothesis, *The Public Interest*, Spring.
[10] An expression attributed to Professor Galbraith.

that give rise to a more favourable climate for recovery and stimulate demand without stimulating inflation. This is undoubtedly
because in the realm of supply-side economics 'the interactions are
so subtle, the feedbacks so complex that we do not have any econometric model capable of handling them'.[11]

DIES IRAE

Public expenditure is at the heart of Britain's economic
problems   *Tory White Paper*

Magic is easily seen as a more limited view of Thatcherism; it contains a kind of Victorian optimism that the Thatcher programme
lacks. A redistribution of output from the public to the private sector
is the essential element. Yet the balanced budget multiplier theorem
tells us that by cutting taxes and government spending by similar
amounts, GNP falls by the size of the budget cut, but disposable
income is unchanged. Even so, this cut, together with deregulation
and a reduced growth of the money supply, is supposed to be sufficient to bring forth the natural increase in output and productivity
and the reduction in inflation everyone has been waiting for. Mrs
Thatcher's programme involves more Draconian measures than a
simple redistribution of output and incomes from the public to the
private sector. Compared to it, Magic is relatively painless and reactionary Keynesianism is pure pleasure.

Under Thatcherism government expenditures must be cut and the
tax burden shifted to the consumer and away from the saver. But
above all the budgetary impact must reduce aggregate demand.
Unemployment rates must be pushed up until 'the inflationary psychology is whipped once and for all' and excess capacity increased
until the inefficient firms have been driven into bankruptcy. Without
the aggregate demand stimulus coming from the budget,
Thatcherism like Magic must find eventual recovery elsewhere. Like

---

[11] Irving Kristol in the *Wall Street Journal,* December 19, 1980. There is a great
temptation to write off supply-side economics as a colossal 'confidence trick'.
Thus one of President Reagan's top economic advisers, David Stockman, was
quoted as saying that the tax features of SSE were merely a 'trojan horse'
designed to bring down the tax rates for the rich. The analysis in the text
attempts to evaluate SSE on its own merits and refrains from dealing with the
motives of its advocates. See W. Greider (1981) The education of David Stockman, *The Atlantic,* December.

all forms of SSE, this is to be achieved in spite of depressed economic conditions and always from rather ill-defined sources. For example, a decline in the governments command over resources is somehow seen to unleash the latent animal spirits of British industry and savers through tax incentives to be sure but more importantly by creating a 'more favourable climate within which business can operate'. Supposedly, not only will an eventual restimulation lead to a revitalized dynamic economy, but labour will have learned its lesson and inflation will not start up again.

1. What if supply increases more than demand?

The budgetary policies advocated in all three types of SSE stress the need for tax cuts in the interests of increasing supply. This, it is believed, will increase living standards and reduce inflation. Assume, for the sake of argument, that any one of the budgetary policies just summarized does result in a bigger increase in supply or potential output than demand because of the initial stimulating effect on investment (work effort effects can be ignored). Such an outcome is easily recast in terms of the 'dual rate of investment' stressed in Harrod–Domar models. Here, investment generates income through the multiplier and also adds to capacity. In supply-side economics, the capacity effects of investment are always assumed to outstrip the multiplier effects. But in Harrod–Domar analysis, this must lead to a decline in investment, not a continued rise, because of the increased excess capacity. This decline then magnifies the initial increase in unemployment resulting from the initial increase in excess supply of output.

SSE is given to stressing the supply effects of its programmes because the creation of additional supply is part of its fight against inflation. The question also arises as to whether such programmes will work in this regard. The answer is found in the earlier analysis of the impact of rising unemployment on inflation. An increase in excess supply of output must act to increase unemployment unless there is some kind of market-clearing, automatic, full-employment mechanism at work. In chapter 6 it was conceded that eventually rising unemployment rates could reduce inflation.

But nothing that was said earlier suggested that this wage and price response would lead to an investment boom. For what must be set against any downward pressure on wages and prices is the impact

of increased unemployment and added excess capacity on the profitability of investment.

Table 9.2 suggests very clearly what can be expected. Annual
figures are given for the rates at which the capacity of industrial

TABLE 9.2   *Wharton indexes of rates of aggregate capacity utilization.*[a]

Year	Belgium (%)	France (%)	West Germany (%)	Italy (%)	Netherlands (%)	UK (%)	Canada (%)	Japan (%)	USA (%)
1973	94.7	96.3	96.9	93.1	94.6	98.2	97.5	98.0	97.0
1974	95.0	93.2	92.4	94.4	93.0	93.7	96.5	89.1	92.8
1975	83.3	81.6	83.9	83.5	83.9	87.2	89.1	74.9	79.3
1976	87.4	85.2	86.8	89.3	85.2	85.9	88.5	77.9	84.5
1977	85.1	81.9	86.3	87.3	81.1	87.6	87.9	77.7	86.6
1978	81.6	80.1	85.1	86.3	78.3	87.8	88.3	77.9	88.9
1979	83.7	81.3	86.7	89.1	77.8	86.9	89.0	80.2	90.2
1980	79.0	76.5	83.5	91.1	74.6	79.5	83.9	82.4	84.9
1981	74.1	71.3[b]	80.0[c]	87.1	71.7	72.8[c]	82.8	81.7	84.5

Source: Wharton Econometric Forcasting Associates, Philadelphia, December 1982.
[a] Based on peaks in industrial production data.
[b] For two quarters.
[c] For three quarters.

plant and equipment has been utilized during the 1970s for several
countries. The impact of depressed demand conditions is clear;
excess capacity has increased markedly since the peak year, 1973.
Even assuming some downward pressure on inflation rates during
this period, the question arises as to why new investment, which will
add to the existing capacity, would ever be undertaken following a
tax cut or any policy that increased supply more than demand. And
without that investment, even SSE economists would hesitate to
predict an acceleration of productivity growth as a result of cuts in
taxes and government expenditures.

2. The unimportance of demand

The general assumption contained in the different 'market solutions'
must be that rates of investment and growth of productivity are not
very sensitive to past and current macro demand pressures. Evi-
dently, unemployment and excess capacity can remain high and
profits low for some time and this will not dampen entrepreneurial
zeal, provided the budgetary reforms are carried out. To say this is

to rephrase an earlier statement; one of the outstanding character-istics of the budgetary theorizing of those advocating a 'market solu-tion' to stagflation is the belief that the current stagnation is not the result of depressed demand conditions, but of too much interference with the market system. As a result both the stagnation and the inflation problems can be resolved by undertaking budgetary (and regulatory) reforms.

As just argued, these programmes will not solve the stagnation problem. Any policy that initially succeeds in increasing the supply or capacity of the economy will lead to more unemployment and excess capacity and an investment slump. But it is not even plausible to assume that there will even be a short-run investment spurt as long as policies have this excess supply impact. Only if budgetary policies result in greater excess demand can it be expected that any kind of investment boom can get started.

3. *Managing the economy*

Earlier chapters argued that rising unemployment (and capacity uti-lization rates) will not solve the inflation problem in the long run. Later chapters will argue that a greater reliance on market solutions aggravates both the productivity and inflation problems by intensify-ing conflict. It will be maintained that no policy can succeed in achieving the macroeconomic goals of growth and price stability (as well as external balance and full employment) without a widely sup-ported cooperative effort. But cooperation is based upon mutual trust and trust comes only when the various economic groups feel that they are being treated fairly, that the distribution of economic outcomes is in some sense fair. For example, there can be no co-operation on the production line between labour and management if one or both feel that they are not the beneficiaries of productivity growth. Nor can there be cooperation between capital and labour and between labour groups in reducing the inflationary pressures if large segments of the economy feel that they must forever struggle to obtain their fair share of national income.

One of the crowning achievements of the modern state has been its ability to soften the blows that the market system would deliver in the absence of government intervention, especially on behalf of those least able to take care of themselves. Measures that have led to high-quality public education, free medical care, adequate retirement pensions, unemployment insurance and the like come to mind. Mea-sures such as these are necessary conditions for the kind of cooperation and national economic consensus that is needed to resolve the dispute over income shares.

Yet each of the three SSE budgets stress tax cuts to business and the wealthy and cut backs on public programmes that help the poor, the unemployed and the elderly. In this day and age this is bound to intensify feelings of distributional unfairness that can only further deplete a dwindling stock of good will. It can only lead to a situation in which economies become increasingly unmanageable.

CHAPTER 10

Demand-side Economics

AGGREGATE DEMAND, UNEMPLOYMENT AND PRODUCTIVITY

This chapter has two main functions. It serves as a corrective to the mistaken policy prescriptions of supply-side economics outlined in chapter 9 and it seeks to justify one important part of a programme to combat stagflation, a stimulative aggregative demand policy. Recall that one of the defining features of SSE is the pre-Keynesian notion that supply creates its own demand. This updated version of Say's law insists that policies to combat stagflation must be designed to create excess supply by increasing supply more than demand. This, its proponents argue, must work to ease the inflationary problem. In effect, this policy is an example of a general class of anti-inflation policies which seek to reduce inflation through creating more unemployment. But as discussed in chapter 6, restrictive aggregate demand policies, which also aim to create excess supply in the economy, at best can combat inflation only in the short run.

But SSE policies will also fail in their attack on stagnation. In a era of widespread excess capacity and unemployment, any policy that increases this slack will retard investment, the keystone to productivity growth. 'Reactionary Keynesianism' is the only version of SSE that has any chance of success against stagnation but then only if such policies (inadvertently) lead to a reduction of excess supply and for familiar Keynesian reasons. In chapter 13 it will be argued that supply-side policies, in contrast to SSE policies, have a definite role to play in any fight against stagflation but only within the context of a full employment world. As formulated by their admirers, SSE policies have little to commend them.

Earlier chapters have stressed how important it is that the true nature of unemployment and inflation be understood. Only when it is realized that most unemployment today is involuntary and that inflation is basically the result of two interacting cost–push mechanisms can a reasonable start be made in combating unemployment and inflation. The fallacies of SSE remind us how important it is that the nature and causes of stagnation be properly understood. SSE sees stagnation as a result of a devil, the welfare state. Rid yourself of that devil and stagnation will end. Quite a different view will be advanced here. It will be argued that stagnation, measured by low and even negative productivity growth, can never be overcome unless unemployment (and excess capacity) rates are greatly reduced to something like their pre-1970s rates.

This is to say that the unemployment and stagnation problems are causally related to the inflation problem. For if growth depends upon reducing unemployment and if the latter will only be permitted by the authorities when accompanied by price and wage stability, then only a policy that reduces unemployment rates without accelerating inflation will lead to higher productivity growth. In short, the key to overcoming stagnation is to find policies that simultaneously reduce inflation and unemployment.

The matter can be put differently. What seems to have been lost sight of in the current period of disillusion with Keynesian principles is that maximum output or supply, i.e. what the economy can produce when labour and capital are fully employed, is itself partially a function of current, past and anticipated levels of aggregate demand. Stagnation is to a large extent the result of a stagnation in the growth of demand.

However, the mechanism of stagflation will be seen to be more complicated than this. Certainly, if inflation can be reduced and at the same time unemployment can be pushed down to something like its full employment rate, there will be an increase in productivity growth. But the causation goes the other way as well. A policy to reduce inflation is only likely to work if productivity growth accelerates, permitting an acceleration in the growth of real wages. This is essential if money wage demands are to be kept down.

This second relationship strengthens the connection between inflation and stagnation but introduces a circularity. At the same time as demand policies are implemented that return the economy to full employment and allow some growth in productivity, policies must be implemented that promote price and wage stability at full employment. But part of the incentive for getting labour and capital to accept a programme leading to price and wage stability will be an increase in productivity, real wages and profits. Without this, powerful economic groups are unlikely to accept programmes aimed at curing the inflation and will intensify their distributional demands thereby accelerating inflation. The question is where to intervene.

In fact the eventual policy recommendation will be to realize several goals simultaneously. But for expositional purposes it is useful to think of breaking out of the circularity by proceeding sequentially. Thus, the analysis formulates a policy sequence to overcome both inflation and unemployment by reducing inflationary pressures at full employment. In other words, policies are developed to reduce inflation at the same time as aggregate demand is stimulated and unemployment reduced. If these policies are successful, productivity growth will increase. And increase it must, since the initial success of the anti-inflation policy may well be lost unless this productivity growth is forthcoming. In chapter 13 it will be conceded that the productivity problem may not be so simply resolved. To handle this a policy sequence is developed which operates directly to increase productivity growth. If these policies are successful, a case can be made that inflationary pressures will be largely eliminated and stagflation overcome.

The rest of chapter 10 deals with the relationship between aggregate demand and stagnation. The main conclusion of the discussion is that any kind of adequate productivity growth depends upon the reduction of unemployment and excess capacity in the economy. Demand-side economics stresses this need to first increase aggregate demand before a supply or productivity response will be forthcoming. Chapters 11 and 12 then consider policies to reduce inflationary pressures while aggregate demand policies are utilized to reduce unemployment and excess capacity. It is argued that the retention of the welfare state is a necessary condition for combating stagflation, as is the pursuit of the public interest by all concerned. Chapter 13 then discusses policies that act directly on productivity growth. Unlike the measures advocated by SSE however, the policies put forth in chapter 13 are designed to be implemented and operate at full employment.

WHY IS PRODUCTIVITY GROWTH IMPORTANT?

Productivity growth is the chief source of rising real wages and per capita incomes. But productivity growth is important for other reasons. First, the higher is the rate of growth of labour productivity, the lower is the basic rate of inflation, i.e. the difference between the rate of growth of money wages and productivity. Second, the basic rate of inflation is also influenced by labour's efforts to realize a growth in real wages, efforts that manifest themselves through demands for money wage increases. When the distribution of output between profits and wage income is constant, the rate of growth of real wages is equal to the rate of growth of labour productivity plus a positive or negative adjustment reflecting changes in the terms of trade. In North America and Britain, especially, productivity growth has declined noticeably since the 1974–75 recession, becoming negative in 1980. In most OECD countries dependent upon the importation of foodstuffs, energy and industrial and agricultural raw materials, movements of the terms of trade have been decidedly unfavourable since the early 1970s.[1] Clearly, with low rates of growth of productivity and adverse movements in the terms of trade, the attempts by labour to achieve a growing real wage will lead to rapid rates of growth of money wages. This will compound the impact of falling productivity growth on labour costs and intensify inflationary pressures.

Third, the rate of growth of productivity in manufacturing has been found to be highly correlated with export success, a matter discussed in chapter 13.[2] High productivity growth, then, is often accompanied by a high and rising external value of the currency as the result of a current account surplus. This reduces the tendency to import inflation but not at the expense of growth, as would be the case if exchange rate appreciation could be traced to rising interest rates. The matter can be put somewhat differently. Rising productivity growth helps free an economy from a payments constraint. Thus, authorities in the trading nations today are reluctant to stimulate aggregate demand not only because of a fear of an immediate impact on domestic costs and prices. They also fear a too rapid rate of growth of imports, as this leads to a depreciation of the exchange rate, and the possibility of importing inflation or an 'exchange rate crisis'. Rapidly growing productivity and the associated successful export performance, therefore, allow the authorities to pursue more expansionary aggregate demand policies.

[1] See *Economic Outlook*, OECD, Paris, July 1980, Table 20.
[2] See G. Ray (1972) Labour costs and international competitiveness, *National Institute Economic Review*, August; R. Gross and M. Keating (1980) An empirical analysis of exports and domestic markets, OECD, *Economic Outlook Occasional Studies*, December; and F. Cripps and R. Tarling (1975) Cumulative causation in the growth of manufacturing industries, Department of Applied Economics, University of Cambridge, June.

DEMAND-SIDE ECONOMICS

Few would take exception to the accounts of the many benefits of higher productivity growth; the question is how it is to be achieved. Broadly speaking, chapter 10 can be thought of as a partial antidote to supply-side economics. SSE has become popular in recent years largely because of the alleged failure of Keynesian policies, whose main emphasis has been the regulation of the economy through demand management. These, it was claimed, can never succeed as they fail to consider the supply side. Now it is certainly true that in the *General Theory* Keynes saw little need to be concerned with policies that would increase maximum output or supply. But as indicated in chapter 13, supply-side policies are easily combined with demand-side or aggregate demand policies in an attack on slow productivity growth.

The charge brought here is that SSE is guilty of overlooking the demand side of the market. More particularly, it assumes that the behaviour of productivity can be analysed independently of what is happening to the actual performance of the economy. The disagreement here can be seen in a wider context as part of the issue of whether growth (of productivity and, therefore, supply or maximum output) is demand or supply-determined, a distinction made relevant by almost a quarter of a century of neoclassical growth theorizing. With demand-determined growth, the rate of technical progress, productivity and maximum output growth are not given exogenously but are the result of the actual performance of the economy. Other things being equal, the stronger are aggregate demand pressures, the greater will be the induced impact on investment, innovation and productivity, largely because strong demand pressures increase profits and reduce macrorisks. Supply then adjusts to demand illustrating 'Say's Law in reverse'. In contrast, the supply-determined growth framework tends to see technical progress, productivity and maximum output growth as something given exogenously or, as in the case of SSE, as something dependent upon the 'business climate' and 'incentives'. Aggregate demand adjusts passively to supply usually through the 'workings of the price mechanism' or some such invisible hand.

Consistent with the supply-determined growth framework is the view that since the late 1960s and early 1970s fundamental structural changes of an exogenous nature have evolved under modern capitalism. One of the most noticeable of these is the shift in the final composition of output to services.[3] By the conventional measures, the rate of growth of productivity in services is slow. Thus, the shift in the composition of output must by the simple arithmetic of the matter progressively bring down productivity growth. Rising energy prices and a greater concern with the environment and work safety beginning in the late 1960s are additional reasons cited for the slow down in productivity and, therefore, output growth.

While there is undoubtedly some truth in these contentions, what must not be forgotten is that a large proportion of the decline in output and productivity growth in the current period compared to the 1950s and 1960s must be attributed to the lack of effective demand. Stagnation in the growth of supply is to a large extent the result of a stagnation in the growth of demand. The matter can be put less strongly. Almost any kind of policy to stimulate productivity growth will be ineffectual if not accompanied by stimulative aggregate demand policies.

Some of the influences of aggregate demand on supply in support of the demand determined view of productivity growth are described on pp. 230–9. Attention is given in the next section to the view that increases in aggregate demand, whatever expenditure category initiates this increase, have supply or maximum output effects even if no increase in investment occurs. The argument is symmetrical, as decreases in aggregate demand lead to decreases in aggregate supply. The impact of higher demand on supply when demand is caused by or causes an increase in investment is shown on pp. 235–9.

SOME GENERAL INFLUENCES OF DEMAND ON SUPPLY

Obviously if there are unemployed resources, demand creates its own supply in the sense that the idle labour and capital can be put to work producing output. But this is not at issue. More to the point, technological improvements, whose implementation is an increasing function of the size of the market, will be realized as a result of greater demand pressures leading to an increase in productivity and, therefore, supply. For example, longer production runs lead to less 'down time' thereby raising productivity.

---

[3] A theoretical model indicating this effect is found in W. Baumol (1967) Macro-economics of unbalanced growth: The anatomy of urban crisis, *American Economic Review*, June.

What has come to be known as 'Okun's Law' also illustrates the impact of increases in aggregate demand on output and productivity. Okun's early finding indicated that if there exists involuntary unemployment and aggregate demand is increased by enough to reduce unemployment by 1 per cent, aggregate output will increase by roughly 3 per cent.[4] Two-thirds of this 3 per cent rise in output is accounted for by an induced increase in labour input as labour participation rates rise as unemployment rates fall. However, the remaining one-third is attributed to an increase in productivity of those already employed. The study explained this in terms of the induced redistribution of labour within the firm towards more productive (production line) jobs.

More recent studies explain the productivity increase in terms of a general 'bumping up' of the labour force.[5] Industries with high income elasticities of demand tend to be high average productivity (and wage) industries while industries that expand relatively slowly following an upsurge in aggregate demand and output tend to have low productivity. Such shifts of workers from low to high average productivity sectors generates an increase in the rate of growth of productivity even if average productivities in each sector are fixed.

This bumping up process is easily seen as the short-run counterpart to the redistribution of labour (and capital) that has been part of the historical process of industrialization. The period from the end of the Second World War until the advent of stagflation in the early 1970s was one of rapid and sustained growth for a large number of mature capitalist economies. What accompanied this growth was a massive movement of labour out of agriculture into industry and the service sector as absolute and relative employment in the latter two sectors expanded rapidly.[6] But in addition high and growing demand pressures led to an economizing of labour in the service sector as vacancies in the higher paying industrial jobs were filled by those who might otherwise have remained in or entered the service sector.[7]

---

[4] See A. Okun (1962) Potential GNP: Its measurement and significance, *Proceedings of the Business and Economic Statistics Section,* American Statistical Society.

[5] A. Okun (1977) Upward mobility in a high pressure economy, *Brookings Papers on Economic Activity,* No. 1; and W. Vroman (1977) Worker upgrading and the business cycle, *Brookings Papers on Economic Activity,* No. 1.

[6] See A. Lewis (1954) Economic development with unlimited supplies of labour, *The Manchester School,* May.

[7] See J. Cornwall (1977) *Modern Capitalism: Its Growth and Transformation,* Martin Robertson, Oxford, chapter 5.

Unfortunately, the bumping up process has a stagnation counterpart. When unemployment rates rise, demand shifts relatively to the
low-wage, low-productivity sectors forcing a scaling-down of career
aspirations and achievements.[8] In important subsectors of the
service sector, namely, retail and wholesale trade, the fact that work
can often be shared reinforces the employment shift derived from the
final-demand shift.

   Another important influence of increased demand on supply is the
impact of reduced unemployment rates on workers' attitudes to
innovation. Technical improvements in the manufacture of capital
goods, learning by doing and the discovery of new, more efficient
production layouts learned on the shop floor are recurring events
whose implementation leads to increased productivity. Yet fear of
being laid-off can and often does lead to worker resistance to even
minor innovations. Attempts to introduce such changes without
prior worker approval leads to a 'work-to-rule' response by labour
thereby negating any possible increase in labour productivity that
would accompany such innovations if prior worker consent had
been obtained.[9] An increase in aggregate demand lessens worker
resistance to innovations because tighter labour markets reduce the
probability of being laid-off in the innovating firm and increase
the probability of finding another job should workers become
redundant.

   The reduction of involuntary unemployment and idle capacity, the
increase in productivity stemming from an increase in the size of the
market, the increase in participation rates as unemployment rates
fall and the greater cooperation of labour when job security is
ensured would appear to be short-run responses of supply to

---

[8] One of the neglected costs of the current stagflation is just this 'bumping down' of
the labour force. See E. Applebaum (1979) The labour market in post-Keynesian
theory, in *Unemployment and Inflation: Institutionalist and Structuralist Views* (Ed.
M. Piore), Sharpe, White Plains, New York.
[9] A resurrected view today argues that the threat of unemployment is what is
required to bring 'labour into line'. The reduction in the incidence of strikes as
unemployment rates rise is often cited as evidence of this. But it is quite a different
matter to argue that high unemployment rates make labour cooperative in other
equally important ways. The text stresses the desirability of cooperation in the
interests of innovational changes. This kind of cooperation is less likely when
workers are concerned that innovation might lead to their redundancy. Hence, an
increase in aggregate demand and a tightening of labour markets reduces this
resistance because alternative job opportunities are more abundant. Job security
increases productivity in a more permanent way than 'cost-cutting' layoffs.

demand. For the most part this is true, although the discussion below of growth as a transformation suggests that some of these responses have a long-run dynamic counterpart. But even if what has been discussed involves only a once over reaction to an increase in aggregate demand, these reactions play a vital role in enabling long-run responses to develop. As discussed in the next section, the major, sustained response of supply to increased demand pressures arises from the latter's influence on investment. Sustained reductions in rates of unemployment and excess capacity, increase the expansionary kind of investment (in contrast to the cost-reducing type) as a share of output and the rate of growth of the capital–labour ratio; these increase the rate of growth of productivity. However, there is an appreciable lag between the decision to invest and the productivity bonus. What is being discussed in this section are short-run supply responses that give a firm, industry or, indeed, the whole economy some short-run supply elasticity when demand picks up. This rising demand is then translated into higher production levels and sales providing the eventual inducement to adjust the capital stock.

However, what has become known as Verdoorn's law reveals that the impact of demand on supply or maximum output need not be limited to the short run. Write:

$$\dot{q}_i = \alpha_0 + \alpha_1 \dot{Q}_i \tag{1}$$

where $\dot{q}_i$ and $\dot{Q}_i$ are rates of growth of labour productivity and output in the ith firm, industry or the economy. Equation (1) expresses the notion of a long-run impact of demand on supply by allowing higher rates of growth of demand which stimulate higher rates of growth of output and eventually productivity. These dynamic economies of scale are often attributed to a learning process in that they are a function of cumulative output increases. Since it is difficult to think of a sustained rate of growth of demand and output generating a sustained rate productivity growth without an expansion of capital, this influence is easily subsumed in the discussion of pp. 235–9.

THE IMPACT OF INVESTMENT ON SUPPLY – THE NEOCLASSICAL VIEW

It is when consideration is given to the impact of greater demand pressures on investment that the long-run impact of demand on supply stands out most clearly.[10] The standard explanation of the investment response runs in terms of higher levels and rates of growth of demand which reduce excess capacity and lead eventually to an adjustment of the capital stock through investment. The basic notion was originally formalized in terms of the 'accelerator relation' and later generalized in numerous ways as the flexible accelerator or capital stock adjustment theory of investment. In the latter, investment is a function of the discrepancy between the desired and actual stock of capital. The desired stock of capital is determined by various influences but a common determinant in most every model is the level of sales and, therefore, demand.

All of this is fairly standard Keynesian dynamics with investment both determining savings through the multiplier and playing a critical role in determining the growth rate of productivity. In contrast neoclassical growth theory rejected both these assumptions. Savings determines investment in neoclassical analysis. Moreover, it is a well-known theorem in neoclassical growth theory that a change in the savings (= investment) ratio cannot permanently affect the rate of growth of output or productivity in the long run.[11]

But much of applied growth theory, with its emphasis on the short run, has continued to assume a theoretical framework that bears important resemblances to neoclassical growth theory and, as a result, concludes that the investment and savings rates are relatively unimportant for growth. In what has become known as 'growth accounting', a framework is adopted that assumes that production functions are linear in logarithms, with no interaction between the growth rates of the inputs.[12] In particular, the contribu-

---

[10] The text ignores the impact of an increase in aggregate demand on the supply of labour.

[11] See, for example, R. Solow (1965) A contribution to the theory of economic growth, *Quarterly Journal of Economics,* February.

[12] The standard accounting framework or production function is,

$$\dot{Q} = \dot{A} + w_1 \dot{K} + w_2 \dot{L}$$

where $\dot{Q}$, $\dot{A}$, $\dot{K}$ and $\dot{L}$ represent rates of growth of output, Hicks neutral technical progress, capital and labour, respectively, and w_1 and w_2 are weights ($w_1 + w_2 = 1$). See E. Denison (1979) *Accounting for Slower Economic Growth: The United States in the 1970s,* Brookings, Washington. Denison's work cannot be described simply as applied neoclassical growth theory. For example, he considers variable returns to scale. Other studies, aimed at explaining the recent slowdown in productivity growth are not so eclectic. See B. Bosworth (1982) Capital formation and economic policy, especially page 284; and M. Baily (1982) The productivity growth slowdown by industry, both in *Brokkings Papers on Economic Activity,* No. 2.

tion of the rates of growth of capital and technical progress are assumed to be additive, thereby disallowing any interaction between the rates of growth of these key variables. Furthermore, the basic contribution of the capital and labour inputs is determined by weighting their growth rates by the income share received by each. This is an assumption that can only be justified by assuming that the real world performs not only according to the competitive assumptions but also in such a way that the economy is always in long-run competitive equilibrium.

These assumptions automatically lead to the conclusion that capital formation is relatively unimportant in its contribution to the growth process. Moreover, recent studies attempting to account for the slowdown in productivity growth during the period of stagflation have adopted these techniques. For example, stagflation gives rise to low rates of capacity utilization of capital. If in measuring the impact of low capacity utilization on the decline in productivity growth this accounting framework (and production function) is employed, then the 'cyclical' impact, i.e. the impact of the current stagnation, will indeed be negligible.[13]

THE IMPACT OF INVESTMENT ON SUPPLY –
A POST-KEYNESIAN VIEW

1. *Investment and productivity growth*

In the basic neoclassical growth model the rate of technical progress is independent of the rate of investment or of any economic events for that matter. Yet any number of studies have revealed that investment is the important and necessary vehicle for implementing new technologies.[14] In an effort to provide some realism in the neoclassical framework, the assumption of embodied technical progress has been invoked whereby increases in productive efficiency require investment if they are to be realized.[15] This has produced the 'vintage' capital models of growth whereby capital goods vary in efficiency depending upon their age, as the most advanced tech-

---

[13] This comes out clearly in Baily, ibid., who allows for a variable relationship between the capital stock and its services.

[14] See L. Nabseth and G. Ray (Eds) (1974) *The Diffusion of New Industrial Processes: An International Study,* Cambridge University Press, Cambridge.

[15] The earliest study is R. Solow (1960) Investment and technical progress, in K. Arrow *et al.,* (Eds) *Mathematical Methods in the Social Sciences,* Stanford University Press, Stanford.

nology is not embodied in all units of the capital stock, but only in units now being constructed. However, the formal models of growth that assume that technical progress can only be realized through investment also assume that the rate at which technical progress proceeds is independent of the size of the investment ratio and, by implication, the kinds of investment projects undertaken. This still leads to the long-run rate of growth of productivity being independent of the size of the investment ratio.[16]

It is the contention here that not only is it difficult to realize technical advance without investment but the rate of technical progress varies directly with the rate and kinds of investment. Further, the separate impacts of capital formation and technical progress on productivity growth are virtually impossible to distinguish.

In explaining why investment and growth of demand are the driving forces behind productivity growth it is useful initially to ignore the historical fact that the long-run growth of an economy is a very unbalanced thing with the composition of output and the distribution of capital and labour across industries regions and firms constantly changing. When growth is seen as a transformation in which resources must constantly be reallocated to new lines of production, the importance of investment for growth is given added significance.

To understand one important way that an increase in aggregate demand leads to an increase in output and investment and so induces an increase in supply through its impact on labour productivity, consider the following sequence. Assume that scale economies and the resultant growth of productivity within a firm are positively related to the capital intensity of the production technique adopted. This can be justified on the grounds that more capital intensive techniques are associated with such things as assembly line and continuous processes and highly developed divisions of labour performing simplified work tasks. Allow further that the production processes available are few in number and that the problem of indivisibilities in production increases with the capital intensity of the production process. Then, an increase in demand for a good, other things being equal, will increase the probability that a firm will opt for the more productive capital intensive technique. This arises because indivisibilities create excess capacity but with demand high

---

[16] See E. Phelps (1962) The new view of investment: A neoclassical analysis, *Quarterly Journal of Economics,* November.

and rising this is only a short-run problem. Investment in this case is undertaken to expand capacity rather than to reduce costs.[17]

Furthermore, the nature of technical progress strengthens this response. Thus, define localized technical progress as improvements in production techniques that increase labour productivity but only for techniques recently or about to be adopted. This follows from the reasonable assumptions that improvements and productivity increases are the result of a learning process in production or result from very specific kinds of research and development prior to production of some capital good, and which will be embodied in that investment project.[18] In this case an increase in demand not only lessens the cost of indivisibilities and excess capacity, thereby encouraging the adoption of more capital intensive techniques, it may force the adoption of such techniques upon a firm. This follows because if a competitor adopts the techniques, rivals must soon follow or permanently experience a cost disadvantage. In contrast, if technical improvements are not localized but apply to any technique and increase steadily over time, then the timing of the adoption of the new technique is not a matter of such consequence.[19]

2. The unbalanced nature of growth

None of this is meant to imply that the ability to achieve scale economies is inexhaustible. It is important at this point to realize that in the course of economic growth the distribution of demand for final output changes markedly.[20] Industries typically experience a sequence of slow, rapid, slow and eventually often negative growth as a good moves from the 'luxury' to the 'necessity' category during the rise of per capita incomes. During the early stages of development of a good, growth of demand will be slow but as the good

[17] This distinction between investment that expands capacity ('enterprise investment') and that which merely aims to reduce costs ('defensive investment') was first emphasized by A. Lamfalussy (1951) *Investment and Growth in Mature Economies,* Macmillan, New York.

[18] This differs from the simple embodiment hypothesis referred to earlier. In the latter case, technical progress or improvement in all techniques, potential and adopted, takes place continuously over time whether adopted or not. As a result, a technique available 20 years ago but not adopted until today will be much more efficient today compared with 20 years ago, even though this technique has been 'shelved' for 20 years.

[19] See A. Atkinson and J. Stiglitz (1969) A new view of technical change, *The Economic Journal,* September.

[20] See Cornwall, op. cit., chapters I and VI.

becomes more of a 'necessity' in the consumer's budget and greater numbers of consumers purchase the good, the overall rate of growth of demand picks up. As just argued it is at this point that economies of scale are likely to be realized leading to an increase in the rate of growth of productivity in the production of this good.

Later, at higher levels of per capita income, when the market becomes relatively saturated and demand shifts to other products, productivity growth will slow down. But this will come at a time when the relative importance of the good in question in the household budget is declining. Hence, the decline in the growth of productivity in the production of the good is less consequential for the overall growth of labour productivity.

Once the market for a good becomes relatively saturated, shifts in consumer tastes and demands to the next group of goods in the hierarchy of purchases lead to a repetition of the demand pattern just sketched. This brings up a consideration which underscores the importance of demand and investment on supply. At any point in time the income elasticities of demand vary between goods, while over time the income elasticity of demand for a large number of individual goods appears to change from low to high and then low again. As a result, an increase in the rate of growth of aggregate demand will set in motion a chain of events such as the following. Initially, employment will expand and excess capacity will be reduced in most industries but especially in those producing goods with high income elasticities of demand. This will lead to an expansion of investment, especially in the industries most affected by the increase in aggregate demand, and an increase in the overall rate of investment.

The impact of a higher rate of investment will be an increase in the rate of growth of productivity throughout the economy and this will be true even if the composition of demand and output is unchanged. However with productivity and per capita income increasing, the composition of demand and output will actually be shifting because of differences in income elasticities of demand. The increase in the rate of growth of overall demand merely acts to speed up this shift or transformation of output. But most capital is neither malleable nor mobile. A more rapid shift in the composition of output involves a more rapid shift in the distribution of capital (and labour) towards the rapid growth sectors. The higher rate of investment serves just this purpose. Indeed, the increment to the investment ratio originally induced by a higher rate of growth of demand can be usefully thought of as an increment to the capital stock in the rapid-growth industries. Moreover, since new technologies are usually embodied in investment, this extra reallocation of capital resources can also be usefully thought of as increasing the rate at which new technologies are exploited, this time in new industries.[21] When growth and investment are seen in this light, the neoclassical separation of the impact of technical progress and capital formation is especially suspect and artificial.

This response becomes even more plausible when account is taken of the behaviour of firms in the capital goods industry. These firms are constantly monitoring demand developments in firms and industries that are potential buyers of their capital goods. When one market becomes saturated and demand begins to shift to other goods, firms in the capital goods industry will expand their research and development activities towards the development of superior capital goods for the growth industries and markets of the future. The stronger is aggregate demand the stronger will be the demand for products of these growth industries and the more active will be the R&D efforts in the capital-goods industry on their behalf.[22]

A SCEPTICAL VIEW

Some critical comments were contained on pp. 234–5 on certain neoclassical elements in growth accounting. In these applied growth studies it is common to assume that there is little if any possibility of an interaction between the rates of growth of the capital stock and technical advance. Moreover the weights chosen to measure the importance of the rate of growth of the capital stock on growth are essentially arbitrary and are such that investment and capital will always be unimportant for growth. For example, the rate of growth of the capital stock could fall to zero and economic growth would be only moderately affected, given the manner in which growth accounting is conducted.

Now these criticisms could be accepted by proponents of the growth accounting approach and there would still remain an important issue, the 'productivity puzzle'. What is meant here is that during the current stagflation period, the investment ratio has

---

[21] See R. Nelson (1981) Research on productivity growth and differences, *Journal of Economic Literature*, September.

[22] See J. Schmookler (1966) *Invention and Economic Growth,* Harvard University Press, Cambridge; and a criticism of Schmookler in N. Rosenberg (1974) Science, invention and economic growth, *The Economic Journal,* March.

remained fairly high (although the rate of growth of capital appears to have been more adversely affected by the current stagnation), yet there has been a pronounced decline in rates of growth of productivity. Thus, the argument can still be made that investment is unimportant for growth, given this lack of correlation between capital formation and productivity growth.

However, critics of the view that investment is unimportant in explaining the current decline in productivity have confused cross-section results, which are relevant, with time-series findings. For example, the positive correlation between the fixed investment ratio averaged over, say, a business cycle and the rate of growth of productivity across countries is strong and widely recognized. However, there is no inconsistency between this finding and the lack of correlation between investment and productivity growth within a country in recent times once two considerations are kept firmly in mind. First, investment not only generates additional productive capacity but determines income through the multiplier. As a result when aggregate investment actually declines, the ratio of investment to output can be little changed. Thus it is important to take note of the direction in which aggregate demand and investment have been and are moving when evaluating the impact of investment on productivity. To take the American experience, business fixed investment as a share of GDP was higher in the period 1980–82 compared to the investment and output boom of 1966–73 (10.6 versus 11.5 per cent). Yet during the period 1980–82 aggregate fixed business investment in constant dollars first rose and then declined so that the level of total investment hardly changed at all. The increase in the investment ratio of 1980–82 hid these stagnant investment conditions.

But equally important were the kinds of investment taking place during this period and earlier. In the USA during the period since 1973 there have been several important changes in the composition of investment. Most commented upon is the rising importance of equipment relative to structures in business fixed investment. This has been largely the result of the growth (absolute and relative) of 'communications and high technology equipment' expenditures (e.g. computers). Accompanying this has been an upsurge in outlays on office buildings, institutional structures and shopping centres ('commercial buildings'). At the same time, expenditures on heavy industrial equipment (e.g. metal-working machinery and turbines) and industrial structures have grown little absolutely since the beginning of the stagflation period and have fallen relatively speaking.[23]

[23] See Business Fixed Investment: Recent Developments and Outlook, *Federal Reserve Bulletin*, January 1983.

These developments are not surprising given the stagnating conditions of the times. New process and product investment, investment that is expansionary in intent, has been replaced by cost-reducing types of investment and investment in the kind of infrastructure associated with affluent capitalism. If the American experience is typical, the 'productivity puzzle' largely evaporates.

THE TECHNOLOGY GAP

Unfortunately, there is one serious qualification that must be made to this analysis of 'demand creating its own supply'. While increased demand pressures do set in motion the kind of sequence described on pp. 237–9, there is an important supply constraint evident today in many countries that was absent during the period of rapid growth of the 1950s and 1960s. Some additional terminology will help bring out this point. Define technological progress as the discovery of new techniques, product designs and ideas that have a potential commercial value. These 'inventions' are to be contrasted with 'innovations' which are the commercial application of inventions in production and can be either process or product innovations.

Consider, then, the sequence sketched above in which an increase in the growth of demand eventually leads to a reallocation of resources including new technologies implemented by investment. Think of this new technology as the introduction of a process innovation based on some previous invention. Looked at this way, it is clear that before the increased growth in productivity can occur, earlier discoveries or inventions relevant for the new technology must have taken place. These inventions are often dependent upon important breakthroughs in basic scientific research. The electronics and chemical industries are most often cited as industries where such scientific discoveries are necessary conditions for inventions and ultimately innovations.

In a closed economy where no international flow of inventions or innovations is possible, i.e. no possibility of borrowing technology, the supply of inventions may well be very inelastic. This would mean that while demand may be shifting towards certain industries, they are unable to respond without excessive cost increases because the ability to satisfy these growing demands with modern technology is absent or available only at a prohibitive cost. In this sense, the rate of growth of supply does not respond noticeably to an increase in the rate of growth of demand, because the supply response must await favourable but as yet undiscovered scientific and technological developments.

Now in the post-war period leading up to the stagflation of the 1970s, many economies found themselves in the enviable position of facing a relatively elastic supply curve of inventions and innovations.[24] This arose primarily because the USA emerged from the Second World War with a level of technology far superior to that of the other modern market economies and was willing to make a large part of its stock of technological and technical knowledge available to would-be borrowers by means of licensing agreements, patent sales or the creation of multinational subsidiaries. Borrowing or imitating countries would thus be subject to less of a supply constraint than the technology leader, provided, of course, that they wished to borrow the leader's technologies. Similar patterns of development of consumption and production at comparable per capita income levels between countries ensured that they did. This ability to borrow had much to do with the success of countries like Japan in the post-war period. The inability to borrow, at least up until recently, also explains a good part of the American failure to keep pace in productivity growth with the technology borrowers.

Today, technology levels have converged, since the rate of growth of productivity was strongly and negatively correlated with the immediate post-war levels of productivity and per capita income of a country. For example, Japan with a per capita income less than 15 per cent of the US level at the beginning of the 1950s experienced a rate of growth of productivity four times that of the USA during the period up to 1973.[25] This convergence means that even without stagnation, the market economies would very likely find it difficult to maintain their pre-1970s rate of productivity growth today. However, this does not mean that a reduction of unemployment to something like the pre-1973 rates will not stimulate productivity growth. To run an economy at high levels of employment stimulates productivity growth because among other things it strains capacity and decreases labour's resistance to technical change, thereby improving profit prospects and stimulating investment.[26] What it does suggest is that those economies that have achieved levels of income and productivity comparable to the USA would do well to

[24] Cornwall, op. cit., chapter VI.
[25] ibid., table 2.1.
[26] For an econometric study supporting this point see P. Clark (1979) Investment in the 1970s: Theory, performance, and prediction, *Brookings Papers on Economic Activity*, No. 1.

embark on a long-run intensive R&D programme. Industry studies reveal that those industries experiencing rapid rates of technical advance and productivity growth are either heavy R&D spenders (e.g. the chemical industry) or are supplied by such heavy spenders (e.g. the aircraft industry).[27]

CONCLUSIONS

What has taken place over the last decade has been a lessening of aggregate demand pressures relative to capacity leading to a decline in the rate of growth of capital per worker, investment and ultimately productivity. Moreover, the investment that has taken place has been more cost-reducing than expansionary, compared to the earlier post-war period, or else in infrastructure. This goes far to explain the slowdown in productivity. Quite possibly other factors have also been at work reducing productivity growth, but that should not detract from the truth of the argument advanced here. Technological breakthroughs, production reorganizations, labour cooperation in the interests of innovative and expansionary investment, require growing markets and profitable business conditions. For this reason, higher levels and rates of growth of aggregate demand would have led to less stagnation over the past decade and would do so today.

Much has been said about basic structural changes beginning in the 1970s that allegedly have led to a permanent slowdown in productivity growth throughout the OECD. But repeated empirical studies have revealed that no such structural change has taken place. Many factors have been found to influence productivity growth, but in all these accounts it is the slowdown in the rate of growth of output and, therefore, aggregate demand that accounts for most of the slowdown in sectoral and aggregate productivity growth.[28]

In chapter 9, the concept of '*ad hoc* crowding out' was briefly considered and rejected. According to this view, a fiscal stimulant,

---

[27] See Nelson, op. cit.

[28] See R. Boyer and P. Petit (1981) Employment and productivity growth in the EEC, *Cambridge Journal of Economics,* March; R. Ruggles (1979) *Employment and Unemployment Statistics as Indexes of Economic Activity and Capacity Utilization,* Background Paper, No. 28, National Commission on Employment and Unemployment Statistics, Washington, April; and G. Wenban-Smith (1981) A study of the movements of productivity in individual industries in the United Kingdom, 1968–79, *National Institute Economic Review,* August.

whether from greater government expenditures or a tax cut, could not generate additional aggregate demand. The main point of this chapter is that there is a role for aggregate demand, as Keynes so long ago taught us. Changes in aggregate demand have symmetrical impacts on output, employment and productivity as long as there is involuntary unemployment. The failure of decreases in aggregate demand to quickly and painlessly reduce inflation only points up the assymetrical response of wages and prices to aggregate demand. Whether this is an argument in favour of 'fine tuning' is another (largely academic) matter, given the millions of unemployed workers today. The goal of full employment is both feasible and basic to a programme to eliminate stagflation. Chapters 11 and 12 turn to the problem of obtaining price and wage stability at full employment.

CHAPTER 11

What Kind of Incomes Policy?

Any fool can deflate the economy and any fool can launch an inflationary boom. The art lies in balancing a whole series of desirable, but sometimes conflicting objectives.
(*Anonymous member of Mrs Thatcher's Cabinet*)

1. The issue is conflict resolution

The message of chapter 10 is that a necessary condition for ending stagnation is an aggregate demand policy that reduces unemployment rates to something corresponding to 'full employment'. Persistent high rates of unemployment and excess capacity lead to poor productivity performance. Since the authorities have chosen to use high unemployment rates in an effort to curb inflation while avoiding payments difficulties, unemployment and stagnation are causally related to inflation. The key to overcoming stagnation is to find policies that reduce inflation as they reduce unemployment.

But if an inflationary bias is a permanent feature of modern capitalism, it cannot be corrected by 'temporarily' depressing aggregate demand. It requires policies of a more permanent nature. Chapters 11 and 12 discuss two types of voluntary incomes policies that share an important belief; that a modern capitalist economy will show no tendency towards acceptable wage and price behaviour at full employment if collective bargaining is not coordinated with government macro policy. The position taken here is that unless one of these policies or some combination succeeds, there is no way to permanently contain inflation and so no way out of stagflation.

The policies proposed are ones that individual countries can implement unilaterally. Their success, however, will depend upon policies pursued elsewhere. Chapter 15 discusses the need for international cooperation and coordination of policies. Transitional problems, which may require statutory wage and price controls, are not considered. Of interest are long-run policies of voluntary wage and price restraint, with minimal recourse to statutory controls. These policies must resolve the conflicts taking place in fix-price markets that aggregate into struggles over income share and relative wages.

Stated this way, it is clear that some kind of national consensus over the need to restrain inflation without creating widespread unemployment is absolutely essential. The consensus, in turn, requires that the parties to an agreement be convinced that the benefits from cooperation will be shared equitably. All parties must be and must be seen to be treated fairly.

Moreover, cooperation is not limited to restraining inflation. A successful policy to combat stagflation must stimulate productivity growth to increase real wages. As will become clear in chapter 13, productivity growth is very much a function of the degree of cooperation achieved by employers and employees.

The fact that cooperation, fair treatment and, ultimately, trust form the basis for a successful policy to restrain inflation and stimulate productivity growth should not be surprising. Essentially cost-push inflation, of both the wage–price and wage–wage kinds, arises out of a conflict over the distribution of income, caused by feelings of unfairness and distrust. Furthermore, the most dramatic example of a lack of cooperation, one leading to disruption of production and, therefore, zero productivity, is the strike and it too can often be interpreted as a manifestation of the struggle over the distribution of income.[1] Rapid inflation, poor productivity performance and widespread and frequent industrial disruptions are the outgrowths of a lack of economic, political and social cooperation, trust and consensus.

2. The importance of the industrial relations system

If, then, the success of policies leading to wage and price restraint as well as productivity growth is critically dependent upon cooperative relations between capital and labour, a brief review of the industrial relations systems (IRS) in the developed economies is most useful. Important differences between countries in their IRS provide clues for understanding past differences in economic performance as well as suggesting suitable policy measures for improvement.

[1] See D. Hibbs (1978) On the political economy of long-run trends in strike activity, *British Journal of Political Science,* April.

Thus, some have suggested that the industrial relations framework of a modern economy should be classified according to whether it is characterized by interactions between adversaries, or whether these same interactions reflect efforts by capital and labour at all levels of organization to first determine areas of common interest as a basis for cooperation.[2] In the former case capital and labour start from the premise that areas of conflicting interests dominate economic relations and these are to be the basis for defining positions of resistance to the adversary's demand as well as formulating their own goals. In the latter case, the two sides start from the position that there are areas of common agreement that must be determined and then protected through compromise and consultation.

All of this, to be sure, is a matter of degree but this distinction illuminates some important issues discussed in chapters 11 to 14. It points up some major differences between the industrial relations systems and economic performances in English-speaking countries and in other developed market economies. In addition, this distinction helps to see what kinds of incomes and industrial policies are appropriate and most likely to be successful, given the existing institutional arrangements.

3. An outline of the chapter

At a general level, then, the analysis of this and the next three chapters deals with some of the basic determinants of successful economic performance and, ultimately, economic and political stability. The common theme is the importance of cooperation and of policies and institutions that foster cooperation.

This chapter focuses on incomes policies that are appropriate for economies in which cooperative industrial relations between capital and labour have developed. The next section briefly discusses two general types of permanent, voluntary incomes policies that differ in the emphasis placed on the methods of compliance. Since these differences are ultimately related to differences in the nature of the IRS, pp. 250–6 outline a cooperative industrial relations system of the

---

[2] See C. Crouch, The conditions for trade-union wage restraint, in *The Politics of Inflation and Economic Stagnation* (Eds L. Lindberg and C. Maier), The Brookings Institution, forthcoming; and E. Kassalow (1980) Industrial conflict and consensus in the U.S. and Western Europe, in *Labour Relations in Advanced Industrial Societies: Issues and Problems* (Eds B. Martin and E. Kassalow), Carnegie Endowment for International Peace, Washington. The first half of chapter 11 has been strongly influenced by the writings of Crouch.

Continental European type. Methods of policy formation and conflict resolution based on the 'Continental model' of industrial relations are discussed on pp. 256–63; i.e. 'Social Democratic
Corporatism'. It is argued on pp. 260–4 that the way to achieve
wage and price stability in countries with strong union movements is
to forego 'union bashing' and seek union cooperation.

The final section turns to an entirely different example of a cooperative IRS; that found in Japan. The extraordinary nature of the
Japanese IRS is the lack of a desire by management to exploit the
weaknesses of the trade unions. The cooperative attitude that exists
between management and the unions is seen as an important influence explaining the favourable inflation record of Japan.

TWO CLASSES OF VOLUNTARY INCOMES POLICIES

However classified or defined, all permanent incomes policies start
from the belief that the interaction of large-scale organizations, each
pursuing its own immediate self-interest, is incompatible with price
stability and full employment. Unlike the monetarist-neoclassical
world, no self-regulating mechanism is assumed. Instead, advocates
of incomes policies seek by various means to cause wages and prices
to behave otherwise than if determined by the 'interplay of market
forces'. Achieving national objectives such as wage and price stability
depends upon either these economic groups internalizing the costs of
potential conflicts in such a way as to lead to cooperation, or the
state intervening with political measures or, most likely, both.[3] An
unconstrained pursuit of private interests unrelated to national goals
is disruptive, not beneficial.

Alternatively, policies can be viewed as a method of coordinating
collective bargaining decisions with government macroeconomic
policy. However stated, policies involve the formulation of norm,
indicating the desired period by period behaviour for wages and
prices, and various methods of achieving compliance.[4] In the past,
the latter has often been no more than patriotic appeals or 'jaw-

---

[3] Crouch, op. cit.

[4] All policies can be said to aim at decreasing the sensitivity of wages and prices to
increases in demand pressures and to increase their sensitivity to declines in aggregate demand. This, if successful, results in inflation being stable upwards and
unstable downwards in response to changes in aggregate demand, an asymmetrical response but one that reverses the relative sensitivities described in
chapter 6.

boning'. The systematic collection and dissemination of information by governing bodies, outlining likely price, wage and productivity movements at home and abroad with an aim to suggesting what is 'reasonable' has also been used.[5] This has been combined with announcements by government as to their intended fiscal and monetary response to domestic wage and price developments.[6] Centralized institutions have been established to coordinate collective bargaining settlements and policy goals. These have ranged from investigatory bodies to tripartite bodies (manned by government, union and employer representatives) to arbitration commissions.[7]

Going further, incomes policies have used various inducement to elicity compliance. These have included tax and subsidy policies, expenditure programmes and the promise of increased political power. Obviously, there is no end to the possibilities, as any compilation of policies adopted in the past will attest.[8] However, in this study it will be found useful to distinguish broadly between two general types of voluntary incomes policies. The distinction is based upon the general method adopted to induce compliance to some norm(s). The method chosen reflects important differences in the IRS of the economies. In the final analysis, however, it will be clear that no incomes policy can have any hope of success without incorporating many instruments of policy. It will be apparent that both kinds of policies involve substantially more in the way of government intervention than simply patriotic appeals and the provision of information.

With this in mind, voluntary incomes policies can be divided into two types; one general class in which the main economic groups are induced to comply with wage and price norms or guidelines by measures that lead them to internalize the costs of their wage and

[5] The success of the 'Scandinavian model' discussed in chapter 4 requires good data of this kind.

[6] The German authorities have set monetary guidelines in an effort to obtain wage restraint. See also J. Meade (1982) *Stagflation, Volume I: Wage-Fixing,* George Allen & Unwin, London.

[7] See C. Blyth (1979) The interaction between collective bargaining and government policies in selected member countries, in *Collective Bargaining and Government Policies,* OECD, Paris, pp. 82–90, for a classification of the various kinds of coordinating machinery.

[8] For a quick summary of policies tried in the post-war period, see J. Addison (1981) Incomes Policy: The recent European experience, in *Incomes Policies, Inflation and Relative Pay* (Eds J. Fallick and R. Elliott), George Allen & Unwin, London. An effort to sift through the various proposals is found in F. Blackaby (1980) An array of proposals, and A. Dean (1980) Roles of governments and institutions in OECD countries, in *The Future of Pay Bargaining* (Ed. F. Blackaby), Heinemann, London.

price behaviour. These will be referred to as consensus policies. The second class of voluntary incomes policies involves legislative and other measures that provide incentives in the form of financial rewards or penalties or both that are directly related to compliance or non-compliance with wage or price norms.[9] These will be referred to as incentive policies. Given that the inflationary mechanism is basically the same in the developed market economies, a consensus or incentive policy or some combination must form the core of any anti-inflation policy. A correct formulation must start from a recognition that these are the only options available. Following a short discussion of industrial relations systems that emphasizes capital and labour cooperation, the analysis in the remainder of the chapter turns to consensus policies.

COOPERATIVE INDUSTRIAL RELATIONS SYSTEMS

1. The 'Continental model'

Many modern capitalist economies outside the English-speaking world have developed institutions fostering cooperation between workers and management at the plant, enterprise, industry and national level. The expression 'concertative institutions' is often used to denote cooperative arrangements at the plant, firm or industry level. Within a particular plant or firm, these are especially relevant for productivity growth but formal and informal arrangements at the firm level are most relevant in achieving wage and price restraint.

Paradoxically, concertative institutions developed in European countries in which the labour movement had a strong anti-capitalist if not socialist orientation. What has come to be known as the 'Continental model' is a system of labour–management relations that has tended to minimize industrial disputes, partly by incorporating concertative institutions.[10] Moreover, this has not been at the cost of a loss of dynamic efficiency as measured, say, by productivity growth.

Consider table 11.1 which shows strike activity in twelve mature market economies in the period leading up to stagflation. Several things stand out. First, there is the extremely high rate of strike

---

[9] Profit sharing schemes are related to local performance, not national wage or price norms. They can be treated as a supplement to any incomes policy.

[10] See E. Kassalow (1977) Industrial conflict and consensus in the United States and Western Europe: A comparative analysis, *IRRA Annual Proceedings*, December; and O. Clarke (1980) The development of industrial relations in European market economies, *IRRA Annual Proceedings*, September.

TABLE 11.1   *Industrial disputes, selected countries, 1965–74 (days lost per 1000 people employed) and rates of unionization*

Country	Days lost in strikes, 1965–74	Percentage of unionization of non-agricultural wage and salary employees (%)
Australia	913	55
Belgium	334	70
Canada	1644	37
Denmark	511	65
Federal Republic of Germany	50	39
Great Britain	743	50
Japan	243	35
Netherlands	65	39–40
Norway	60	63
Sweden	46	82–83
Switzerland	1	37
USA	1305	28–29

Source: E. Kassalow, Industrial conflict and consensus, op. cit.
Man-days lost per 1000 employed is a comprehensive index of strike volume that is the product of the frequency, duration and size of strikes. Thus,

$$\frac{\text{Man-days lost per}}{\text{1000 employed workers}} = \frac{\text{Strikes}}{\text{Employed workers (in thousands)}} \times \frac{\text{Man-days}}{\text{Workers involved}} \times \frac{\text{Workers involved}}{\text{Strikes}}$$

or:
Strike volume   = Frequency   × Duration   × Size

See Hibbs, On the political economy, op. cit.

activity in the four English-speaking countries. Second, there is the relatively low rate of strike activity in the Continental countries, Belgium, Denmark, West Germany, the Netherlands, Norway and Sweden. Third, there is the very impressive record for Switzerland and to a lesser extent for Japan. If Denmark is ignored, what is also remarkable is the tremendous gap between the extent of strike activity in the English-speaking group and the others.[11] Moreover, the fact that the Continental group of countries is heavily unionized with high-level bargaining and highly centralized or federated union movements, while Japan and Switzerland are economies with a weak, fragmented union structure appears to be of minor conse-

[11] Italy and France have experienced a high incidence of strikes. They do not fit the Continental model of an IRS largely because of the importance of communist-dominated trade unions and the weak development of the welfare state.

quence.[12] Similarly, the English-speaking group contains the North American countries with a low density of unionization as well as the highly unionized Australian and British economies. Clearly, neither the degree of centralization of the union movement nor the density of unionization of the labour force are correlated with the degree of disruption. The question is why economies with highly centralized, powerful union movements of socialist origins experience so much less disruption than the English-speaking economies.

Several factors leading to a more successful record of conflict resolution in Continental systems can be cited. First, the union movement in Continental Europe emerged as part of a struggle by the working class for voting rights and the realization of a socialist society, as well as economic protection and gain. It more readily identified with a political party compared, say, with North American unions. This fostered greater reliance by unions on legislation to achieve economic goals, rather than a more exclusive reliance on collective bargaining as in North America.[13] The heavier reliance on collective bargaining in North America quite naturally led and continues to lead to a bargaining situation that was more conflict prone, since a wider number of issues would be under dispute.

Second, the rise of unions was accompanied on the Continent by a rise of employers' associations whose attitudes towards unions differed from attitudes elsewhere in at least two important respects. While the attitude towards unions as late as the turn of the century was strongly antagonistic, acceptance came swiftly and more easily soon after. This in itself would be important in eventually creating more harmonious industrial relations, especially as unionization was extended to new industries in the more recent period. In addition, the national scope of the employers' associations helped to deflect unions from organizing at the enterprise level.[14]

The latter point is particularly relevant to a third issue. What has evolved in Continental countries is an IRS that has established a distinction between issues on which labour and management clearly disagree and those on which there is broad agreement. This division has become associated with separate institutions for handling matters of conflict and those of common interest.[15] In particular,

---

[12] There is a high correlation between the fraction of the labour force unionized, the degree of centralization in decision making and the level at which collective bargaining is carried out. See Blyth, op. cit., appendix.

[13] The lack of legislation to secure economic goals also helps explain the extremely high numbers of lawyers per capita in the USA.

[14] See Kassalow in Martin and Kassalow, op. cit., p. 53.

[15] Clarke, op. cit.

matters of conflict, of which pay is the critical one, tend to be handled through collective bargaining at the industrial, national or regional level instead of in the plant or firm. This gives unions a much diminished direct role inside the plant and firm. Instead, alternative structures have developed whose chief function is to discuss and resolve issues of common interest.[16] Furthermore, by removing matters of conflict from the plant and firm and placing them at a higher organizational level, any concessions made during the process of collective bargaining is less likely to lead to a felt loss of authority or 'face'. This must lead to a quicker and more satisfactory resolution of conflict in collective bargaining and allow a cooperative spirit at the enterprise level to remain intact.

In sum, the 'Continental model' of industrial relations is one in which matters of conflict over wages and other matters tend to be dealt with through collective bargaining at the industry, national or regional level, while matters of common interest are discussed within the plant and enterprise. Furthermore, the number of conflicts to be resolved has been reduced because legislative enactments have led to prior achievements of certain goals. Add to this the greater willingness of employers to accept unionism in Europe and a general unwillingness to do so in English-speaking countries and the outlines of two alternative forms of industrial relations systems emerge, one cooperative, the other adversarial.

2. Cooperation and distributional issues

The structure of employee and employer associations goes far to explain relative strike activity. So do differences in the number of issues that need to be settled through collective bargaining. Unions and employers operating in a society in which social and economic benefits other than wages are not at issue in bargaining arrangements are more likely to minimize conflict. However, this presupposes that these same benefits have been secured through legislations. The point is that much of the industrial harmony found in the Continental economies must be attributed to the welfare state. Without these welfare programmes, collective bargaining would likely resemble that in North America, as discussed below.

For example, using a sample of nine OECD countries in which the IRS and welfare programmes differed greatly, a strong negative correlation was found between non-defence government spending as a

---

[16] The importance of these structures in enhancing productivity growth is discussed in the next chapter.

share of GNP and strike activity. This was true whether comparing changes between the inter-war and post-war period or across countries in the post-war period. A companion study reaffirmed the need of governments, be they friendly to labour or not, to deliver tangible rewards to labour if they wished to discourage labour militancy.[17] These results were confirmed by a similar study employing a larger sample of countries in the post-war period.[18] In all cases, the industrial harmony in the Continental model economies was clearly related to welfare benefits available to all. Similarly, the widespread industrial strife in North America was largely attributable to a failure of government to provide these benefits.

Figure 11.1 portrays changes over time in the volume of strikes in eleven countries and helps illustrate the impact of developments in industrial relations.[19] The strike measure is designed to take account of the frequency of strikes, their duration and their size. What stands out is the increase in disruptions in North America, Finland, Italy and France and the noticeable decline in strike volume in the other countries. Strikes, like cost–push inflation, are interpreted largely as a manifestation of conflicts over the distribution of incomes. Their sharp reduction in some countries is attributable to a change in the way distributional outcomes are determined. What is involved here is simply the evolution of one facet of the Continental model. In the post-war period, many countries introduced social legislation guaranteeing all citizens certain public goods and services that hitherto had been sought after in collective bargaining, if at all. The result was to transfer areas of conflict from collective bargaining to parliament.[20]

---

[17] 'The core of the argument is that *long-run changes in the volume of industrial conflict are largely explained by changes in the locus of the struggle over distribution'* (italics in original), Hibbs On the political economy . . . , op. cit., p. 165; and D. Hibbs (1976) Industrial conflict in advanced industrial societies, *The American Political Science Review,* December.

[18] Crouch, op. cit.

[19] Hibbs, On the political economy . . . , op. cit.

[20] The British record would seem to be at variance with most of what has been said up to this point. The industrial relations system is strongly adversarial, yet the strike record has improved measurably according to figure 11.1, an improvement attributed to the implementation of the welfare state. However, while the British record reveals a noticeable improvement when the period 1918–36 is compared to 1944–72, events within the post-war period reveal a counter trend. Thus a steady increase in strike activity beginning in the late 1960s took place in Britain. As table 11.1 indicates, by 1974 the record in industrial relations was relatively poor. In contrast, the 1965–74 period revealed no such deterioration in industrial relations in Belgium, the Netherlands, Norway and Sweden.

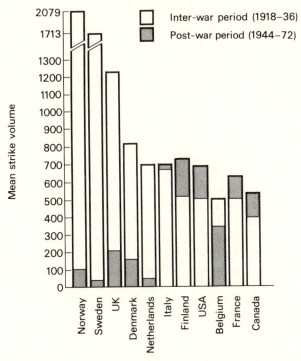

FIGURE 11.1   *Changes in strike volume over time*

Source: D. Hibbs (1978) On the political economy of long-run trends in strike
activity, *British Journal of Political Science.*
Note: Mean strike volume for the post-war period is measured by the distance from
the horizontal axis to the top of the striped bar. See comments to table 11.1 for
definition of strike volume.

France and Italy are countries with industrial relations that do
not fit the cooperative pattern nor the pure, adversarial, unconstrained collective bargaining model. The industrial relation system
is adversarial in these two countries and intensified by the existence
of communist trade unions (as in Finland), but the state has often
intervened in the bargaining process in a unilateral way, setting
wages, etc. However, intervention in this sense, and a lack of intervention to create the welfare state, has intensified adversarial relations, generating a poor strike record similar to that of the
English-speaking countries.

The point is that there is more to harmonious industrial relations
than the existence of bargaining institutions that enhance cooperation between workers and management. The installation of a com-

prehensive welfare programme has also been characteristic of Continental economies. This guarantees workers certain benefits that are only available (if at all) in a country such as the USA as part of a collective-bargaining settlement. Together, the Continental model of industrial relations and the rise of the welfare state have enhanced industrial peace.

3. *Capitalism and industrial conflict*

Events have a way of creeping up on economics. The ability of so many developed economies, outside the English-speaking countries, to avert strikes and in general to maintain harmonious industrial relations has set businessmen and government officials (if not economists) to thinking more seriously about the importance of co-operation in industrial relations. Capitalist economies come with widely different kinds of industrial relations systems and these differences are reflected in widely different levels of industrial harmony. Some economies have been highly strike prone but it is clear that this is not inevitable under capitalism. What is becoming clear in the English-speaking countries is that their records of bad labour–management relations is a record they can ill afford.

The case to be made now is that not only does the welfare state lead to industrial peace but other things being equal, it improves price stability.[21] In the next three sections incomes policies undertaken by and appropriate for economies with strong, centralized trade union movements are discussed. Following that the study turns to Japan, an economy with harmonious industrial relations and a successful voluntary incomes policy, but one with a fragmented labour movement.

CONSENSUS INCOMES POLICIES AND SOCIAL
DEMOCRATIC CORPORATISM (SDC)

1. *The Continental model and policy formation*

Consider, then, a developed capitalist society in which institutions of cooperation between labour and capital are widespread. Allow that

---

[21] The contrary view has been stated by Friedman: 'Governments have not produced high inflation as a deliberately announced policy but as a consequence of other policies – in particular, policies of full employment and welfare-state policies raising government spending.' See M. Friedman (1977) Nobel lecture: Inflation and unemployment, *Journal of Political Economy*, June.

the trade union movement is strong as measured by union membership. Collective bargaining is highly centralized so that, if there is not national bargaining, there is industrial and region-wide bargaining with a likelihood of coordination at the national level. Next, assume that individual employers are willing to delegate their bargaining rights to central confederations of employers which are able to ensure obedience. Finally, allow for widespread compliance by the rank and file with any collective agreement worked out.

What has evolved in these economies with a Continental model of industrial relations is the rejection of individualistic, adversarial industrial relations of the kind to be described in chapter 12. Moreover, institutions have evolved at the national level that assist the development of cooperation and common interests. To some extent this was taken up in the previous section in the discussion of the redistributional function of the modern welfare state. But there is more to it than this. There has developed an industrial relations system that relies, very strongly, not only on cooperative relationships between centralized capital and labour organizations, but also between these two and the central government. The aim has been and continues to be the realization of industrial peace and other national goals. Political scientists and politicians have increasingly been given to use the expression 'democratic', 'liberal' or 'social democratic corporatism' (SDC) in describing societies with centralized collective bargaining and strong union movements in which the aims and wishes of capital and labour are accommodated in state policies.

Social democratic corporatism is seen by some as a natural part of the evolution of capitalism, greatly abetted by the commitment of many governments to full employment. It has been variously defined but is summarized adequately as:

an institutionalized pattern of policy-formation in which large interest organizations cooperate with each other and with public authorities not only in the articulation (or even 'intermediation') of interests, but . . . in the implementation of such policies.

And:

liberal corporatism should not be confounded with simply more consultation and cooperation of government with organized interest groups which is, of course, common in all constitutional democracies with a highly developed capitalist economy. The distinguishing trait of liberal corporatism is a high degree of collaboration among these groups themselves in shaping economic policy.[22]

An important defining feature is the coordination of aims and efforts within each of a limited number of groups, for present purposes capital and labour, allowing highly centralized decision-making organizations to operate. This centralizing tendency is often encouraged by the state which grants a representational monopoly to an organization in its dealings with other centrally organized bodies. Once organized, the interests of capital and labour are allowed to influence policy and the state expects their consent and their collaboration in implementing those policies. But the state is an active force influencing the behaviour of these interest groups as well.

2. The origins of SDC

Historically, corporatism has been associated with fascism (corporatism from 'above' or 'state' corporatism) and the term is often avoided in English-speaking countries by labour when characterizing its political programmes. However, corporatist developments have emerged in even the most democratic capitalist countries. Modern writers in affixing a prefix such as 'liberal', 'democratic' or 'social democratic' to the term inevitably stress the voluntary nature of the association with the government.

Organizations are highly centralized but autonomous (i.e. free to enter or withdraw from some arrangement), wielding strong powers in an environment of equals. Thus, in fact, the proper contrast here is not between corporatist and democratic systems, but between corporatism and economic pluralism. In the latter, the pattern of policy formulation entails a government that is relatively passive, reacting to demands by special interests. A reluctance to lead is justified by vague references to countervailing power or some other form of the invisible hand that allegedly brings about harmonious political and economic relations.

Social democratic corporatism developed largely in Continental Europe after the First World War. Thus,

---

[22] See G. Lehmbruch (1977) Liberal corporatism and party government, *Comparative Political Studies,* April, p. 94. The entire April 1977 issue of this journal is devoted to 'Corporatism and policy making in contemporary Western Europe'.

in a few Continental European cases, the intervening period of individualistic liberalism was quite short and incomplete as monarchic autocracies and conservative oligarchies attempted to make over from above medieval corporations into modern interest associations (e.g. West Germany, and especially, Austria).[23]

Often its development was associated with open, highly exposed economies which modernized relatively late.[24] The basis of its wide appeal in the post-war period was and is a desire to maintain full employment and to solve the inflationary problems generated by full employment.

3. Corporatism and incomes policy

Today, SDC manifests itself most clearly in the coordination of collective bargaining with national policy. This often takes the form of a tripartite arrangement in support of voluntary incomes policies, earlier referred to as consensus policies. Labour, capital and government, represented by organizations with decision-making power cooperate, consult and implement policies of wage and price stability. Behind these developments lies a commitment to full employment and the welfare state and the desire today to reaffirm this commitment. Incomes policies are needed since full employment increases the power of labour, especially when centrally organized, to put strong pressure on wages and prices. Social democratic corporatism strives to restrain this potential power. The success of an incomes policy, therefore, requires the cooperation, acceptance and assistance of unions in implementing and monitoring it.[25]

4. Acceptance of consensus policies in the post-war period

One study of eleven economies in the 1950s and 1960s concluded that two conditions must be met before labour unions would 'accept'

---

[23] See P. Schmitter (1981) Interest intermediation and regime governability in Western Europe and North America, in *Organizing Interests in Western Europe: Pluralism, Corporatism, and the Transformation of Politics* (Ed. S. Berger), Cambridge University Press, Cambridge.

[24] Crouch, op. cit.

[25] Interested observers of economic policy in the English-speaking countries often have great difficulty in understanding the workings of any kind of incomes policy other than one framed in explicit legal terms. An incomes policy involves an attempt to influence wage and price decisions so that they are more consistent with the aims of macro policy. The point is this is often done in European economies through 'gentlemen's agreements'.

a consensus incomes policy, framed largely in terms of wage norms.[26] Acceptance was defined as ten consecutive years of operation of a policy in which labour acquiesced in regular and direct government intervention in an effort to influence wage settlements. First, it was required that a pro-labour (usually socialist) government governed or shared power for most of the policy period. Second, a strong centralized union movement was required in which confederation leaders were involved in the administration of the policy, bargaining tended to be at the national level and discipline and compliance of the member unions was enforced through confederation control of strike funds and dues of the member units. The Scandinavian countries, Austria (but not West Germany), the Netherlands and Belgium were found to satisfy the two conditions most fully in the period considered. The English-speaking countries in the sample, the UK, the USA and Ireland, together with West Germany, France and Italy did not satisfy both conditions.[27]

Consensus incomes policies where accepted varied from guidelines with no retroactive government powers to strike down wage increases to those that included such power. In some cases, tripartite groups were given power to advise on wage (and price) increases. In others, the Scandinavian approach was adopted in which government played a less-active role. The common feature, however, was the acceptance by unions as well as others of the view that unconstrained 'free' collective bargaining was not an acceptable means of determining wage settlements. Governments regularly and directly confronted both union and employer representatives in an effort to influence bargaining outcomes.

UNION COOPERATION AS A SUBSTITUTE FOR
UNION BASHING

Those who believe that SDC policies can ensure relatively harmonious industrial relations, as evidenced by strike activity, also see them as advancing the cause of wage and price stability. Just how successful these policies were in the past is difficult to determine with any exactness.

---

[26] See B. Heady (1970) Trade unions and national wages policies, *The Journal of Politics*, May.

[27] Crouch, op. cit., disputes Heady's finding that decision-making within the German labour movement is not highly centralized.

A casual comparison of the inflationary performances of the OECD economies up until the end of the 1960s leads only to the negative conclusion that rates of wage inflation, and more importantly rates of growth of unit labour costs, did not appreciably differ between those countries with SDC incomes policies and the rest. It is worth emphasizing, however, that economies in which SDC policies were used had exceptionally low rates of unemployment and strong unions. It is also worth emphasizing that the issue is not whether countries with consensus incomes policies experienced inflation, but whether inflationary conditions would have been noticeably worse without regular and direct (but not necessarily statutory) intervention in wage and price setting.[28]

More revealing is the record in the period of stagflation. Before the early 1970s productivity growth had been substantial in all OECD countries allowing a rapid growth of real wages. Following the recession of the early 1970s (1973 marked the peak in activity in most countries) real wage growth slowed noticeably. In chapter 6, the possibility of 'real wage resistance' was discussed. Any deviation below trend in growth rate of real wages would be likely to accelerate money wage demands as part of an effort by workers to maintain what had come to be considered a normal increase in real wages.

The observation that under SDC arrangements the existence of strong, centralized union movements, paradoxically, is consistent with wage and price stability suggests that real wage resistance would be least in countries in which cooperation was a normal pattern of events. With cooperation at the national level between the major economic groups, falling real wages would be less likely to set off accelerated money wage demands and settlements as the major economic groups learned to come to terms with stagflation.

This view has been tested in an econometric study of eighteen OECD economies.[29] The increase in the rate of price inflation in the 1970s over the 1971–72 inflation rate was regressed on strike activity

[28] A common technique used to reveal whether incomes policies do or do not make a difference is to introduce dummy variables as regressors. However, SDC incomes policies involve a gradual process of developing institutions of cooperation and consultation. Even when one of the parties to the consensus formally refuses to take part in the implementation of the policy there is a carry over of attitudes from the past. Similarly, before a policy is about to be implemented there is no marked abrupt change in the institutions or attitudes of the participants.

[29] See C. Barber and J. McCallum (1982) *Controlling Inflation: Learning from Experience in Canada, Europe and Japan*, Canadian Institute for Economic Policy, Ottawa, chapter 1. See also Crouch, op. cit.

in the 1960s (a measure of consensus or willingness to cooperate). The hypothesis tested was that economies with a high degree of social consensus would adjust best to the supply shocks beginning in 1972–73. This would be revealed by a negative relation between the acceleration of inflation rates in the 1970s (compared with 1971–72) and strike activity in the 1960s.

According to the hypothesis, efforts to resist real wage decline through accelerated wage settlements and, therefore, price inflation, would be reduced when consensus was strong.[30] The hypothesis was supported by the usual statistical criteria as almost 80 per cent of the variance was explained by the strike variable alone. This compared favourably with an alternative monetarist hypothesis.

Recall the conclusions of chapters 6 and 7. Trade unions (and oligopolies) functioning in an environment of sustained full employment have led to a situation in which modern economies suffer from an inflationary bias. This derived from the ability of labour to push for fairness considerations in their wage settlements which was contingent upon the rise of unions and their development of 'staying power'. This was the final link in the development of the cost–push inflation mechanism. Such a mechanism is at work today in all economies in which trade unions and large scale corporations exist side by side.

Under discussion here are policies that might greatly restrain these inflationary tendencies. Comparing one country with another, economies with high density unionism and centralized union organizations but pursuing SDC policies, are seen to be more likely to experience lower rates of inflation than other economies with other structures and policies at comparable rates of unemployment. A case can be made that the welfare state, far from generating inflationary tendencies, may well be leading to a favourable inflation record.

Although these cross-country studies are only in a development stage and the data is subject to more than one interpretation, the

[30] The relevant regression results were:

$$\dot{p}_t = \dot{p}_{t-1} - 5.26 + 1.865S \qquad R^2 = 0.79$$
$$ (4.0) \quad\;\; (7.2)$$

and

$$\dot{p}_t = 3.20 + 0.76(\dot{M} - \dot{Q}) \qquad R^2 = 0.68$$
$$ (2.7) \quad (6.1)$$

where $\dot{p}_t$, $\dot{p}_{t-1}$, S, $\dot{M}$ and $\dot{Q}$ represent the average rates of price inflation in 1973–79 and 1971–72, the logarithm of average number of working days lost per thousand non-agricultural workers 1950–69, the average rate of growth of the narrowly defined money supply for 1972–78 and the trend rate of growth of real GNP for 1972–78, respectively. Figures in parentheses are t − statistics.

issue is basic. What is being suggested is that serious inflation at low rates of unemployment is more probable in one kind of social structure than another. If this is true, policies to reduce inflation on a permanent basis may involve long-term structural changes. Curtailing the power of unions, primarily through restrictive aggregate demand and policies, is one possible policy response to inflation. The discussion here suggests quite a different one.

THE PARADOX OF UNION POWER

The success of any kind of consensus incomes policy requires the cooperation of labour, especially the unions, on wage constraint. Yet, an important implication of SDC incomes policy is, paradoxically, that the more centralized and coordinated and, therefore, the more powerful is the union movement, the more likely is wage restraint to result. The paradox has been resolved by many writers along the following lines.[31] Compared with a world of perfect competition, a world of trade unions is more inflationary. But with a centralized union movement the leaders will likely be aware of the macroeconomic effects of their activities. In these circumstances they may be willing to cooperate in efforts to achieve national goals such as wage and price stability.[32] In addition, the problem of individual unions disregarding the generally accepted wage norm in order to improve their relative wage is lessened. In effect centralization achieves synchronized wage settlements.

Labour may not cooperate, to be sure, but it is even more difficult to see a fragmented union movement adhering to a consensus policy of wage restraint, unless unions are very weak. Hence, the apparent paradox that the more centralized is the labour movement the greater is the possibility that the costs of excessive wage demands will be internalized by unions. In the post-war period, the ability of governments to attract and maintain the support of unions in a policy of wage restraint, industrial peace, etc., has necessitated concessions to labour, usually in the form of welfare measures such as free medical care, generous retirement and unemployment benefits, but often in the form of shared responsibility; e.g. an influence on government policy and trade union representation in the cabinet. If

---

[31] See Blackaby, op. cit., chapter IV; Blyth, op. cit., pp. 75–77 and Crouch, op. cit.

[32] The same general reasoning helps explain why, even if deflationary policies achieve the status of 'credibility', they are not likely to be terribly effective in a country with a fragmented labour movement. They might still work in a country like West Germany (where they have been tried) with its highly centralized, coordinated union decision-making. See chapter 12, pp. 282–4.

union bashing seems counterproductive, so might dismantling of the welfare state.[33] This important point will be discussed further below.

BOURGEOIS DEMOCRATIC CORPORATISM

1. The Japanese IRS

Internalizing the social costs of inflationary wage and price setting requires that the participants recognize that certain types of behaviour may directly lead to adverse consequences at the national level, or at least contribute to an unfavourable result if imitated on a wide scale. Somewhat paradoxically, wage restraint in the interest of national well-being may be enhanced by concentrated market power. But the experience of Japan in the post-war period strongly suggests there are other means to price and wage stability. The Japanese experience reveals that economies characterized by cooperative IRS fall into two distinct types; one with a strong and highly centralized trade union movement as in the Continental model; and one in which the trade union movement is weak and highly fragmented.

The Japanese trade union movement is composed of several hundred autonomous unions in which collective bargaining is carried out by individual unions whose decisions are usually unco-ordinated with decisions made in other collective agreements. Yet the available evidence indicates that labour at the enterprise and plant level in Japan is very much concerned about the impact of the collective bargaining decisions on the welfare of both the company and the country. The ultimate effect is that a consensus incomes policy has been operative in Japan throughout the post-war period. 'Free' collective bargaining has not been carried out in the adversarial manner common in English-speaking countries, but in a manner in which wage setting is highly constrained as in the Continental European countries pursuing SDC policies.

2. Built-in stabilization

To see the extraordinary nature of this system, note that with a fragmented labour movement, the social costs of any single wage settlement, e.g. the effect on the aggregate rate of price inflation or national export performance, will be slight. But if all settlements are influenced by immediate financial gain alone and if there is a strong tendency to ignore any suggested national guideline or norm, the social costs can be very great. Now any one union stands to lose

---

[33] Compare the text view with the quote of Friedman's views in footnote 21 above.

substantially in its ranking in the wage structure if all other wage settlements are made with total disregard of the national norm and it alone is constrained by a form of public spirit.[34] And it has much to gain by joining the others. Considerations such as this that have led economists to argue that consensus incomes policies are not likely to be even moderately successful when the labour movement is fragmented.

Yet consider the data in table 11.2 for Japan. Earnings in Japanese industry are made up of three components of which the contractual earnings are about two-thirds and bonuses a little less than one-third of the total. Bonus payments are based on the profitability of the company and therefore vary with the phases of the business cycle. During 1974 the Japanese authorities intensified their restrictive aggregate demand policies causing industrial profits (but not employment) to decline sharply in 1974 and recover, moderately, in 1975. The lagged impact on bonus payments in 1975 and 1976 is seen in table 11.2.[35]

TABLE 11.2 *Wages, productivity and unit labour costs percentage changes from previous year*

	Percentage of total[b]	1973	1974	1975	1976
Total cash earnings[a]	100.0	21.5	27.2	14.8	12.8
Contractual cash earnings[c]	67.3	18.0	27.6	19.6	11.7
Overtime pay	6.0	24.8	4.4	1.1	25.2
Special cash payments	26.6	29.5	32.8	6.6	13.1
Productivity[d]		20.1	0.8	−5.1	13.6
Unit labour costs[d]		2.8	25.2	17.5	0.9
Consumer prices – industrial goods		12.3	28.3	7.4	6.6

Source: Economic Survey of Japan, OECD, Paris, 1975, p. 22 and 1977, pp. 15, 16.
[a] Firms with more than thirty regular employees.
[b] In fiscal year 1976.
[c] Excluding overtime pay.
[d] In manufacturing industry.

[34] The general problem here is one of a class of problems collectively known as the Prisoner's Dilemma. In this case, if each union pursues only its immediate self-interest (in this case pushing for the highest wage increase possible), a less favourable result obtains than if every union and labour group followed a different principle of behaviour (wage restraint). However, for any one group to not pursue economic self-interest while all others do, would cause harm to the former.

[35] Additional data to that cited in table 11.2 is taken from *Economic Survey of Japan,* 1976, OECD, Paris, p. 24.

The beneficial effects of this on-unit labour cost, and therefore prices, are also shown; such profit (and productivity) related wage payments automatically decline when restrictive policies are in force. Of equal interest is the impact of anti-inflationary policies on contractual pay earnings, this in a country of lifetime employment security. The growth rates of these fell by almost two-thirds from 1974 to 1976. Moreover, productivity growth accelerated after 1975, indicating that if unions were dissatisfied with the behaviour of earnings, this did not seem to cause any difficulties on the shop floor. The impact of all this on unit labour costs and prices is quite dramatic as indicated.

No other country succeeded in reducing inflation following the events leading up to 1974 as well as the Japanese. Yet this was done without markedly driving up unemployment rates, and without statutory wage and price controls or the kind of tripartite agreement found in some Continental European economies. Some clues to understanding this phenomenal achievement are discussed in chapter 13. There it is pointed out that no other IRS has been able to match the Japanese in its ability to develop what was termed concertative institutions which foster cooperation.

Japanese unions were readily accepted by management from the very beginning of the post-war period. Not only that, they receive concessions from management in the form of company benefits that match in many cases what workers in Continental countries obtain through legislation.[36] What has developed is a 'Japanese model' of industrial relations that largely parallels at the enterprise level what has evolved at the national level in Continental Europe. The origins of such a system are vastly different from their European counterparts but its impact has been similar.

The success of efforts to bring down inflation beginning in 1975 is but another aspect of the whole process.[37] Cooperation in industrial

---

[36] It should be noted that the Japanese economy can be described (somewhat metaphorically) as a 'dual economy' in which a large share of enterprises can be described as in the text, but in which another large part of industry is made up of 'marginal firms' which do not treat their workers quite as well.

[37] Rates of wage ($\dot{w}$) and price ($\dot{p}$) inflation in Japan for the relevant years were:

	1974	1975	1976	1977	1978	1979	1980	1981
$\dot{w}$	25.8	15.0	11.0	9.2	6.5	5.8	7.7	7.6
$\dot{p}$	24.5	11.8	9.3	8.1	3.8	3.6	8.0	4.9

Source: Economic Outlook, OECD, Paris, July 1982, table R10 and OECD private correspondence. Wage data is for manufacturing.

relations is based on trust between workers and management and when management has obtained the workers' trust, their statements about the need to adjust wage demands downwards would have a high degree of credibility.[38] That, plus the fact that Japanese management in large industrial concerns is constantly made aware of the government's policy aims and is willing to cooperate with government.

The success of the Japanese policy arrangements is most apparent in its performance in recent times. Unemployment and inflation rates remain low, the former in spite of some relaxation of the lifetime employment provision in large firms. Many have cited the uniqueness of the Japanese culture and history as an explanation of its economic success. The conclusion here, and in chapter 13, is that Japan's uniqueness lies in its highly cooperative IRS and the fragmented nature of the labour union movement. To put it differently, what is unique about the Japanese example is a concern by Japanese management for its workers in spite of the weakness of their unions. This has made unnecessary a policy to reduce union power to combat inflation.

The analysis turns now to a discussion of a voluntary incomes policy for an economy with a fragmented union movement but with adversarial industrial relations, a useful description of the situation in English-speaking countries. As might be expected, in economies in which trust and cooperation are conspicuous by their absence, in which unions have been and continue to be opposed strenuously, in which invisible hands are thought to be standing by, and in which reducing the power of unions is considered a remedy for a number of ills, a different kind of incomes policy is needed to combat inflation. The concern is to formulate a policy that has some chance of success in spite of the existing adversarial IRS and fragmented labour movement.

Chapter 12 concludes with some remarks and policy recommendations for lessening price and wage pressures whatever the IRS. In keeping with a general theme of the study, changing economic structures are seen to lead to economic problems that can only be resolved by political means.

---

[38] See Barber and McCallum, op. cit., chapter I.

Incomes Policies in English-speaking Countries

ADVERSARIAL INDUSTRIAL RELATIONS SYSTEMS

1. *Economic pluralism*

Men could safely be trusted to pursue their own self-interest without due harm to the community not only because of the restrictions imposed by the law, *but also because they were subject to built-in restraint derived from morals, religion, custom and education.*[1] (*my italics*)

The competitive model of general equilibrium is a formalization of Smith's invisible hand with one important difference; the formal version, indeed most of economic theory, has nothing to say about the importance of the conditions set forth in the italicized part of the quote. Supposedly the workings of the market ensure that any kind of restraints, other than legal ones, are inconsequential. As long as the different participants obey the law, unrestrained, non-cooperative, non-collusive behaviour, in other words, the invisible hand leads to the best of all possible worlds. The adversarial industrial relations of the competitive model are of no consequence, since the 'forces of competition' will ensure that only the most competitive sort of behaviour survives.

The competitive model of general equilibrium has great elegance and mathematical sophistication. It shows how, given some very strong assumptions, an economy with decentralized decision-making, carried out by agents unable to influence market outcomes, can efficiently organize itself. The analysis is carried out with both grace and a technical flair which no doubt accounts for its appeal

---

[1] Taken from Adam Smith's *The Theory of Moral Sentiments*, quoted by F. Hirsch (1976) *The Social Limits to Growth*, Harvard University Press, Cambridge, p. 137.

among a large number of theorists. Unfortunately the real world is one of highly organized powerful groups, interacting in such a way that economic relations must be conducted by administrative and organizational rules of behaviour, not through responses to impersonal price signals.

To handle this consideration, an organizational, aggregative analogue to the competitive model has been put forward as a description of market processes. This view, influenced by the increased power of unions in recent times, sees important economic outcomes as the result of a competitive interaction of large-scale, powerful organizations. Pluralism, in its economic aspects, visualizes the industrial relations system in terms of a number of organized, special interest groups pursuing specific, narrowly defined goals that enhance the welfare of their constituent members. And even though economic (and political) outcomes are seen as the result of competing demands of these groups, social scientists who advance this picture of how markets work have, until recently, tended to be optimistic. The functioning of an economy dominated by the organized, uncoordinated pursuit of self-interest is alleged to work satisfactorily. Differences of interests lead to bargaining and compromise and even though the concerns of the different groups may be pragmatic and parochial, limited and selfish, a common good somehow emerges. But instead of being the result of the forces of atomistic competition, the invisible hand in this version shows itself in the form of a system of checks and balances or countervailing economic and political power groups, such that none is able to dominate others. The contrast with social democratic corporatism is obvious.

2. The invisible hand made flesh

The truncated version of Adam Smith's belief in a self-regulating economy, in which any concern for internal restraints can be conveniently ignored, has gained its greatest acceptance in English-speaking countries, particularly the USA. This belief functions as a powerful political and economic ideology among leaders in these countries and has provided a framework for theorizing among academic economists. Its wide acceptance as valid description of (and justification for) capitalism in the USA and, to a lesser extent, the other English-speaking economies partly derives from important features of the industrial relations systems in these countries. Unlike Continental Europe and Japan, trade unions were and continue to be resisted in the English-speaking countries. The lack of a centralized union movement and of high-level collective bargaining did not allow issues of conflict between management and labour to become separated from issues that led to cooperation. Moreover, in the USA the development of the welfare state was limited. Consequently, labour has had to seek many of the benefits associated with the welfare state through collective bargaining. The IRS that developed was quite different from the Continental model. What evolved was a 'them' versus 'us' psychology in which capital and labour looked upon one another as natural combatants in collective bargaining and on the shop floor. The resulting adversarial industrial relations system put a minimal value on labour–management cooperation.

Another factor that explains the persistence of the belief in an invisible hand and the failure to recognize the importance of restraints on economic behaviour has been the economic success of English-speaking countries as reflected in relative income *levels*, again with the USA the outstanding example. Until the last decade or so, the USA was thought to be a model of successful capitalist development because of its high income levels, the working out in real life of the truncated form of Adam Smith's parable. This lent support to the view that an economy with an adversarial industrial relations system was not on a mission of self-destruction but was supportive of dynamic efficiency.

Given, then, the relatively high levels of incomes (until very recently) achieved in countries with a strong anti-union history and a highly adversarial IRS, it is not surprising that economists and political leaders would find support and take comfort in the notions of the invisible hand, economic pluralism and countervailing powers. Such optimism was and continues to be responsible for a lack of concern that market relations and the industrial organization system be supported by 'morals, religion, custom and education'. Something more will be said in chapter 14 about the relative success of US capitalism.

3. The breakdown of economic pluralism

Recently, social scientists outside of economics have challenged the optimistic view of those who see the world in terms of economic pluralism.[2] The interaction of uncoordinated, interest groups, uncon-

---

[2] See, for example, J. Goldthorpe (1978) *The current inflation: Towards a sociological account,* in *The Political Economy of Inflation* (Eds F. Hirsch and J. Goldthorpe), Harvard University Press, Cambridge; and S. Berger, Introduction, op. cit.

strained by considerations of national welfare, is increasingly seen to be destabilizing as competing demands, motivated by limited, selfish aims, lead to a malfunction of the economy. This emergent pessimism is quite in keeping with the analysis of inflation presented here. The earlier chapters have, in effect, argued that successful economic performances are unlikely in economies dominated by the uncoordinated pursuit of self-interest by powerful organizations. The inflationary bias of modern times was seen in chapter 6 as one manifestation of conflicts of interests between powerful organizations capable of destabilizing the economy.

The discussion in chapters 6 and 7 pointed out that such an inflationary bias might be permanently eliminated if the power of unions were greatly reduced. The next three sections offer an alternative strategy, one that rejects weakening the powers of unions through persistently high unemployment. It starts from the belief that the English-speaking economies have been particularly prone to disharmony and non-cooperation, leading to severe inflation and other malfunctions such as strikes and dynamic inefficiencies. This makes the task of combating inflation more difficult to be sure, but recognition of these difficulties suggests what options might be available. For example, this alternative strategy sees the strengthening and extension of cooperative structures and institutions as an important basis of an anti-inflation programme. But when capital and labour have been locked in an adversarial relationship historically, a workable, permanent incomes policy cannot place as much reliance on voluntary cooperation as under, say, a social democratic corporatist regime.

The first step, therefore, is to formulate an alternative set of policies for compliance with wage and price norms. The analysis proceeds by taking into account another important feature of countries with an adversarial IRS. The union movement in the English-speaking countries is highly fragmented, characterized by decentralized decision-making. In this respect it resembles the Japanese development but only in this respect. Because of the fragmentation, tripartite agreements in the interests of wage and price restraint of the kind discussed in chapter 11 are not possible in the near future. Should labour and management groups centralize their decision-making, the emphasis in incomes policy might shift towards that of SDC. But here a policy is formulated under the assumption that no unified voice speaks for labour or for management that can promise compliance with agreed-upon price and wage norms or guidelines. Furthermore, the adversarial nature of the IRS precludes a Japanese solution in which costs are internalized.

To be considered are incomes policies that include, as mechanisms for achieving compliance with wage and price norms, known financial punishments and rewards. The outstanding characteristic of these programmes, according to some of their advocates, is that the participants can operate according to their own self-interest without having to take account of the impact of their behaviour on the likely realization of national goals.

Several types of incentive schemes have been offered and the next section merely outlines one example, a type of tax-based incomes policy (TIP). However, one example is quite sufficient to indicate how unlikely is the success of all such policies unless reinforced by additional policies. It therefore is unnecessary to exhaustively discuss the relative merits of the various forms of TIP, other incentive schemes such as MAP or the 'not-quite-compulsory-arbitration' system. None can succeed without institutions of cooperation.[3] In this, policies for English-speaking countries resemble consensus policies.

A TAX-BASED INCOMES POLICY (TIP)

1. *The basic ingredients*

While the tax-based incomes policy (TIP) finds its intellectual roots in the USA, its alleged applicability is not so limited.[4] Increasingly it is being discussed elsewhere as an alternative to an induced recession to control inflation, to voluntary guidelines, and to compulsory wage and price controls. The general idea behind TIP is to provide economic incentives for adherence to some guidelines either in the form of a tax penalty (if the guidelines are exceeded) or a tax reward (if the guidelines are followed or improved upon). Almost every version has been formulated in terms of a wage guideline, although some wage guidelines are addressed to the employer, others to workers in the firm. Thus, an employee reward programme would give workers a

---

[3] The general ideas behind MAP (Market-based Incomes Policies) is found in D. Colander (1981) Tax and market-based incomes policies: The interface of theory and practice, and A. Lerner and D. Colander (1981) There is a cure for inflation, in *An Incomes Policy for the United States: New Approaches* (Eds R. Cornwall and M. Claudon), Nijhoff, Boston. The arbitration solution is offered in J. Meade (1982) *Stagflation Volume 1: Wage-fixing*, George Allen & Unwin, London.

[4] An early study is that of H. Wallich and S. Weintraub (1971) A tax-based incomes policy, *Journal of Economic Issues*, June. Studies of a TIP for other countries include R. Bodkin (1981) Would a tax-based incomes policy help? *Canadian Public Policy*, supplement; and R. Layard (1982) Is incomes policy the answer to unemployment? *Economica*, August.

tax rebate if they agreed to follow the wage guideline or a variable tax rebate depending upon the extent to which their wage settlements fall below the guidelines. Most versions stress the 'neutral' role of prices, in the sense that when product markets are fix-price and the mark-up constant, the rate of price increase will differ from the rate of wage increase by the rate of growth of productivity. A corollary of this is that the way to stop price inflation is to stop wage inflation. The impact of flex-price product markets, terms of trade effects and upward trends in food–energy prices on the formulation of such an incentive policy has not yet been well worked out.

Common elements running through the different versions include the following. First, TIP rejects direct government intervention in the wage bargaining process, maintaining instead 'free' collective bargaining. In this way, it differs from both a consensus incomes policy in which wages are to be determined by a norm agreed upon by labour and management groups, and statutory incomes policies in which wages (and prices) are regulated directly by law. Second, TIP allows changes in relative wages to occur as part of the natural course of events, thereby allowing the 'price mechanism' to continue to serve in its alleged capacity as a resource allocative mechanism. Third, one of the prime functions of TIP is to increase the resistance of management to excessive wage demands and to decrease union aggressiveness.

Fourth, TIP advocates believe that inflation is best treated as a micro problem, arising out of collective agreements in individual markets. If the wage settlement raises money wages at a rate greater than some agreed-upon guideline, then labour or management or both will be penalized in the form of higher taxes. Alternative schemes have been worked out for handling settlements in which wage increases are less than the guidelines. Given, then, that TIP will utilize a wage norm, any combination of employer and employee penalties and rewards is a possible incentive incomes policy.

Finally, by restraining inflation, TIP is alleged to lead to a full-employment situation which should result in a more rapid rate of growth of labour productivity and therefore real wages and living standards. As with the consensus incomes policy, TIP (and other incentive policies) are meant to be part of a policy package that aims for full employment as well as price and wage stability.

2. An employer TIP

Most formulations of TIP are framed in terms of corporate income taxes. Thus, let T_c and P_c represent corporate tax yields and corporate profits before taxes, respectively and α_1 and α_2 represent the 'basic' corporate tax rate and the 'multiple' that is used to penalize firms whose wage increases exceed the wage increase guidelines, $\dot{w}_g$. Then the following simple algebraic relations can be derived outlining the essentials of an employer reward–employer penalty form of TIP. The corporate tax rate is given by:

$$T_c/P_c = \alpha_1 + \alpha_2(\dot{w} - \dot{w}_g) \tag{1}$$

where $0 < \alpha_2 < 1$;

and corporate profits after taxes can be represented by:

$$P_c - T_c = [(1 - \alpha_1) - \alpha_2(\dot{w} - \dot{w}_g)]P_c. \tag{2}$$

Clearly whatever the agreed upon wage guideline, $\dot{w}_g$, if it is less than the actual wage rate increase, $\dot{w}$, corporate tax rates increase.

To see how the programme works assume that in the absence of TIP the basic corporate tax is a flat rate, α_1 per cent. Then if the firm sets its wages at the guideline its tax rate remains at α_1 per cent. But if its actual wage settlement exceeds the wage guideline, it will be penalized by an increase of its tax rate of $\alpha_2(\dot{w} - \dot{w}_g)$ per cent. As written equation (1) allows for an employer tax reward when $\dot{w} < \dot{w}_g$. If it is desirable to remove the tax reward but retain the tax penalty features, then the condition, $T_c/P_c = \alpha_1$ if $\dot{w} \le \dot{w}_g$ can be added.

The importance of the size of the multiple in determining the tax rate and, in the minds of the advocates of TIP, the degree of resistance or backbone of employers to wage demands is clear. The larger is α_2, the greater is the tax penalty incurred by firms that exceed the guideline. A related argument is that the multiple can always be made large enough to keep the higher corporate tax burden (due to exceeding the guideline) from being passed on to the consumer in the form of higher prices. Thus, since $P_c = T_c + P_n$ where P_n is profits after tax, the equation for profits after tax as a share of gross profits P_c, is easily seen to be:

$$P_n/P_c = [1 - \alpha_1 - \alpha_2(\dot{w} - \dot{w}_g)]. \tag{3}$$

As α_2 increases, P_n/P_c approaches zero; i.e. no amount of price rise can compensate for the stiffness of the tax penalty. Having handled that problem, however, proponents of TIP have raised another one. The effectiveness of a TIP in preventing higher taxes from being passed on in prices is negatively related to the ability of the programmes to allow firms to generate internal savings for investment.

3. *Some problems*

The problems associated with TIP have been extensively debated, largely in terms of implemental and administrative detail.[5] For example, there is the matter of coverage. In the original formulation of TIP, the coverage extended only to the larger corporations.[6] This means that government bodies and unincorporated businesses (some of which face powerful unions) would not be covered. This has led to a suggestion that changes in payroll tax rates rather than the corporate tax rates be used as the basis of the TIP guideline and penalty formula since this would extend coverage in most countries. Related to this is the notion of an earlier mentioned employee-rewards TIP whereby firms granting wage increases below the wage guideline would be able to pass the difference on to the workers in the form of a tax rebate.

Also, there has been the suggestion that price guidelines be formulated as well as wage guidelines, usually with the price guideline less than the wage guideline by the rate of growth of labour productivity. This critical issue is discussed further in the next section.

Various kinds of administrative problems also have been cited. For example, since the labour market is always in disequilibrium with regards to relative wages, how would such initial inequities be eliminated? Or assume some union has previously signed a multi-year contract with a firm or an entire industry that exceeded the guidelines. How would this be handled? How would the problem of low-wage workers be dealt with?

The list of problems and considerations is formidable, but to explore them in any depth or breadth would detract from the central problem. And that is that the workability of an incentive programme in an economy characterized by adversarial industrial relations and a fragmented labour movement requires that it be widely accepted, particularly by labour. To put it otherwise, it is an illusion to think that financial incentives alone can bring compliance with an incomes policy, just as it is illusory to believe that market incentives alone (the invisible hand), can lead to industrial peace, full employment and price stability. A corollary is that if some policy is widely supported, the required details of any particular programme as well as the correct implemental and administrative features can be determined through trial and error process. The next section indicates why labour's acceptance is so critical.

[5] See the special issue of the *Brookings Papers on Economic Activity*, No. 2, 1978.
[6] See Wallich and Weintraub, op. cit.

WHY INCENTIVES ARE NOT ENOUGH

1. *Price norms or wage norms*

Whatever the form of incentive income policy adopted, a crucial decision is whether the authorities seek to induce money wages, prices or both to behave in a certain way. Thus, because of pass through and feedback effects, any measure that directly influences wages will indirectly influence prices in fix-price markets and vice versa. But any effort to work directly on wages or product prices alone runs the risk of antagonizing labour or capital. Yet, almost all incomes policies discussed, whether consensus or incentive, have emphasized a wage norm or guideline. The nature of the inflationary process indicates why this has been so.

The argument of the earlier chapters suggests that the pass-through relation from the rate of growth of wages to prices is more firmly established than the feedback effect of price inflation on wage inflation. This means that any growth of money wages in excess of productivity growth faced by firms passes through to prices with a short lag. On the other hand, individual wage bargains and, therefore, aggregate wage inflation are influenced not only by the nature of past, current and expected rates of price inflation and but also by past, current and expected changes in the wage structure. As a result, the response of wage inflation to price inflation must be considered to take the form of a complicated and perhaps variable distributed lag. The exact nature of the response is not known so that trying to indirectly influence wage inflation through directly attacking price inflation will be less successful than trying to indirectly influence price inflation by directly working on wage inflation.

But there is also the ability of the authorities to have a direct influence on price inflation. As chapter 7 made clear, much of the impetus to the acceleration of inflation during the 1970s must be traced to the acceleration of food and energy prices and the wide cyclical swings in prices in other commodity markets. In most economies the movements in prices in these markets do not reflect movements in wages or even labour costs at all well. For example, exogenous 'supply' factors have often played an important role and these forces are beyond the influence of the authorities who might otherwise like to implement a price target or norm. Any discussion of food–energy price movements suggests how difficult it is to directly influence the prices of two important components of the CPI. For many countries, heavy dependence on imports make it close to impossible to influence directly the rate of price inflation of a wide number of goods. As indicated below, changes in the exchange rate are not always a solution. However, there is no such limitation on the ability to directly influence wages of the domestic labour force.

Arguments related to the administration of the two norms have also been made. It has been said that in an age of affluence, style and quality changes are recurring events in the production of most goods and services. A price norm would influence the mark-up over costs. Yet quality changes in new products raise problems of correct mark-ups as do increases in productivity. Other problems can be added.[7] In general, the conclusion must be that 'a prices policy is certain to fail without a wages policy, whereas a wages policy can work without a price policy'.[8]

2. Some further difficulties

Having noted the likelihood of adopting a wage guideline, it is possible to focus more clearly on the important difficulties of incentive policies. For example, given the fact that most forms of TIP utilize a wage norm, such policies must be structured so as to appeal to labour. Now while much has been made of the fact that under an employer-penalty TIP employers would be penalized if labour demands and gets more than the wage norm, the argument for an employer-reward system seems hardly acceptable to labour. Neither is an employee-penalty TIP. That leaves only an employee-reward TIP and an employer-penalty TIP. Both should have more appeal to labour and such a combined TIP has the advantage of possibly altering the behaviour of both employees and employers in the desired direction. Thus, the employee-reward part would reduce labour's aggressiveness in tighter labour markets. The employer-penalty part would penalize employers for bidding up wages and earnings above a norm.

But such considerations, while important, only begin to come to grips with the main obstacles to success of an incentives incomes policy. With price movements seemingly uncontrolled or not subject to tax penalties (or rewards), it is difficult to see why labour has much incentive to cooperate with an adversary to ensure that the

[7] See, for example, W. Nordhaus (1981) Tax-based incomes policies: A better mousetrap? in *An Incomes Policy for the United States: New Approaches* (Eds R. Cornwall and M. Claudon), Nijhoff, Boston.

[8] Layard, op. cit., p. 231.

latter is not penalized. As individual labour groups will see it, wage increases above the norm will be passed on in the forms of higher prices. To argue that the reward of full employment is enough to ensure labour's cooperation is hardly convincing. With a fragmented labour movement in an adversarial industrial relations setting, it would be extremely difficult to convince individual labour groups that wage demands and settlements in excess of a guideline would be counter-productive if widespread, as the full employment goal of the programme would then have to be abandoned. Rather each labour group will continue to be concerned about their ranking in the wage structure. Synchronized wage bargaining is only part of the solution.

Clearly, then, it seems most unlikely that a TIP of any form will work if the participants continue to operate without some regard to the public interest. This is but to say that the market incentives of a TIP are not sufficient to generate widespread compliance. Given the long history of adversarial industrial relations and the fragmentation of the labour movement in the English-speaking countries, some kind of incentives incomes policy is surely necessary but more is needed. Not surprisingly, this something more includes measures that lead to a more cooperative industrial relations system. But more fundamentally this something more is an effort to achieve a distributional fairness in the interests of promoting a national consensus.

THE DISTRIBUTIONAL ISSUE

1. *A tax on non-wage incomes*

Prolonged periods of full employment bring affluence and affluence brings higher aspirations and power. This was one of the important conclusions of chapter 6, in which the evolving pattern of the relative strengths of capital and labour was summarized. The rising relative power of labour culminated in the post-war period of 1950 to the early 1970s. The one critical result of this ascent towards economic parity with capital was a strong inflationary bias. Basically this was seen as a struggle over the distribution of income. Because an incentive incomes policy based on a wage norm must be implemented in this institutional setting, additional measures must be taken that are seen by all, but especially labour, to promote a fair distributional outcome. Three such measures are considered briefly. Each promotes a greater equality in the distribution of incomes than would arise out of a pure market determination of the income distribution. Given the redistribution of power that comes with full employment, no other kind of programme would be consistent with the aim of price and wage stability at full employment.

First, a strong effort must be made to control the growth of non-labour after tax incomes. Specifically, this requires the retention of a progressive tax on personal incomes. It does not require a progressive tax on profits, only dividends. Thus, an additional argument against a price norm is that without it the 'price mechanism' can function as a means of regulating the available internal corporate funds for investment. Expanding industries and industries in general may have a preference for financing investment outlays internally. Allowing the price mark-up over costs to vary for this reason provides a positive benefit, provided dividends (and corporate salaries) are subject to a tax that is consistent with the desired after-tax distributional goals. It is important to note that these tax measures need not lead to a decline in total non-labour incomes. Rather, a failure to control inflation through an incomes policy will lead to an effort to control it by creating unemployment. And widespread unemployment means restricted output and sales, excess capacity and low profits.

2. Real-wage insurance

Another problem in making the incentive policy work is that it is difficult for labour to believe that the rate of price inflation will not exceed the rate of money wage increase determined by the wage norm. In an age of price rises in commodity (flex-price) markets, OPEC cartels and currency devaluations, it is all too apparent that the rate of domestic price inflation can be increased by forces other than wages. Some kind of insurance or guaranteed real-wage provision is required for labour's cooperation. This holds true whether an incentive or consensus policy is adopted.[9]

Real-wage insurance programmes, whereby wages are automatically increased should rates of price inflation exceed some threshold, are a means of handling this concern. Various possibilities arise

[9] The text neglects any consideration of the use of buffer stock programmes that might allow stimulative policies to be implemented without setting off a sharp rise of prices in commodity markets. It is important to note that in Sweden a measure of agreement has been reached in handling energy price changes. Since these are largely outside the control of participants in collective bargaining, the cost-of-living index computed for determining 'fair' money wage settlements excludes energy prices.

here.[10] The insurance could be made available to all wage earners, irrespective of their wage settlements, or it could apply only to those who abide by the wage norm. The adjustment of money wages could allow money wages to grow in line with productivity or allowances could be made for adverse movements of the terms of trade, etc.

Any real-wage insurance scheme has as its rationale the view that in order to ensure acceptability, a programme of wage restraint must be seen to be fair. By relating money wage adjustments to productivity growth, for example, an effort is made to ensure that labour shares in the benefits of rising real incomes. These kinds of measures certainly get to the heart of the matter. In the earlier chapters, inflation was described as a struggle over the distribution of income. Any anti-inflation programme with any chance of success must always reduce this struggle. A real-wage insurance policy attempts to reduce labour's dependence on higher money wage demands as the only means to protect real wages.

3. The welfare state

The discussion of strike behaviour among the OECD economies and especially the finding that industrial disputes fell sharply in several European economies that adopted the modern version of the welfare state is also relevant here. The temptation to reduce welfare programmes has proved to be very great in the 1970s and early 1980s. Partly this is due to the absence of growth, the zero-sum game situation; partly it is due to a misunderstanding of the benefits of the welfare state. In the next chapter something will be said about policies aimed at stimulating productivity growth and breaking out of the zero-sum game. At issue is the role that the welfare state plays in fostering a national consensus in the interests of compliance with an incomes policy. Here, some of the findings of chapter 11 are critical. Economic and social harmony increased greatly after the implementation of the welfare state in several European countries. The state intervened in order to redistribute incomes in a more equal manner in response to rising agitation against market-determined distributional outcomes. Policies such as supply-side economics advocate a redistribution of income that increases inequality in the name of increased growth. As argued in chapter 9, such policies will do little

---

[10] See A. Rees (1978) New policies to fight inflation: Sources of skepticism, *Brookings Papers on Economic Activity*, No. 2; and L. Seidman (1981) Insurance for labor under tax-based incomes policy, in *An Incomes Policy for the United States: New Approaches* (Eds R. Cornwall and M. Claudon), Nijhoff, Boston.

for growth, and they intensify conflict and potential inflationary pressures if the economy ever moves back to full employment. In a full-employment world, the one way to reduce this (inflationary) struggle is to maintain the welfare state, not abandon it.

Ending stagnation requires a return to full employment which cannot be maintained unless wage bargaining is carried out so as to ensure wage and price stability. In this important sense the inflation and stagnation problems are related. What has just been argued is that before an incentive incomes policy has any chance of success, additional (political) programmes must be implemented that reduce the struggle over income shares. Not surprisingly, the programme for ending inflation (and therefore stagnation) in the English-speaking countries emphasizes the need for more cooperation between capital and labour, as in the countries considered in chapter 11, and for a widespread belief in the fairness of the programme. Naturally, the message for those countries considered in chapter 11 is to do everything possible to preserve those institutions and programmes that have been the basis of a national consensus.

Clearly, all of this indicates how much ending stagflation is a political problem. Structural changes in labour markets, attributable to changes in the relative power of labour and capital, have made capitalist systems inflation prone at or near full employment in the absence of government intervention. But the desired policy response is only likely if government leaders can articulate and administer a policy that has widespread acceptance. The success of any kind of incomes policy, whether consensus or incentive, therefore, depends upon the quality of political leadership. Strong, conciliatory leadership rather than the divisive kind that accompanies supply-side economics policies is required. This holds equally true for countries with cooperative or adversarial industrial relations systems, centralized or fragmented labour movements and, therefore, concensus or incentive incomes policies.

Much debate has taken place within the economics profession over some of the finer points of an incomes policy. The discussions surrounding TIP are a case in point. But these fine points are really just that, fine points. Given a strong, conciliatory political leadership, the details of the correct incomes policy will be determined by trial and error and based on perceptions of fairness. The importance of political factors in solving stagflation cannot be underestimated and will be reflected in the details of any incomes policy. Today, inflation (and stagnation) is always and everywhere a political phenomenon.

CAN ECONOMISTS PLAY A ROLE IN ENDING STAGFLATION?

If the success of an incomes policy depends so much upon political factors, the question is what role is left for economists. In answering this, a page can be taken from the book of those monetarists who place so much faith in the credibility hypothesis. They have argued that before a restrictive aggregate demand policy can be expected to bring down inflation, there must be widespread belief that: (1) the authorities will not deviate from their announced goal of wage and price stability; and (2) the authorities have no acceptable alternative policy for realizing wage and price stability.[11]

The chief role of the economist in the programme advanced here is to foster an understanding of the correct credibility conditions. In contrast to credibility conditions of the monetarists, what must be recognized is: (1) if the incomes policy cannot be made to work, the authorities will revert to a programme of restrictive demand measures which guarantees continuous stagnation, if not stagflation; and (2) there is no alternative to a permanent incomes policy for achieving wage and price stability at full employment. Once these conditions are met, an incentives or a consensus incomes policy can be said to be 'credible' and an important step will have been taken in ending inflation.

The first condition affirms a belief that the fear of (accelerating) inflation, especially by governments and national and international financial groups, is pervasive and strong. So much so that it cannot be expected that governments will implement full employment policies unless there is some supplementary policy that will handle the inflation problem. 'Inflation without stagnation' is not a feasible alternative. The behaviour of the authorities from the early 1970s

[11] See W. Fellner, op. cit. The first condition is somewhat ambiguous since it implies that the authorities may push up unemployment through restrictive measures to whatever levels are needed to 'wipe out the inflationary psychology once and for all'. While unemployment today has been allowed to rise to levels that would have been considered politically unacceptable only a short time ago, even the most staunch advocate of the credibility hypothesis would balk at, say, a Chilean solution to the inflation problem.

until the present attests to this unwillingness to seriously deal with unemployment until there are reasonable assurances that inflation is and will be controlled. A necessary condition for a return to low unemployment and high profits is an incomes policy. Economists will have accomplished a great deal if this point is made clear.

The realization that a permanent incomes policy is needed and the only possible strategy requires an understanding of why current policies will not work in the long run. Ultimately, this is only possible if there is a better understanding of the true nature of the inflation. Although speculative, it was argued that even if attempts to reduce inflation to acceptable rates through depressed demand conditions actually succeeded, this would be a short-lived gain. High rates of unemployment teach labour a lesson, to be sure, but not the one usually cited. What labour learns today is that it has been singled out to play a special role in fighting inflation and that role involves either the threat of unemployment or its realization. The perceived unfairness of it all leads to the development of an unflinching desire to recapture past losses whenever the economy returns to full employment.

Close to a decade of attempts to reduce inflation to acceptable rates in most countries through high unemployment should strongly suggest that restrictive aggregate demand policies are a clumsy instrument akin to blood-letting. To justify such policies by an appeal to some beneficial 'long-run' effects is to ignore human psychology and the lessons of the recent past.

Underlying this belief in the inability of current policies to permanently cure inflation is a recognition of a changed institutional structure. The nature of this change can be summarized by pointing up how important it is to reject certain influential but erroneous notions about the nature of modern capitalist economies. Implicit throughout the earlier chapters was the view that modern economies are not blessed with self-correcting mechanisms that guarantee price stability any more than they guarantee full employment. Keynes argued that once capitalist economies reach a stage of affluence, there is no necessary tendency for investment to equal full employment savings. Interventionist policy would then be necessary to bring the economy to full employment.

And if, as argued, inflation is a struggle over income shares, the idea that an invisible hand is at work bringing social, political and economic harmony irrespective of the IRS must also be discarded. With the rise of large-scale organizations, conflicts do not take the benign form posited by the competitive model in which some kind of

social optimum emerges. Rather conflict has more malevolent consequences, one of which is inflation. Order and stability in this sense
are no longer maintained by the 'impersonal forces of the market'.
This is another important message for economists to make known.

CONCLUSIONS

Figure 12.1 summarizes the two most important characteristics of an
IRS to be considered in designing an incomes policy. The degree of
centralization of decision-making in wage settlements and the attitudes of labour and capital towards each other are constraints that
cannot be ignored in structuring a voluntary incomes policy. No
country has been assigned the cell for highly centralized union and
employer organizations and an adversarial IRS. Without too much
exaggeration, this situation describes nothing less than class warfare.
No attempt has been made to assign all the OECD countries to any
one of the other cells. Consensus incomes policies have been operative in the post-war period in economies with both fragmented and
centralized labour and employer decision-making institutions. This
suggests that the basic consideration in designing an incomes policy
is whether the IRS can be characterized as cooperative or adversarial. As argued above, the IRS that has evolved in the English-
speaking countries greatly increases the difficulties of finding a
workable incomes policy. It was maintained that the welfare state

Union-employer
decision making

Fragmented   Centralized

		Fragmented	Centralized
	Adversarial	English speaking countries	
Industrial relations system			
	Cooperative	Japan	Continental Europe

FIGURE 12.1   Institutional determinants of an incomes policy

was a precondition for social and economic harmony and trust between capital and labour along with some guarantees about income distribution. This would lead to an economic environment similar to many countries in Continental Europe. However, because of the adversarial nature of industrial relations in the English-speaking countries new incentive schemes would also be needed. An example was TIP.

Neoclassical theorizing ignores the enormous differences in the industrial relations systems between countries in modelling the manner in which an economy is organized. As a result it lends support to the beliefs that cooperation and fair treatment are of secondary concern in industrial relations and that somehow the proper functioning of the economy is automatic, provided government remains on the sidelines. According to this view, market forces would lead to the replacement of any economic configuration of institutions and beliefs inconsistent with price and wage stability, as well as with full employment and dynamic efficiency.

The historical record suggests something different. Economies continued to malfunction throughout the post-war period (and earlier for that matter) with no evidence of self-correcting institutional and legislative changes. Strikes, inflation and low productivity were the clearest manifestations of the malfunction. Only recently, with the advent of stagflation has serious concern been given to the need for adaptation. The point made here is that the English-speaking countries will find themselves at a disadvantage in trying to implement a workable incomes policy. Their adversarial IRS and their ideological views about the role of government make it difficult to even see what must be done.

As it may turn out, countries with adversarial industrial relations may never be able to implement successful incomes policies. The English-speaking countries suffer a great handicap in any effort to combat stagflation. A long history of mistrust is certainly the major impediment. If the world is to escape stagflation, the English-speaking countries may have to be dragged along by the other developed capitalist economies.

But if unconstrained collective bargaining at full employment reveals an inflationary bias, and if full employment is still desired, then the cure of inflation and stagnation involves more not less government intervention to offset the political and institutional as well as economic developments that lead to an inflationary bias. In chapter 13 additional reasons are given for supporting the view that more government intervention is now required to prevent a general malfunctioning of the economy.

CHAPTER 13

A Real Wage Policy

INTRODUCTION

Chapters 10–12 sought to establish two pillars of an anti-stagflation policy; an aggregate demand policy to achieve the full employment target and an incomes policy to deal with the problem of inflation. What remains is to formulate an industrial policy to generate an increase in the growth of productivity and, ultimately, real incomes. Thus, while a strong case can be made that the rate of growth of productivity is positively related to the employment rate, there is no guarantee that a return to full employment will be sufficient to generate a satisfactory growth in productivity, per capita incomes and real wages. This is critical since rising real wages and per capita incomes are necessary, along with full employment, for acceptance of a wage norm. Growing productivity is also a means for preserving the welfare state, a prerequisite for social harmony. Less obvious, but of critical importance, it will be argued in this chapter that in a world economy of relatively free trade, international competitiveness requires rapid productivity growth. Without this kind of success, full employment policies would soon have to be abandoned.

There are two problems here. Table 13.1 reveals that the period since the boom of the early 1970s has seen a sharp reduction in productivity growth. For example, the Japanese record of nearly 3 per cent growth in labour productivity is high compared with the other six large OECD countries but less than one-half its own earlier performance in 1963–73. This difficulty has been compounded recently by adverse movements in the terms of trade against the OECD countries, largely due to rising oil prices. In every country, movements have been such as to reduce real income growth. In table 13.1 the column headed Warranted real wage shows that if factor shares had remained constant during the 1974–81 period, real wages

TABLE 13.1   Annual average rates of growth of real wages, productivity and the terms of trade in the seven large OECD economies

Country	Money wages		Real wages		Productivity[a]		Terms of trade[b]		Warranted real wage[c]		Real wage gap[d]	
	1963–73	1974–81	1963–73	1974–81	1963–73	1974–81	1963–73	1974–81	1963–73	1974–81	1963–73	1974–81
USA	4.97	7.75	1.40	−0.20	1.9	0.19	n.a.	−0.17	n.a.	0.02	n.a	−0.22
Canada	6.52	10.10	2.85	0.70	2.4	0		−0.15		−0.15		0.85
Japan	14.20	11.08	8.04	2.21	8.7	2.99		−0.91		2.08		0.13
France	9.48	14.18	4.75	2.70	4.6	2.48		−0.55		1.93		0.77
West Germany	8.60	6.84	5.12	1.85	4.6	2.51		−0.37		1.14		0.81
Italy	11.58	19.53	6.65	1.45	5.4	1.49		−0.58		0.91		0.54
UK	8.47	16.93	3.14	1.75	3.0	1.36		0.17		1.53		0.22

Sources: OECD, *Economic Outlook* (July 1980); OECD, *Main Economic Indicators* (March 1966 and March 1980); OECD, Private Correspondence.
[a] Rate of growth of real GDP per employed person.
[b] Income effect of changes in terms of trade.
[c] Growth of real wages consistent with initial factor shares = productivity + terms of trade effect.
[d] Actual real wage − warranted real wage.

would have grown more slowly than productivity because of the adverse movements of the terms of trade everywhere but the UK. In actual fact, income shifted towards labour in every country listed in table 13.1 except the USA as seen in the last column. Even so, real wages grew much more slowly in the recent periods compared with 1963–73.

But there is another serious problem involved, one so far ignored, and that has to do with the balance of payments. At given exchange rates, any policy that succeeds in reducing unemployment rates is bound to stimulate the demand for imports. This raises the distinct possibility of encountering a balance of payments constraint in which the current account turns decisively negative before the employment target is reached.

To assume that this can be handled by a depreciation of the currency is, unfortunately, question begging. The early optimism that flexible exchange rates would automatically allow a country to pursue independent domestic policies has long since been abandoned. Today there is strong support for the view that a depreciation of the currency, especially, is at best only a partial solution to a payments disequilibrium and at worst a measure leading to a crisis of confidence in the currency. There are several problems here.[1] First, as just suggested, attempts to pursue full-employment policies unilaterally lead to speculations against the currency, especially in countries starting from weak payments positions. The rise in imports may lead initially to a modest devaluation, which hopefully will allow the current account to clear. But in the recent past the international banking community has taken a dim view of such stimulative policies, which has contributed to a lack of confidence in the currency and further depreciations. Restrictive policies then have had to be reintroduced, as the examples of the USA under the Carter Administration and France under Mitterand attest.

But even if speculative movements against a currency were not a

---

[1] In addition to the difficulties in using exchange-rate adjustments to maintain external balance cited in the text, there is another argument. Depreciating the currency leads to 'trading down' in which countries unable to compete in the exchange of sophisticated, highly fabricated goods, whose non-price characteristics are so important, will find upon depreciation that the only goods that they are able to sell abroad are those which are relatively price-sensitive. These are goods less-clearly distinguished from their nearest substitute in terms of non-price characteristics. Some of the relevant literature discussing this point as well as those cited in the text are found in M. Posner and A. Steer (1979) Manufacturing industry, in *De-Industrialization* (Ed. F. Blackaby), Heinemann, London; and A. Thirlwall and R. Dixon, A model of export-led growth with a balance of payments constraint, in *Inflation, Development and Integration* (Ed. J. Bowers), Leeds.

problem there are other difficulties. For example, allowing the external value of the currency to fall in hopes of correcting the current account deficit runs into all the short-run problems associated with the so-called J-curve effects; i.e. low price elasticies of demand for both imports and exports. To assume this can be handled by short-term borrowing brings the analysis back to the subject of 'credit worthiness' or its extreme form, 'confidence in the currency'.

But even if the price elasticities are right, there is an additional problem. The increase in costs of imported finished goods and raw materials directly and indirectly generates price increases which becomes generalized once the induced effect of rising living costs on money wages take place. This leads to a rise in prices of exports in the home currency that may be sufficient to bring the price of exports in foreign currency back to their former level.

Finally, even if it is possible to alter the real exchange rate, the fear of importing inflation has often been enough to discourage the use of stimulative policies coupled with a depreciation of the currency. The result is a situation under flexible exchange rates whereby countries have not been able to pursue independent domestic policies, in this case a return to full employment.

The problem of devising instruments for maintaining external balance at full employment and accelerating productivity growth is the concern of this chapter. Fortunately, the problems are related since many measures that succeed in achieving one goal will help in realizing the other. But while an industrial policy that succeeds in raising labour productivity growth is likely to bring about adjustments in exports and imports that relieve a possible payments constraint and vice versa, two qualifications must be mentioned. First, designing a successful policy to relieve the economy of a payments constraint must take precedence over a policy that works directly on productivity growth. A necessary condition for the acceptance and success of an incomes policy is the ability of the authorities to 'deliver' full employment, as labour and management will never accept a permanent incomes policy otherwise. But in addition, no industrial policy to raise productivity growth will have much impact unless the economy is operating at high levels of capacity utilization and employment. Thus, a policy that succeeds in relieving a constraint on the balance of payments, thereby permitting full employment, is a precondition for the success of both an incomes policy and one aimed at raising productivity growth.

Second, it will become clear, relieving an economy of a payments constraint in most countries requires less dependence upon the importation of primary products, especially energy. But policies that

succeed in reducing energy dependence need not stimulate productivity growth except to the extent that their success allows policy-
makers to increase aggregate demand. On the other hand, raising the
payments ceiling also involves expanding export markets for manu-
facturers and import substitution at home. Success here will permanently increase the rate of growth of productivity. The payments
ceiling will be discussed first.

THE PAYMENTS CONSTRAINT

In chapter 7 the impact of rising oil prices on inflation in the recent
period was discussed. No less important has been the impact of
rising energy prices on the balance of payments of countries exporting and importing oil. Table 13.2 summarizes the behaviour of
current accounts from 1973–81 for the industrial countries, the oil
exporting countries and the non-oil developing countries. The rapid
increase in oil prices (and raw material prices in general) in 1974 and
again at the beginning of the 1980s is reflected in the large increase
in deficits on current account for most of the industrial countries and
the non-oil developing countries. Its counterpart is the increase in
current account surpluses by the oil exporting countries. During
the middle 1970s, the industrial countries (but not the non-oil
developing countries) were on the whole able to eliminate their deficits, the notable exception being the USA. The success of industrial
countries other than the USA can be largely attributed to restrictive
demand policies. Lower rates of growth of demand reduced production, especially in heavy industry, which led to a decrease in
demand for energy inputs.[2]

---

[2] The impact of changes in world-wide spending, together with rising prices of oil
and other primary commodities, on trade and payments flows comes out clearly
from simulation experiments. Based on a model in which imports of manufactures
vary in proportion to domestic spending, primary commodity demands are negatively related to prices and positively to real domestic spending, an effort was
made to determine the nature of trade imbalances following a world-wide increase
in rates of growth of spending above the rates of the 1970s. This was done within a
context in which no country (or bloc) was faced with a financial constraint on its
ability to finance trade deficits. The overall effect was a radical loss of trade
surplus for Japan and an increase in trade deficits as a percentage of GDP in
Western Europe and a more pronounced rise in the deficit for non-oil developing
countries compared with the actual performance during the 1970s. These differences were attributable to the higher aggregate spending, indicating that much of
the actual 'improvement' in trade balances in recent times, outside the oil exporting countries, can be attributed to the relative stagnation in these countries. See P.
Atkinson *et al.* (1980) World trade and finance: Prospects for the 1980s, *Cambridge
Economic Policy Review,* December, chapter 1.

TABLE 13.2 Summary of payments balances on current account, 1973–81[a] (In billions of US dollars)

	1973	1974	1975	1976	1977	1978	1979	1980	1981[b]
Industrial countries	19.3	-12.4	17.1	-2.1	-5.5	30.1	-10.7	-44.0	-29.5
Canada	—	-1.6	-4.7	-4.0	-4.0	-4.1	-4.5	-1.6	-3.0
USA	9.9	7.6	21.2	7.5	-11.3	-11.1	2.8	8.4	13.0
Japan	0.1	-4.5	-0.4	3.9	11.1	18.0	-8.0	-9.5	-0.5
France	-0.1	-4.9	1.0	-4.9	-1.6	5.2	2.9	-5.9	-7.0
Fed. Rep. of Germany	7.1	13.0	7.7	7.7	8.5	13.5	0.9	-8.5	-6.5
Italy	-2.2	-7.4	-0.2	-2.5	3.1	7.8	6.4	-9.5	-9.0
UK	-1.2	-7.2	-3.0	-0.5	1.6	4.6	1.0	10.1	12.0
Other industrial countries	5.8	-7.4	-4.7	-9.3	-12.8	-3.8	-12.2	-27.5	-28.5
Developing countries									
Oil exporting countries	6.6	67.8	35.0	40.0	31.1	3.3	68.4	112.2	96.0
Non-oil developing countries	—	—	—	—	-28.6	-37.5	-57.6	-82.1	-97.0
(excluding People's Rep. of China)	-11.5	-36.8	-46.5	-32.9	-29.6	-37.1	-56.1	-80.4	-96.5
Total[c]	14.4	18.6	5.6	5.0	-3.0	-4.1	0.1	-13.9	-30.0

Source: World Economic Outlook, International Monetary Fund, Washington, DC, 1981.
[a] Goods, services and private transfers.
[b] Figures are rounded to the nearest $0.5 billion.
[c] Reflects errors, omissions and asymmetries in reported balance of payments statistics, plus balance of listed groups with other countries (mainly the Union of Soviet Socialist Republics and other non-member countries of Eastern Europe and, for years prior to 1977, the People's Republic of China).

Throughout the stagflation period, strong currency countries have been reluctant to pursue full employment policies for fear that the higher rate of growth of imports would lead to a depreciation of the currency and the importation of inflation, while the weak currency economies had to be concerned about currency crises as well as inflation. This has led to the imposition of a payments constraint or ceiling for many countries. The effect of such a constraint on output and its growth within a country can be seen more formally using a simple model.[3] Consider the following model describing trade between some country and the rest of the world:

$$\dot{X} = \eta(\dot{p}_d - \dot{p}_f - \dot{e}) + \xi\dot{Z} \tag{1}$$

$$\dot{M} = \theta(\dot{p}_f - \dot{p}_d + \dot{e}) + \pi\dot{Q} \tag{2}$$

$$w_1(\dot{p}_d + \dot{X}) + w_2\dot{K} = \dot{p}_f + \dot{M} + \dot{e} \tag{3}$$

where

$\dot{X}$ = rate of growth of exports
$\dot{p}_d$ = rate of growth of domestic prices
$\dot{p}_f$ = rate of growth of foreign prices
$\dot{e}$ = the rate of growth of the domestic price of foreign currency
ξ = world income elasticity of demand for a country's exports ($\xi > 0$)
$\dot{Z}$ = rate of growth of world income
$\dot{M}$ = rate of growth of imports
π = income elasticity of demand for imports ($\pi > 0$)
$\dot{Q}$ = rate of growth of domestic output
$\dot{K}$ = rate of growth of net capital inflows
η = price elasticity of demand for exports ($\eta < 0$) and
θ = price elasticity of demand for imports ($\theta < 0$).
w_1 and w_2 are weights with $w_1 + w_2 = 1$

Equations (1) and (2) are derived from conventional multiplicative import and export demand functions with constant elasticities. The equations have been transformed into their growth-rate counterparts. Equation (1) asserts that the rate of growth of a country's exports depends positively on the rate of growth of world income and negatively on the rate of growth of the relative price of its exports measured in a common currency. Equation (2) states that the rate of growth of a country's imports depends positively on the rate

[3] See Thirlwall and Dixon, op. cit.; and A. Thirlwall (1979) The balance of payments constraint as an explanation of international growth rate differences, *Banca Nazionale del Lavoro Quarterly Review*, March.

of growth of its output and negatively on the rate of growth of the relative price of foreign goods, again measured in a common currency. Equation (3), which ignores net income from abroad, is a payments constraint indicating a balance that must be satisfied if foreign reserves are to be maintained. Its slightly unusual form derives from the need to assign relative weights to the rate of growth of exports and capital inflows both measured in domestic currency.[4]

Substituting equations (1) and (2) into (3) and rearranging terms gives:

$$\dot{Q} = (1/\pi) \cdot [(w_1\eta + \theta)(\dot{p}_d - \dot{p}_f - \dot{e})$$
$$+ (\dot{p}_d - \dot{p}_f - \dot{e}) + w_1\xi\dot{Z} + w_2(\dot{K} - \dot{p}_d)] \qquad (4)$$

Equation (4) gives the rate of growth of output that maintains the balance of payments equilibrium described by equation (3). If the rate of growth of output given by equation (4) is less than that required to maintain full employment, then the country in question is said to be subject to a payments constraint or ceiling.

To see the essential issues, assume a zero growth of net capital inflows and an inability to alter relative foreign and domestic prices measured in a common currency; i.e. the real exchange rate. Then equation (4) reduces to:

$$\dot{Q} = (1/\pi) \cdot (\xi\dot{Z}) = \dot{X}/\pi. \qquad (4')$$

Studies have indicated that the actual growth performance of several mature capitalist economies in the post-war period can be approximated by equation (4').[5] This indicates that changes in the real income are the means whereby imports and exports are brought into line and not changes in the real exchange rate.

Relief from a payments constraint (other than capital inflows) can be obtained by a higher rate of growth of exports, which can be achieved if the rate of growth of world incomes, $\dot{Z}$, increases or by an increase in the income elasticity of demand for a country's exports, ξ. A reduction in the income elasticity for imports, π, leads to the same result. In the absence of internationally coordinated policies, an increase in ξ and a decrease in π are the correct strategies. In the concluding chapter consideration is given to international cooperation for recovery.

[4] See A. Thirlwall and M. Hussain (1982) The balance of payments constraint, capital flows and growth rate differences between developing countries, *Oxford Economic Papers*, November, fn 2.
[5] Thirlwall, op. cit.

Obviously, reducing a country's dependence on oil imports acts to reduce π, thereby raising its payments ceiling. The importance of finding substitutes for oil in production technology and final consumption has been the subject of much discussion elsewhere.[6] An alternative strategy that complements a policy of reducing dependence on foreign sources of primary products is one that reduces a country's dependence on foreign sources of manufactures. Such policies, if successful, lead to import substitution in manufactures and simultaneously raise exports. These will be considered here.

Such a policy is critical if full employment is to be restored and if an incomes policy is to have a chance of success. To some extent, a return to full employment will enhance this goal as argued in chapter 11. A reduced dependence on oil imports relaxes the payments constraint and works in the same direction. But an industrial policy directed at raising productivity growth, especially in manufacturing, is needed.

POLICIES TO RELIEVE THE SUPPLY AND
PAYMENTS CONSTRAINT

1. *The correlation between productivity and output growth*

The important task of this section is to argue that policies which increase the rate of growth of productivity and, therefore, aggregate supply also act to relieve a balance of payments constraint through the impact of these policies on trade in manufactures. This issue will be seen to revolve primarily around whether or not the increased rate of growth of productivity is induced by an increased rate of growth of output and sales (Verdoorn's law) and, ultimately, innovations, rather than 'defensive' cost-reduction measures. The analysis will proceed first within the context of a closed economy and then to the open economy with trade in manufactures alone. It has already been mentioned that a policy to reduce dependence on imports of oil may be critical also.

It must be noted that trade between countries has been shifting increasingly towards more highly fabricated goods, especially dura-

---

[6] Among the other studies published there is, The European community: problems and prospects, *Cambridge Economic Policy Review,* December 1981, especially chapter 5. The neglect of energy policies as well as the neglect of manpower policies and commodity price stabilization policies throughout the text is solely due to a desire to focus on other policies.

bles.[7] With these goods, non-price competition is particularly important, making it necessary to alter the definition of 'competitiveness'.
Recognition of this slightly complicates the analysis. For while an
increase in productivity growth will, other things being equal, reduce
rates of increase of unit labour costs and prices of goods, it is not
clear why it must be associated with an improvement in the non-
price elements of competition. If it is not, then greater productivity
growth need not be associated with expanding sales, unless the price
reductions are outstanding.

However the likelihood of a positive correlation between the rate
of growth of productivity in the production of a good and the
enhanced appeal of non-price qualities associated with the good, e.g.
design, dependability, reliable servicing, short delivery dates, etc., will
be strong if there is a positive correlation between rates of growth of
output and sales on the one hand, and productivity on the other; i.e.
Verdoorn's law applies. For in an age of highly fabricated finished
goods, the goods with favourable non-price characteristics will be
the most marketable. Initially this may involve sales only to high
income groups, but as the good increases in popularity, because of a
successful product innovation, longer production runs and learning
economics will reduce unit labour costs while raising productivity,
thereby reinforcing the tendency for rapid expansion of markets.

There are other explanations of the correlation between productivity growth and 'quality'. Studies of Japanese factories reveal
that efforts on the part of Japanese workers to produce high-quality
products lead not only to a reduction in the number of rejects but
also a reduction in the number of workers needed to maintain
quality control.[8] Second, higher rates of growth of productivity generate higher rates of growth of profits and cash flows, allowing
greater expenditures on product improvement and marketing.[9]

However, the essential common element in all these examples is
that productivity growth be induced by sales expansion and that,
ultimately, innovation lies behind it all. This is to be contrasted with
productivity improvements of a more static kind resulting from a
policy of 'financial stringency'. The latter policies reduce costs at
given levels of output by reducing 'over-manning', 'eliminating frills',

[7] See A. Maizels (1970) *Growth and Trade*, Cambridge University Press, Cambridge.
[8] See the description of a Japanese manufacturing factory in R. Hayes (1981) Why
Japanese factories work, *Harvard Business Review*, July–August.
[9] See D. Stout (1979) De-industrialization and industrial policy, in *De-
Industrialization* (Ed. F. Blackaby), Heinemann, London, p. 181 for this and
related points.

etc. As the discussion below of the Japanese IRS will indicate, these kinds of productivity policies may well be counter-productive in the long run. The retained labour force, following layoffs, is liable to be unreceptive to future innovations, thereby leading to a long-run reduction in productivity growth.

2. Sales success in domestic and foreign markets

Whether associated with process or product innovation, it seems clear that higher rates of growth of productivity and expanding markets will be correlated. This remains true for product innovations even if productivity gains are 'eaten up' by a more rapid growth of money wages. Quality improvements will still be important. The issue now is whether this sales success will be as likely abroad as at home. After all, Heckscher–Ohlin trade theory teaches us that for export success everything depends upon relative factor endowments, not such mundane matters as product designs and quality.

Consider, then, a large conglomerate in a closed economy with domestic competition and producing a range of manufactures. In an effort to expand its share in existing markets, but especially in markets of the future, the firm in question is naturally keen to develop and improve product and process technologies. Suppose that a superior product design is invented and a successful innovation results. This innovation then creates a technology gap in the sense that the firm will have put into production a product of superior design and captured a larger share of the market for it and similar goods, which can only be imitated after some lapse of time.

Sooner or later, however, this gap may well be eliminated as competing firms learn to produce a product of similar quality. The length of 'imitation lag' will depend upon the complexity of the technology involved in the innovation, whether patent laws exist and restrain potential imitators from producing close substitutes, etc. Efforts to simplify the technology will also be taking place in the interests of productivity growth, quality control, etc. This will make it easier eventually for potential competitors to introduce similar products since the technology to be 'borrowed' will be less complex and have most of the 'bugs' worked out of it. Indeed, if these potential competitors are located in low-wage areas within the country, they may soon find that they can more than compete with the innovator.

Consider next the identical situation except for the fact that the firm in question exists in a country that engages in international trade. Import substitution is now a possibility for the firm, as it may drive out foreign competitors with its new product. But it may also venture into foreign markets and realize export success. These possibilities suggest that the distinction between resolving payments problems through import substitution rather than export expansion and vice versa is overdrawn when dealing with manufactures. More important, these options suggest that the distinction between sources of sales success in manufactures in a closed economy and an open one are also overdrawn. Whatever the source of rapid expansion in demand, sales success depends upon successful product and process innovations implemented by investment. The possibility of dynamic-scale economies reinforces the initial success at home and abroad.

Certainly there is nothing to force local firms to move into foreign markets. Greater familiarity with the local market may in fact lead to feeble efforts to exploit abroad the profit possibilities of innovations. But even so, successful innovations in the home market should lead to import substitution. This also will relieve the payments constraint by reducing the income elasticity of demand for imports. What a sensible industrial policy must do is to combine a policy to encourage investment and innovation with one emphasizing and rewarding the exploitation of that innovation abroad.

But if growth is to continue unconstrained by a balance of payments ceiling, international competition will force the innovating economy into engaging in vigorous and continuous efforts in export markets. To use the previous example, suppose that successful innovations have allowed local producers to greatly increase their share of the domestic market for some type of good. It is most likely in the case of manufactures that this will stimulate interest in producing similar goods abroad, especially in low-wage countries, either by local producers or others wishing to take advantage of relative wage differences. The geographical shift in production must await, however, the development of a less complex technology, just as in the earlier example of developments within the country. Once this technology has been developed, buyers in the country in which the innovation was first developed will likely find themselves unable to resist the now cheaper products and the trade balance will deteriorate, other things being equal.

This is simply the working out of the 'product-cycle' theory of international trade, in which the comparative advantage in production of some good changes, not because total resource endowments alter between countries but because the human capital requirements of a specific technology change. Alternatively, the sequence can be expressed as the development of a dynamic comparative advantage in that the usual neoclassical trade assumptions of fixed tastes and technologies can, fortunately, be discarded. The message for the country originating the innovations is straightforward. In order to pay for imports at full employment new sources of export success are required and this involves a 'trading-up' process.[10] But this trading-up is, in turn, merely a facet of the transformation process referred to in chapter 10. As growth proceeds and per capita incomes rise, demands shift towards the high-income elasticity sectors. In response to these changing demands, local producers reallocate resources. But in an open economy, in order to pay for full employment imports, i.e. relieve the economy of a payments constraint, this transformation and reallocation must be accelerated as forages must be made into new export markets. The extent to which this effort is successful will determine both the extent to which a country is or is not constrained by a payments ceiling and the rate of growth of productivity.

SUPPLY-SIDE POLICIES

1. *Policies for transformation*

The issue is how to construct a policy that will successfully increase the rate of innovation, investment and transformation, especially in manufacturing, all in the interests of raising the payments ceiling, productivity and real wages. An important clue in developing a successful policy is suggested by an inspection of the nature of the growth process itself, a theme of chapter 10. The rate of growth of productivity and, therefore, output, was seen to reflect the rate of transformation of the economy; i.e. a changing composition of output (and inputs), as the economy moved through an hierarchy of goods spurred on by rising per capita incomes and productivity. A higher rate of growth of productivity, on this reading, reflected a higher rate of movement through this hierarchy. Shifts in the composition of demand and output lead to declines in industries that at one time may have been pace setters and the rise of others (the

---

[10] Much of the relevant literature is summarized by C. Freeman, Technical innovation and British trade performance, in *De-Industrialization* (Ed. F. Blackaby), Heinemann, London, pp. 57–9. The categories 'sunset' and 'sunrise' industries are somewhat misleading. Trading up, for example, will often involve developing special product lines that require special skills in established industries, e.g. textiles and steel.

'sunrise' industries) that produce goods with high income elasticities of demand at prevailing levels of per capita incomes. Naturally, this kind of growth involves a transfer of capital within the economy from declining to expanding firms, industries and sectors. Since most of the capital stock is non-malleable and immobile, being designed for specific lines of production and located in specific geographic areas, this involves new capital goods, often of a different kind.[11] Hence, the earlier emphasis given to investment in accelerating the growth process. Moreover, the higher is the rate of investment, other things being equal, the more rapidly can this transformation and the growth process proceed. Verdoorn's law indicates that higher rates of growth of output are associated with higher rates of growth of productivity. The unbalanced nature of the growth process suggests that innovational investment is an important link in this causal chain.

2. The rate of innovation and labour-management relations

Now it is fairly obvious that merely carrying out unchanged day-to-day routine production operations with a minimum of interruptions is directly related to the degree to which relations between capital and labour are harmonious. To take some examples, absenteeism, strike activity and lesser disruptions such as work slow-downs, all manifestations of bad labour morale, cause various degrees of inter-ruption of production. Clearly, if plant activities even of a routine nature are constantly being interrupted, reorganization of the work place in order to introduce new processes and products becomes difficult and lengthy if not impossible. It follows that the prod-uctivity performance in any enterprise and any economy is very much dependent upon the level of labour-management conflict over acceptable reorganizations of production. In particular the ability to innovate, should management want to, is greatly reduced and as a consequence productivity suffers when labour relations are bad. Thus, even if entrepreneurial zeal leads management to desire an expanded investment programme in the interests of innovation, cost reduction and productivity growth, such desires will be at least par-tially thwarted.

If growth is to proceed, product and process innovations must continuously be introduced and the rates of growth of output and

---

[11] To the extent that the labour force is immobile or cannot be retrained, to that extent does growth of the labour force become important.

productivity will be directly related to the pace at which these innovations are introduced and diffused throughout the economy. One
element missing in chapter 10 was an explicit recognition that industrial relations at the work place are a critical factor in this innovational process, as they very much determine the speed at which not
only new production processes are introduced, but new work rules
accepted and jobs reclassified. A highly mobile and flexible labour
force, allowing workers to be readily and quickly retrained and
moved to new tasks within the enterprise is just as unlikely as
intense innovational activity in an enterprise and an economy characterized by an adversarial industrial relations system. Intra-firm
mobility takes on a role as critical as inter-firm.[12]

3. Supply-side policies and supply-side economics

A second element omitted in chapter 10 was a supply-side counterpart to the demand policies advocated there. Aggregate demand
policy was the instrument assigned the task of returning the
economy to full employment. It is now clear that demand policies
need to be supplemented by methods that help relieve an economy
of the payments constraint and that act directly to increase productivity. What must be implemented is an industrial policy that
works essentially on the supply side. One important part of such a
policy is to provide means for maximizing the rate of innovation and
investment in rapid growth sectors. This must also be an industrial
policy that, put negatively, acts to discourage entrepreneurs from
moving 'down market' and attempting to bolster 'sunset' industries.
The ability of higher rates of growth of aggregate demand to be
translated into higher rates of growth of output or supply depends
upon the ability to shift resources into the growth industries of the
future both home and abroad. This is partly a matter of growth in
factor supplies, given a high degree of non-malleability and non-
mobility of factors. But once growth is recognized as a transformation, taking place in the face of foreign competition, accelerating
rates of sectoral and aggregate growth requires a definite industrial
policy, built upon measures to increase labour's acceptance of innovation and management's desire to direct it into the right sectors. It
is in this sense that supply-side policies, in contrast to supply-side
economics, must not be neglected. The seemingly obvious position

---

[12] The Japanese experience suggests that pay scales based primarily on work experience rather than job content helps in this regard.

that labour's cooperation is important in stimulating the growth potential of an economy is discussed further in the next section.

COOPERATION AGAIN

1. *Controlling inflation and advancing productivity*

One of the central themes of chapters 11 and 12 was that countries in which a cooperative industrial relations system had evolved were in a much better position to implement a successful voluntary incomes policy than the English-speaking countries, because of a tradition of cooperation between labour and management. But this cooperation required a high degree of trust, fostering the internalization of national goals by participants in the bargaining process. What was just suggested on pp. 298–301 was that a cooperative IRS is critical in achieving a relatively favourable productivity performance in any economy. Furthermore, while productivity growth is certainly related to other factors as well, harmony in industrial relations will have a stimulative effect on productivity growth. In any country improved industrial relations will accelerate the rate at which firms can invest and innovate.

In the next two sections, examples of cooperative institutions will be discussed and offered as support for the view that greater dynamic efficiency results from the strengthening of these kinds of arrangements. However, there is a shift in emphasis from cooperation at the industry or national level to the enterprise and especially the plant level. An industrial policy to improve the rate of growth of labour productivity cannot hope to succeed unless due regard is given to conditions at the work place. This does not mean that the cooperative collective bargaining institutions and the kind of welfare programmes discussed in chapter 11 are not important also. Even under the best working conditions in the plant, labour will be much less inclined to cooperate in an effort to raise productivity if wage bargaining is carried out in adversarial industrial relations setting and if it does not feel that distributional issues have been fairly resolved.

2. *Job security and productivity*

There is another important common feature enhancing inflation control and productivity advance. The realization of each goal will require cooperation but cooperation requires that labour be guaranteed job security. In chapter 11 it was argued that before it could be expected that labour would accept a wage norm, various kinds of inducements would be required. These included insurance against unfavourable movements of their real wages, income distribution changes and other welfare measures. An obvious additional inducement was the inclusion of a full employment policy in a package that demanded wage restraint.

But consider the requirements of labour cooperation in reorganizing production. The impact of innovations on employment, especially those that raise productivity, can cut two ways. On the one hand, it offers an opportunity for passing along monetary and real gains to workers when markets are expanding. On the other hand, it suggests to the worker, and rightly so, that his job may be in jeopardy if markets are not expanding.

Thus, whether dealing with measures to bring about wage restraint or measures to stimulate productivity and eventually real-wage growth, success requires cooperation and trust. And from labour's point of view these attitudes are not likely to be generated by restrictive aggregate demand policies. Quite the contrary, they require job-security measures. As argued in earlier chapters, attempts to reduce inflation through creating unemployment will only be successful in the short run if at all. The important related point is that efforts to increase productivity through creating unemployment, 'bashing' or, more politely, 'shaking-out' labour, are also likely to be short-run gains. The eventual reflation of the economy will tend to generate actions that protect jobs at the expense of productivity. What is required is productivity growth induced by expanded sales, not by reduction of employment.

CO-DETERMINATION

Consider again some of the points made about the Continental model of industrial relations. A greater reliance on legislation to achieve economic goals, the importance of centrally directed employers' and employees' associations and the removal of matters of conflict from plant-level negotiations were seen to be important in generating labour–management cooperation, particularly so because these developments have taken place in countries in which the trade unions are strong. The contrast with Italy brings this out. Strikes and disruptions increased in frequency and intensity in the post-war period as the union movement grew in importance. The antagonism of the communist trade unions towards capitalism, the declining importance of worker participation and the tendency for unions to play a strong role within the plant in wage bargaining, illustrated the importance of concertative industrial relations features in other Continental economies with strong trade unions.[13]

But there are additional factors at work in the latter economies and elsewhere which have much to do with explaining not merely the reduction in industrial conflict, but the development of cooperative efforts at the plant level as well. The so-called principle of codetermination refers to certain institutional features of the IRS, those which aim to develop harmonious labour–management relations and cooperative efforts by the sharing of decision-making at the plant and, to a more limited extent, the enterprise level. Generally speaking, the principle of co-determination allows labour to act as a lesser partner of management in a joint determination of work arrangements.[14] This may involve membership on supervisory boards at the enterprise level, as in West Germany, whose task it is to appoint the managers of the enterprise. But in the main, codetermination refers to plant-level partnerships as reflected in works councils, committees representing and elected by workers in the plant. Such councils are either required by law or are recognized as part of a central collective agreement throughout Europe with the UK, Ireland and Switzerland notable exceptions.[15] One of the chief aims of a works council is to get workers to feel a vested interest in the welfare of the plant.

While they cannot call a strike, the councils have a say on such important matters as hiring and firing policy, production policies and even investment programmes. However, co-determination is not to be confused with 'industrial democracy', where the latter implies a form of decision-making in which members of management and labour groups have an equal voice. Instead the emphasis is one of consultation and communication between the two groups and the encouragement of suggestions for improvement of working condi-

---

[13] See C. Pellegrini (1980) Co-determination and its contribution to industrial democracy: A critical evaluation-discussion, *IRRA 33rd Annual Proceedings,* September.

[14] See C. Crouch, The conditions for trade-union wage restraint, in *The Politics of Inflation* . . . op. cit., for a discussion of these kinds of institutions fostering industrial cooperation in several European countries.

[15] See O. Clarke (1980) The development of industrial relations in European Market economics, *IRRA Annual Proceedings,* September. For a description of a British attempt along these lines in the mid-1970s see Stout, op. cit., pp. 189–96.

tions and productivity. Co-determination constrains management's decision-making but with the aim of improving performance at the plant. Works councils are, thus, more than agencies for handling grievances and resolving conflict; they are agencies for generating cooperation in the interests of change.[16]

THE SACRED TREASURES OF INDUSTRIAL RELATIONS

Link the world together with all our hearts and technology   (*motto of Matsushita Electric – UK branch*)

The Japanese system of industrial relations, at least with respect to the large corporations, involves the most pronounced and extensive effort to date to develop concertative or cooperative institutions and to develop a working environment conducive to innovation and productivity growth through trust. At the basis of this system are what have been called the 'sacred treasures' of the Japanese IRS; lifetime employment, a length-of-service rewards system, enterprise unionism and 'social norms within the enterprise', i.e. essentially, the worker considers himself a part of a community centred around the company, non-wage benefits and decision-making is a joint task between workers and management.[17] For present purposes, the life-time employment treasure is best seen as a safety net for the worker ensuring him that he will not be adversely affected by productivity growth resulting from his cooperation. This, in turn, relieves the

---

[16] Thus, in the West German case,

> co-determination is a rather pragmatic approach toward influencing work condi-
> tions in highly organized and dynamic structures. The effects of investment
> policy, for example, upon work structure and workers' qualifications cannot be
> influenced by traditional bargaining techniques. Instead, the whole process of
> arriving at investment decisions and implementing them by technological, eco-
> nomic, and possibly social planning needs to be accompanied by steady commu-
> nication and consultation in order to avoid an outcome detrimental to workers'
> basic interests. It is precisely this communication and consultation structure,
> combined with changes for greater influence, that co-determination at present
> provides.

F. Furstenberg (1980) Co-determination and its contribution to industrial democracy: A critical evaluation, *IRRA Annual Proceedings,* September.

[17] See T. Shirai and H. Shimada (1978) Japan, in *Labor in the Twentieth Century*
(Eds J. Dunlop and W. Galenson), Academic Press, New York.

worker of any need to identify himself with one particular job, thereby increasing the intrafirm mobility. Consequently, large numbers of Japanese workers follow non-specialized career paths. Lifetime employment together with the second treasure, the length-of-service promotions and rewards system, minimizes competition between workers, an important consideration for maximizing on-the-job training. Together, these 'treasures' gently increase worker co-operation and flexibility at the work place.

In and of themselves, tenure and an absence of merit-pay increases based on individual job performance might result in a poor productivity performance, at least according to one school of worker motivation. However, the social norms within the enterprise treasure has led to an attachment by workers to their company that has been almost enough to ensure a most superior job performance. As has been documented quite thoroughly by now, the company is more than merely a place to work in the eyes of the Japanese worker; it is part of his extended family. How well the company does, reflects not only on management but on himself. This community spirit is greatly enhanced in Japan by lifetime employment guarantees but also by an egalitarianism unknown in other capitalist countries, e.g. both blue and white collar workers belong to the company union and management has had shop-floor experience.

This feeling of attachment and concern with the well-being of the company, reciprocated by the company's employment guarantees, is further strengthened by constant consultation at all levels of authority on production problems and their resolution. If these various social norms are not sufficient to guarantee superior performance, one final element may be cited; bonus systems are widespread in the modern sectors of industry that relate overall pay to the profitability and ultimately the productivity of the firm.[18]

To set against these factors leading to a sense of cooperation and trust is the fact that bargaining over contract wages takes place to a larger extent at the enterprise level compared to Continental economies. As argued in chapter 11, local pay bargaining tends to intensify industrial relations conflict, other things being equal. However, in actual fact this third treasure has not been an outstanding problem, as it might be under the Continental system.

The social norms within the enterprise treasure of the Japanese IRS is a more intensive and extensive version of the works councils found in Continental European economies. The lifetime-employment

---

[18] See chapter 11, pp. 264–7.

guarantee is also an exaggerated version of a kind of implicit contract prevalent in European economies.[19] It is the polar opposite of
a labour relations system where workers are guaranteed little
security against depressed demand conditions. What needs to be
added is the element of limited ports of entry into the job structure
of a company (almost always the lowest rung of whatever promotion
ladder is relevant) and the basic elements of a highly structured
'internal labour market' are in place. This has commanded a great
deal of attention in North American writings.[20] Limited ports of
entry, promotion from within, relative job stability for skilled
workers in the face of market fluctuations have been seen as a
rational response to firm-specific training, learned on the job and
financed by the employer. Together, these elements reduce turnover
and allow firms to more easily recoup their investment in human
capital. The Japanese system entails all this, but in a pronounced
form.

The considerable financial and economic success of Japanese companies indicate that this kind of IRS at the plant and enterprise level
gives far superior results in terms of productivity and costs to those
achieved under an adversarial IRS in which a 'them versus us' psychology develops. Pay according to length of service rather than 'job
content', job security rather than short-run layoffs, profit and divi-
dend rather than employment variability, cooperative, consultative
rather than unilateral decision-making, social and psychological as
well as economic attachment to the job are arrangements that have
been adopted partly because of a greater concern in Japan, and to a
lesser extent in other non-English-speaking developed economies,
with the welfare of the workers. Paradoxically to outsiders, arrangements by which the Japanese enterprise allows its profit-making
activities, e.g. price, output and employment adjustments, to be
highly constrained by a concern for the welfare of its labour force
turn out to be highly profitable.[21]

---

[19] See R. Kaufman (1979) Why the U.S. unemployment rate is so high, in *Unemployment and Inflation – Institutionalist and Structuralist Views* (Ed. M. Piore),
Sharpe, Armonk, New York.

[20] See P. Doeringer and M. Piore (1971) *Internal Labor Markets and Manpower
Analysis,* D. C. Health, Lexington, Massachusetts.

[21] It has even been argued that works councils and labour membership on supervisory boards has induced German management to be more successfully innovative than their American counterparts. This has allowed them to move
'up-market' expanding their share of sales in international markets. See R. Hayes,
and W. Abernathy (1980) Managing our way to economic decline, *Harvard
Business Review,* July–August.

The results are not so surprising, however, once one simple fact is recognized; the attitudes of workers towards productivity enhancing behaviour and work reorganization and various forms of disruption are not 'given'. Rather they are very dependent upon the desire to cooperate and the strength of this desire varies with worker morale and feelings of fair treatment. What the Japanese IRS has shown the world is that conflict between the two sides of the labour market is detrimental to productivity growth (as well as wage restraint). Japanese firms compete fiercely with one another but for some time have stressed cooperation within the firm. The recent interest in Japanese industrial relations, especially in English-speaking countries, is but a belated recognition that impersonal market forces will not ensure dynamic efficiency regardless of institutional arrangements. The invisible hand needs a great deal of guidance in the form of cooperative institutions and motivations that not only give rise to a more humane capitalism, but also contribute to a higher productivity and profit performance. Economic theory at its more elevated neoclassical level deals with a structureless labour market in which 'there is no attachment except the wage between the worker and the employer. No worker has any claim on any job and no employer has any hold on any man.'[22] The Japanese experience suggests that what is being modelled in this kind of economic analysis is a set of labour markets and an industrial relations system in perpetual disorder.

The recent lessening of employment guarantees in Japan and elsewhere entails a warning; short-run cost reductions, if achieved through reduction of workers, are likely to have detrimental medium and long-run effects on productivity. Attempts to reduce the importance of works councils will have similar effects. The means to rapid productivity growth lie elsewhere.

AN OUTLINE OF A WELL-FUNCTIONING ECONOMY

1. *The programme in place*

In order to tie some of the important policy recommendations together it is useful to describe the manner in which a successful policy response to stagflation by an individual country would reveal itself. First of all, allow that stimulative aggregate demand policies

---

[22] The quotation is from C. Kerr (1954) The Balkanization of labor markets, in *Labour Mobility and Economic Opportunity* (Eds E. W. Bakke *et al.*), Cambridge, Technology Press, p. 101n.

have been introduced and the unemployment rate has been reduced to more or less the overall job vacancy rate.[23] Wage and price inflation have also been reduced to an acceptable rate because of the simultaneous implementation of a successful incomes policy.

The achievement of full employment has helped to stimulate productivity growth compared with the present stagnation period but other measures have been necessary as well. Thus, the effect of stimulative aggregate demand policies on imports (and exports) together with the need to guarantee some minimum rate of growth of productivity has necessitated the use of additional policy instruments of the kind suggested in this chapter. These included measures to lessen energy dependence, but in addition measures that resulted in an improved export performance and import substitution in manufactures. Both measures have worked to relieve the economy of any kind of payments constraint thereby allowing full employment.

Because the sources of trade success in manufactures are little different from those stimulating productivity growth, the successful industrial policy has led to an acceleration of productivity growth, per capita incomes and real wages. This, in turn, has allowed the maintenance of the many welfare programmes developed during the 1950s and the 1960s that had much to do with the relatively harmonious industrial relations during that period. In the present situation their maintenance has helped to guarantee the continued acceptance of the permanent incomes policy. The dynamics of this 'Japanese model of perpetual growth and transformation' can be sketched as follows.

2. The dynamics of success

Productivity growth has accelerated compared with the current stagflation period reflecting full employment conditions but also a successful industrial policy that stimulates innovation and investment and relieves the economy of a payments constraint. This higher rate of growth of productivity and output is best seen as a more rapid transformation of the economy, a more rapid movement through what was described in chapter 10 as an hierarchy of goods. This is spurred on by a more rapid rate of investment which embodies the new technologies and product innovations in the present and future rapid-growth sectors of the economy.

---

[23] If this unemployment rate is deemed too high, manpower policies of the Swedish variety can be introduced as a supplementary policy instrument.

But continued innovational success at home requires forays into the export market and import substitution as well, otherwise restrictive aggregate demand policies would have to be invoked in a world in which exchange-rate policy has only a limited role to play. It is certainly true that the initial export success and import substitution in manufactures leads to cumulative effects because of the importance of dynamic economies of scale. Rates of growth of productivity are very much influenced by rates of growth of sales so that superior product design and dependability lead to expanded sales, mass production and cost-saving technologies and prolong competitive success.

But even so the initial success in ending stagflation can only be maintained by a reorientation and redirection of both domestic and foreign sales. As new products and processes come on to the market, a learning experience plus an ability to borrow technologies enables 'late starters', i.e. foreign competitors, to duplicate innovations once the novelty and difficulties of the production process are mastered. Technology innovators in the various sectors of our successful country cannot expect, therefore, to maintain their competitive advantage permanently, since low-wage countries will eventually have a distinct potential competitive advantage. Hence the need for the country under discussion to continuously move up market whenever other less-affluent, less-industrialized countries are themselves moving up market.

But by continuously seeking new markets at home and abroad for new products and processes, the probability of maintaining high productivity growth and being able to finance full employment imports is strengthened. What is being described is nothing more than a 'virtuous circle' of rapid growth of output leading to rapid growth of productivity, leading to a rapid growth of exports and the maintenance of a strong current account, all of which allows rapid growth of output to continue indefinitely. Comparative advantage is not a fixed situation that can be modelled by static analysis. It is a dynamic process entailing and prescribing an ever-changing adaptation by entrepreneurs and policy makers to new conditions.

3. *Cooperation and the growth of productivity*

One of the important lessons of chapters 11 and 12 is that success at every stage in the growth process is contingent upon cooperation between government, capital and labour at the plant, industry and national level. This is necessary to insure the successful working of

an incomes policy, to strengthen the ability of management to innovate and to maximize the rate at which this takes place. The greater
is this cooperation, the more rapidly can innovations be implemented through investment, productivity growth be speeded up and the
economy move through an hierarchy of goods.

Those countries trapped by history in an adversarial industrial-
relations system will find themselves at a distinct disadvantage compared with the well-functioning economy just described. Chronic
current account deficits, restrictive fiscal and monetary policies, high
unemployment and low productivity growth will characterize their
development. And the important point is that the loss suffered by
these countries is not simply a one-time loss that can be measured,
say, in terms of a one-time reduction in the level of output. By
improving upon the degree of harmony of the IRS, the rate of innovation and investment is speeded up. This increases the rate of
growth of productivity, not just its level, because the higher rate of
investment and innovation speeds up the rate at which the economy
transforms itself. More concretely, this higher rate of productivity
growth is translated into higher rates of growth of real wages and
per capita incomes. This means that demand and output will now be
shifting more rapidly towards the high income elasticity sectors. The
higher growth of demand and output in these rapid growth sectors,
which now realize a higher level of demand and output at an earlier
point in time, causes a higher rate of investment than otherwise in
these sectors, again at an earlier point in time. This also spurs productivity, real wage and per capita income growth as the economy
moves through an hierarchy of goods at a more rapid rate. Another
Japanese lesson to the world is that a cooperative industrial-
relations system must be the basis of any sound industrial policy, a
lesson independently learned in many Continental European economies.

Marx's view that the accumulation of capital is essential to capitalism's survival finds support in what has just been said. Export
success requires rapid productivity growth and this requires high
rates of investment. Without this accumulation a payments ceiling
would be operative in a highly integrated economic world. And with
a payments ceiling comes unemployment, excess capacity and stagnation.

ELEMENTS OF AN INDUSTRIAL POLICY

Given this basic consideration, additional clues for the construction
of a successful industrial policy emerge from the brief sketch of the

well-functioning economy. The general thrust of any successful industrial policies must be aimed at speeding up the rate of transformation of the economy. This has two parts. First, it is necessary to speed up the rate of transfer of resources out of declining industries into the growth industries of the future (while minimizing the costs). Here, the allocation of a large share of resources to investment is essential, as most capital is non-malleable and immobile. High rates of growth of output and productivity are, therefore, dependent upon a rapid transfer of capital into new sectors of the economy. A similar recommendation applies to labour. Manpower programmes to retrain and relocate workers serve to speed up the rate of transfer of labour. Second, it is necessary to increase the rate of growth of productivity within the newly expanding industries. This involves assistance largely in the form of R&D support and guidance, to increase the rate of invention and innovation, or more technically, the rates of growth of technological and technical progress. With the closing of the technology gap, rapid rates of growth of productivity and supply require larger outlays on research and development in all economies, not just the technology leaders. Thus, greater malleability and mobility of capital and labour, i.e. greater flexibility, need to be complemented by measures that stimulate the rate of inventions and innovations in the new industries.

But a successful industrial policy in an economy undergoing transformation requires that there be a speedy release of resources in the declining industries and sectors of the economy as well.[24] There are at least two problems here. First, vested interests seeking to protect the declining sectors of an economy will be more powerful politically in retarding transformation than the interests seeking assistance in new industries and sectors will be in accelerating change.[25] Second, in the absence of definite policies for adaptation to change, the various groups involved in adapting to decline, i.e. management, workers and the communities, do so at vastly different rates. The mobility of capital, often increased by tax breaks to business, is much greater than that for workers and both are infinitely more mobile than the community infrastructure that has been built up to support local industry. As a result, 'market signals' indicating the greater profitability of new industrial ventures do not generate

---

[24] See I. Magaziner and R. Reich (1982) *Minding America's Business,* Harcourt, Brace, Jovanovich, New York. What becomes most clear in this study is how important it is for a government agency to merely collect data on industrial developments at home and abroad at the firm, industry and national levels.

[25] The remainder of this section relies heavily on the reference in fn 24 and R. Reich (1980) Making industrial policy, *Foreign Affairs,* Spring.

parallel responses that allow all resources in the declining sectors to be utilized.

A successful industrial policy must take account of these differences by coordinating the required capital and industrial adjustment to the kinds of adjustment by labour and communities that are feasible. Besides the obvious need for manpower policies, feasibility may imply locating new industries in the same area as declining industries so that a maximum utilization of resources is maintained throughout the transformation process. A coordinated effort of this sort is absolutely essential if the political and economic forces resistant to change are to be neutralized. But whether discussing the need to accelerate the expansion of new industries or the contraction of old, industrial policies to accelerate the rate of transformation and growth require coordinated efforts agreement between government, labour and business, just as does the working out of a successful incomes policy. And as with an incomes policy, only the government is in a position to bring about the kind of cooperative arrangement essential for success. It alone is in a position to provide a consistent, long-run plan for growth, to collect and disseminate the information needed to put the plan into effect and to reconcile the seemingly competing interests.

CONCLUSIONS

All of this would appear to be very general and belabour the obvious. An industrial policy aimed at increasing productivity and real wage growth by means of greater cooperation between labour, management and government, greater emphasis on growth in the industries of the future and greater government leadership in shaping industrial policy is hardly provocative. Yet a belief persists that the best policy for industrial development is a 'hands off' policy in which something called 'the market' provides the information needed for reallocating resources, including R&D expenditures.

Unfortunately, this suggests a false choice and leads to undesired results. For a belief that market forces or an invisible hand can function as a substitute for a well-thought-out (and permanent) industrial policy of the type sketched here has had a destructive impact on the dynamic efficiency of at least one economy, the USA. Far from leading to a 'hands off', *laissez-faire* industrial policy, an alleged belief in an invisible hand has facilitated the reception of demands by special interests for political and economic protection.

As a result the denial of the need for any activist policy for industrial prosperity has led to a multiplication of *ad hoc* government measures in support of certain groups.[26] In the economies of today, the choice is not between a market solution to the productivity problem versus 'planning', but between a private, *ad hoc* industrial policy that retards growth and a consistent public policy to exploit market forces.

[26] ibid.

CHAPTER 14

The US Model of Development

The central point of the second half of this study is that if the goals of price stability, full employment and rising living standards are ever to be realized in development capitalist economies again, more not less government intervention is required. There is no inherent self-regulating mechanism within capitalism that guarantees the realization of these goals if, say, the authorities will only balance the budget and carefully regulate the money supply. Full employment, as Keynes pointed out, may require discretionary demand management. Price stability at or near full employment will necessitate even greater government concern and activism, as the affluence generated by prolonged periods of full employment causes new problems for capitalist economies. In particular, sustained full employment greatly increases the power of labour relative to capital and if full employment without inflation is to be achieved a whole new set of attitudes, institutions and policies must be developed. Chapters 9 to 13 outlined some of the necessary changes in attitudes, institutions and policies that are required for realizing the goals of price stability, full employment and growing per capita incomes.

In those chapters it was also argued that current policies of restricting aggregate demand would not work in any long-run sense. Even if unemployment rates are pushed high enough and maintained at those high levels until the inflation is squeezed out of the system, there is every reason to believe that any subsequent restimulation of the economy would set off accelerating rates of inflation long before involuntary unemployment had been appreciably reduced.

And even if, after inflation rates have been reduced to something approaching those that prevailed before the mid-1960s, economies could be magically transported back to full employment there are difficulties. As argued in chapter 6, the inflationary process at work in modern capitalist economies today is unstable upwards. Outside disturbances set in motion the inflationary mechanisms but only in an upward direction.

This view of an inflationary bias stands in sharp contrast to the monetarist scenario which relies heavily on the 'credibility hypothesis' (CH) first discussed in chapter 3. According to the monetarist version of the CH, if the (monetary) authorities can convince the public that, first, it will adhere to restrictive aggregate demand policies until inflation is brought under control, and second, there is no alternative means to achieve price stability, then inflation will be brought under control rapidly. But the monetarist scenario also assumes that once this condition is met, the introduction of a sensible monetary rule will be shortly followed by a return to full employment without inflation starting up again.

The belief in an inflationary bias implies a rejection of both parts of the monetarist scenario. Leaving aside the fact that the CH is a non-refutable hypothesis (i.e. if restrictive policies do not quickly bring down inflation rates it is because the authorities have not yet acted credibly enough), the ability to vote out of office those associated with a restrictive demand policy places limits on how far and how quickly unemployment rates can be allowed to rise and bankruptcies allowed to pile up and how long all this can be allowed to go on. As discussed on pp. 324–6 the USA (and other English-speaking countries) have shown a greater tolerance for unemployment than most other developed economies but limits exist none the less.

The belief that the economy will automatically move back to full employment without inflation provided a monetary rule is followed can only be based on the assumptions of the make-believe world of perfect competition. The real world, as the economy moves towards full employment, will be one of strong and affluent trade unions and oligopolies that will wish to make up for all they lost during the restrictive policy period. Labour, especially, will not likely have learned the virtue of piety through unemployment. Rather the lesson the authorities will have taught them through their policies is that the rational person presses his advantages whenever he can and the best way to do this is through accelerated wage demands. To be credible the credibility hypothesis and the monetarist scenario require a 'Chilean solution'.

A third possible policy, one not considered here, is to push the economy back to full employment through stimulative aggregate demand policies and let inflation take whatever course it might. Unfortunately, such a policy would most likely generate a 'currency crisis', and a widespread speculation against the currency, unless foreign exchange controls are simultaneously introduced following depreciation. But even if such policies were undertaken in a closed economy, there is reason to be sceptical of their workability. Given the inflationary bias inherent in the workings of modern economies, it is doubtful if anything other than an acceleration of inflation rates would result.

To say this is not to assume that this acceleration must be of a South American variety. No doubt such a policy would be accompanied by periodic statutory incomes policies. But if full employment is pursued in earnest, it is doubtful that temporary incomes policies can do more than lead to temporary pauses in the acceleration of inflation rates. And unless one is willing to make the unrealistic assumption that inflationary rates will be correctly anticipated and acted upon by all, such inflationary developments are bound to generate feelings that the gainers and losers have reaped gains and borne losses that bear no relation to any acceptable criterion of fairness. Such feelings would sooner or later provide the monetary authorities and the financial community with support for their view (assuming they ever needed any) that restrictive policies in the interests of price stability were now essential.

The implicit assumption throughout this study has been that no such policy of 'curbing' stagflation by eliminating stagnation but allowing inflation would be acceptable under modern democracies in the long run. Thus, the policy advocated in chapters 10 to 13 rejects as unacceptable both a policy of stagnation without inflation and a policy of inflation without stagnation.

THE UNITED STATES MODEL

Those who advocate a programme of less government intervention as a means of curing stagflation are prone to point for support to the historical record of the USA, a country with one of the least-developed welfare states, one of the most adversarial industrial relations systems and the country most given to preaching the value of *laissez-faire* policies among the OECD economies. According to this view, the absence of welfare programmes, harmonious industrial relations and the sort of industrial policy advocated in chapter 13 has not been an impediment to the dynamic efficiency required for high living standards. Admittedly, the USA, along with the other English-speaking countries listed in table 11.1, were the most strike prone of all those considered. But, so the argument goes, conflict as measured by strikes and other means is the price that must be paid to enjoy other economic benefits of a dynamic, vigorous economy, benefits inevitably measured in terms of productivity and living standards.

Now it is important here to emphasize an elementary but fundamental distinction. And that is between levels and rates of growth of labour productivity and, ultimately, per capita incomes. Thus, allowing for the fact that international comparisons of incomes levels are notoriously subject to error and misinterpretation, it still remains true that a powerful argument supporting the American model of development has been the relatively high *levels* of labour productivity and per capita incomes.

However, this finding overlooks the important fact that at the beginning of what can be considered the period of industrialization and modernization of the US economy, i.e. the period following the Civil War, per capita incomes were already often double or even triple those of other OECD economies outside of England, France and West Germany. To a large extent this was the result of an abundance of fertile agricultural land and industrial and agricultural raw materials. By comparison with the natural endowments bestowed upon post-Civil War USA, the North Sea oil is a minor gift of nature. What has become clear recently is that this superior comparative performance in terms of productivity and income levels has been accompanied by a relatively poor performance in terms of growth of these levels, a point made clear by repeated findings that the US ranking in terms of international per capita incomes levels has been falling for some time.

This whole point can be made more concrete with the help of table 14.1 in which rates of growth of labour productivity are given for eleven countries for periods of up to a century or more. As is quite clear, during the period of widespread steady growth from 1950 and 1973, the US growth record was the worst of the eleven. The period since 1973 is little better in relative terms. The picture emerging from the pre-1913 and 1913–50 is rather unclear since in the former period many countries such as Italy had not even begun to industrialize, while growth rates in the latter period were dominated by extraordinary events, especially the Second World War. Even so, the period from 1950 to the present represents over three decades, long enough to reveal long-term trends, and during this period the record of the US economy, as measured in terms of its dynamic efficiency, i.e. productivity growth, suggests that 'the American way' has not been a superior model of development.

TABLE 14.1   *Average annual percentage*

Growth rates of GNP or GDP worker[a]

	Starting year	Pre-1913[b] (%)	1913–50[c] (%)	1950–73[c] (%)	1973–81[c] (%)
USA	1871	2.2	1.7	2.2	0.5
Canada	1872	1.9	1.0	2.8	0.3
Japan	1880	3.4	1.7	7.8	3.4
France	1855	1.5	0.9	4.4	2.5
Germany	1853	1.5	0.6	4.6	2.6
Italy	1863	0.7	0.9	5.5	1.9
Norway	1865	1.3	1.6	3.2	2.9[d]
Denmark	1872	2.1	1.0	2.7	1.3[d]
Netherlands	1900	0.7	0.7	4.0	2.2
Sweden	1863	2.4	1.4	3.0	0.8
UK	1857	1.6	0.6	2.5	1.0

[a] The real growth rate of GNP (or GDP) per employed civilian.
[b] From *National Institute Economic Review,* July 1961.
[c] Calculated from *National Institute Economic Review,* July 1961; OECD, *Economic Outlook,* December 1981; OECD, *Labour Force Statistics,* 1972, 1981; IMF, *International Financial Statistics,* 1981.
[d] 1973–79.

To see matters in a different way, consider the following hypothetical example. Assume that in 1981 some country, A, had achieved more or less the same level of labour productivity (and per capita income) as the USA. Then, given some historical rate of growth of productivity from 1950 to 1981 (1950–73 and 1973–81 as in table 14.1), it is a simple matter to extrapolate backwards to obtain the relative productivity levels in 1950 for country A compared with the USA. For example, productivity grew at an average rate of 2.2 and 4.6 per cent from 1950–73 and 0.5 and 2.6 per cent from 1973–81 in the USA and West Germany, respectively. Assuming that productivity levels in 1981 were the same in the two countries, a reasonable approximation, then using the historical growth rates of productivity from 1950–81, it is found that the level of productivity in West Germany in 1950 relative to the USA was only 47.6 per cent.[1]

What this exercise is meant to suggest is that in a period free from major wars and depressions, relative productivity levels and, therefore, per capita incomes remain as high as they do today in the USA because of high relative levels in 1950 (and earlier).

TECHNOLOGICAL LEADERSHIP

A counter-argument to that just made is readily available. It is true that the USA was generously endowed with natural resources, and a large expanding domestic market foster high initial income levels. This favourable start, together with the relatively decent productivity performance in the early stages of industrialization, as seen in table 14.1, would lead to relatively high per capita income levels in the USA for much of the total period covered in table 14.1. If it can be assumed that the relative level of technical sophistication is strongly correlated with relative income levels, then it follows that during much of the period of capitalist development up to the present, the USA was the technology leader.[2] More important, countries industrializing later but following similar patterns of development would have been in a position to borrow the technology already developed by the USA. Not only that, they would have borrowed the best technology from the leader, leading to a wider and faster diffusion of this superior technology throughout the imitative countries compared with the USA. Given some very plausible additional assumptions, the conclusion can then be drawn that the ability to borrow technology confers a tremendous bonus upon imitating countries and a large relative handicap for the innovative country.

---

[1] Using this kind of exercise for Denmark, France, the Netherlands, Norway and Sweden (countries with productivity levels comparable to the USA in 1981) gives relative productivity levels in 1950 as a percentage of those in the USA of 85.0, 50.2, 56.6, 67.8 and 80.7 per cent, respectively. The computations are derived as follows. Assuming each country had an average level of labour productivity of 100 in 1981, productivity levels in 1950 are given by: $q = 100/[(1 + r_1)^{24} \times (1 + r_2)^9]$ where r_1 and r_2 are annual average rates of growth of productivity from 1950 to 1973 and 1973 to 1981, respectively, in some countries. This figure is then expressed as a percentage of average productivity levels in the USA in 1950, similarly computed.

[2] See J. Cornwall (1977) *Modern Capitalism: Its Growth and Transformation,* Martin Robertson, Oxford, 1977, chapter VI.

By this argument, the USA has been penalized over the past 30 years, much the same way that England earlier was penalized.[3] On this reading the poor productivity growth performance in the post-Second World War period should not be attributed to a perverse form of capitalism but to an accident of history. Besides, the growth of productivity in America before the post-Second World War period was relatively good as seen in table 14.1.

Now there is much that is sound in this argument, but it is also true that new technologies do not fall like manna from heaven but must be discovered, often through costly search processes, refashioned by local producers and implemented on the shop floor. All of this requires large amounts of investment, a labour force that does not impede innovation and a management class that has a keen interest in the development of product and process technologies. This desire and determination to innovate would reveal itself in the rate of capital formation and it is here that the US record (and that of UK and Canada) is very poor.[4] While the USA may have paid a price for being the industrial and technology leader through most of the post-war period, it is also true that little effort was made to compensate for this penalty.

Nor is the relatively high rate of growth of productivity up to the post-war period evidence that the American model of development leads to dynamic efficiency under modern conditions. What must not be overlooked is the historically weak bargaining position of labour before widespread unionization, a weakness accentuated by the fact that such a large proportion of the US labour force was composed of newly arrived immigrants. Large-scale unionization only came to the USA in the 1930s. In this situation, labour was not in a position to respond negatively to any bad treatment handed to it or to impede innovation.

But one of the points made in earlier chapters is that with the formation of strong unions, especially when operating under conditions of full employment, industrial relations must be harmonious if innovation is to be widespread and productivity growth rapid. Disruption of the unionization of new industries, efforts to break the power of existing unions, the absence of institutions promoting co-operation such as works councils, the absence of a developed welfare state and the presence of a strong *laissez-faire* ideology, all of these

---

[3] ibid., chapter VI.

[4] When comparing the ratios of business investment and manufacturing investment to output, these three English-speaking countries inevitably figure at the bottom of the rankings in the OECD countries.

must be added to the penalty of an early start in explaining the US record of dynamic inefficiency. The real message of US development in the recent period is that future industrial and technology leaders must retain and support any elements of a cooperative IRS and refrain from adopting some harmful ideological baggage if productivity and real wage growth are to be preserved.[5]

THE LOSS OF THE WORK ETHIC

But it is becoming clear that the US model of development has been associated with additional problems of more recent origin or, at least, have only become apparent recently. These are the widespread relative failures of US managers as entrepreneurs and the comparative inability of the US system of government to articulate and enact consistent policies for achieving desired economic ends. Both difficulties have contributed to the impairment of the dynamic efficiency of the US economy. The failure of entrepreneurship among US management will be considered in this section and the inability to make use of long-run economic policies on pp. 326–30.

Consider first the allegation that US management has failed to perform in an entrepreneurial capacity, which is then cited as an important cause of the decline of US competitiveness.[6] This is easily related to the discussion of the nature of the growth process in chapters 10 and 13. As indicated there, growth is a very unbalanced process with new industries developing continuously and established industries subject to eventual decline. The rate at which this transformation proceeds was seen to depend heavily upon the rate at which resources were transferred into the new industries. This, by definition, requires new process and product technologies illustrating the defining features of entrepreneurship; the ability and willingness to innovate.

The charge brought against US businessmen is that at some time, midway through the post-war period, top management lost its

---

[5] This last point finds casual empirical support in the change in productivity and product quality in formerly American firms that have been taken over by parent Japanese companies. With most of the former production personnel unchanged, but modified Japanese management techniques introduced, productivity improved partly as a result of a much lower rate of rejection of produced goods by the quality control division.

[6] R. Hayes and W. Abernathy (1980) Managing our way to economic decline, *Harvard Business Review*, July–August.

'organizational commitment to compete in the marketplace on tech-nological grounds'.[7] Instead of searching for new markets and allo-cating the R&D and investment funds necessary for the new product and process innovations needed to develop these markets, US mana-gers at best have been more concerned than their foreign com-petitors with short-run cost reductions and 'promotional gimmicks' in existing, safe markets. At worst, they have been guilty of an almost total neglect of the production or technology side of corporate oper-ations, devoting most of their attention to financial manipulation. This often takes the form of mergers and acquisitions involving some of the most desperate types of product lines.

This redirection of the tasks of management from long-run con-cerns with innovations, growth and profitability has been attributed to bad management techniques, techniques that emphasize detach-ment from day-to-day production routines, the unimportance of familiarity with these same routines and the adoption of modern theories of financial portfolio management to the management of corporate production portfolios (e.g. 'diversify your product line to reduce risk').

This explanation naturally raises the more basic question of just why American management has chosen such techniques. A plausible explanation runs in terms of the adoption by corporate management of goals that place little value on entrepreneurship. Recognition of this has, in turn, led to less charitable explanations of the decline of US international competitiveness. Thus, consider the following fea-tures of corporate management in the USA; a widespread separation of management from ownership, a lack of job security for top corpo-rate management, executive performance evaluated largely in terms of recent behaviour of share prices, and executive salaries and bonuses tied to short-run profit performance. Add to this a business environment with a large accumulation of tax loopholes or benefits available through financial manoeuvrings (as distinct from outright cheating) and the stage is set for the recruitment of lawyers and accountants to run corporations.

Now such recruits, even with little or no knowledge of production considerations, may succeed quite admirably in the short run in generating large paper profits and rising share prices, e.g. changing accounting rules following an acquisition or merger. And if such aims are the overriding considerations of business executives, Amer-ican management techniques are well-suited to the task. Where they

---

[7] ibid., p. 68.

do very badly, naturally, is in the role of Schumpeter's entrepreneur. But the management techniques adopted by corporate officials are more the symptoms of the problem than the cause; good old-fashioned greed.

Whether a symptom or a cause, and allowing for the fact that the evidence is 'soft' and impressionistic, this relative loss of the work ethic has compounded the difficulties for the American economy in the recent past and will likely continue to do so in the future. A second additional barrier to successful economic development, also of recent origin, will be taken up on pp. 326–30. Its relevance for future development of the US economy is highlighted.

WHAT WILL UNITED STATES' ECONOMIC POLICY BE IN THE FUTURE?

The conditions, institutions and beliefs that have shaped US economic development throughout its recent history will have much to do in determining its probable policy response to future economic conditions. And because of its immense economic importance, the US response is relevant to the success or failure of any policy pursued in other OECD economies and the rest of the world. It is therefore of some value to speculate on US policy towards stagflation over, say, the next decade.

Consider one of the trends discussed in chapter 7. By 1982 a noticable deceleration in the rate of wage and price inflation had begun in the USA, especially in the second half of that year. As argued in chapter 6, this would be the result primarily of creating nineteenth-century labour markets in which fairness considerations did not have a strong influence on wage demands and settlements. With unemployment reaching such high rates for so long, it would no longer be a problem confined solely to marginal workers. Not only the young, females, the elderly and minorities would feel unemployment, but also members with seniority in their jobs. As a result wage demands based on past cost-of-living increases or wage settlements elsewhere would be less frequent and pushed with less force as employers would increasingly have the upper hand.

Let it be assumed then that some time in 1983 inflation in the USA is considered under control. The issue is what policies will US governments be willing to adopt now that the fight against inflation has finally been won. The question cannot be ignored since the powerful influences of the US economy on the rest of the world acts as a constraint on policy options open to the other economies. There are two possibilities which, when due account is taken of the conclusions reached in chapter 6, come to the same thing.

The American authorities, fearful of inflation accelerating once again, may choose to run the economy at rates of unemployment of around, say, 10 per cent and rates of capacity utilization similar to those of the early 1980s. Alternatively, an attempt will be made to restimulate the economy since profits rise with the level of economic activity and the unemployed can vote. However, given the likelihood that price and wage inflation will begin to accelerate long before involuntary unemployment and excess capacity have been eliminated, restrictive aggregate demand policies will soon be reintroduced. Inflation may be reduced but the depressed economic conditions will again act as a strong impediment to any kind of investment boom. Stagnation without inflation will become a long-run feature of the US economy.

THE LACK OF PRESSURE FOR MAINTAINING FULL EMPLOYMENT

All of this predicts the US Government will choose long-run stagnation over the kind of policies advocated in the last several chapters. This conclusion is based on a recognition of the various influences previously cited to explain the inferior US performance. But there are two additional factors at work, not yet discussed; the lack of effective political pressure for maintaining full employment, and an inability to formulate and implement any kind of coherent long-run economic policy under the present political system in the USA.

There are several reasons for the relative unimportance of maintaining full employment in the USA. First, the union movement, which has a strong stake in reducing unemployment, has always been relatively weak both politically and economically. Its political 'clout' has been made even weaker recently by the increased importance of money in US elections, a matter to be discussed shortly. Second, and related, not only is the union movement weak, the USA has, throughout its industrialization, been strongly anti-union. One important aspect of this anti-union sentiment is a strong desire to reduce union power even if it requires high rates of unemployment.

Third, in chapter 8 it was noted that rising unemployment has a discouraged-worker effect, as many potential workers withdraw from the labour force when job prospects deteriorate. In the USA, the impact of stagnation on voter participation is also decidedly negative, i.e. when unemployment rates rise, participation falls. Rising unemployment rates in the USA affect not only how people vote but strongly influence whether or not they vote.[8] The explanation is threefold: (1) the opportunity cost of political participation rises when the returns for attending to a serious personal problem such as unemployment increase; (2) unemployment disrupts social relationships and this cuts off sources of political information and the encouragement to participate; and (3) unemployment causes such deep psychological problems, e.g. loss of self-confidence and self-esteem and guilt, that the unemployed find participation in any kind of normal activity extremely difficult.[9] While it is true that adverse economic conditions tend to influence the way people vote if they do vote, the decline in voter participation can be strong enough to swamp the impact of economic conditions on how people vote. In effect some of those hurt by stagnation disenfranchise themselves and fail to support those candidates that are concerned with the unemployment problem. Those most likely to disenfranchise themselves are the poor, minority groups, manual workers and the young and the old.

Fourth, the fear of government deficits is more pronounced in the USA than in any other developed economy. Discussion in the Congress and the Reagan Administration and throughout the business community in the 1980s reveals an attitude about deficits that can only be considered irrational. Large deficits are seen by influential groups in and out of government as a sign of national bankruptcy, government spending out of control, and even 'an unwillingness by government to share in the hardships of mass unemployment'. They are also viewed as a cause of accelerating inflation and a crowding out of productive private investment, as discussed earlier in chapter 9. As a result, any attempt to reduce unemployment that requires large increases in the deficit will meet strong resistance.

---

[8] This part of the text is based on the study by S. Rosenstone (1982) Economic activity and voter turnout, *American Journal of Political Science*, February. Rosenstone employs both cross section and time series data to test his various hypotheses.

[9] A large proportion of the economics profession has an extremely difficult time understanding that the 'cost' or 'loss' from unemployment is more than the difference between the wage while employed and the unemployment benefits received when out of work. In the concluding section of chapter 8 it was suggested that this might be partly attributed to the overwhelming use of secondary data when studying the unemployment problem.

Finally, if these various factors are combined with an ideological view that the unemployed are somehow manifesting 'a lack of inward grace' and some faulty notions about the nature of unemployment as discussed in chapter 8, the lack of political pressure to resolve the unemployment problem is obvious. There will be limits to how far unemployment rates can be pushed. These limits will be reached very likely when unemployment begins to adversely affect the middle classes; their employment prospects, bankruptcies of their business and foreclosures of their mortgages. But before this occurs the conditions generating stagnation will already have been achieved.

TO FORM A GOVERNMENT

But even if it could be assumed that full employment was considered to be an essential goal of economic policy and that deficits of, say, 5–7 per cent of GNP are not too high a price to pay for reducing unemployment, there are additional reasons for expecting that the USA will choose (in effect) a policy of continued stagnation over the next decade or so.

Merely to cite the historical suspicion of government, intensified greatly by 'Reaganism', makes it difficult to see a strong coalition of political forces in the USA even proposing the kinds of incomes and industrial policies needed to realize price and wage stability and accelerated productivity growth. Both these policies require substantially more government intervention not less and policies must be clearly articulated and permanent. But there is a more serious, fundamental concern, a result of influences that have intensified in force over the past 15 years or so. These influences, which involve institutional developments and the spread of the corruption of the political processes, make the use of rational, long-run government policy as a corrective force virtually impossible. In particular, the policy for recovery without inflation outlined in the last few chapters will be politically unacceptable in any country confronting such problems.

The problem of institutions is conveyed by the belief that under the American Constitution it is no longer possible for a US government to 'propose, legislate and administer a balanced program of governing'.[10] In the first instance, this is due to the separation of executive and legislative powers, in which the chief executive is not

---

[10] See L. Cutler (1980) To form a government, *Foreign Affairs,* Fall.

chosen from the majority party in the legislative branch but is elected separately. This can and often does lead to representatives of different political parties heading the two branches which, in turn, can and often does lead to political stalemates. The two branches of government are then unable to use the political process to implement even those economic programmes supported by a majority of the voters.

But clearly this is only the beginning of the political difficulties. Even if the two branches of government were represented by members from the same political party (as under a parliamentary system), there is no guarantee that programmes can be enacted and governments held responsible without party discipline. And what has become most apparent in the post-war period is a steady decline in party discipline as well as in political parties.[11]

Under the US system of government there is no constitutional duty and increasingly no practical need for members of the legislative branch to support the executive branch, even when both are controlled by the same party. This development has been greatly accelerated by the increasing tendency since the early 1970s for campaign financing to be handled outside of the political parties (which is partly responsible for their declining importance). Instead, campaign money is raised and dispensed increasingly through political action committees (PAC), groups of people with similar interests who raise funds to give to individual candidates for the American Congress. But as might be expected the money is raised and dispensed in an effort to influence legislation.[12] And there is evidence that the effort has been successful; at least changing votes at the margin and intensifying the degree of support for a bill. As the proportion of special interest money in campaign financing rises 'a candidate entering politics now must systematically make the rounds of the interest groups and win their approval, and their money, by declaring himself, usually in very specific terms, in favor of the legislative goals they seek'.[13]

[11] This and other institutional problems are developed in J. Sundquist (1981) *The decline and Resurgence of Congress,* The Brookings Institution, Washington, DC.

[12] Money has also been used in this way to induce legislative vetoes of rulings by regulatory agencies. For example, the Federal Trade Commission had ruled that used-car dealers must give notice of known defects in cars they sell. This ruling received a legislative veto by the US House of Representatives following the payment of substantial sums of money by the National Auto Dealers Association to key House members.

[13] See E. Drew (1982) *A reporter at large (Politics and money – Part I), The New Yorker,* December 6, p. 146.

The impact of this form of 'vote buying' was clearly brought out during the tax-cut bill of 1981. What was known as the 'bidding war' between Democrats who controlled the House of Representatives and the Reagan White House was an auction. The two branches of government tried to outbid one another in the tax breaks they wished to put into the tax bill to obtain campaign money from the special interests that would eventually benefit.[14] The manner in which congressmen often chose to indicate their desire to exchange votes for funds, in this case and others, was the 'fund raiser'.

The word in the Washington lobbying community was that the fund-raisers were the congressmen's way of letting it be known that they were open for business. Even if, to be charitable, this was a cynical interpretation, it does suggest the problem; that congressmen, desperate for funds, had to raise money over the full two years of their term, and, while they were writing a tax bill, allowed themselves to be seen as asking for funds from people seeking to influence the substance of that bill.[15]

The end result is the corruption of the political process: 'a process where . . . campaign contributions are not terribly different from a bribe. The only reason it's not bribery is because Congress defines what bribery is.'[16]

All this has concentrated on the legislative branch of government. When account is taken of the media-dominated method of selecting presidential candidates, rather than by selection from within the political party, the difficulties are merely compounded. In both cases the raising and disposal of campaign funds is increasingly handled by special interests in contrast to public financing or financing through a political party.

To argue that from such a process will come a balancing of forces so that a common good emerges is to overlook several important facts. Obviously not all special interests obtain equal access to government officials; e.g. the poor almost none, business far more than

---

[14] This process has been detailed in the now famous 'Stockman interview' in which one of President Reagan's top economic advisers analysed the vote-buying side of the 1981 tax-cut bill. See W. Greider (1981) The education of David Stockman, *The Atlantic,* December.

[15] Drew, op. cit., p. 90.

[16] The quotation is from M. Green (1982) Political Pac-man, *The New Republic,* December 13, p. 24.

labour. Furthermore, these special interests seeking access to candidates and elected representatives are usually seeking immediate, highly parochial goals. This means a lack of pressure and influence from any constituency that might be said to speak for the national interest or even to represent a position that could represent a consistent point of view.

Furthermore, the amounts of money that must now be raised are enormous. Congressional elections in 1982 were estimated to cost $300 million in the USA compared with $3 million in 1979 for British parliamentary elections.[17] The result is that US congressmen spend a high proportion of their time merely raising money for their campaigns. To do otherwise would expose them to great risk; their challengers might be able to outspend them in the next election. The result is a lack of understanding of the value and effects of the proposed legislation, other than the financial gain for the special interests fostering the legislation.[18]

Within the context of proposing, enacting and administering a workable incomes and industrial policy, the results are devastating. The executive and legislative branches of government, often in the hands of different political parties, represented by elected officials whose campaign financing comes largely from special interests seeking immediate financial gain through legislation, must be able between the two of them to propose, enact and administer policies designed to realize the long-run goals of full employment, price and wage stability and increased dynamic efficiency. All this at a time when the members of the legislative branch are increasingly ignorant of the relative merits of such programmes and the executive branch is likely headed by a 'personality' with mass media appeal.

But even if reasonable, consistent policies were somehow adopted, there are ample reasons to be pessimistic. As argued in chapters 11 to 13, no incomes or industrial policy will work without widespread acceptance based on a widely shared belief in the fairness of the policies. Yet with legislation constantly being enacted that heaps economic benefit on those contributing to the election of the legislatures, the resulting cynicism on the part of the electorate can only lead to various forms of non-compliance and non-cooperation with the policies.

All things considered, it is difficult to escape the conclusion that the political resolution of the inflation problem will be carried out

[17] ibid., p. 25.
[18] Drew, op. cit.

through long-run depressed demand conditions and, therefore, stagnation.

What is being predicted is a role for the USA that stands in marked contrast to that which it played in the 1950s and 1960s. As US exports as a share of world trade declined and import penetration increased, US policy during this period was relatively passive. The growing demand by Americans for foreign goods thereby stimulated the demand pressures needed to bring about full employment growth elsewhere. The large and persistent current account deficits that accompanied this facilitated and reinforced the world-wide expansionary trends by providing the international liquidity needed to carry out expanding world trade.

The scenario for the future suggested here is that out of fear of inflation (and possible payments difficulties), aggregate demand will be restricted in the USA, thereby leading to a slow growth in demand for the exports of others. Even if energy substitutes for oil are developed and energy conservation becomes a high domestic priority everywhere, the American 'strategy' of stagnation will have international repercussions, particularly for those economies heavily dependent upon trade with the USA. It will also require a special structuring of any internationally coordinated relation policy.

CHAPTER 15

When Economists Do Harm

This is a moment – the early eighties – of peculiar sordidness. It's as if the spirit of the old robber barons had been triumphantly resurrected, as if the most calloused notions of Social Darwinism were back with us, as if the celebrations of greed we associate with the late nineteenth century were reenacted a century later...

Irving Howe *A Margin of Hope*

NEW PROBLEMS, NEW SOLUTIONS

Reflecting on the last 100 years of economic development, it is clear that capitalism raises new macroeconomic problems at least as rapidly as it solves existing ones. Rising per capita incomes and increased affluence in particular are the driving forces. As Keynes noted half a century ago, once incomes have risen enough to allow consumption of something more than the necessities of life, problems of aggregate demand arise.

More recently, rising income levels have made it possible to introduce a welfare state in most capitalist economies while at the same time allowing private consumption to rise. But as argued earlier, when this takes place during an extended period of full employment, an inflationary bias develops. Without the right kind of government intervention, inflation rates tend to accelerate.

Moreover, this inflationary bias is such that it cannot be eliminated on a long-term basis by restrictive aggregate demand policies. These policies are neither a necessary nor sufficient condition for a return to price stability at full employment. In order to eliminate inflation while at the same time guaranteeing full employment a permanent incomes policy must be implemented. In this basic sense inflation, unemployment and stagnation are always and everywhere political phenomena.

Part II has been devoted to formulating a policy response to inflation that allows price stability, full employment and growth. This involves the acceptance of more government intervention, including strong, conciliatory political leadership and a concerted, national effort based on trust and cooperation. A policy response of inflation without stagnation has been hardly touched upon in this study. Increasing aggregate demand to return to full employment without simultaneously finding a means to restrain wage and price inflation is not a policy likely to be adopted in any of the mature capitalist economies. It is ruled out by a fear of accelerating inflation, currency crises and payments disequilibria.

It is evident from Part II that some economies are in a better position than others to implement those policies that are necessary conditions for ending stagflation. Thus, in chapter 14 it was predicted that the most powerful capitalist economy will choose a policy of stagnation without inflation in response to the stagflation conditions of the 1970s and early 1980s. Fearful of a renewal of inflation (and rightly so) and unwilling and unable to employ an incomes policy, the likely behaviour of US governments in the next decade or so will be to run the economy at rates of unemployment approaching double figures. This will eliminate inflation to be sure but, if the arguments of chapter 10 are correct, only at the expense of economic growth.

AN ERA OF PECULIAR SORDIDNESS

Economists must share some of the blame for this perverse conduct. A substantial part of the profession in its writings has fostered and articulated a view that there are automatic, self-correcting tendencies in capitalist economies. This view has now become a barrier to sensible analysis of our ills.

One of the recurring themes of Part II is that a belief in invisible hands, countervailing powers and economic pluralism has been an opiate of governments (and of the people) in many countries. These are the notions that have lulled the authorities into the belief that capitalist economies are for the most part self-regulating. According to this view, the private pursuit of private interests must lead to the best of all possible worlds irrespective of such things as the prevailing industrial relations system, the distribution of incomes and whether business and labour engage in corrupt and frivolous activities. Such considerations are alleged to be of little consequence, since the inexorable workings of the price mechanism will eliminate inefficient behaviour and institutions.

When things go wrong, for example when inflation rates accelerate and growth slows to a halt, there is a natural tendency to assign blame to an easily identifiable source such as central bankers, trade unions or government. To make things right, it is only necessary to exorcise a devil. During the current crisis this amounts to measures such as stricter control of the money supply, lower government budget deficits and dismantling of the welfare state.

But such an unqualified faith in an invisible hand that provides efficient and satisfying outcomes, even in the presence of organizations with great market power who are also unconstrained by considerations of fairness, is more than just an opiate. It is a malignant force promoting the spread of a permissive commercial ethos and eventually leading to economic anarchy. For such a faith generates a belief that however one behaves, something good will come out of it sometime, somehow. As with any religion that finds the source of perfection and salvation outside the practitioner's own behaviour, such beliefs downplay the importance of personal responsibility in the conduct of day-to-day activities and of anti-social behaviour as a cause of disruption. Norms of honesty, cooperation and fairness need not be internalized or even considered in economic affairs, beyond the narrowest legal requirements. Even criminal behaviour can reflect nothing more than the workings of the price mechanism under this ethical imperative.[1]

Much was made in chapter 5 of the use of implicit and explicit contracts in commercial dealings to realize satisfactory outcomes, as reliance solely on impersonal market forces is not efficient. A commercial ethos that divests market participants of any need for honest, fair behaviour undermines this contract system and seeks to replace it by a concern with nothing more than short-term gain. The resulting lack of continuity and increased uncertainty, far from fostering an orderly conduct of economic affairs, promotes discord and dissension and leads in the end to economic anarchy. A necessary condition for ending stagflation is to discard an economic ideology that is inherently destabilizing.

---

[1] A member of the Department of Transportation in the Reagan Administration, when informed that bribes were being paid in the trucking industry, responded that this reflected the price mechanism at work.

The chief difficulty today in adopting long-term policies to correct the stagflation problem can be seen by way of contrast with a policy for combating simply mass unemployment, the problem of the 1930s. When inflation is of little consequence, the private pursuit of private interests is quite compatible with the achievement of the macroeconomic goal of full employment. In the absence of any ideological impediment to expansionary fiscal policy, private conduct would not have to be public spirited. But when the main macroeconomic problems of the day can be traced to a competition for the distribution of full employment income and output, the success of policy requires as a necessary condition the private pursuit of public interests. Cooperation and trust are required, not an invisible hand, with government the main source of leadership and reconciliation. These are the points that must be made clear. However, the likelihood that such views will receive a fair hearing, let alone be incorporated into a policy for recovery, is unfortunately slight in many countries.

INTERNATIONAL COORDINATION

What about the prospects of those economies with a fairly long history of cooperative industrial relations, unencumbered by a self-destructive *laissez-faire* ideology that prevents the use of long-range policies, in short those countries which might be predisposed to implement the policies package advanced here? There is reason for pessimism about recovery here also, as even these countries are likely to be forced into a strategy of stagnation without inflation. This arises because of an absence today of any internationally coordinated aggregate demand, trade and foreign lending programmes. The immediate formulation and implementation of such a programme is vitally important. Given the complexity of the issues, a separate lengthy study would be necessary to do the subject justice. Only a few remarks are possible here.

A little reflection should reveal that the various policy measures advocated in chapters 10–14 are only necessary conditions for overcoming stagflation, at least in most countries. Given the present international monetary arrangements, a likely and common scenario following a restimulation of the economy can be inferred from attempts by the USA in the late 1970s and by France in the early 1980s. In fact, when stimulative policies are implemented unilaterally the most likely outcome will be speculation against the currency which accelerates the rate of its depreciation, giving rise to a currency crisis. This undermines any incomes policy as the rising exchange rate is likely to lead to the importation of inflation. A sharp reversal of aggregate demand policy will soon follow, accompanied by some temporary support from the international financial community, e.g. the IMF, conditional upon the initiation of restrictive measures. Only if the country in question is fortunate enough to start from a very strong payments position could such a chain of events be averted.

All of this suggests the need for coordinated expansionary policies on a broad front so that the 'leakages' into imports for each country are offset to the maximum extent possible by rising exports. Furthermore, a coordinated expansionary policy must be accompanied by measures that prevent the importation of inflation that could arise if widespread expansion is allowed to drive up prices in international commodity markets. Commodity price stabilization programs are needed here. But even a general expansionary programme runs up against a powerful payments constraint today due to a limited rate of growth of imports, first, in most of the oil-producing countries and, second, in those countries such as the USA, who through fear of inflation will likely restrict imports indirectly by restricting aggregate demand.[2] Relief from this constraint depends critically upon adequate borrowing facilities for the oil-importing countries on a fairly long-term basis.[3]

In chapters 1 and 7 it was pointed out that a leading factor in the world-wide recession of the early 1970s was a fear of inflation in the OECD countries.[4] The large current account deficits induced by the two oil price rises forced these same countries to continue and even intensify their restrictive policies. Unfortunately international lending agencies, in particular the IMF, in adopting monetarist principles, have caused the recession to be more prolonged and deeper than need be the case.

---

[2] Imports into the oil-producing countries are limited by the rate at which these underdeveloped countries can absorb them. Imports into countries with an overriding fear of inflation will be limited by the amount of aggregate demand deficiency thought necessary to drive up unemployment rates to a level consistent with the inflation target. In contrast, imports into other countries will be limited by their export performance and ability to borrow.

[3] See F. Cripps (1978) Causes of growth and recession in world trade, *Economic Policy Review*, March.

[4] This is not meant to deny that the downturn in some countries in 1973 might have been initiated by an over-accumulation of capital.

The basic fallacy of IMF policy is no different from that contained in the policies pursued today in the individual capitalist economies. That is to assume that restrictive aggregate demand policies can permanently eliminate inflation, thereby permitting economies to eventually return to full employment. Based on this erroneous assumption, the IMF has assumed that payments deficits can be eliminated permanently through devaluation, tight money policies and fiscal retrenchment.[5] The importance of devaluation as an instrument for achieving external balance need not be considered further. The role of tight money and restrictive fiscal policy is, in the eyes of the IMF, to reduce the adverse effects of inflation on the balance of payments.

The argument made earlier is that if restrictive policies are pushed far enough they will certainly bring down inflation but always at the expense of employment. Furthermore, inflation rates will again accelerate if stimulative policies are then introduced. Even assuming that the reduction of inflation rates will achieve some kind of balance of payments equilibrium, other things being equal, any attempt to return to full employment will not only bring back accelerating inflation but external disequilibrium.

Making loans conditional upon the borrowing country adjusting to external imbalance through restrictive policies is, on this reading, short-sighted. It leads to a most unsatisfactory domestic performance without permanently achieving what the policy set out to do. But matters are much worse than this. Adjustments through restrictive policies merely set in motion or intensify beggar-your-neighbour policies, the kind that have now become endemic. The lesson of the earlier chapters is that if conditions for borrowing from international lending agencies are required, then conditionality should be based on the willingness of the country to maintain full employment, to pursue an incomes policy and to reduce its imports from those economies who are restricting imports for reasons other than balance of payments consideration, e.g., OPEC and the USA. But this is nothing more than a programme suggested for individual economies.

Clearly, constructing a new international order in which external and internal (full employment) balance in the various countries again becomes a distinct possibility is a formidable task involving a large number of preconditions. But basic to the acceptance and implemen-

---

[5] See S. Dell (1982) Stabilization: The political economy of overkill, *World Development*, No. 8.

tation of any correct program is a recognition at the international level that monetarist policies cannot succeed in curing stagflation but can only create world-wide stagnation.

RECOVERY OR STAGNATION

The list of necessary conditions for ending stagflation has by now become formidable. Not only are there policies that individual countries can and must implement unilaterally, but coordinated policies are also needed. This requires pronounced changes in attitudes and institutions and only an optimist would predict that such policies will be adopted in the near future. But again, consider the only politically feasible alternative – world-wide stagnation. An unwillingness to implement a permanent incomes policy in spite of the presence of an inflationary bias means, at best, short-term stimulative programmes in the individual countries whenever inflation rates have been markedly reduced through restrictive aggregate demand policies and the payments position is very strong. More likely, the failure to adopt the programme advocated here will simply lead to perpetual stagnation world-wide. Moreover, there are reasons to believe that an economy caught in a condition of stagnation is subject to increased economic instability as well.[6] Recessions beginning from a high rate of unemployment are very likely to lead to unemployment rates like those of the 1930s before reaching the trough of the cycle. Even if this possibility is ignored, it is difficult to see why unemployment at, say, a 10–12 per cent rate, stretching from one decade to the next can be considered any less of a breakdown of the economic system than that of the 1930s. In each case, capitalism must be judged to have failed.

What the economist can do in the face of such a bleak possibility has already been discussed earlier in this chapter and in chapter 12. He can help rid the world of some pernicious 'fairy tales'. If this sounds flippant, it is nevertheless true. An important task is to convince those in authority that programmes of the kind outlined here can provide a long-term answer to current economic problems and that continuation of prevailing policies will cause stagnation and recession to persist. To a large extent this involves economists coming to a better understanding of the true nature of inflation and the impact of restrictive demand policies on the economy. But one of

[6] See J. Cornwall, *Growth and Stability*, op. cit., chapters VI and VII.

the central points of the first half of this book was that this will never come about until economists have discarded the larger part of neo-classical analysis. To assume that atomistic competition prevails in most markets, that markets are flex-price and that price signals are sufficient to organize economic activities efficiently, that utility functions are independent, that tastes and technologies are exogenous, that optimizing behaviour can be adequately captured within a framework that ignores most institutional constraints, all leads not just to bad science. As the monetarist application of the neoclassical precepts reveals, this kind of analysis contributes to economic breakdown.

Bibliography

Ackley, G., *Macroeconomics: Theory and policy,* Macmillan, New York, 1978.

Addison, J. and Siebert, W., *The Market for Labor: An Analytical Treatment,* Goodyear, Santa Monica, 1979.

Addison, J., 'Incomes Policy: The Recent European Experience', in J. Fallick and R. Elliott (Eds), *Incomes Policies, Inflation and Relative Pay,* George Allen & Unwin, London, 1981.

Akerlof, G., 'The Case Against Conservative Macroeconomics: An Inaugural Lecture', *Economica,* August, 1979.

Applebaum, E., 'The Labour Market in Post-Keynesian Theory', in M. Piore (Ed.), *Unemployment and Inflation: Institutionalist and Structuralist Views,* M. E. Sharpe, New York, 1979.

Arrow, K., 'Towards a Theory of Price Adjustments', in M. Abramovitz *et al., The Allocation of Economic Resources,* Stanford University Press, Stanford, 1959.

Artes, M. and Miller, M., 'Inflation, Real Wages and the Terms of Trade', in J. Bowers (Ed.), *Inflation, Development and Integration: Essays in Honour of A. J. Brown,* Leeds, 1979.

Atkinson, A. and Stiglitz, J., 'A New View of Technical Change', *The Economic Journal,* September, 1969.

Atkinson, P. *et al.,* 'World Trade and Finance: Prospects for the 1980s', *Cambridge Economic Policy Review,* December, 1980.

Baily, M., 'The Productivity Growth Slowdown by Industry', in *Brookings Papers on Economic Activity,* No. 2, 1982.

Barber, C. and McCallum, J., *Controlling Inflation: Learning from Experience in Canada, Europe and Japan,* Canadian Institute for Economic Policy, Ottawa, 1982.

Barro, R. and Grossman, H., 'A General Disequilibrium Model of Income and Employment', *American Economic Review,* March, 1971.

Baumol, W., 'Macroeconomics of Unbalanced Growth: The Anatomy of Urban Crisis', *American Economic Review,* June, 1967.

Blackaby, F., 'An Array of Proposals', in F. Blackaby (Ed.), *The Future of Pay Bargaining,* Heinemann, London, 1980.

Blaug, M., 'Kuhn versus Lakatos, or Paradigms versus Research Programmes in the History of Economics', *History of Political Economy*, No. 4, 1975.

Blyth, C., 'The Interaction between Collective Bargaining and Government Policies in Selected Member Countries', in *Collective Bargaining and Government Policies*, OECD, Paris, 1979.

Bosworth, B., 'Capital Formation and Economic Policy', in *Brookings Papers on Economic Activity*, No. 2, 1982.

Bowers, J., 'The Theory of the Cost of Inflation', in J. Bowers (Ed.), *Inflation Development and Integration: Essays in Honour of A. J. Brown*, Leeds, 1979.

Bowers, N., 'Probing the Issues of Unemployment Duration', *Monthly Labor Review*, July, 1980.

Boyer, R. and Petit, P., 'Employment and Productivity Growth in the EEC', *Cambridge Journal of Economics*, March, 1981.

Branson, W. H., *Macroeconomic Theory and Policy*, 2nd ed., Harper & Row, New York, 1979.

Brooks, J., 'Annals of Finance', *The New Yorker*, April, 1982.

Buiter, W. and Miller, M., 'The Thatcher Experiment: The First Two Years', *Brookings Papers on Economic Activity*, No. 2, 1981.

Cagan, P., *The Hydra-Headed Monster*, American Enterprise Institute, Washington, 1974.

Chaplin, G., 'Unemployment Insurance, Job Search and the Demand for Leisure', *Western Economic Journal*, March, 1971.

Christofides, L., Swidinsky, R. and Wilton, D., 'A Microeconometric Analysis of Spillovers within the Canadian Wage Determination Process', *Review of Economics and Statistics*, May, 1980.

Clark, K. and Summers, L., 'Labour Market Dynamics and Unemployment: A Reconsideration', *Brookings Papers on Economic Activity*, No. 1, 1979.

Clark, P., 'Investment in the 1970s: Theory, Performance, and Prediction', *Brookings Papers on Economic Activity*, No. 1, 1979.

Clarke, O., 'The Development of Industrial Relations in European Market Economies', *IRRA Annual Proceedings*, September, 1980.

Clower, R. W., 'The Keynesian Counter-Revolution: A Theoretical Appraisal', in F. Hahn and F. Brechling (Eds), *The Theory of Interest Rates*, Macmillan, London, 1965.

Colander, D., 'Tax and Market-Based Incomes Policies: The Interface of Theory and Practice', in R. Cornwall and M. Claudon (Eds), *An Incomes Policy for the United States: New Approaches*, Nijhoff, Boston, Mass., 1981.

Cornwall, J., *Modern Capitalism: Its Growth and Transformation*, Martin Robertson, London, 1977.

Coutts, K., Godley, W. and Nordhaus, W., *Industrial Pricing in the United Kingdom*, University of Cambridge, Cambridge, 1978.

Cripps, F. and Tarling, R., *Cumulative Causation in the Growth of Manufac-*

turing Industries, Department of Applied Economics, University of Cambridge, Cambridge, June, 1975.

Crouch, C., 'The Conditions for Trade-Union Wage Restraint', in L. Lindberg and C. Maier (Eds), *The Politics of Inflation and Economic Stagnation,* The Brookings Institute, Washington, forthcoming.

Cutler, L., 'To Form a Government', *Foreign Affairs,* Fall, 1980.

Danziger, S. and Haveman, R., 'The Reagan Budget: A Sharp Break with the Past', *Challenge,* May–June, 1981.

Danziger, S. 'President Reagan's Economic Policy', *Midland Bank Review,* Summer, 1981.

Dean, A., 'Roles of Governments and Institutions in OECD Countries', in F. Blackaby (Ed.), *The Future of Pay Bargaining,* Heinemann, London, 1980.

Denison, E., *Accounting for Slower Economic Growth: The United States in the 1970s,* The Brookings Institute, Washington, 1979.

Doeringer, P. and Piore, M., *Internal Labour Markets and Manpower Analysis,* Lexington, Mass., D. C. Heath, 1971.

Drew, E., 'A Reporter at Large (Politics and Money – Part I)', *The New Yorker,* December, 1982.

Duesenberry, J., 'The Mechanics of Inflation', *Review of Economics and Statistics,* May, 1950.

Duesenberry, J., 'Worldwide Inflation: A Fiscalist View', in D. Meiselman and A. Laffer (Eds), *The Phenomenon of Worldwide Inflation,* American Enterprise Institute, Washington, 1975.

Eatwell, J. *et al.,* 'Money Wage Inflation in Industrial Countries', *Review of Economic Studies,* October, 1974.

Eckstein, O. and Brinner, R., *The Inflation Process in the United States,* A Study Paper for the Use of the Joint Economic Committee, US Congress, February, 1972.

Eckstein, O. and Wilson, T. A., 'The Determination of Money Wages in American Industry', *Quarterly Journal of Economics,* August, 1962.

Ehrenberg, R. and Oaxaca, R., 'Unemployment Insurance, Duration of Unemployment and Subsequent Wage Gain', *American Economic Review,* December, 1976.

Federal Reserve Bulletin, 'Business Fixed Investment: Recent Developments and Outlook', January, 1983.

Feige, E. and Johannes, J., 'Was the United States Responsible for Worldwide Inflation Under the Regime of Fixed Exchange Rates?' *Kyklos,* No. 2, 1982.

Feldstein, M., 'Lowering the Permanent Rate of Unemployment', Joint Economic Committee, US Congress, Washington, 1973.

Feldstein, M., 'Government Deficits and Aggregate Demand', *Journal of Monetary Economics,* January, 1982.

Fellner, W., 'The Valid Core of the Rationality Hypothesis in the Theory of Expectations', *Journal of Money, Credit and Banking,* November, 1980.

Fellner, W., 'The Credibility Effect and Rational Expectations: Implications of the Gramlich Study', *Brookings Papers on Economic Activity*, No. 1, 1979.

Freeman, C., 'Technical Innovation and British Trade Performance', in F. Blackaby (Ed.), *De-Industrialization*, Heinemann, London, 1979.

Friedman, M., 'The Methodology of Positive Economics, in *Essays in Positive Economics*, University of Chicago Press, Chicago, 1953.

Friedman, M., 'The Role of Monetary Policy', *American Economic Review*, March, 1968.

Friedman, M., 'Some Comments on the Significance of Labour Unions for Economic Policy, in D. Wright (Ed.), *The Impact of the Union*, Harcourt, Brace, New York, 1951.

Friedman, M., 'Nobel Lecture: Inflation and Unemployment', *Journal of Political Economy*, June, 1977.

Frisch, H., 'Inflation Theory, 1963–1975: A Second Generation Survey', *Journal of Economic Literature*, December, 1977.

Furstenberg, F., 'Co-determination and its Contribution to Industrial Democracy: A Critical Evaluation', *IRRA Annual Proceedings*, September, 1980.

Gilder, G., *Wealth and Poverty*, Basic Books, New York, 1979.

Godley, W., 'Inflation in the United Kingdom', in L. Krause and W. Salant (Eds), *Worldwide Inflation: Theory and Recent Experience*, The Brookings Institute, Washington, 1977.

Goldberger, A., *Impact Multipliers and Dynamic Properties of the Klein-Goldberger Model*, North-Holland Publishing Co., Amsterdam, 1959.

Goldthorpe, J., 'Social Inequality and Social Integration in Modern Britain', in D. Wedderburn (Ed.), *Poverty, Inequality and Class Structure*, Cambridge University Press, Cambridge, 1974.

Goldthorpe, J., 'The Current Inflation: Towards a Sociological Account', in F. Hirsch and J. Goldthorpe (Eds), *The Political Economy of Inflation*, Harvard University Press, Cambridge, Mass., 1978.

Gordon, D., *Theories of Poverty and Underemployment*, Lexington, Mass., D. C. Heath, 1972.

Gordon, R. J., 'Wage-Price Controls and the Shifting Phillips Curve', *Brookings Papers on Economic Activity*, No. 2, 1972.

Gordon, R. J., 'Recent Development in the Theory of Inflation and Unemployment', *Journal of Monetary Economics*, No. 2, 1976.

Gordon, R. J., 'World Inflation and Monetary Accommodation in Eight Countries', *Brookings Papers on Economic Activity*, No. 2, 1977.

Gould, F., 'The Development of Public Expenditures in Sweden: A Comparative View', *Skandinaviska Enskilda Banken Quarterly Review*, No. 3, 1982.

Green, M., 'Political Pac-Man', *The New Republic*, December 13, 1982.

Greider, W., 'The Education of David Stockman', *The Atlantic*, December, 1981.

Gross, R. and Keating, M., 'An Empirical Analysis of Exports and Domestic Markets', *Economic Outlook Occasional Studies*, OECD, December, 1980.

Grossman, H., 'Why Does Aggregate Employment Fluctuate?' *American Economic Review*, May, 1979.

Hall, R., 'Employment Fluctuations and Wage Rigidity', *Brookings Papers on Economic Activity*, No. 1, 1980.

Handra, J., 'Rational Expectations: What Do they Mean? – Another View', *Journal of Post Keynesian Economics*, Summer, 1982.

Hassan, A. and de Broucker, P., 'Duration and Concentration of Unemployment', *The Canadian Journal of Economics*, November, 1982.

Haveman, R., 'Unemployment in Western Europe and the United States: A Problem of Demand, Structure, or Measurement?' *American Economic Review*, May, 1978.

Hayes, R. 'Why Japanese Factories Work', *Harvard Business Review*, July–August, 1981.

Hayes, R. and Abernathy, W., 'Managing Our Way to Economic Decline', *Harvard Business Review*, July–August, 1980.

Heady, B., 'Trade Unions and National Wages Politics', *The Journal of Politics*, May, 1970.

Heilbroner, R., 'The Demand for the Supply Side', *New York Review of Books*, June 11, 1981.

Hibbs, D., 'Inflation, Political Support and Macroeconomic Policy', in *The Politics of Inflation and Recession*, The Brookings Institute, Washington, forthcoming.

Hibbs, D., 'On the Political Economy of Long-run Trends in Strike Activity', *British Journal of Political Science*, April, 1978.

Hibbs, D., 'Industrial Conflict in Advanced Industrial Societies', *The American Political Science Review*, December, 1976.

Hicks, J. R., *The Crisis in Keynesian Economics*, Basic Books, New York, 1974.

Hicks, J. R., 'What is Wrong with Monetarism', *Lloyds Bank Review*, October, 1975.

Hines, A., 'The Micro-economic Foundations of Employment and Inflation Theory: Bad Old Wine in Elegant New Bottles', in G. Worswick (Ed.), *The Concept and Measurement of Involuntary Unemployment*, George Allen & Unwin, London, 1976.

Hines, A., *On the Reappraisal of Keynesian Economics*, Martin Robertson, London, 1971.

Hirsch, F., *The Social Limits to Growth*, Harvard University Press, Cambridge, Mass., 1976.

International Monetary Fund, *International Financial Statistics*, IMF, Washington, various issues, 1970–82.

Jacobson, L. and Lindbeck, A., 'On the Transmission Mechanism of Wage Change', *Swedish Journal of Economics*, September, 1971.

Kalecki, M., 'Political Aspects of Full Employment', in *Selected Essays on the Dynamics of the Capitalist Economy 1933–1970*, Cambridge, 1977.

Kassalow, E., 'Industrial Conflict and Consensus in the U.S. and Western Europe', in B. Martin and E. Kassalow (Eds), *Labour Relations in*

Advanced Industrial Societies: Issues and Problems, Carnegie Endowment for International Peace, Washington, 1980.

Kaufman, R., 'Why the U.S. Unemployment is So High', in M. Piore (Ed.), *Unemployment and Inflation – Institutionalist and Structuralist Views,* M. E. Sharpe, New York, 1979.

Kerr, C., 'The Balkanization of Labor Markets', in E. W. Bakke *et al., Labour Mobility and Economic Opportunity,* Technology Press, Cambridge, 1954.

Keynes, J. M., *The General Theory of Employment, Interest and Money,* Macmillan, London, 1936.

Korliras, P., 'Disequilibrium Theories and their Policy Implications: Towards a Synthetic Disequilibrium Approach', *Kyklos,* No. 3, 1980.

Kuhn, T., *The Structure of Scientific Revolutions,* University of Chicago Press, Chicago, 1970.

Lamfalussy, A., *Investment and Growth in Mature Economies,* Macmillan, New York, 1951.

Layard, R., 'Is Incomes Policy the Answer to Unemployment?' *Economica,* August, 1982.

Lehmbruch, G., 'Liberal Corporitism and Party Government', *Comparative Political Studies,* April, 1977.

Leibenstein, H., *Beyond Economic Man,* Harvard University Press, Cambridge, Mass., 1976.

Leijonhufvud, A., *On Keynesian Economics and the Economics of Keynes,* Oxford, N.Y., 1968.

Lerner, A. and Colander, D., 'There is a Cure for Inflation', in R. Cornwall and M. Claudon (Eds), *An Incomes Policy for the United States: New Approaches,* Nijhoff, Boston, Mass., 1981.

Lester, R., 'Wage-Price Dynamics, Inflation, and Unemployment – Discussion', *American Economic Review,* May, 1969.

Lewis, A., 'Rising Prices: 1899–1913 and 1950–1979, *Scandinavian Journal of Economics,* No. 4, 1980.

Lewis, A., 'Economic Development with Unlimited Supply of Labour', *The Manchester School,* May, 1954.

Lewis, W., *Growth and Fluctuations: 1870–1913,* George Allen & Unwin, London, 1978.

Lipsey, R., 'The Relation between Unemployment and the Rate of Change of Money Wage Rates in the United Kingdom, 1862–1957: A Further Analysis', *Economica,* February, 1960.

Lucas Jr., R., 'Unemployment Policy', *The American Economic Review,* Paper and Proceedings, May, 1978.

Magaziner, I. and Reich, R., *Minding America's Business,* Harcourt, Brace, Jovanich, New York, 1982.

Main, B., 'The Length of Employment and Unemployment in Great Britain', *Scottish Journal of Political Economy,* June, 1981.

Maizels, A., *Growth and Trade,* Cambridge University Press, Cambridge, 1970.

Marston, S., 'The Impact of Unemployment Insurance on Aggregate Unemployment', *Brookings Papers on Economic Activity*, No. 1, 1975.

Mayer, T., *The Structure of Monetarism*, Norton, New York, 1978.

Meade, J., *Stagflation Volume 1: Wage-Fixing*, George Allen & Unwin, London, 1982.

Mulvey, C. and Trevithick, J., 'Trade Unions and Wage Inflation', *Economic and Social Review*, January, 1973.

Musgrave, A., 'Unreal Assumptions in Economic Theory: The F-Twist Untwisted', *Kyklos*, No. 3, 1981.

Nabseth, L. and Ray, G. (Eds), *The Diffusion of New Industrial Processes: An International Study*, Cambridge University Press, Cambridge, 1974.

Negishi, T., *Microeconomic Foundations of Keynesian Macroeconomics*, North Holland Publishing Co., Amsterdam, 1979.

Nelson, R., 'Research on Productivity Growth and Differences', *Journal of Economic Literature*, September, 1981.

Nickell, S., 'The Effect of Unemployment and Related Benefits on the Duration of Unemployment', *Economic Journal*, March, 1979.

Nordhaus, W., 'The Political Business Cycle', *Review of Economic Studies*, April, 1975.

Nordhaus, W., 'Tax-Based Incomes Policies: A Better Mousetrap?' in R. Cornwall and M. Claudon (Eds), *An Incomes Policy for the U.S.: New Approaches*, Nijhoff, Boston, Mass., 1981.

OECD, *Economic Outlook*, Paris, various issues.

OECD, *Economic Survey of Japan*, Paris, 1976.

OECD, *Labour Force Statistics*, Paris, various issues.

OECD, *Main Economic Indicators*, Paris, various issues.

OECD, *Towards Full Employment and Price Stability*, Paris, 1978.

Okun, A., 'Rational Expectations with Misperceptions as a Theory of the Business Cycle', *Journal of Money, Credit, and Banking*, November, 1980.

Okun, A., 'Inflation: Its Mechanics and Welfare Costs', *Brookings Papers on Economic Activity*, No. 2, 1975.

Okun, A., *Prices and Quantities: A Macroeconomic Analysis*, The Brookings Institute, Washington, 1981.

Okun, A., 'Potential GNP: Its Measurement and Significance', *Proceedings of the Business and Economic Statistics Section*, American Statistical Society, 1962.

Okun, A., 'Upward Mobility in a High Pressure Economy', *Brookings Papers on Economic Activity*, No. 1, 1973.

Osberg, L., *Economic Inequality in America*, M. E. Sharpe, New York, 1983.

Papola, T. A. and Bharadwaj, V. P., 'Dynamics of Industrial Wage Structure: An Inter-Country Analysis', *Economic Journal*, March, 1970.

Parkin, M., *Modern Macroeconomics*, Prentice Hall Canada, Scarborough, Ontario, 1982.

Patinkin, D., *Money, Interest and Prices*, Harper & Row, New York, 1965.

Pellegrini, C., 'Co-determination and its Contribution to Industrial Democracy: A Critical Evaluation – Discussion', *IRRA 33rd Annual Proceedings*, September, 1980.

Perry, G., 'Slowing the Wage-Price Spiral: The Macroeconomic View', *Brookings Papers on Economic Activity*, No. 2, 1978.

Perry, G., 'Wages and Guideposts', *American Economic Review*, September, 1967.

Perry, G., 'Unemployment Flows in the U.S. Labor Market', *Brookings Papers on Economic Activity*, No. 2, 1972.

Pesaran, M., 'A Critique of the Proposed Tests of the Natural Rate – Rational Expectations Hypothesis', *The Economic Journal*, September, 1982.

Phelps, E., 'The New View of Investment: A Neoclassical Analysis', *Quarterly Journal of Economics*, November, 1962.

Phelps, E., 'Okun's Micro-Macro System: A Review', *Journal of Economic Literature*, September, 1981.

Phelps, E. *et al.*, *Microeconomics Foundations of Employment and Inflation Theory*, Norton, New York, 1970.

Phelps Brown, E., *A Century of Pay*, Macmillan, London, 1968.

Phelps Brown, E., 'The Analysis of Wage Movements Under Full Employment', *Scottish Journal of Political Economy*, November, 1971.

Phillips, A., 'The Relation between Unemployment and the Rate of Change of Money Wage Rates in the United Kingdom, 1861–1957', *Economica*, November, 1958.

Piore, M., Unemployment and Inflation: An Alternative View, in M. Piore (Ed.), *Unemployment and Inflation: Institutionalist and Structuralist Views*, M. E. Sharpe, New York, 1979.

Piore, M., 'Wage Determination in Low-Wage Labour Markets and the Role of Minimum-Wage Legislation', in M. Piore (Ed.), *Unemployment and Inflation: Institutionalist and Structuralist Views*, M. E. Sharpe, New York, 1979.

Pollon, W., 'Wage Rigidity and the Structure of the Austrian Manufacturing Industries: An Econometric Analysis of Relative Wages', *Weltwirtschaftliches Archiv*, No. 4, 1980.

Posner, M. and Steer, A., 'Manufacturing Industry', in F. Blackaby (Ed.), *De-Industrialization*, Heinemann, London, 1979.

Pratten, C., 'Mrs Thatcher's Economic Experiment', *Lloyds Bank Review*, January, 1982.

Ray, G., 'Labour Costs and International Competitiveness', *National Institute Economic Review*, August, 1972.

Rees, A., 'New Policies to Fight Inflation: Sources of Skepticism', *Brookings Papers on Economic Activity*, No. 2, 1978.

Reich, R., 'Making Industrial Policy', *Foreign Affairs*, Spring, 1980.

Ripley, F., and Segal, L., 'Price Determination in 395 Manufacturing Industries', *Review of Economics and Statistics*, August, 1973.

Rosenberg, N., 'Science, Invention and Economic Growth', *The Economic Journal,* March, 1974.

Rosenstone, S., 'Economic Activity and Voter Turnout', *American Journal of Political Science,* February, 1982.

Ross, A. and Wachter, M. L., 'Wage Determination, Inflation, and the Industrial Structure', *The American Economic Review,* September, 1973.

Ruggles, R., *Employment and Unemployment Statistics as Indexes of Economic Activity and Capacity Utilization,* Background Paper, No. 28, National Commission on Employment and Unemployment Statistics, Washington, April, 1979.

Santamero, A. M. and Seater, J. J., 'The Inflation-Unemployment Trade-off: A Critique of the Literature', *Journal of Economic Literature,* June, 1978.

Sargent, T. J. and Wallace, N., 'Rational Expectations and the Theory of Economic Policy, Studies in Monetary Economics', *Federal Reserve Bank of Minneapolis,* Minneapolis, 1975.

Schmitter, P., 'Interest Intermediation and Regime Governability in Western Europe and North America', in S. Berger (Ed.), *Organizing Interests in Western Europe: Pluralism, Corporatism, and the Transformation of Politics,* Cambridge University Press, Cambridge, 1981.

Schmookler, J., *Invention and Economic Growth,* Harvard University Press, Cambridge, Mass., 1966.

Schultze, C., *Demand–Pull versus Cost–Push Inflation, Recent Inflation in the United States,* Study Paper No. 1, Joint Economic Committee, Washington, 1959.

Scitovsky, T., 'Market Power and Inflation', *Economica,* August, 1978.

Seidman, L., 'Insurance for Labor under Tax-Based Incomes Policy', in R. Cornwall and M. Claudon (Eds), *An Incomes Policy for the U.S.: New Approaches,* Nijhoff, Boston, Mass., 1981.

Shirai, T. and Shimada, H., 'Japan', in J. Dunlop and W. Galenson (Eds), *Labor in the Twentieth Century,* Academic Press, New York, 1978.

Simon, H., 'Rationality as Process and as Product of Thought', *American Economic Review, Papers and Proceedings,* May, 1978.

Smith, W., 'On Some Current Issues in Monetary Economics: An Interpretation', *Journal of Economic Literature,* September, 1970.

Solow, K., 'Comments on Stein', in J. Stein (Ed.), *Monetarism,* Vol. 1, North-Holland Publishing Company, Amsterdam, 1976.

Solow, R., 'Alternative Approaches to Macroeconomic Theory: A Partial View', *Canadian Journal of Economics,* August, 1979.

Solow, R., 'A Contribution to the Theory of Economic Growth', *Quarterly Journal of Economics,* February, 1965.

Solow, R., 'Investment and Technical Progress', in K. Arrow *et al.* (Eds), *Mathematical Methods in the Social Sciences,* Stanford University Press, Stanford, 1960.

Soskice, D., 'Strike Waves and Wage Explosions, 1968–1970: An Economic

Interpretation', in C. Crouch and A. Pizzorno (Eds), *The Resurgence of Class Conflict in Western Europe Since 1968*, Vol. 2, Holmes & Meir, New York, 1978.

Stout, D., 'De-Industrialization and Industrial Policy', in F. Backaby (Ed.), *De-Industrialization*, Heinemann, London, 1979.

Sundquist, J., *The Decline and Resurgence of Congress*, The Brookings Institute, Washington, 1981.

Swoboda, A., 'Monetary Approaches to Worldwide Inflation', in L. Krause and W. Salant (Eds), *World Wide Inflation: Theory and Recent Experience*, The Brookings Institute, Washington, 1977.

Sylos-Labini, P., 'Industrial Pricing in the United Kingdom', *Cambridge Journal of Economics*, No. 3, 1979.

Tarling, R. and Wilkinson, F., 'The Movement of Real Wages and the Development of Collective Bargaining in the U.S.: 1855–1920, *Contributions to Political Economy*, No. 1, 1982.

Thirlwall, A., 'The Balance of Payments Constraint as an Explanation of International Growth Rate Differences', *Banca Nazionale del Lavora Quarterly Review*, March, 1979.

Thirlwall, A. and Dixon, R., 'A Model of Export-Led Growth with a Balance of Payments Constraint', in J. Bowers (Ed.), *Inflation, Development and Integration Essays in Honour of A. J. Brown*, Leeds, 1979.

Thirlwall, A. and Hussain, M., 'The Balance of Payments Constraint, Capital Flows and Growth Rate Differences Between Developing Countries', *Oxford Economic Papers*, November, 1982.

Thurow, L., *On Generating Inequality*, Basic Books, New York, 1975.

Tobin, J., 'Stabilization Policy Ten Years After', *Brookings Papers on Economic Activity*, No. 1, 1980.

Tobin, J., *Assets Accumulation and Economic Activity: Reflections on Contemporary Macroeconomic Theory*, Yrjo Jahnsson Lectures, Basil Blackwell, Oxford, 1980.

Tobin, J., 'Are New Classical Models Plausible Enough to Guide Policy?' *Journal of Money, Credit, and Banking*, November, 1980.

Tobin, J., 'Inflation and Unemployment', *American Economic Review*, March, 1972.

Tobin, J., 'The Wage-Price Mechanism: Overview of the Conference', in O. Eckstein (Ed.), *The Econometrics of Price Determination: Conference, Board of Governors of the Federal Reserve System and Social Science Research Council*, 1972.

Tobin, J., 'Deficit Spending and Crowding Out in Shorter and Longer Runs', in H. Greenfield *et al.* (Eds), *Theory of Economic Efficiency: Essays in Honour of Abba P. Lerner*, MIT, Cambridge, Mass., 1979.

Trevithick, J., 'Inflation, The Natural Unemployment Rate and the Theory of Economic Policy', *Scottish Journal of Political Economy*, February, 1976.

Turner, H. and Jackson, D., 'On the Stability of Wage Differences and

Productivity Based Wage Policies: An International Analysis', *British Journal of Industrial Relations*, No. 1, 1969.

Ulman, L., 'Union Behavior and Incomes Policy', unpublished paper, McGill University, Montreal, 1980.

Vroman, W., 'Worker Upgrading and the Business Cycle', *Brookings Papers on Economic Activity*, No. 1, 1977.

Wachter, M., 'The Wage Process: An Analysis of the Early 1970s', *Brookings Papers on Economic Activity*, No. 2, 1974.

Wachter, M., 'Cyclical Variation in the Interindustry Wage Structure', *The American Economic Review*, March, 1970.

Wachter, M. and Williamson, O., 'Obligational Markets and the Mechanics of Inflation', *Bell Journal of Economics*, Autumn, 1978.

Wallich, H. and Weintraub, S., 'A Tax-Based Incomes Policy', *Journal of Economic Issues*, June, 1971.

Walsh, B., 'Unemployment Insurance and the Labour Market: A Review of Research Relating to Policy. Report to OECD', *Manpower and Social Affairs*, May, 1981.

Wannicki, J., 'The Mundell-Laffer Hypothesis', *The Public Interest*, Spring, 1975.

Wenban-Smith, G., 'A Study of the Movements of Productivity in Individual Industries in the United Kingdom, 1968–79', *National Institute Economic Review*, August, 1981.

Wood, A., *A Theory of Pay*, Cambridge, 1978.

Author Index

Subject Index